REX MUNDI
Book Four

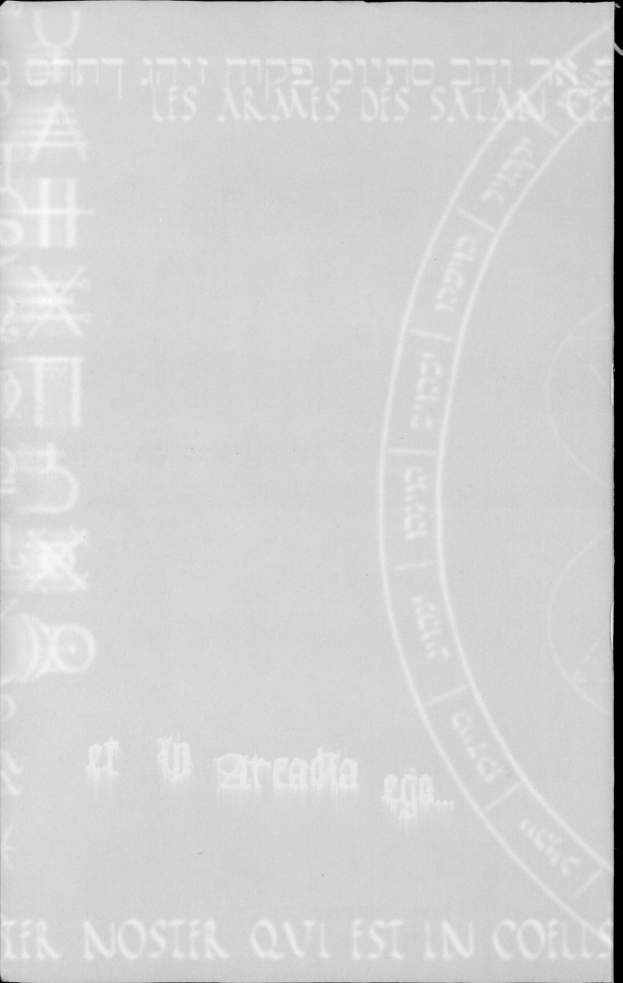

LES ARMES DES SATAN CE

et in Arcadia ego...

NOSTER QVI EST IN CŒLIS

RexMundi

· BOOK FOUR ·

Crown and Sword

writer ARVID NELSON
artist JUAN FERREYRA

Rex Mundi created by ARVID NELSON and ERICJ

DARK HORSE BOOKS®

publisher
MIKE RICHARDSON

editor
SCOTT ALLIE

assistant editor
RYAN JORGENSEN

man in the shadows
MATT DRYER

letterer and newspaper designer
ARVID NELSON

book designer
AMY ARENDTS

art director
LIA RIBACCHI

Special thanks to Jason Hvam and Jason Rickerd
Archival photographs: Eugène Atget

character profiles • summaries of past issues • much more: www.rexmundi.net

Errata

In *Book 2: The River Underground,* the fourth artist featured in the Gallery section was incorrectly named Freddie *William.* Freddie's last name is, in fact, Williams.

Also, the introduction to "Brother Matthew: Welcome to Paris" incorrectly stated "Brother Matthew" first saw print in the Dark Horse edition of *Book 1: The Guardian of the Temple.* In fact, the magazine *Comics International* first printed "Brother Matthew."

Rex Mundi's author prays Freddie Williams, the management of *Comics International,* and the Holy Inquisition will have mercy on his body and his soul.

REX MUNDI BOOK FOUR: CROWN AND SWORD

This volume collects issue eighteen of *Rex Mundi* originally published by Image Comics, and issues one through five of *Rex Mundi* published by Dark Horse Comics. Also, the story "To Weave a Lover" which appeared in the *Dark Horse Book of Monsters* published by Dark Horse Comics.

Published by
Dark Horse Books
A division of Dark Horse Comics, Inc.
10956 SE Main Street
Milwaukie, OR 97222

darkhorse.com

To find a comics shop in your area, call the Comic Shop Locator
Service toll-free at 1-888-266-4226

First edition: December 2007
ISBN: 978-1-59307-824-9

10 9 8 7 6 5 4 3 2 1

Printed in China

INTRODUCTION

by Bill Whitcomb

Doctor Julien Saunière, Gnostic Detective

There is a curious resemblance between the mystic's quest for gnosis and the detective's search for truth, but rarely have the two paths overlapped as they do in *Rex Mundi*. This is a mystery spanning the bloodline of Christ, the nature of sorcery, and the struggle for mastery of the world.

The word *gnosis* comes from the Greek word for knowledge, referring to illumination or direct knowledge of God through awareness of the divine spark within. While gnosis itself cannot be taught or expressed in words, some think it can be obtained through knowledge of secret words, names, signs, and rituals. This esoteric knowledge, hidden and warded, could enable the seeker to break through myriad layers to the real underlying truth. The path, however, is filled with obstacles.

The secret knowledge is hidden, encoded, and protected. The seeker must win past guardians both hostile and well meaning, overcoming deceptions and dangers without and the seeker's own fears and temptations within. Each step toward enlightenment reveals new illusions and perils that increase exponentially as one nears the truth. This is the path of the magician as well as the mystic, though for the magician, the emphasis is on mastery of self and the power that it brings.

The detective walks along a similarly tangled and dangerous road. The detective must separate facts from lies, enduring beatings and close calls, refusing to be bought off, and wading through corruption and death until the darkness and horror are peeled away and he finally knows the score.

It is perhaps this similarity of maps that has so often resulted in initiatory magical and mystical organizations becoming enmeshed in conspiracy, espionage, revolution, and politics. The vital secrets are concealed, both from outsiders and from would-be initiates not yet advanced or proved loyal enough for arcane knowledge. Only those in the inner circle, those with the secret keys, codes, words, and names, are permitted to know the order's real history and goals.

As with many who enter the search for secret knowledge, Dr. Julien Saunière's journey might not have seemed so serious at the beginning. He wanted to help an old friend, Father Gérard Marin, find a missing manuscript. He was curious. As with many of us seeing an issue of *Rex*

Mundi for the first time, he might have casually wondered, "What's this, now?" I only encountered *Rex Mundi* recently, but like the good doctor, I also looked too long, and now I can't seem to look away. Now the stakes are higher.

Like the search for enlightenment, like all good mysteries, the story of *Rex Mundi* becomes ever darker and more convoluted even as it seems to promise revelation. Julien Saunière faces pain and danger as he seeks the secret of Rennes-le-Château, while Dr. Genevieve Tournon walks a razor's edge between her love for Julien and her desire for wealth and influence. David-Louis Plantard de St. Clair, the Hitleresque Duke of Lorraine, is poised to achieve his dreams of glory, seemingly oblivious to the world's catastrophic peril and the pain of his daughter, the Lady Isabelle. So many have died and the remaining players spiral into terror, betrayal, and disillusion toward their ultimate destiny. Will the final secret provide power, knowledge, or simply the ability to survive? Is there really any difference?

Is Rex Mundi Jesus? God? Will the Duke of Lorraine, the possible heir of Jesus and the Merovingian kings, become the Lord of Europe and the Holy Land? Could Dr. Julien Saunière, purified by the alchemical fires of his quest, become the true king, if only within his own soul? Or will the jealous and hateful demiurge believed by the Gnostics to be the creator of the material world be revealed as the true Rex Mundi, triumphant over all the characters' hopes and aspirations?

As Doctor Julien Saunière, the Duke of Lorraine, and the various other characters each travel through their own Dark Night of the Soul, we go with them because, in the end, like both the detective and the mystic, we just have to know!

Bill Whitcomb isn't a descendant of the Merovingian kings and, if he knows the secret of the Templars, he's not aware of it. He is, however, the author of *The Magician's Companion* and *The Magician's Reflection*, two worthwhile books about magic and symbolism, published by Llewellyn Worldwide, Ltd. www.llewellyn.com

REX MUNDI BOOK FOUR:
CROWN AND SWORD

Paris, 1933. The Protestant Reformation failed. Europe is in the grip of feudalism, and sorcerers stalk the streets at night. It is the world of *Rex Mundi*.

The Duke of Lorraine, a powerful French aristocrat and grand master of a secret society born in the murky history of the First Crusade, has manipulated rising political tensions to ignite a devastating world war.

Lorraine has seized power from the unpopular King Louis XXII, and the duke's co-conspirators in the French parliament have appointed him to lead the French armed forces in the burgeoning conflict. Lorraine and his followers are united by the secret of the Holy Grail itself.

Master Physician Julien Saunière devoted himself to uncovering that secret when an encrypted medieval scroll connected to the Grail was stolen from longtime friend Father Gérard Marin. A mysterious assassin in a white suit murdered Marin soon after, leaving Saunière no choice but to investigate.

Saunière's prying has aroused the ire of the powerful Archbishop of Sens, head of the Holy Inquisition in Paris. The archbishop, also in search of the Grail, impressed Saunière into service. Saunière is withholding some of his findings from the Inquisition, at great personal risk.

Saunière continues his dangerous investigation with the help of Genevieve Tournon, an old flame and fellow doctor. Tournon also happens to be Lorraine's personal physician. She is having an affair with the powerful duke, spying on Saunière while trying to protect him at the same time.

What's more, Tournon bears a striking resemblance to the duke's dead wife, awakening long-dormant feelings in Lorraine.

Tournon and Saunière have used the cover of a party at the duke's Paris estate to break into his family chapel. There they discover part of the Grail's secret: Lorraine may be a direct lineal descendant of King David and Jesus Christ.

But the chapel's guardian, a magical golem, badly hurt Julien in the process. Now he and Genevieve must flee Lorraine's estate before the Duke learns of their snooping . . .

"For there is nothing hid, which shall not be manifested; neither was anything kept secret, but that it should come abroad."

— Mark 4:22

CHAPTER ONE
TO KISS AND TO KILL

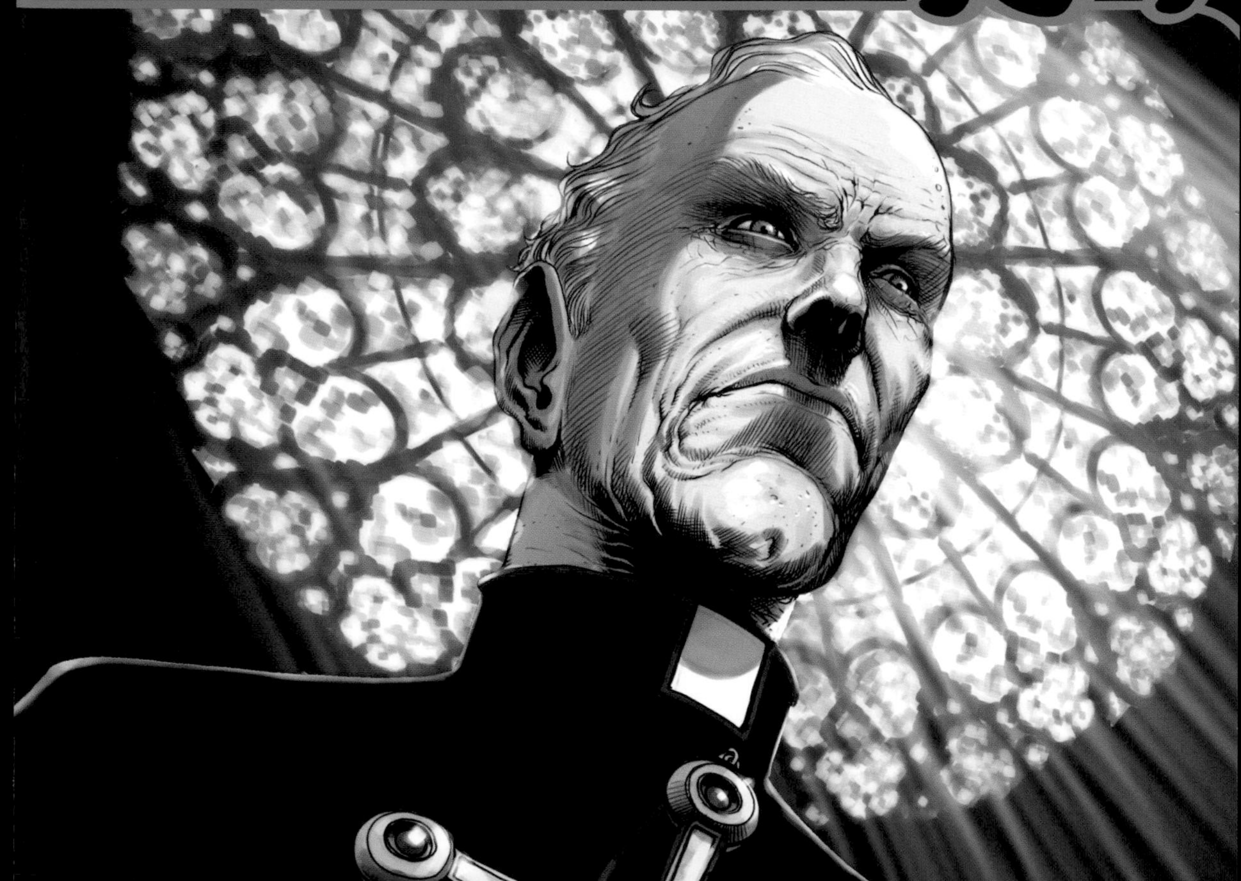

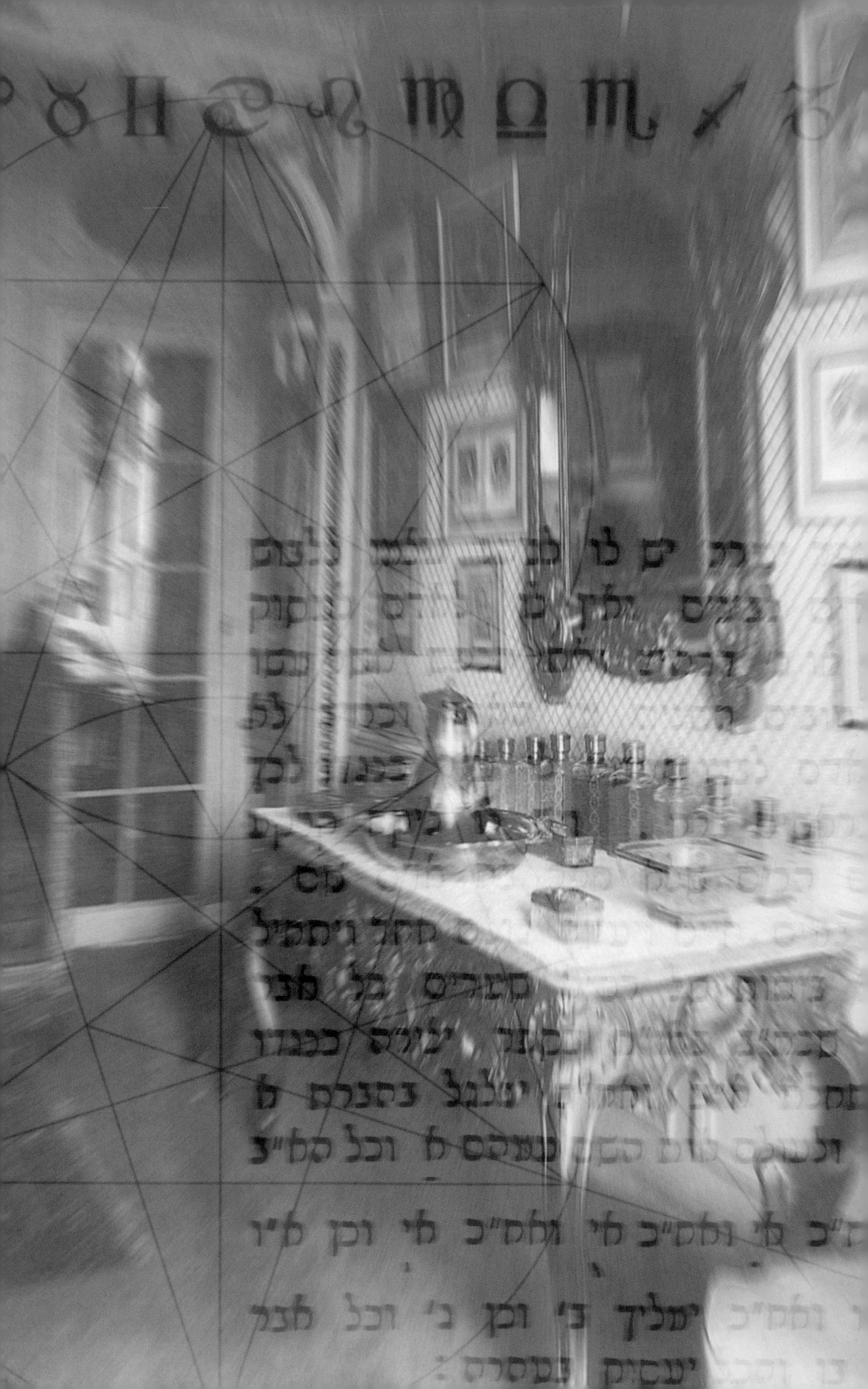

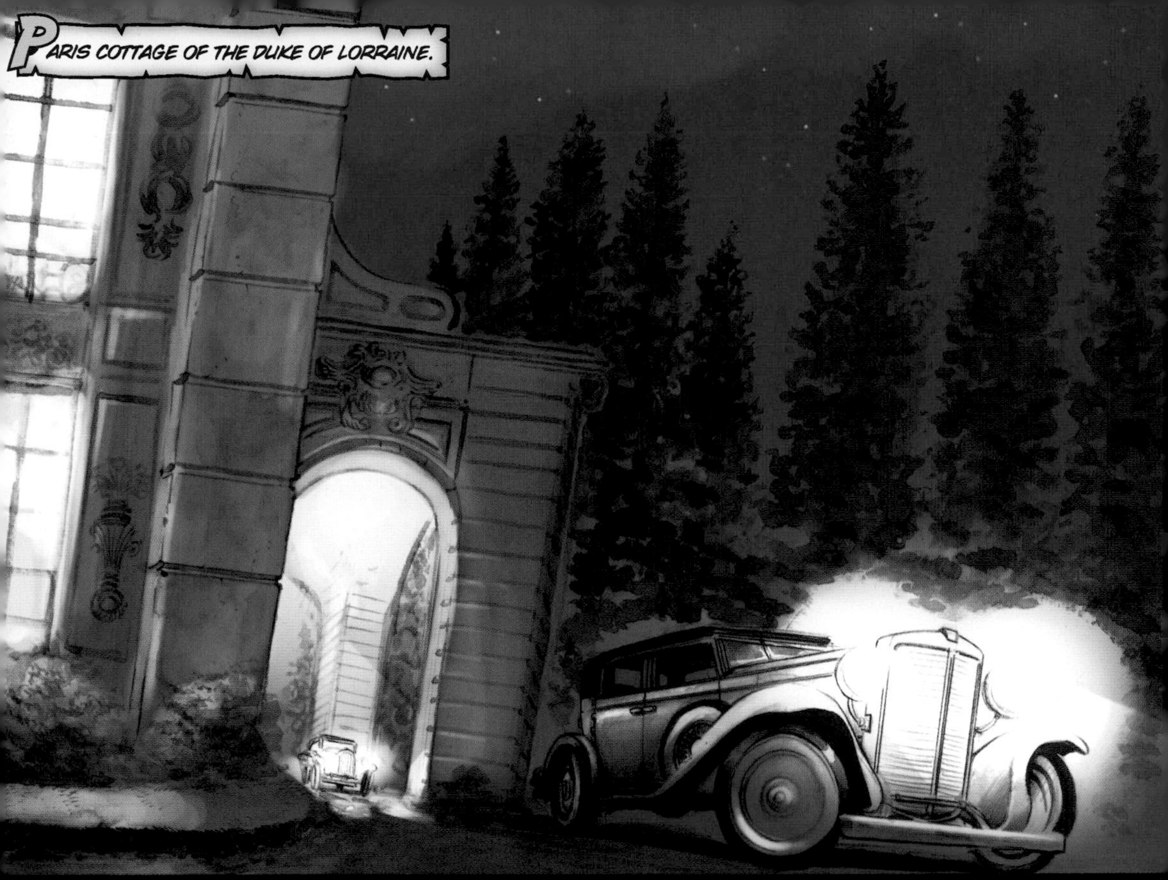
PARIS COTTAGE OF THE DUKE OF LORRAINE.

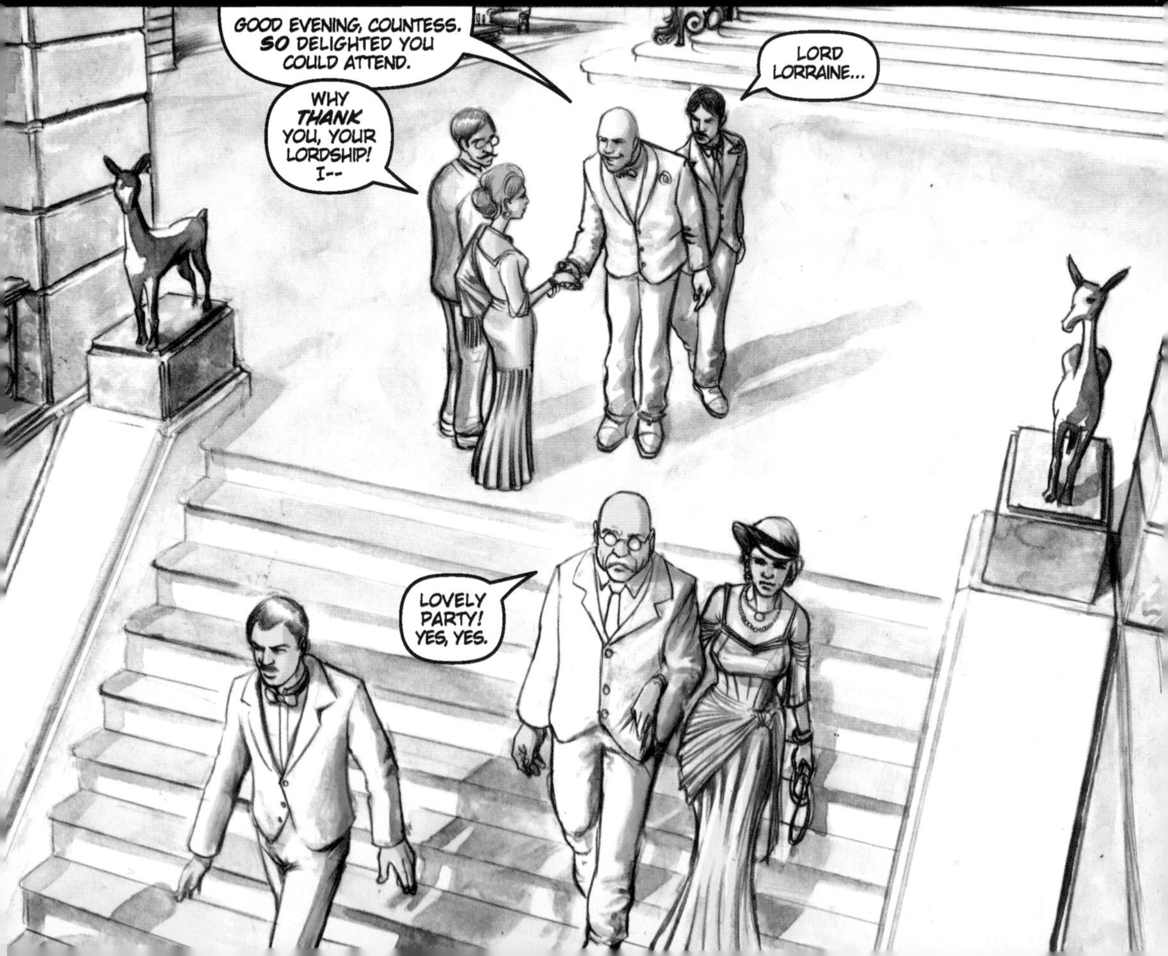
GOOD EVENING, COUNTESS. SO DELIGHTED YOU COULD ATTEND.
WHY THANK YOU, YOUR LORDSHIP! I--
LORD LORRAINE...
LOVELY PARTY! YES, YES.

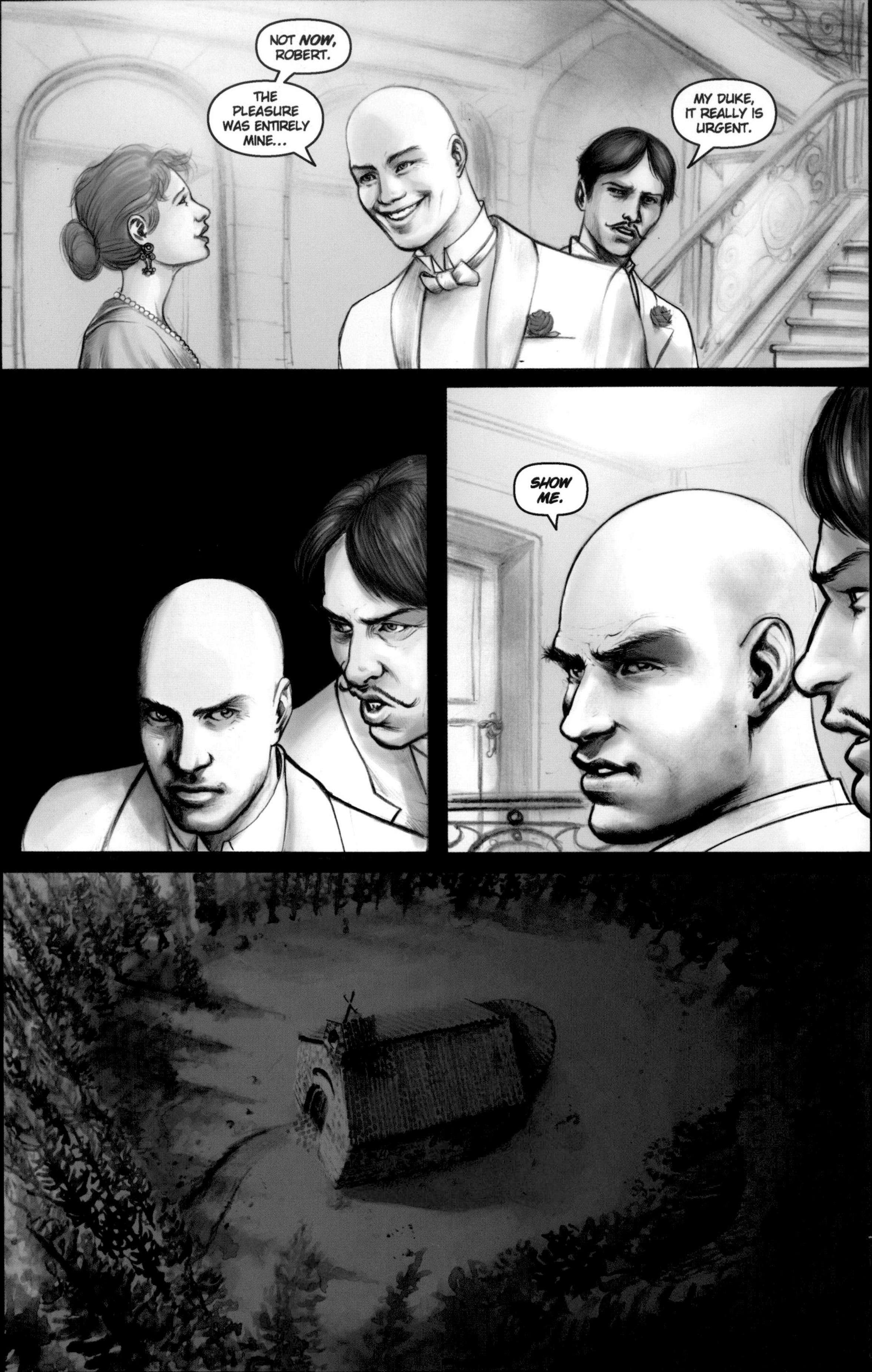
NOT NOW, ROBERT.
THE PLEASURE WAS ENTIRELY MINE...
MY DUKE, IT REALLY IS URGENT.
SHOW ME.

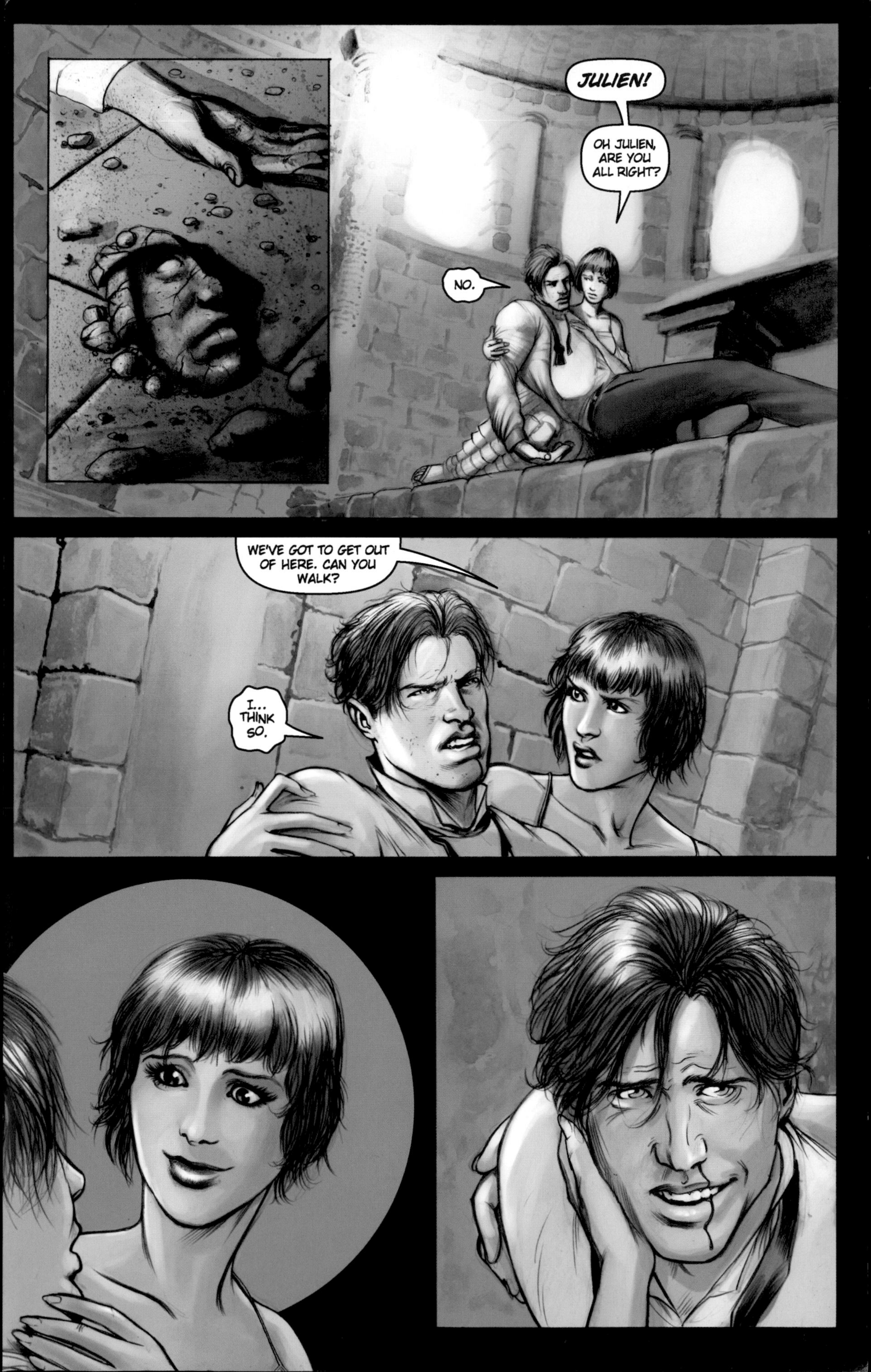
JULIEN!
OH JULIEN, ARE YOU ALL RIGHT?
NO.
WE'VE GOT TO GET OUT OF HERE. CAN YOU WALK?
I... THINK SO.

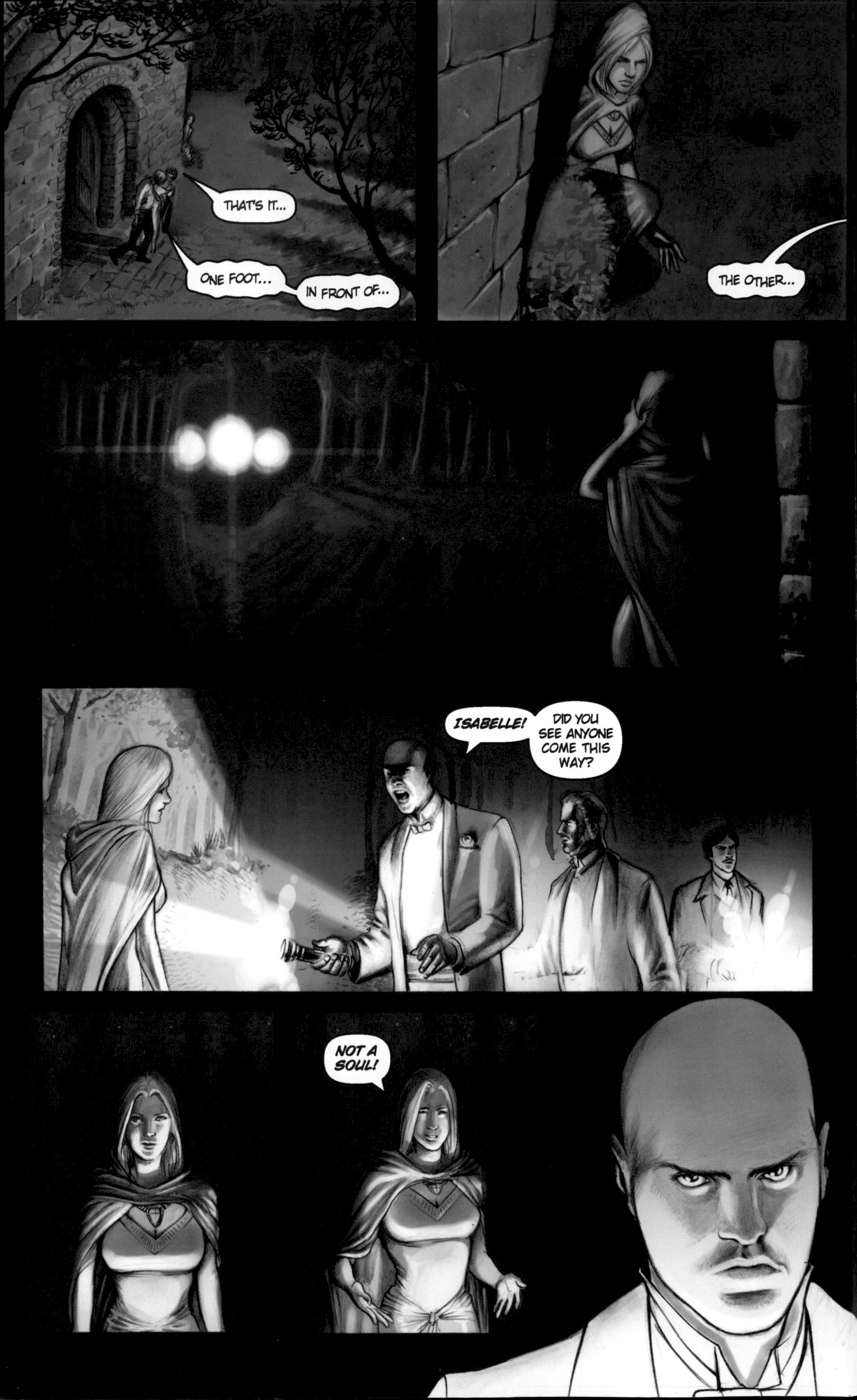
THAT'S IT...
ONE FOOT...
IN FRONT OF...
THE OTHER...
ISABELLE!
DID YOU SEE ANYONE COME THIS WAY?
NOT A SOUL!

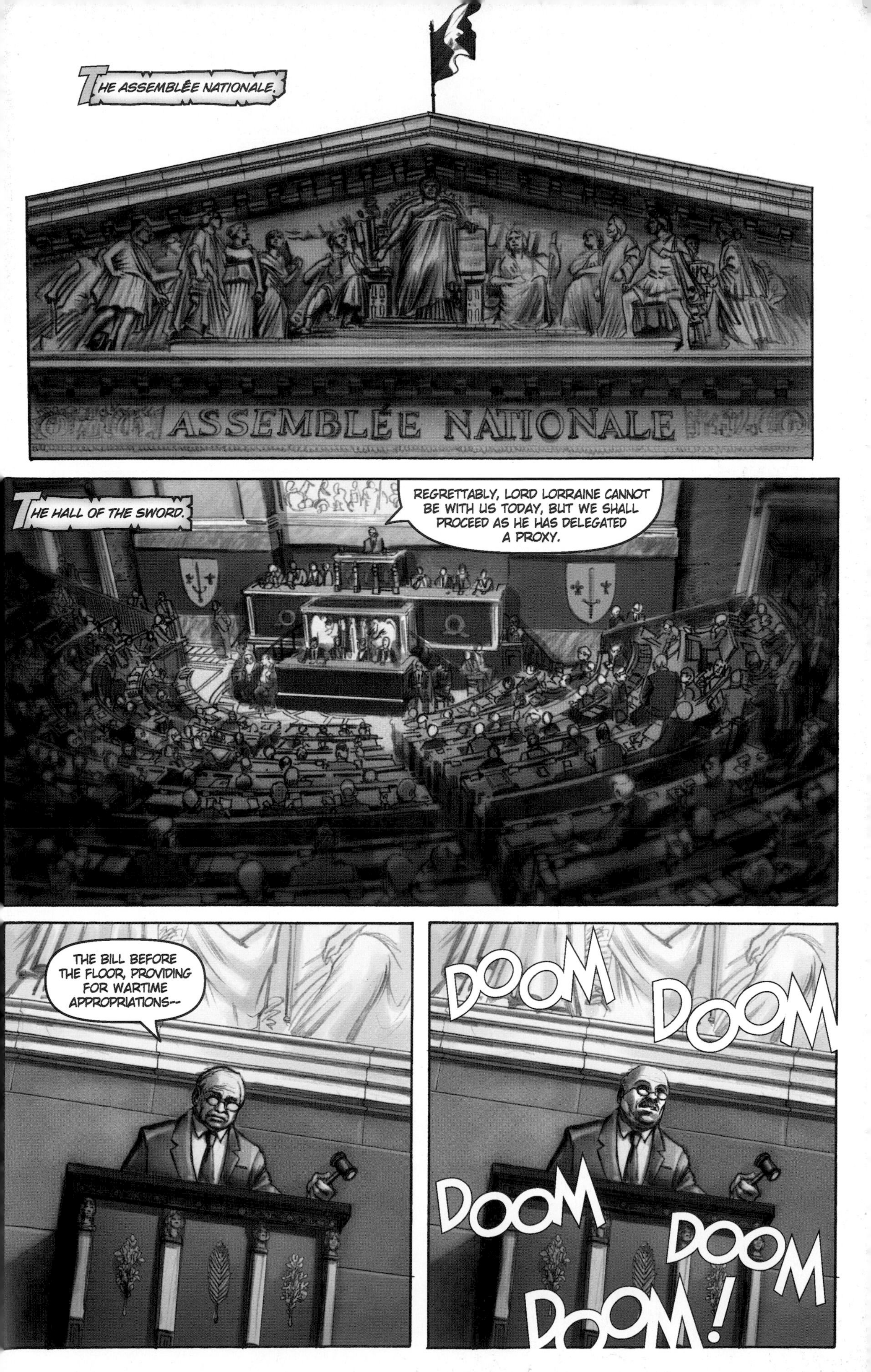
THE ASSEMBLÉE NATIONALE.
ASSEMBLÉE NATIONALE
THE HALL OF THE SWORD.
REGRETTABLY, LORD LORRAINE CANNOT BE WITH US TODAY, BUT WE SHALL PROCEED AS HE HAS DELEGATED A PROXY.
THE BILL BEFORE THE FLOOR, PROVIDING FOR WARTIME APPROPRIATIONS--
DOOM DOOM
DOOM DOOM
DOOM!

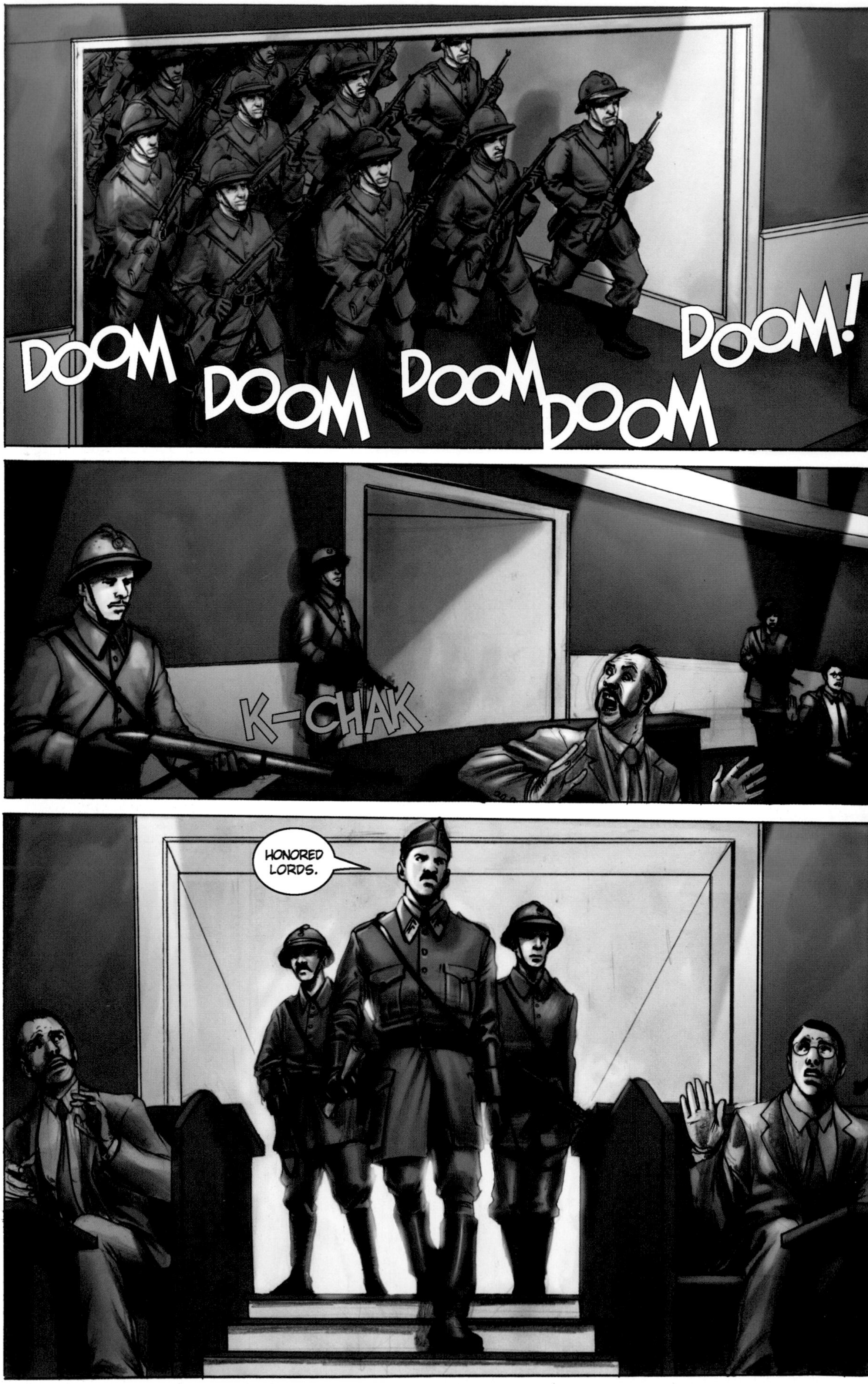
DOOM
DOOM
DOOM
DOOM
DOOM!
K-CHAK
HONORED LORDS.

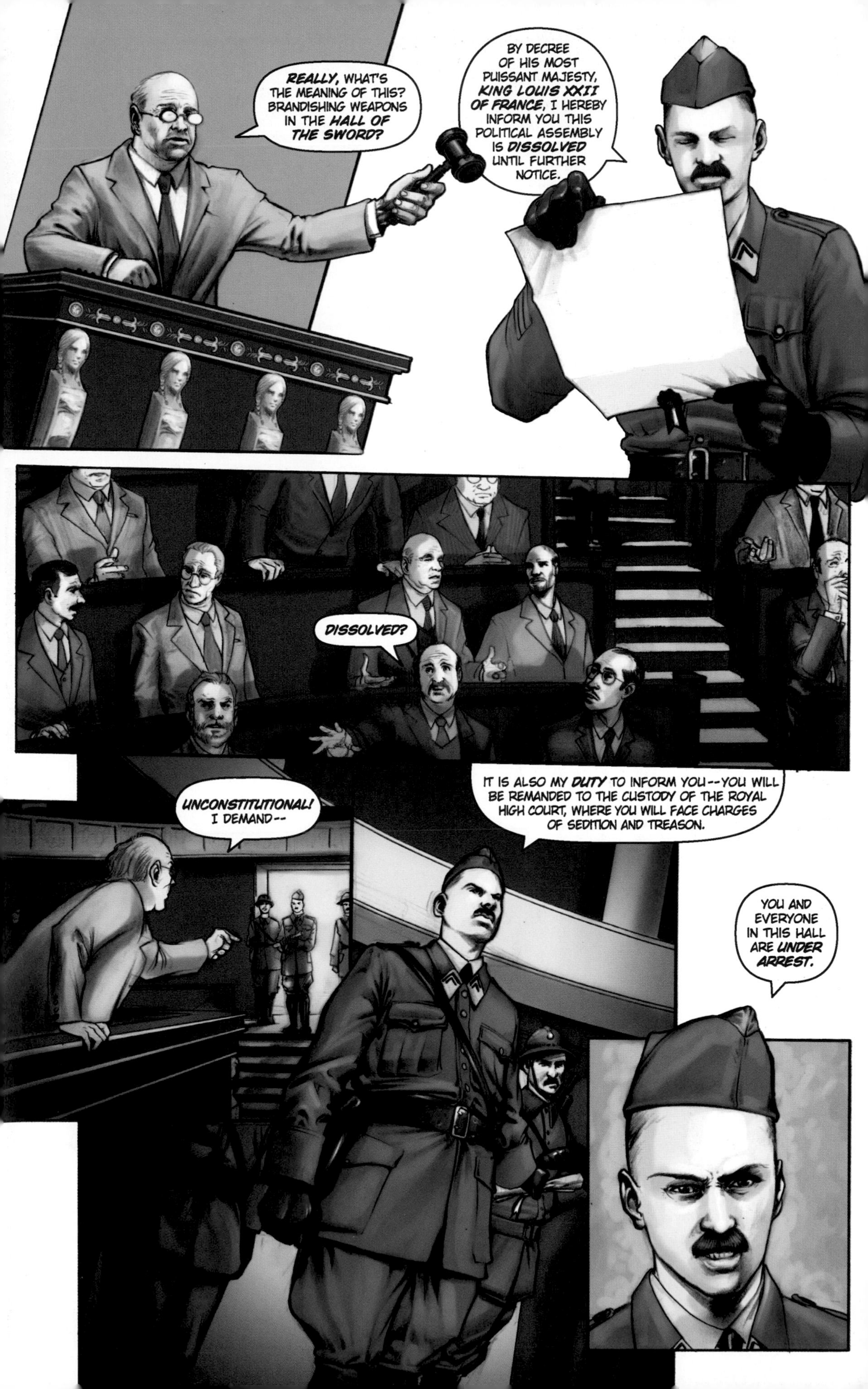
REALLY, WHAT'S THE MEANING OF THIS? BRANDISHING WEAPONS IN THE HALL OF THE SWORD?
BY DECREE OF HIS MOST PUISSANT MAJESTY, KING LOUIS XXII OF FRANCE, I HEREBY INFORM YOU THIS POLITICAL ASSEMBLY IS DISSOLVED UNTIL FURTHER NOTICE.
DISSOLVED?
UNCONSTITUTIONAL! I DEMAND--
IT IS ALSO MY DUTY TO INFORM YOU--YOU WILL BE REMANDED TO THE CUSTODY OF THE ROYAL HIGH COURT, WHERE YOU WILL FACE CHARGES OF SEDITION AND TREASON.
YOU AND EVERYONE IN THIS HALL ARE UNDER ARREST.

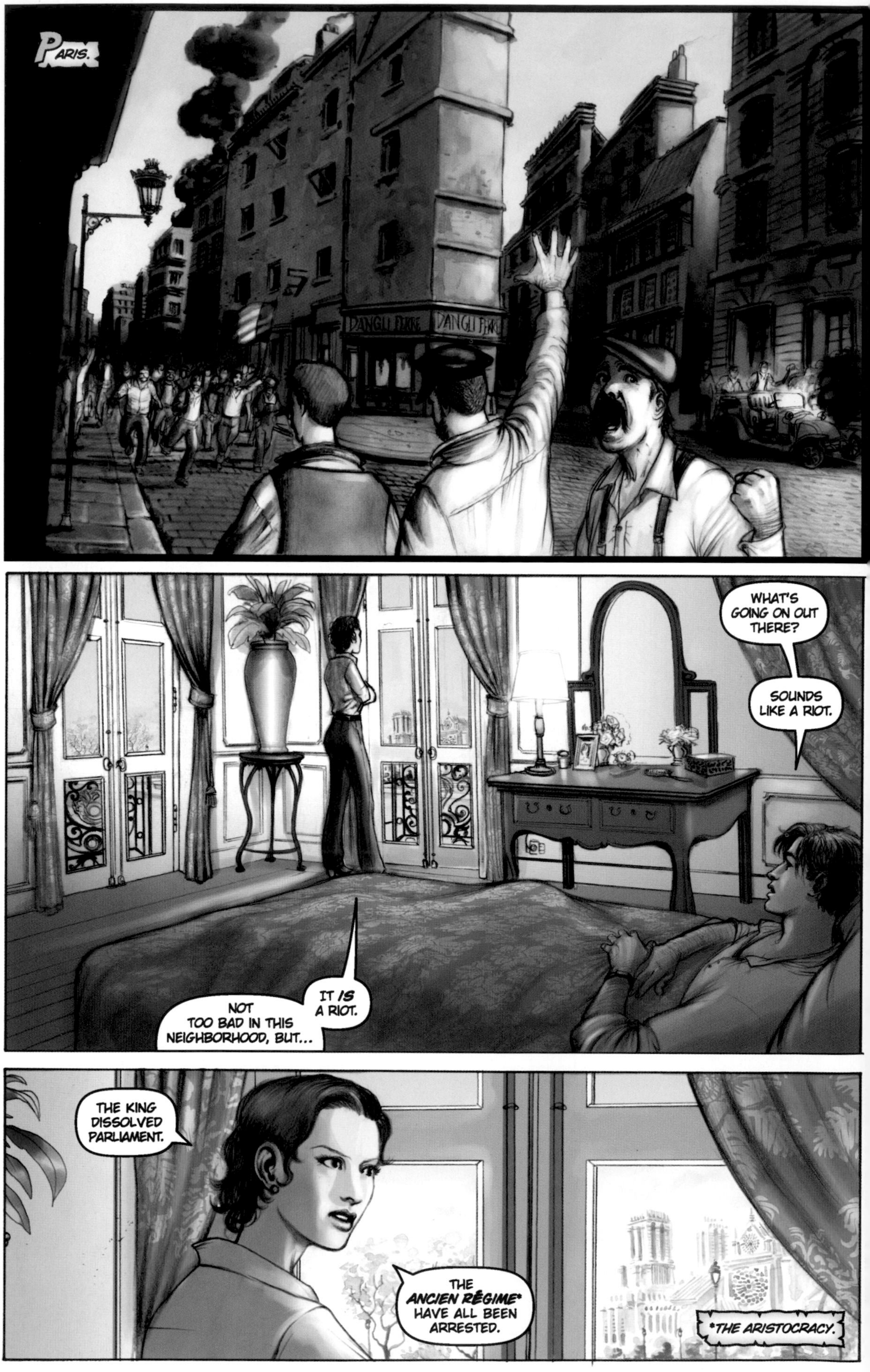
PARIS.
WHAT'S GOING ON OUT THERE?
SOUNDS LIKE A RIOT.
IT IS A RIOT.
NOT TOO BAD IN THIS NEIGHBORHOOD, BUT...
THE KING DISSOLVED PARLIAMENT.
THE ANCIEN RÉGIME* HAVE ALL BEEN ARRESTED.
*THE ARISTOCRACY.

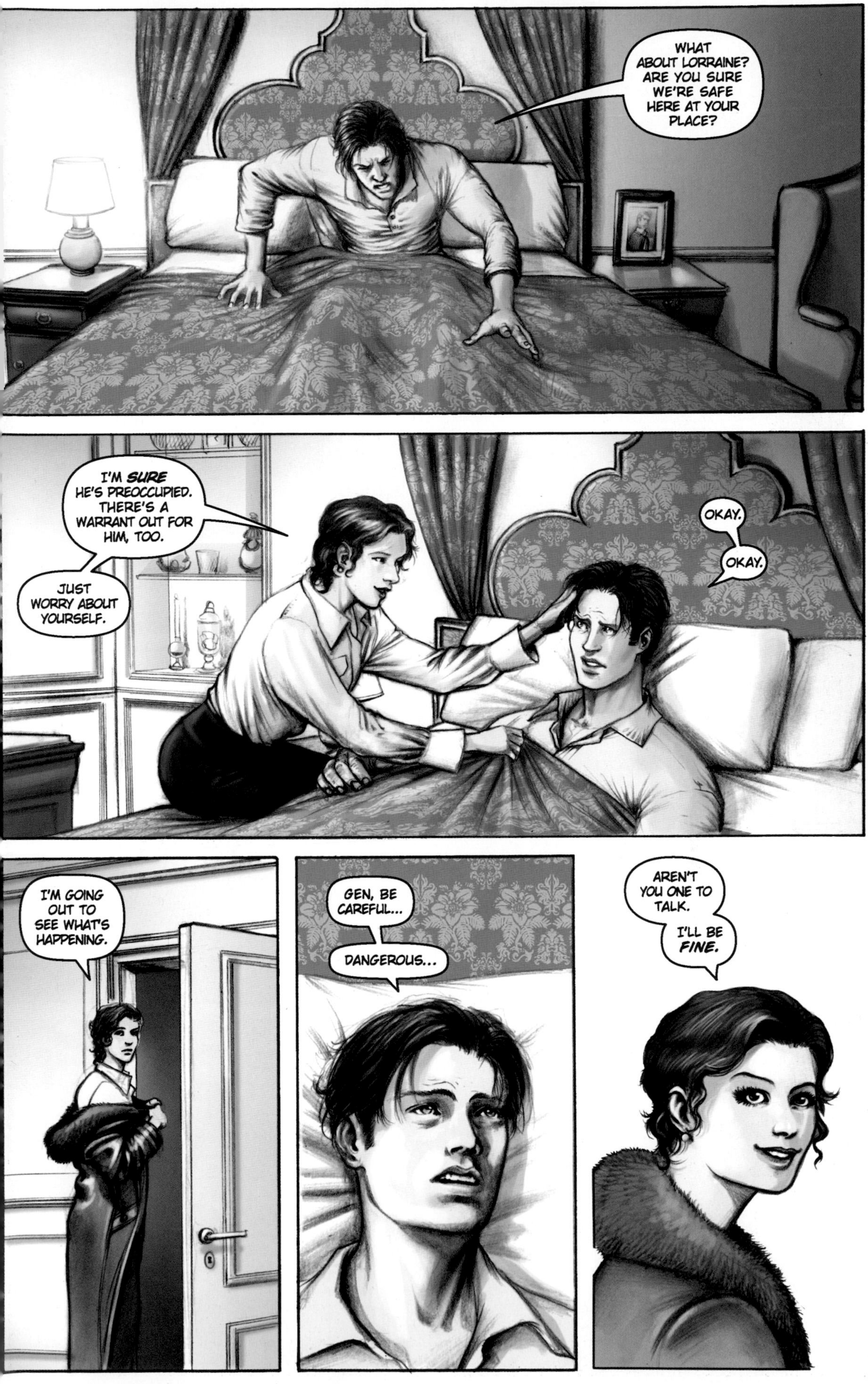
WHAT ABOUT LORRAINE? ARE YOU SURE WE'RE SAFE HERE AT YOUR PLACE?
I'M *SURE* HE'S PREOCCUPIED. THERE'S A WARRANT OUT FOR HIM, TOO.
JUST WORRY ABOUT YOURSELF.
OKAY.
OKAY.
I'M GOING OUT TO SEE WHAT'S HAPPENING.
GEN, BE CAREFUL...
DANGEROUS...
AREN'T YOU ONE TO TALK.
I'LL BE *FINE.*

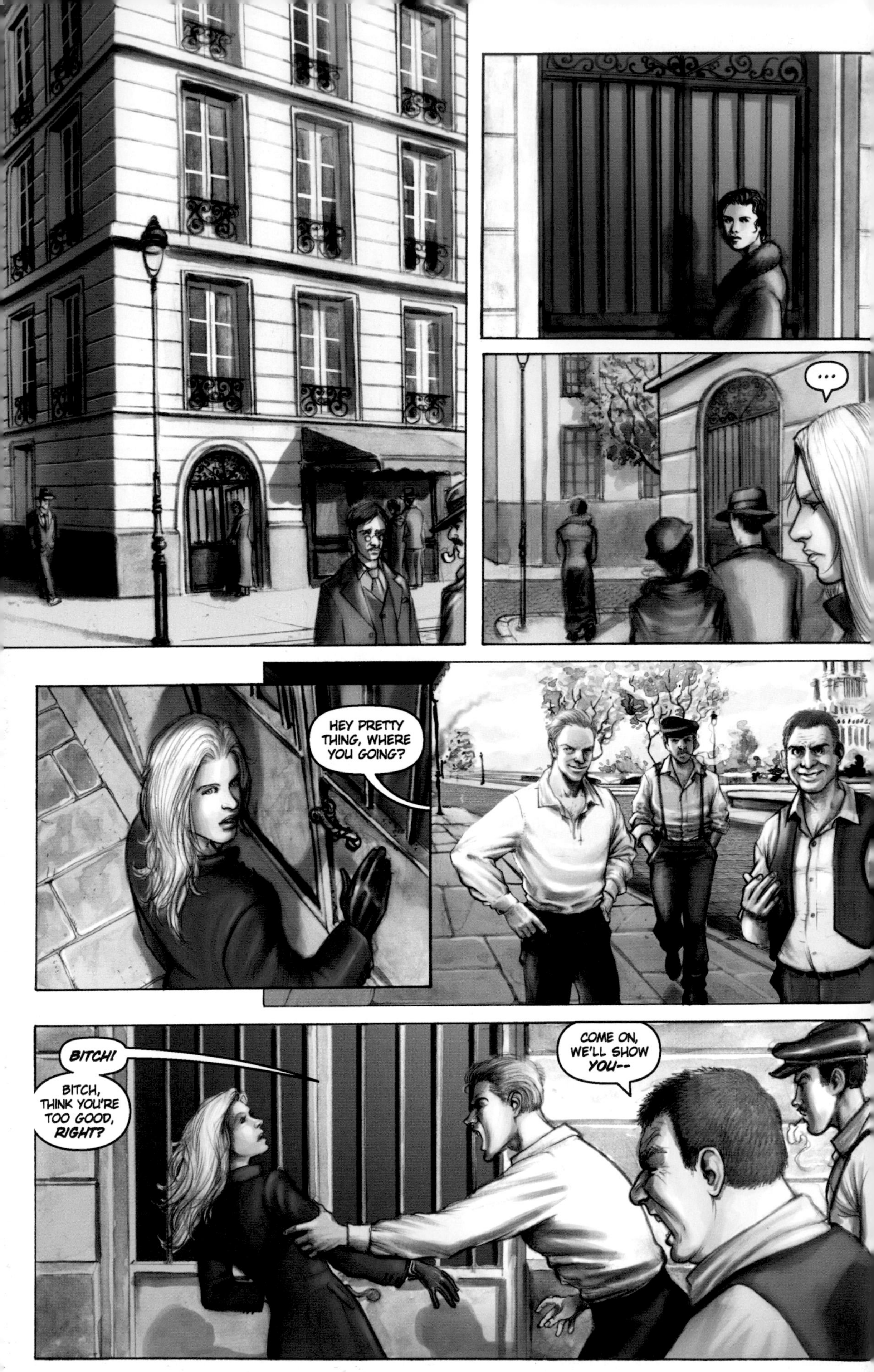
...
HEY PRETTY THING, WHERE YOU GOING?
BITCH!
BITCH, THINK YOU'RE TOO GOOD, RIGHT?
COME ON, WE'LL SHOW YOU--

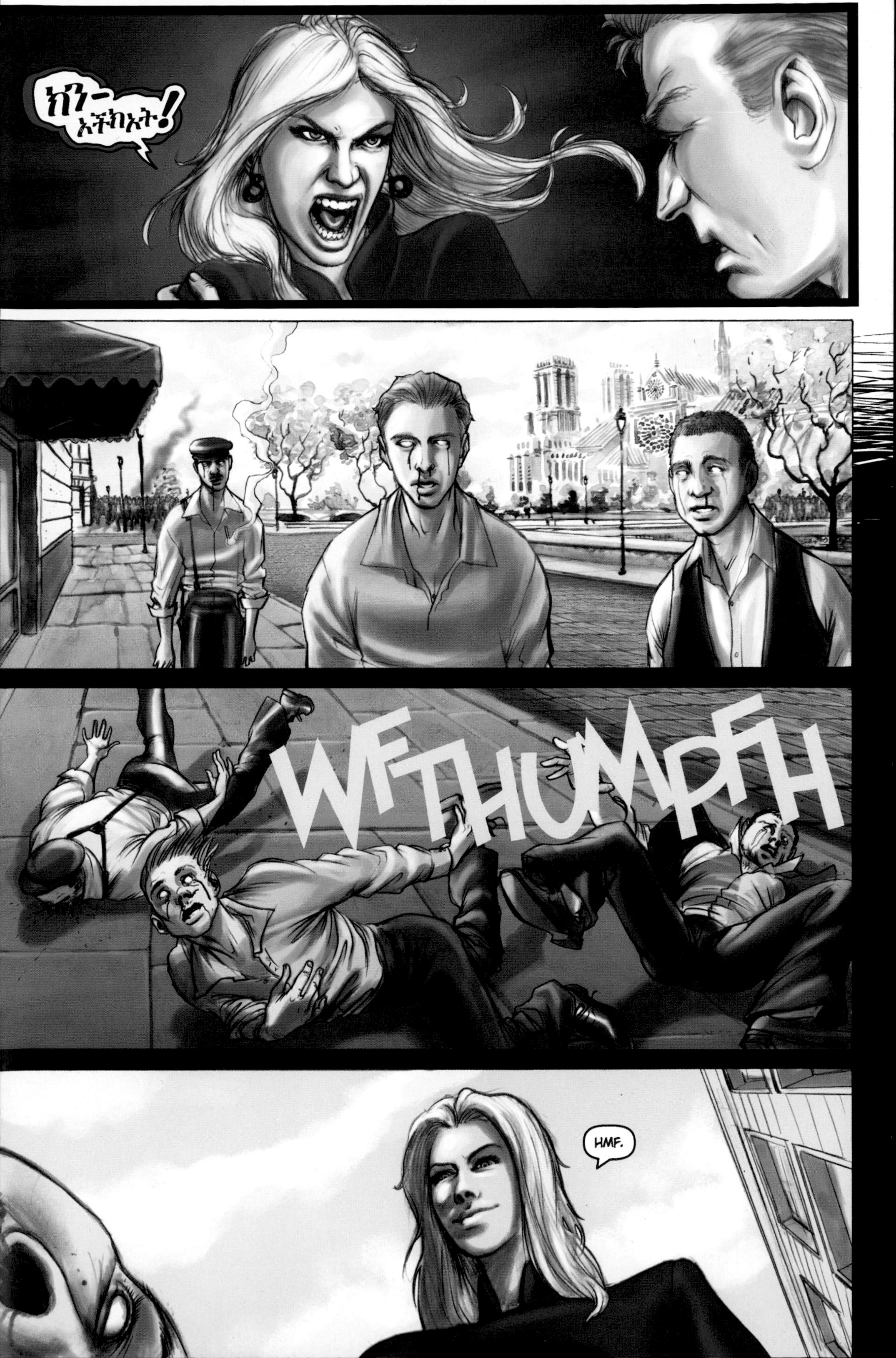
ክን— አችክአት!
WFTHUMPFH
HMF.

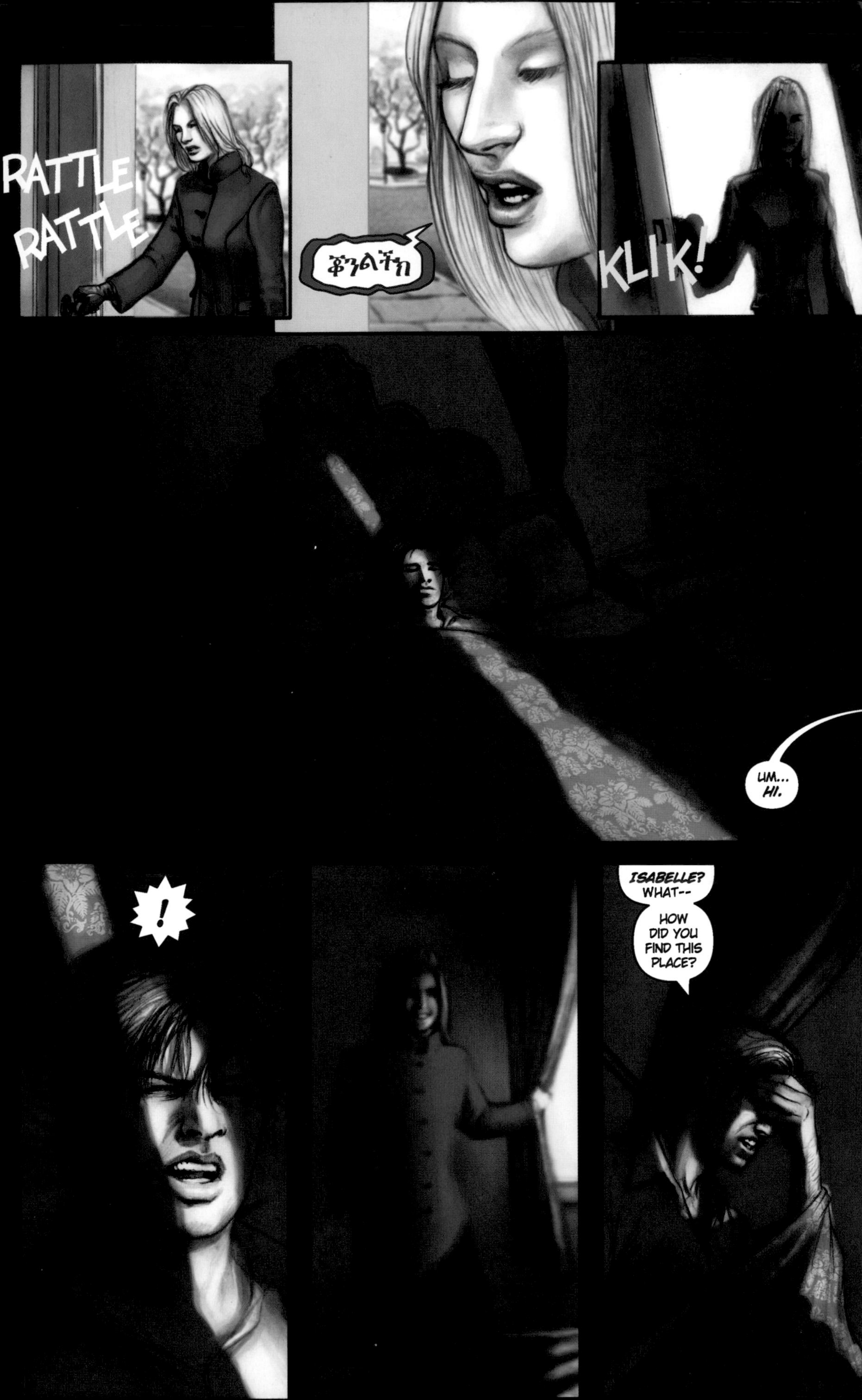
RATTLE
RATTLE
ቆንልችክ
KLIK!
UM... HI.
!
ISABELLE? WHAT--
HOW DID YOU FIND THIS PLACE?

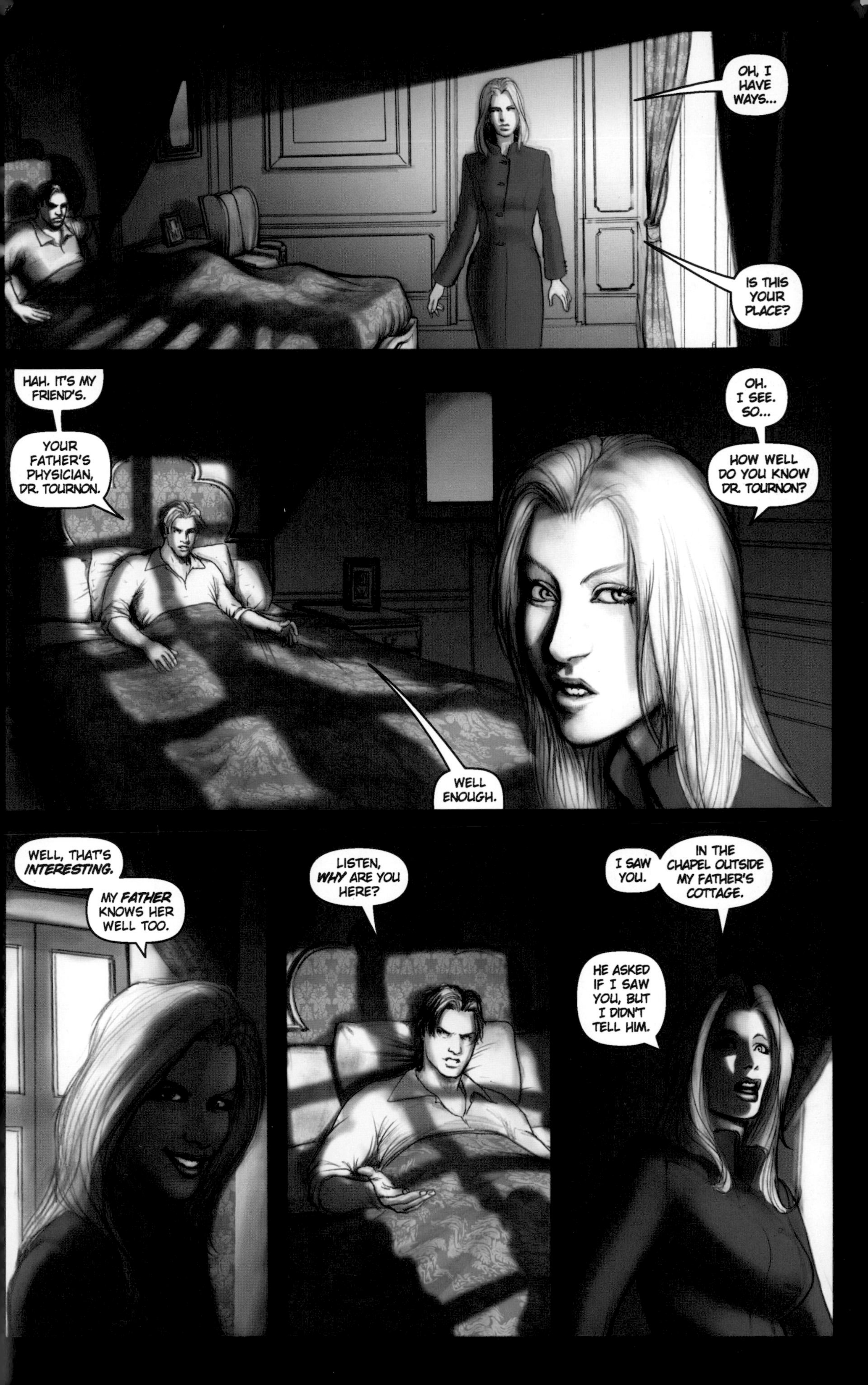
OH, I HAVE WAYS...
IS THIS YOUR PLACE?
HAH. IT'S MY FRIEND'S.
YOUR FATHER'S PHYSICIAN, DR. TOURNON.
OH. I SEE. SO...
HOW WELL DO YOU KNOW DR. TOURNON?
WELL ENOUGH.
WELL, THAT'S INTERESTING.
MY FATHER KNOWS HER WELL TOO.
LISTEN, WHY ARE YOU HERE?
I SAW YOU.
IN THE CHAPEL OUTSIDE MY FATHER'S COTTAGE.
HE ASKED IF I SAW YOU, BUT I DIDN'T TELL HIM.

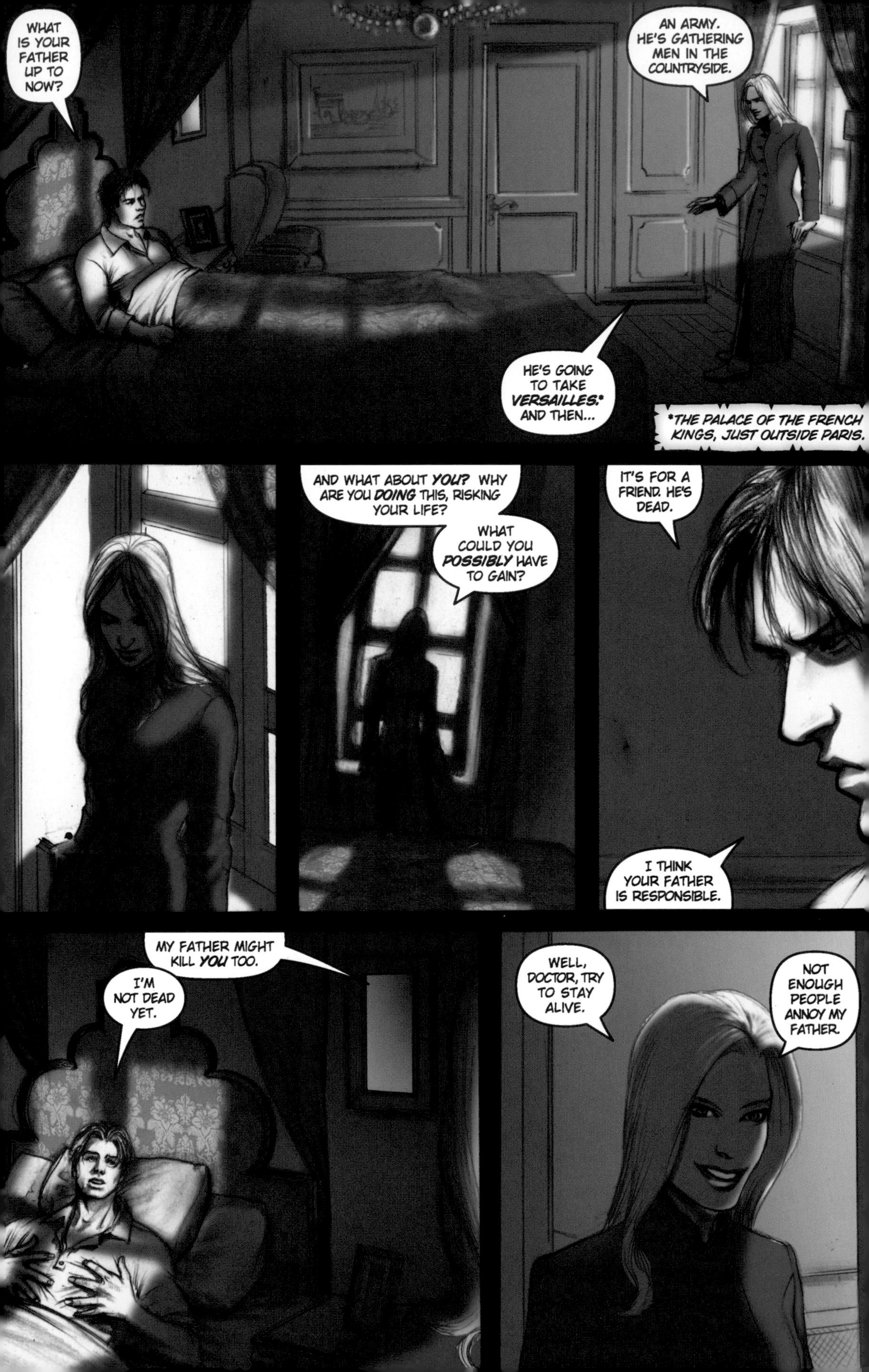
WHAT IS YOUR FATHER UP TO NOW?
AN ARMY. HE'S GATHERING MEN IN THE COUNTRYSIDE.
HE'S GOING TO TAKE **VERSAILLES.*** AND THEN...
*THE PALACE OF THE FRENCH KINGS, JUST OUTSIDE PARIS.
AND WHAT ABOUT **YOU?** WHY ARE YOU **DOING** THIS, RISKING YOUR LIFE?
WHAT COULD YOU **POSSIBLY** HAVE TO GAIN?
IT'S FOR A FRIEND. HE'S DEAD.
I THINK YOUR FATHER IS RESPONSIBLE.
MY FATHER MIGHT KILL **YOU** TOO.
I'M NOT DEAD YET.
WELL, DOCTOR, TRY TO STAY ALIVE.
NOT ENOUGH PEOPLE ANNOY MY FATHER.

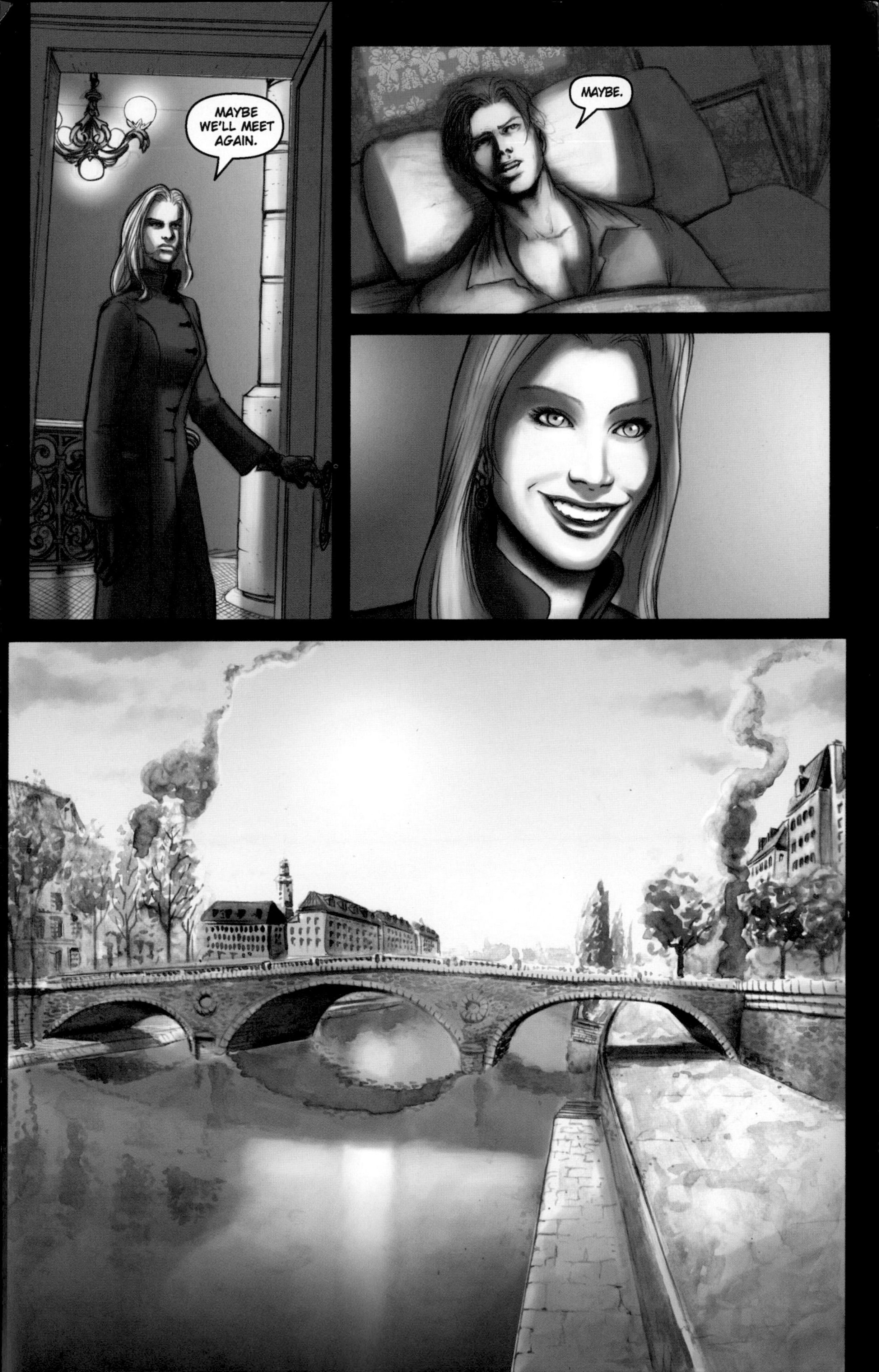
MAYBE WE'LL MEET AGAIN.
MAYBE.

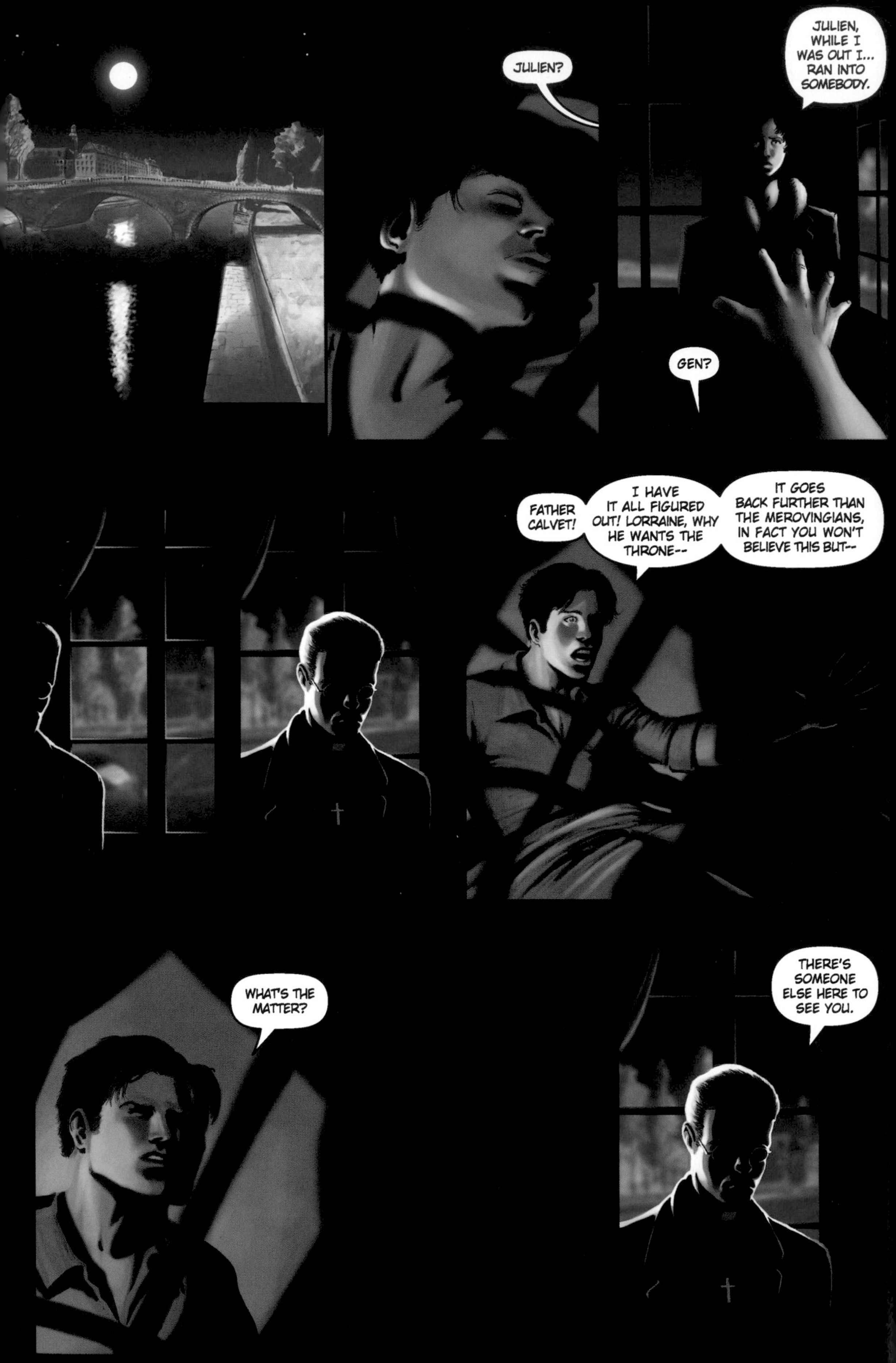
JULIEN?
JULIEN, WHILE I WAS OUT I... RAN INTO SOMEBODY.
GEN?
FATHER CALVET!
I HAVE IT ALL FIGURED OUT! LORRAINE, WHY HE WANTS THE THRONE--
IT GOES BACK FURTHER THAN THE MEROVINGIANS, IN FACT YOU WON'T BELIEVE THIS BUT--
WHAT'S THE MATTER?
THERE'S SOMEONE ELSE HERE TO SEE YOU.

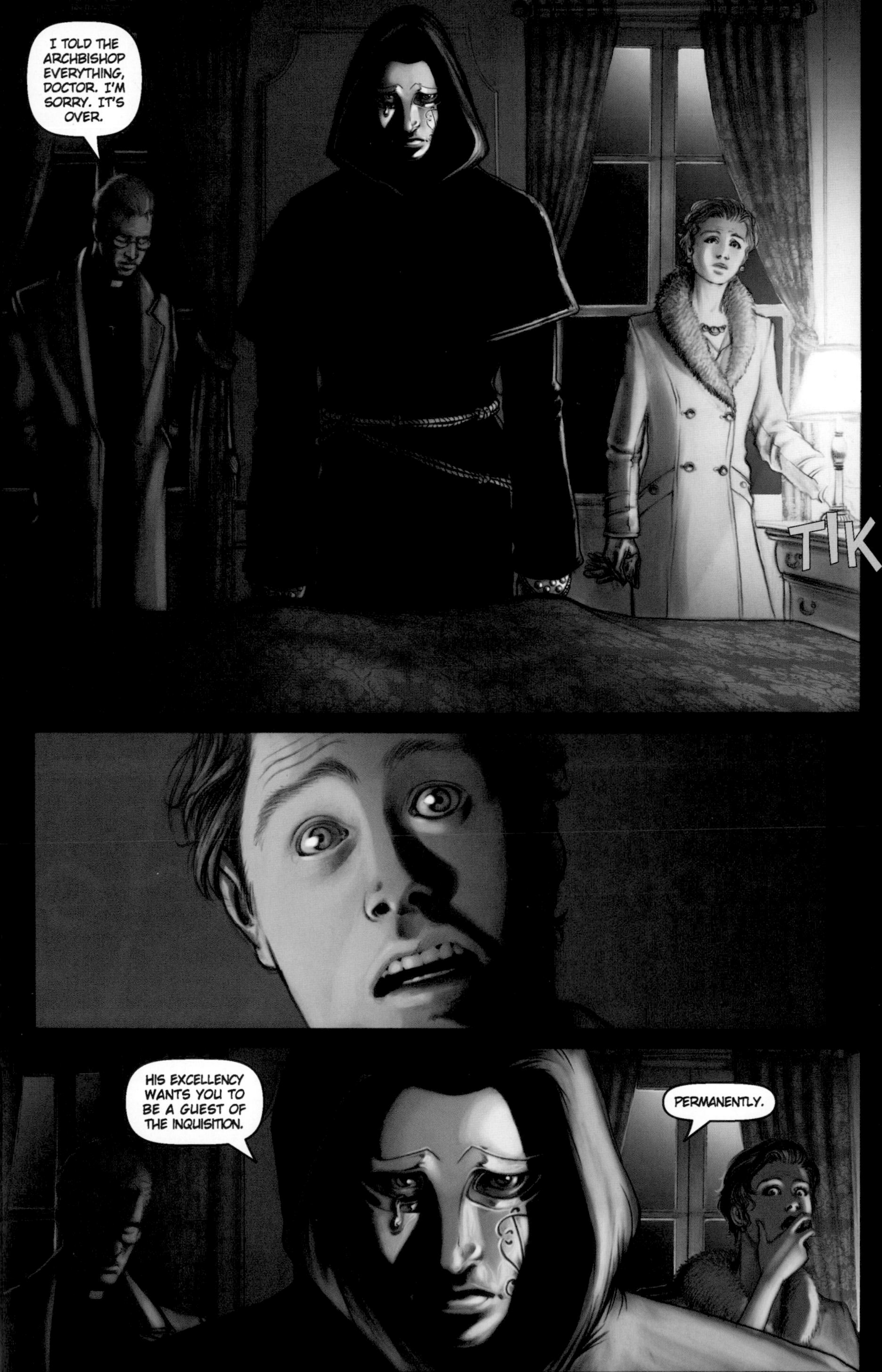
I TOLD THE ARCHBISHOP EVERYTHING, DOCTOR. I'M SORRY. IT'S OVER.
TIK
HIS EXCELLENCY WANTS YOU TO BE A GUEST OF THE INQUISITION.
PERMANENTLY.

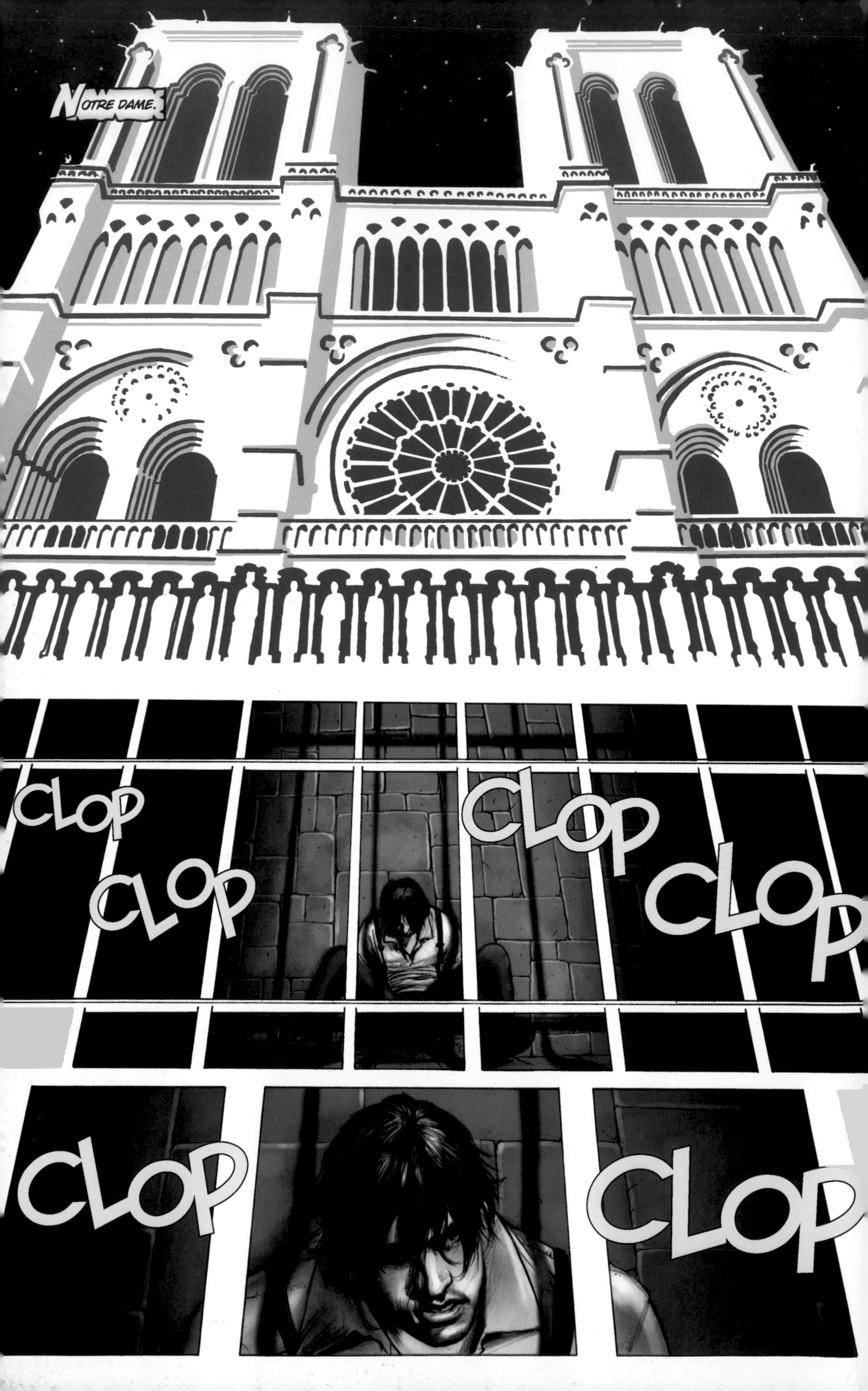
NOTRE DAME.
CLOP
CLOP
CLOP
CLOP
CLOP
CLOP

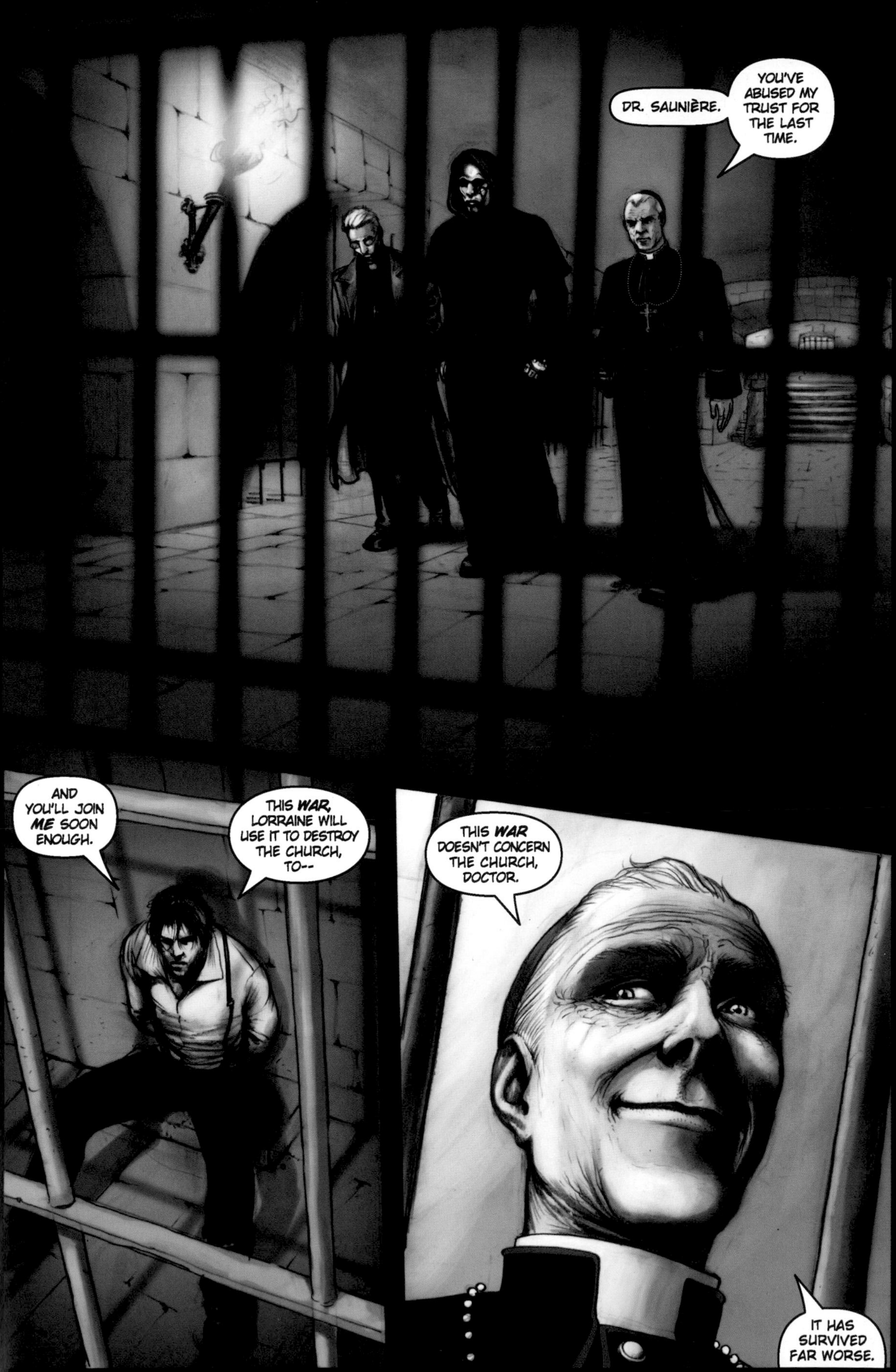
DR. SAUNIÈRE.
YOU'VE ABUSED MY TRUST FOR THE LAST TIME.
AND YOU'LL JOIN ME SOON ENOUGH.
THIS WAR, LORRAINE WILL USE IT TO DESTROY THE CHURCH, TO--
THIS WAR DOESN'T CONCERN THE CHURCH, DOCTOR.
IT HAS SURVIVED FAR WORSE.

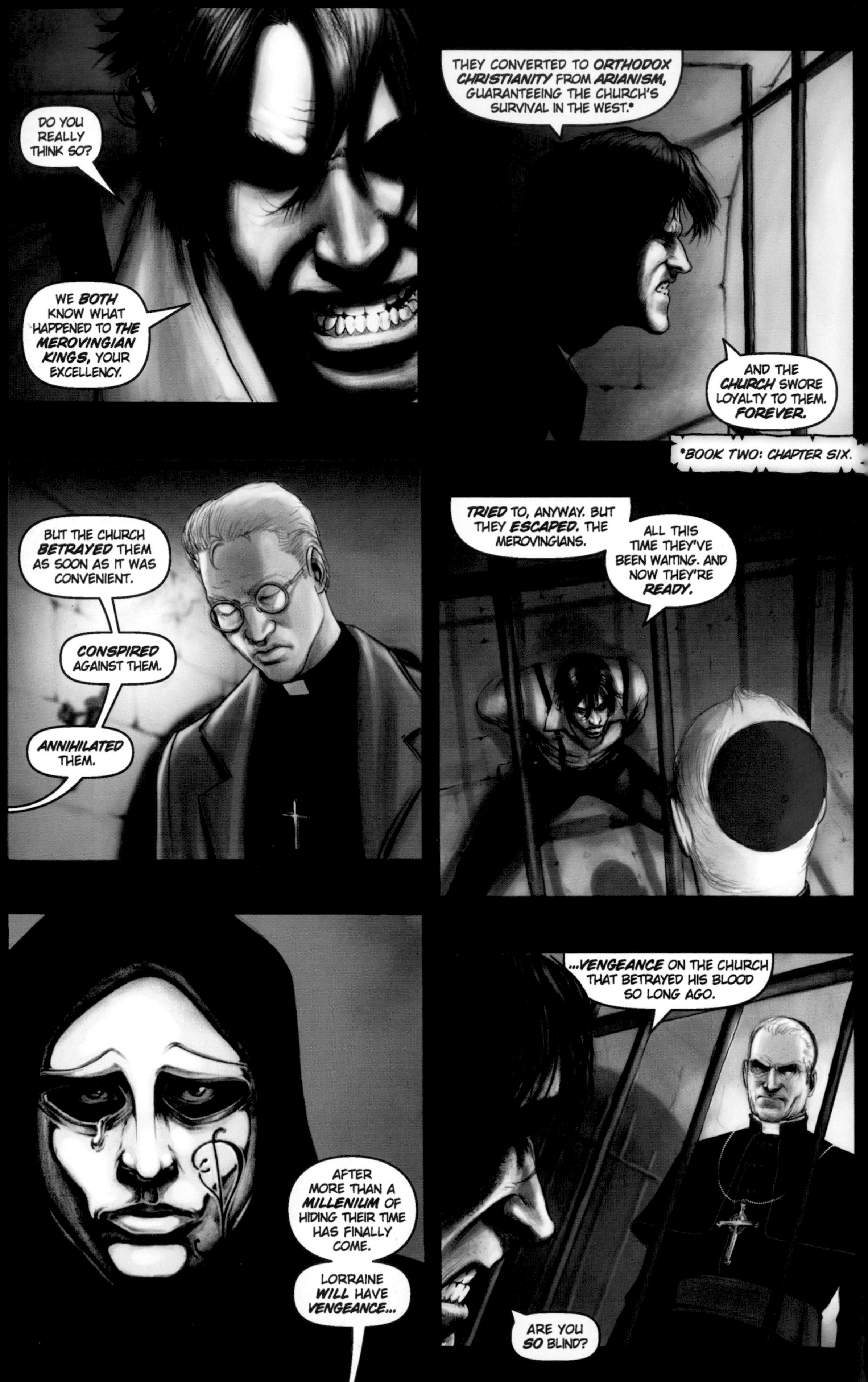
DO YOU REALLY THINK SO?
WE BOTH KNOW WHAT HAPPENED TO THE MEROVINGIAN KINGS, YOUR EXCELLENCY.
THEY CONVERTED TO ORTHODOX CHRISTIANITY FROM ARIANISM, GUARANTEEING THE CHURCH'S SURVIVAL IN THE WEST.*
AND THE CHURCH SWORE LOYALTY TO THEM. FOREVER.
*BOOK TWO: CHAPTER SIX.
BUT THE CHURCH BETRAYED THEM AS SOON AS IT WAS CONVENIENT.
CONSPIRED AGAINST THEM.
ANNIHILATED THEM.
TRIED TO, ANYWAY. BUT THEY ESCAPED. THE MEROVINGIANS.
ALL THIS TIME THEY'VE BEEN WAITING. AND NOW THEY'RE READY.
AFTER MORE THAN A MILLENIUM OF HIDING THEIR TIME HAS FINALLY COME.
LORRAINE WILL HAVE VENGEANCE...
...VENGEANCE ON THE CHURCH THAT BETRAYED HIS BLOOD SO LONG AGO.
ARE YOU SO BLIND?

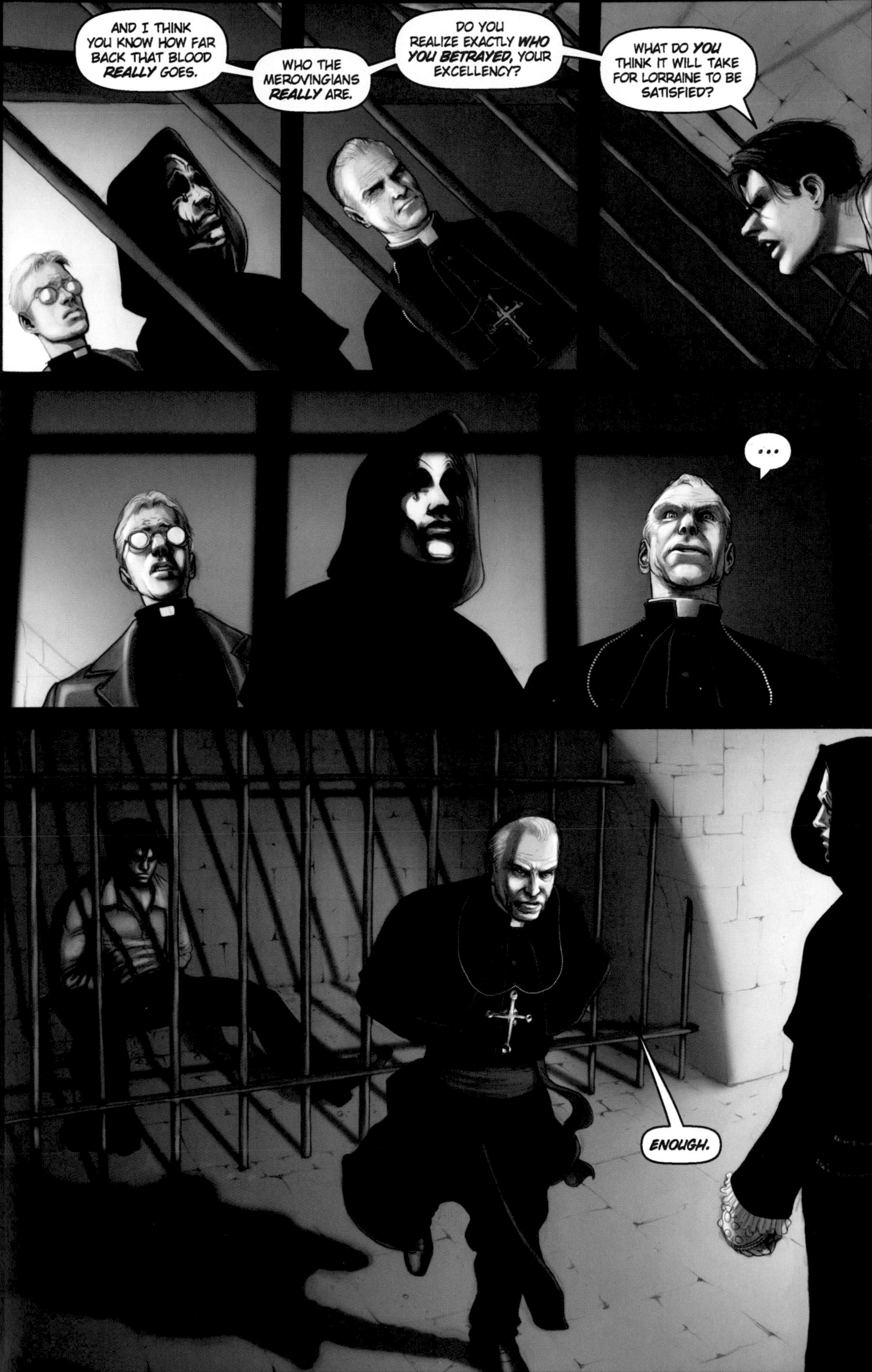
AND I THINK YOU KNOW HOW FAR BACK THAT BLOOD REALLY GOES.
WHO THE MEROVINGIANS REALLY ARE.
DO YOU REALIZE EXACTLY WHO YOU BETRAYED, YOUR EXCELLENCY?
WHAT DO YOU THINK IT WILL TAKE FOR LORRAINE TO BE SATISFIED?
...
ENOUGH.

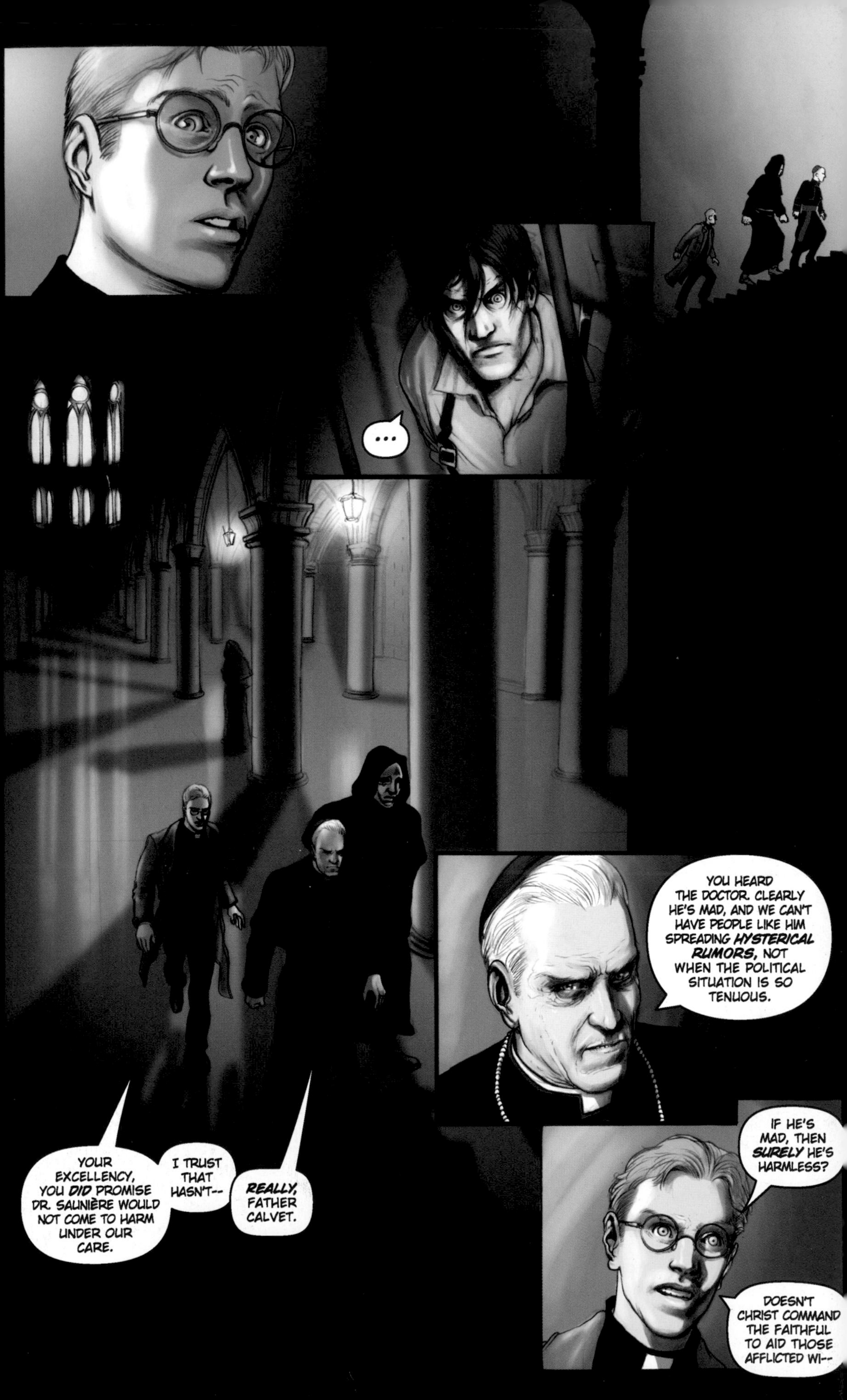
...
YOUR EXCELLENCY, YOU DID PROMISE DR. SAUNIÈRE WOULD NOT COME TO HARM UNDER OUR CARE.
I TRUST THAT HASN'T--
REALLY, FATHER CALVET.
YOU HEARD THE DOCTOR. CLEARLY HE'S MAD, AND WE CAN'T HAVE PEOPLE LIKE HIM SPREADING HYSTERICAL RUMORS, NOT WHEN THE POLITICAL SITUATION IS SO TENUOUS.
IF HE'S MAD, THEN SURELY HE'S HARMLESS?
DOESN'T CHRIST COMMAND THE FAITHFUL TO AID THOSE AFFLICTED WI--

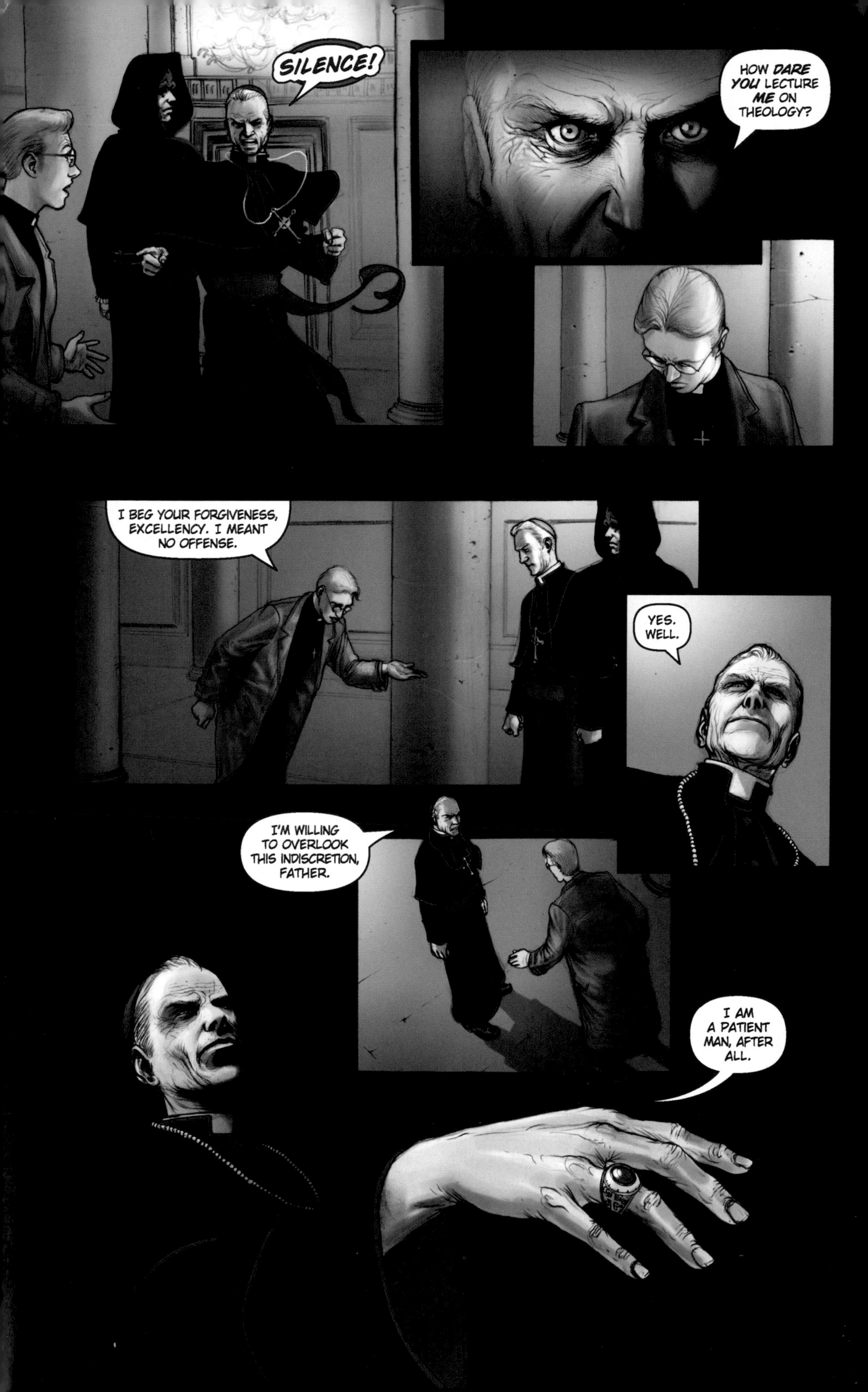
SILENCE!
HOW DARE YOU LECTURE ME ON THEOLOGY?
I BEG YOUR FORGIVENESS, EXCELLENCY. I MEANT NO OFFENSE.
YES. WELL.
I'M WILLING TO OVERLOOK THIS INDISCRETION, FATHER.
I AM A PATIENT MAN, AFTER ALL.

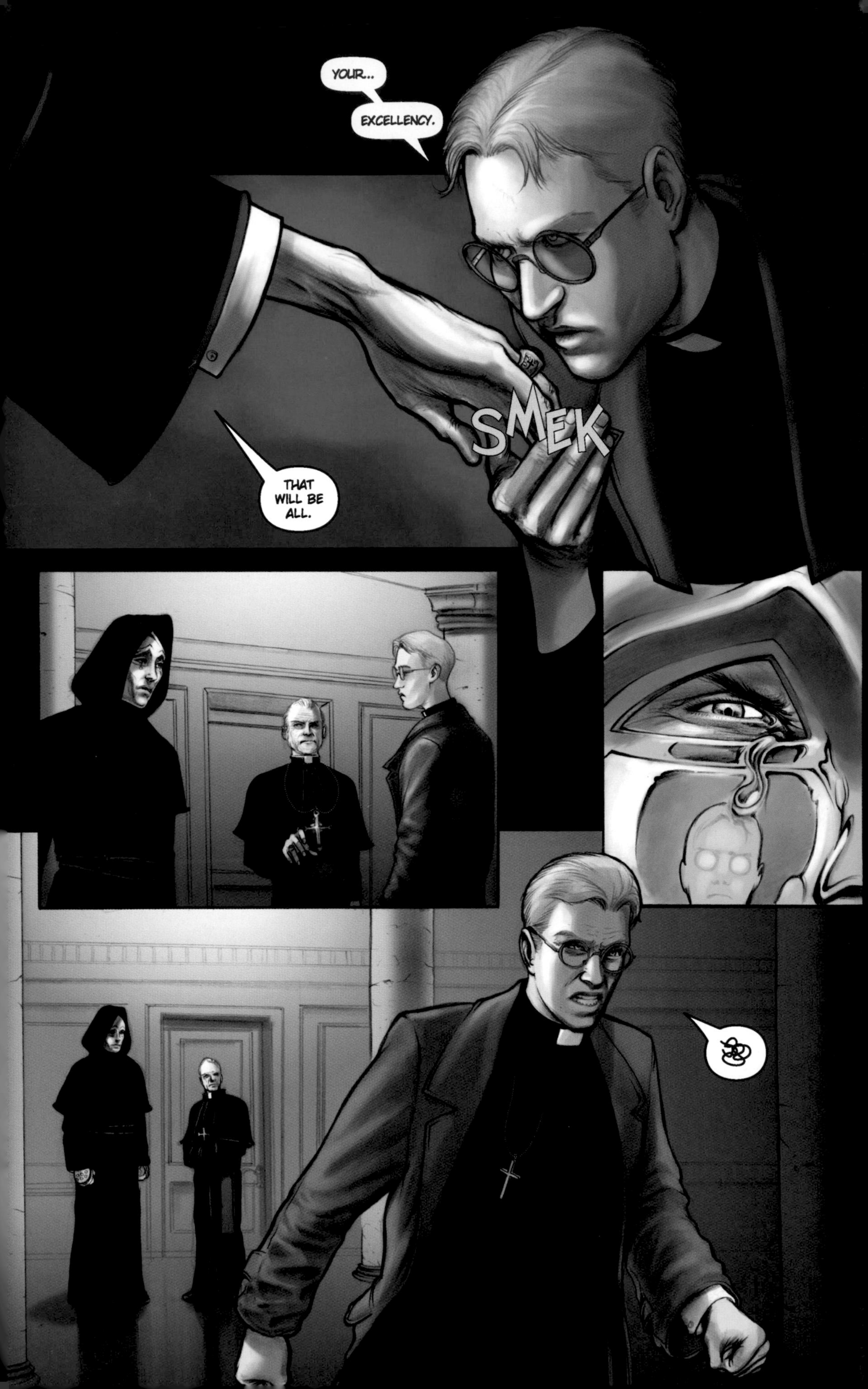
YOUR...
EXCELLENCY.
SMEK
THAT WILL BE ALL.

Le Journal de la Liberté

Paris' leading anglophone newspaper • vol. 205, no. 102 • Nov. 8, MCMXXXIII

Editors in Chief: M. Tait Bergstrom, M. Matthew Pasteris. **Story Editor:** M. Arvid Nelson.
Art Editor: M. Juan Ferreyra. **Photography Editor:** M. Alexander Waldman.
Layout Supervisor: M. William Kartalopoulos. **Editors Emeritus:** M. Clark A. Smith,
M. Howard P. Lovecraft, M. Robert E. Howard. Redacted by the Holy Inquisition under the direction
of His Excellency Archbishop Emile-Jean Ireneaux. *Le Journal de la Liberté* is printed under the benign
auspices of his most puissant majesty KING LOUIS XXII of FRANCE. GOD SAVE THE KING.

Papal seal

of Approval

KING LOUIS DISBANDS PARLIAMENT, ARRESTS NOBLE FAMILIES, DUKE OF LORRAINE'S SUPPORTERS

Lorraine Escapes Initial Roundup

The Duke of Lorraine has so far avoided capture by royalist forces.

Lorraine is very popular with the military, having commanded successful colonial expeditions in Indochina and Algiers. His grandfather was a distinguished commander in the Thirty Years War, waged from 1861 to 1891.

Speculation Lorraine might be gathering an army loyal to him for an assault on Versailles abounds.

On the eve of the invasion of Cordova, parliament named Lorraine supreme commander of all French forces. Lorraine ordered all troops deployed to France's borders, leaving the interior of the country virtually undefended.

Lorraine has also gained enormous political power and popular support in recent years for his confrontational foreign policy and tough stance on Islam.

Lorraine outmaneuvered King Louis in a stunning series of political upsets which culminated in the annexation of the hinterlands of Aragon, Navarre and Catalonia several weeks ago.

The Marquis of Aragon was assassinated shortly thereafter, prompting Lorraine to issue an ultimatum to the Cordovan Emirate which was quickly ratified *Continued on page A21*

☙ INSIDE ☙

Riots broke out in Paris as a result of the arrests. The crown authorized Royal Gendarmes to "use all means available" to restore order.

Facing an increasingly rebellious parliament, King Louis yesterday ordered the arrest of all members of the Hall of the Sword. The move was intended to be "swift and surprising," officials said.

A few Sword members escaped the initial roundup. There are outstanding warrants for those still at large, including the Sword's leader, the Duke of Lorraine.

King Louis also suspended parliament indefinitely.

"The king is acting in the interests of his subjects," Sir Charles Martel, King Louis' mayor of the court, said. "The crown must have absolute control in times of war."

The Sword members were taken to a Royal Gendarmerie prison for "temporary holding." Martel would not speak as to their ultimate fate.

"King Louis reserves all rights in this matter. We will attend to each case individually and fairly," he said.

At the time this edition went to press, the men had not been arraigned, and they had not been granted access to family members or legal counsel.

The mass arrests were carried out as a reaction against the king's political opponents, Guy-Manuel Bangaltier, King Louis' interior minister, said.

"The King regrets the necessity of these arrests," Bangaltier said. "But His Majesty had no choice. He personally appeared before parliament, urging the rejection of the Spanish Marches, but the Robe betrayed him. It was a catastrophic mistake."

The Hall of the Robe, the lower house of parliament and the king's traditional support base, defied the king's wishes and voted for the annexation of the Spanish Marches with the Hall of the Sword.

The unprecedented vote was largely due to the efforts of the Duke of Lorraine, de facto leader of the Hall of the Sword. The annexation was part of Lorraine's larger goal of ridding the Iberian peninsula of the Cordovan Emirate and then "marching to the Holy Land."

What remains of that plan is in serious doubt.

The Hall of the Sword is made up of the members of France's ancient noble houses. The Sword is usually opposed to the Crown's policies, but always *continued on page A2*

PRUSSIANS ADVANCE ACROSS ALSACE

The Western Front, Ardennes Forest – Prussian troops moved relentlessly westward, taking advantage of the political instability in France to overwhelm the bewildered Lorrainer troops defending the western marches.

The Prussian army has advanced ten miles in two days. If it continues at its current rate, the army will arrive in Paris in a few weeks.

Effective use of artillery has facilitated the Prussian offensive, according to French commanders fleeing the onslaught.

"The big guns hit us without warning. The infantry assault comes soon after, and it's been devastating. I've lost a lot of good men," a Lieutenant Colonel coordinating a desperate relief effort for a company of Royal Grenadiers pinned down by Prussian artillery said.

Casualty reports vary widely, ranging from the low hundreds to the thousands.

"It's bad, I'll tell you that much," a captain in the medical corps said. "We're seeing a lot of traumatic injuries from the shrapnel. A lot of amputations."

Civilians have not been spared in the advance of the Prussian hosts, and a steadily growing stream of refugees moves westward in advance of the German hosts.

Survivors tell horror stories of indiscriminate slaughter of women, children and the infirm, of rape, and widespread looting.

"We've lost everything, everything. The Germans burned down our house," Yvette Duchamp, a woman fleeing the destruction, said. "I was separated *continued on page A7*

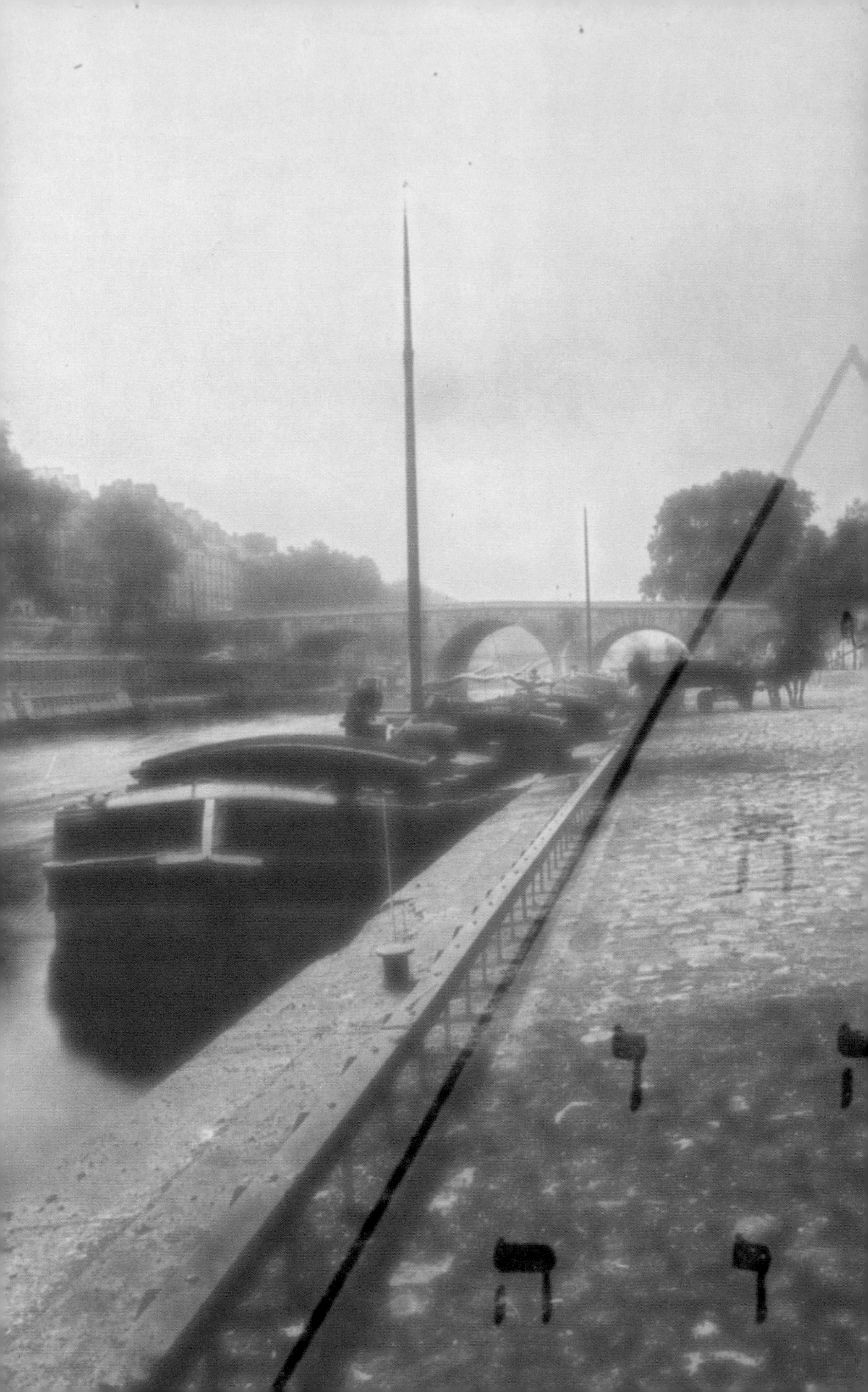

CHAPTER TWO
CROWN AND SWORD

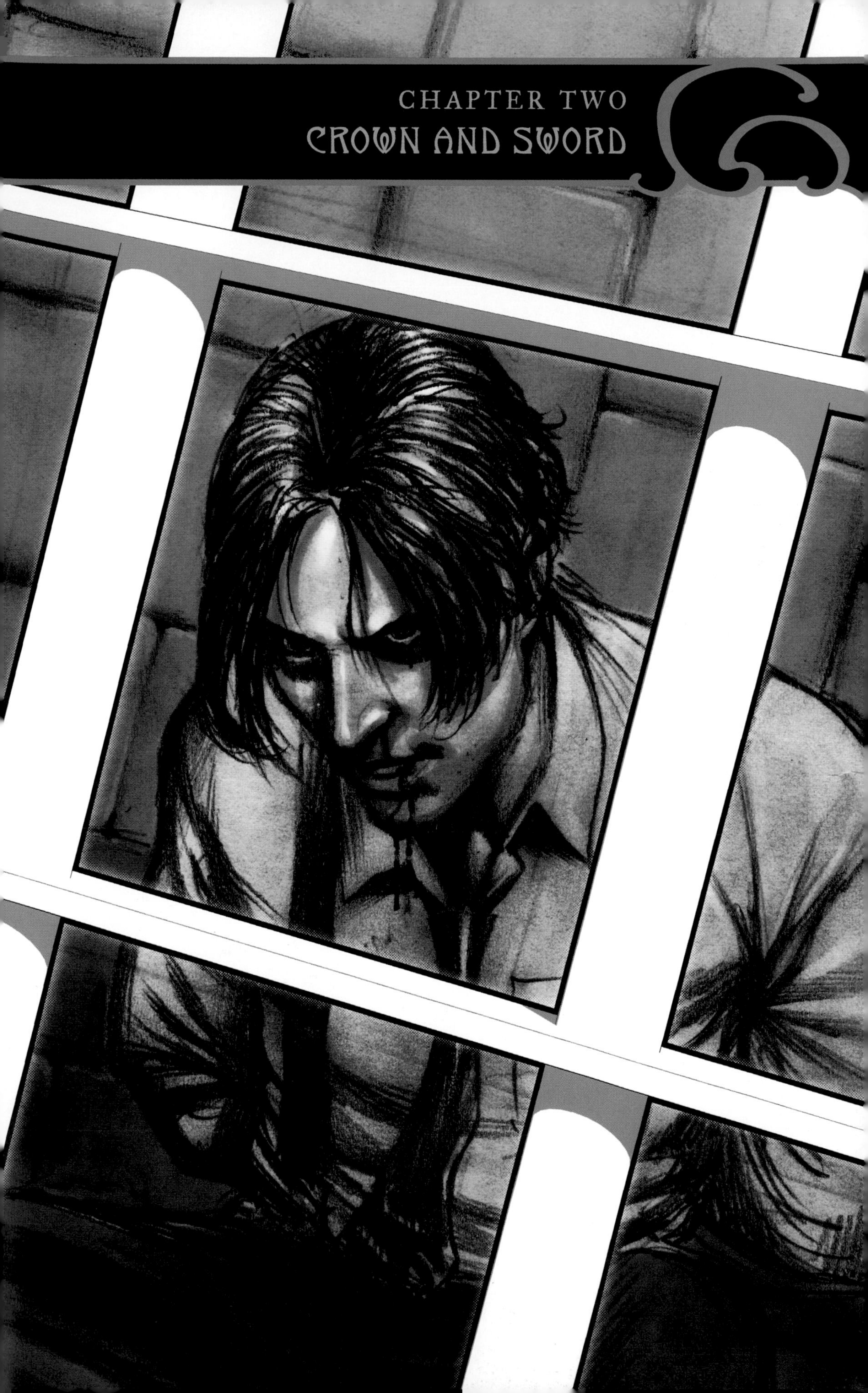

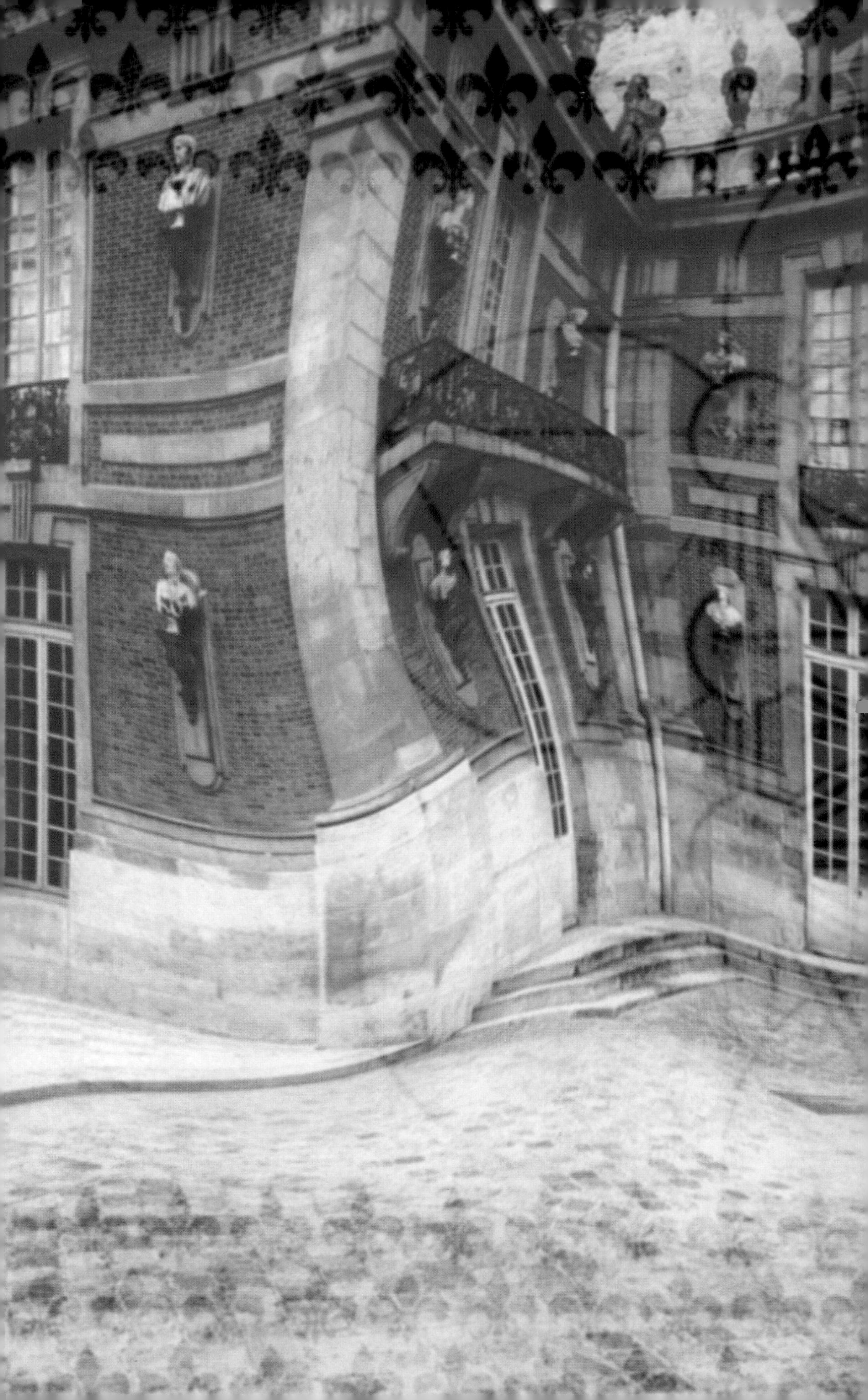

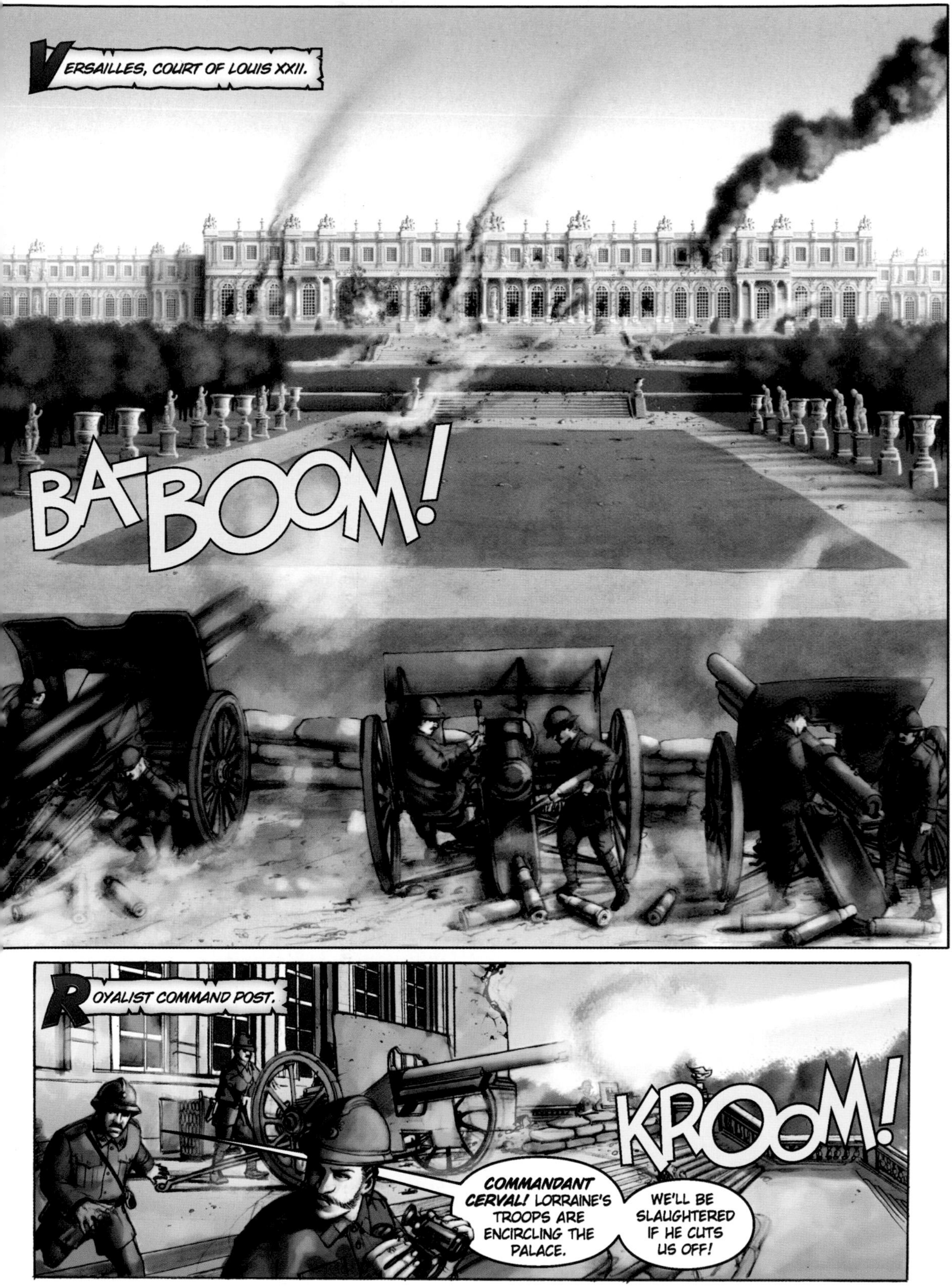
VERSAILLES, COURT OF LOUIS XXII.
BA-BOOM!
ROYALIST COMMAND POST.
KROOM!
COMMANDANT CERVAL! LORRAINE'S TROOPS ARE ENCIRCLING THE PALACE.
WE'LL BE SLAUGHTERED IF HE CUTS US OFF!

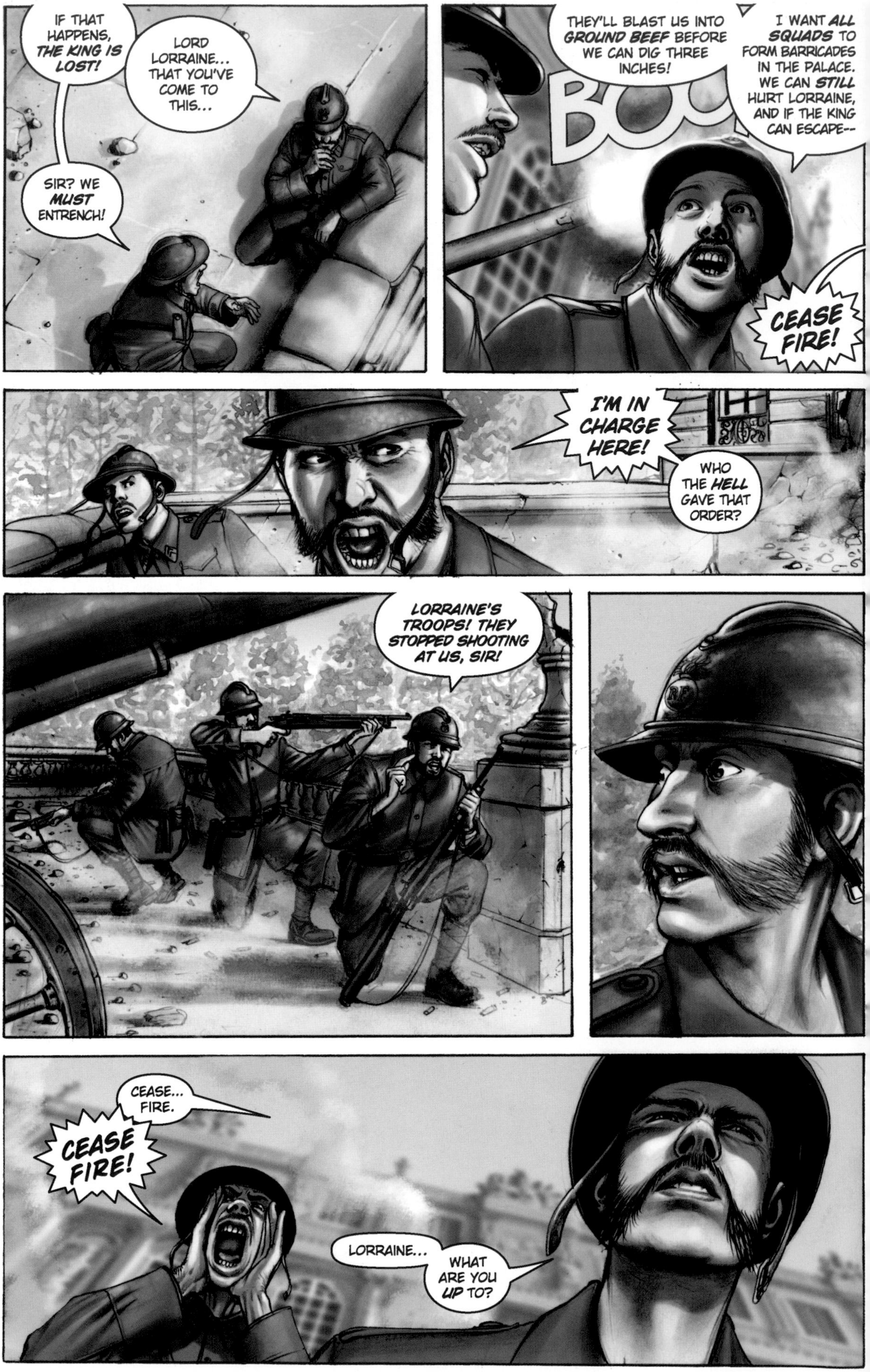

IF THAT HAPPENS, THE KING IS LOST!
LORD LORRAINE... THAT YOU'VE COME TO THIS...
SIR? WE MUST ENTRENCH!
THEY'LL BLAST US INTO GROUND BEEF BEFORE WE CAN DIG THREE INCHES!
BOO
I WANT ALL SQUADS TO FORM BARRICADES IN THE PALACE. WE CAN STILL HURT LORRAINE, AND IF THE KING CAN ESCAPE--
CEASE FIRE!
I'M IN CHARGE HERE!
WHO THE HELL GAVE THAT ORDER?
LORRAINE'S TROOPS! THEY STOPPED SHOOTING AT US, SIR!
CEASE... FIRE.
CEASE FIRE!
LORRAINE...
WHAT ARE YOU UP TO?

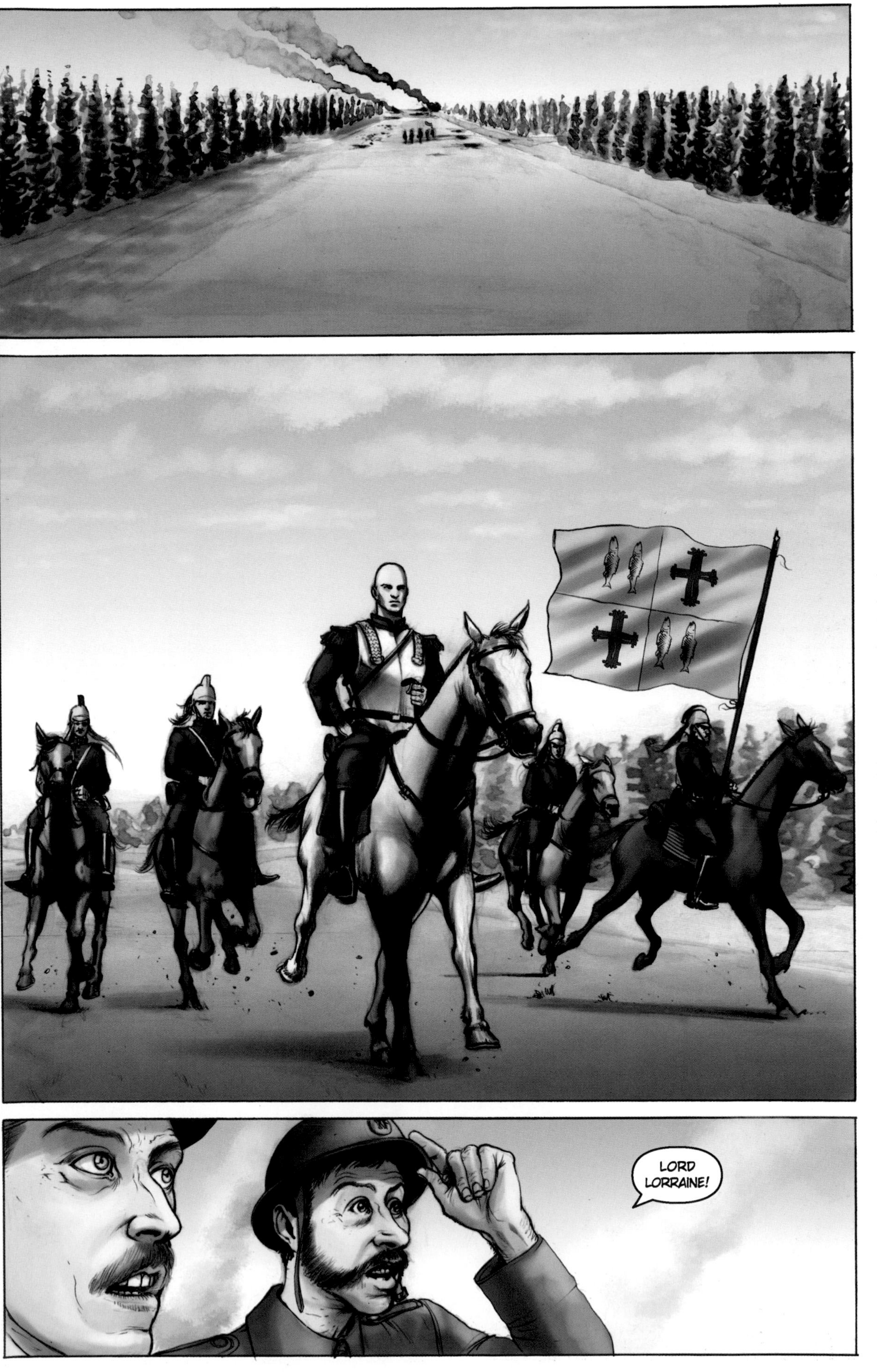
LORD LORRAINE!

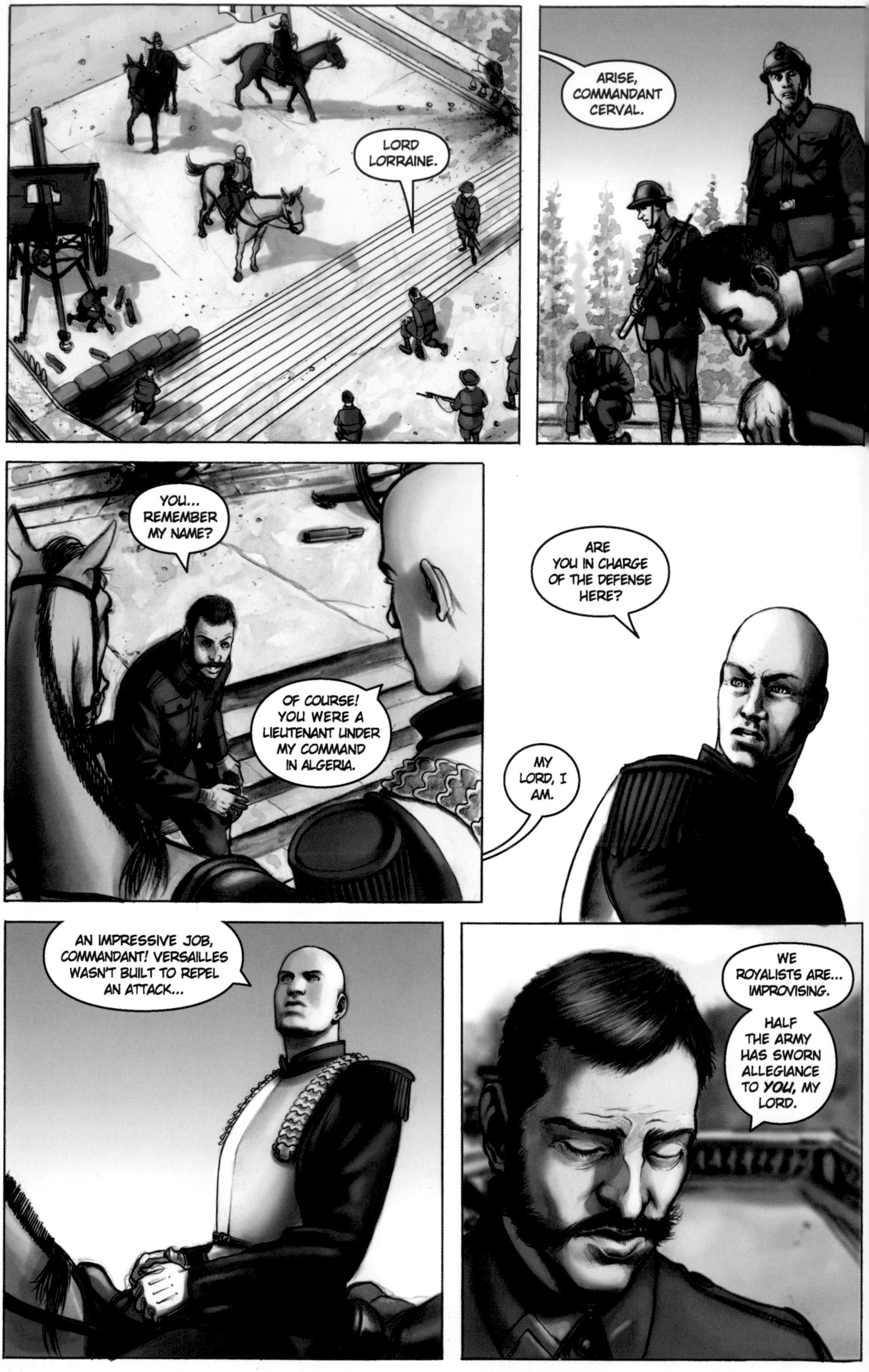
LORD LORRAINE.
ARISE, COMMANDANT CERVAL.
YOU... REMEMBER MY NAME?
OF COURSE! YOU WERE A LIEUTENANT UNDER MY COMMAND IN ALGERIA.
ARE YOU IN CHARGE OF THE DEFENSE HERE?
MY LORD, I AM.
AN IMPRESSIVE JOB, COMMANDANT! VERSAILLES WASN'T BUILT TO REPEL AN ATTACK...
WE ROYALISTS ARE... IMPROVISING.
HALF THE ARMY HAS SWORN ALLEGIANCE TO *YOU*, MY LORD.

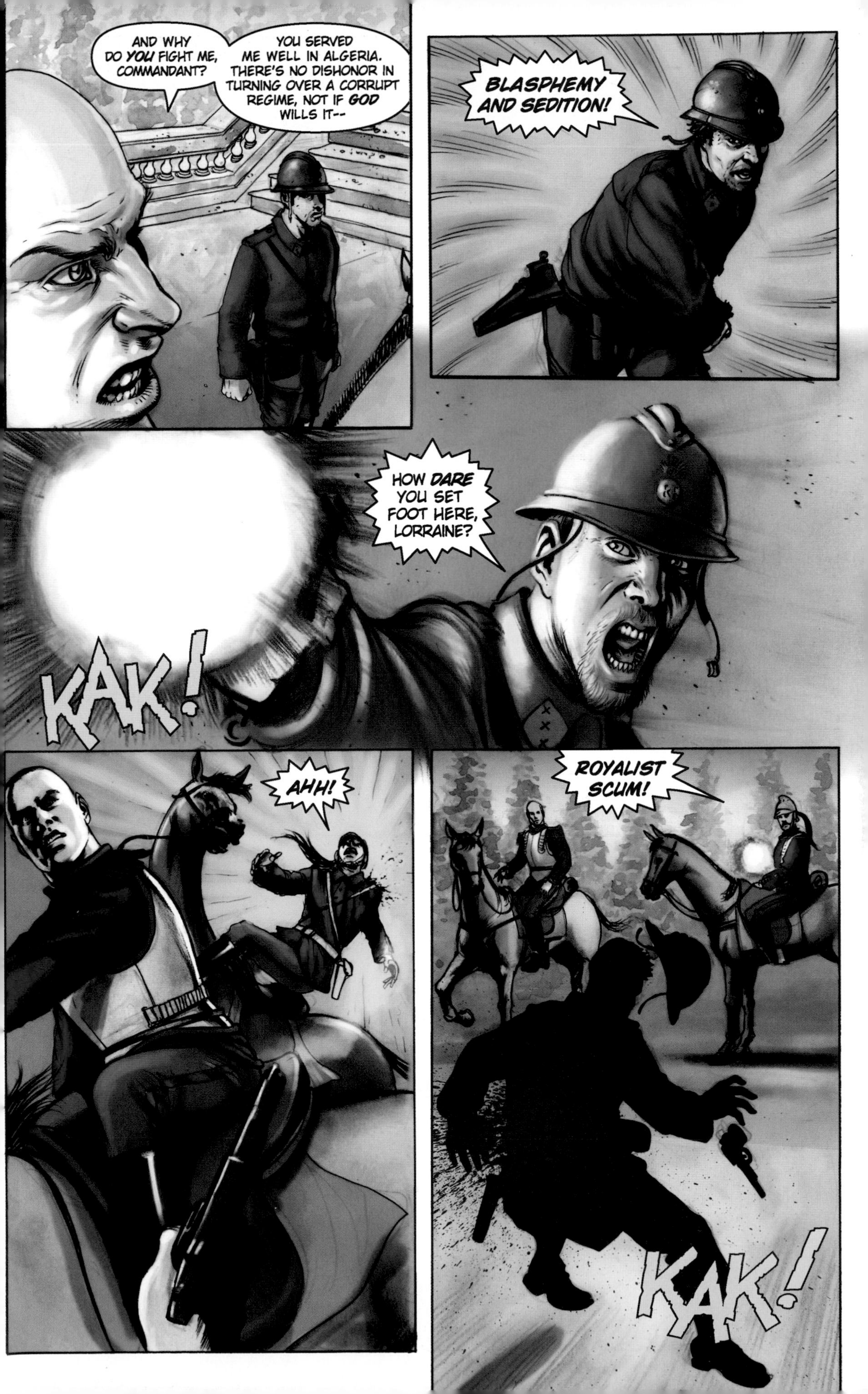
AND WHY DO YOU FIGHT ME, COMMANDANT?
YOU SERVED ME WELL IN ALGERIA. THERE'S NO DISHONOR IN TURNING OVER A CORRUPT REGIME, NOT IF GOD WILLS IT--
BLASPHEMY AND SEDITION!
HOW DARE YOU SET FOOT HERE, LORRAINE?
KAK!
AHH!
ROYALIST SCUM!
KAK!

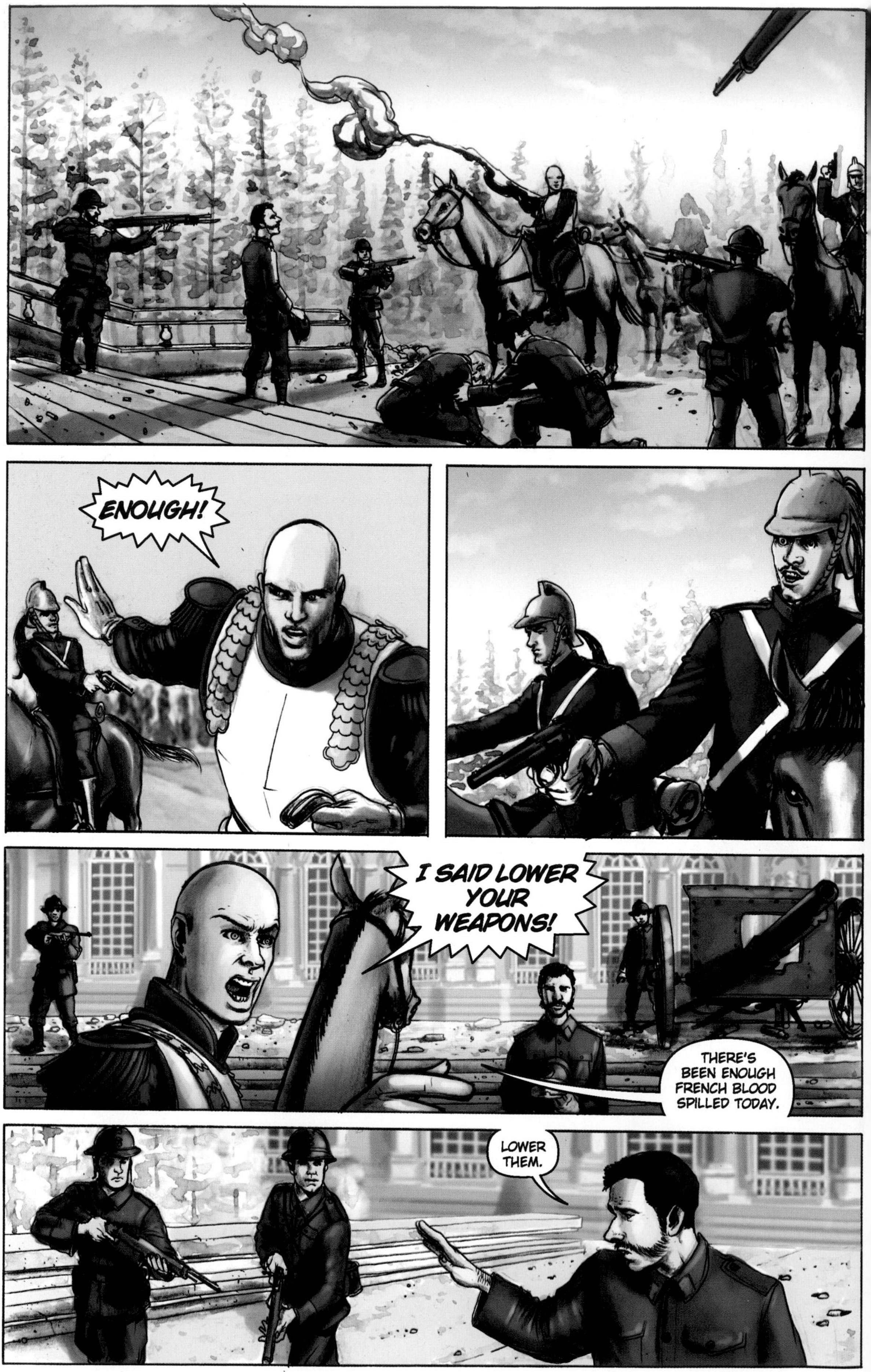
ENOUGH!
I SAID LOWER YOUR WEAPONS!
THERE'S BEEN ENOUGH FRENCH BLOOD SPILLED TODAY.
LOWER THEM.

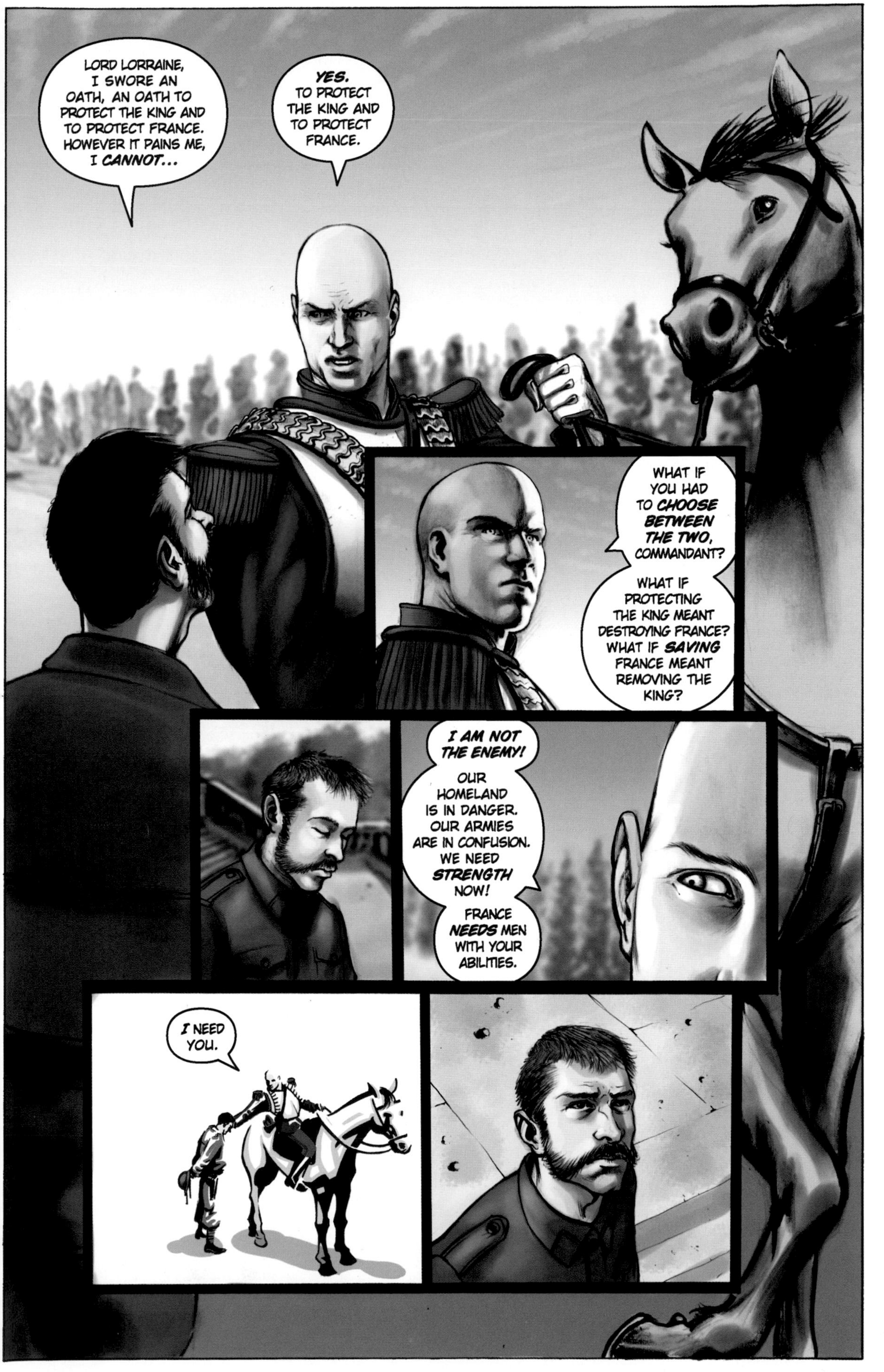
LORD LORRAINE, I SWORE AN OATH, AN OATH TO PROTECT THE KING AND TO PROTECT FRANCE. HOWEVER IT PAINS ME, I CANNOT...
YES. TO PROTECT THE KING AND TO PROTECT FRANCE.
WHAT IF YOU HAD TO CHOOSE BETWEEN THE TWO, COMMANDANT?
WHAT IF PROTECTING THE KING MEANT DESTROYING FRANCE? WHAT IF SAVING FRANCE MEANT REMOVING THE KING?
I AM NOT THE ENEMY!
OUR HOMELAND IS IN DANGER. OUR ARMIES ARE IN CONFUSION. WE NEED STRENGTH NOW!
FRANCE NEEDS MEN WITH YOUR ABILITIES.
I NEED YOU.

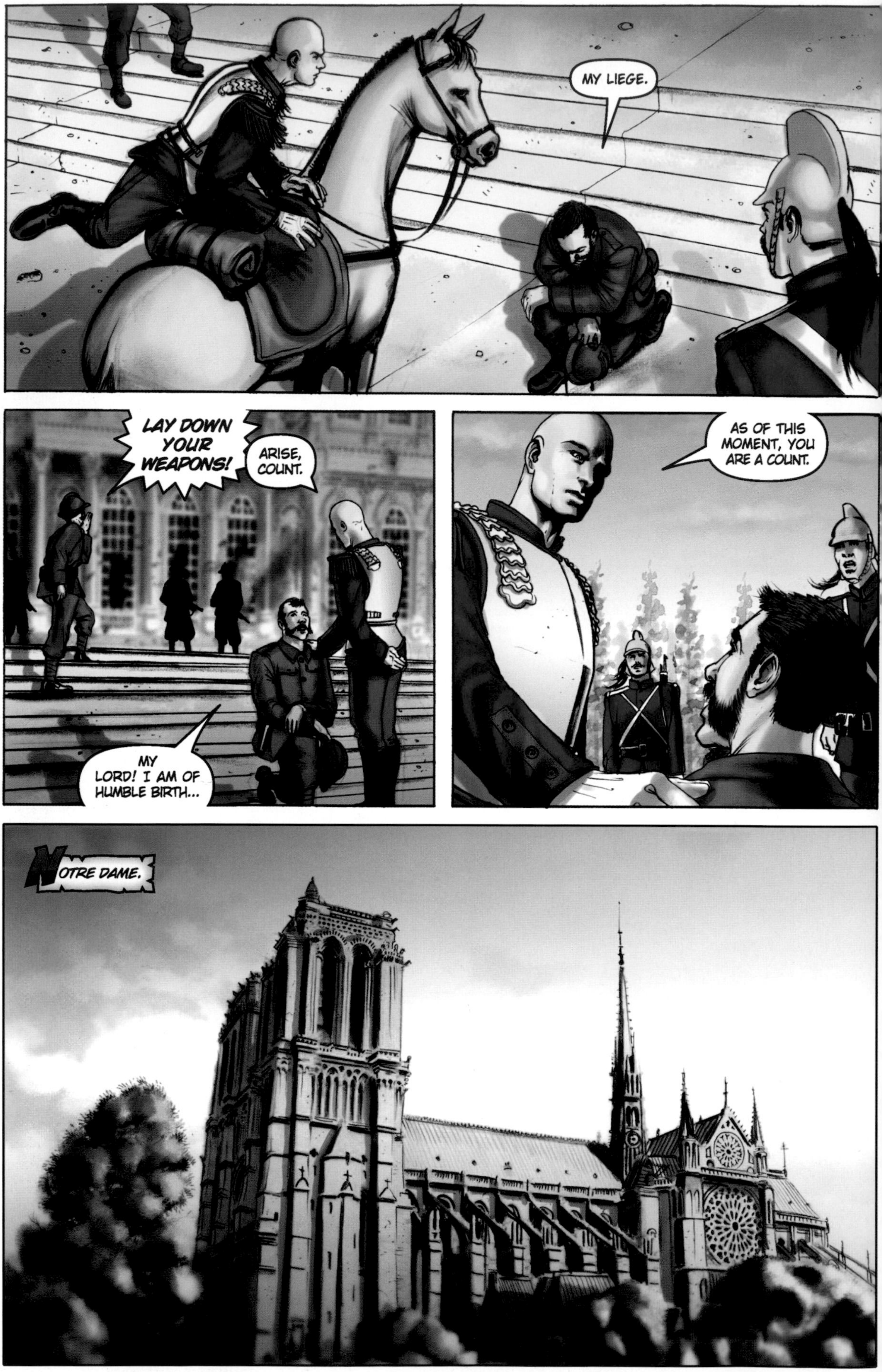
MY LIEGE.
LAY DOWN YOUR WEAPONS!
ARISE, COUNT.
MY LORD! I AM OF HUMBLE BIRTH...
AS OF THIS MOMENT, YOU ARE A COUNT.
NOTRE DAME.

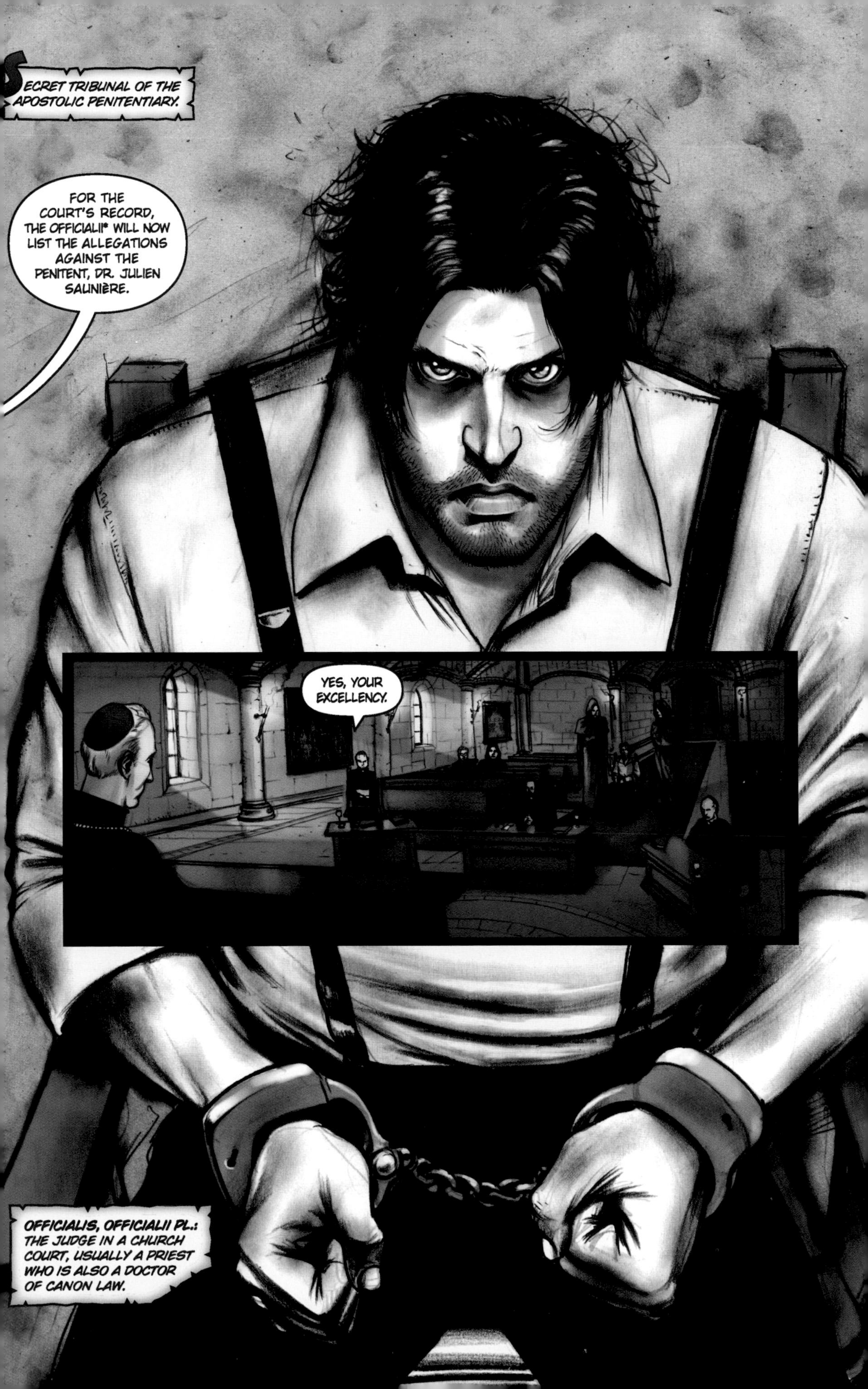
SECRET TRIBUNAL OF THE APOSTOLIC PENITENTIARY.
FOR THE COURT'S RECORD, THE OFFICIALII* WILL NOW LIST THE ALLEGATIONS AGAINST THE PENITENT, DR. JULIEN SAUNIÈRE.
YES, YOUR EXCELLENCY.
*OFFICIALIS, OFFICIALII PL.: THE JUDGE IN A CHURCH COURT, USUALLY A PRIEST WHO IS ALSO A DOCTOR OF CANON LAW.

DR. SAUNIÈRE IS ACCUSED OF VIOLATING THE SANCTITY OF THE CHURCH OF THE MAGDALENE, AFTER HE AND FATHER GÉRARD MARIN, NOW DECEASED, DISCUSSED FORBIDDEN ECCLESIASTICAL INFORMATION.

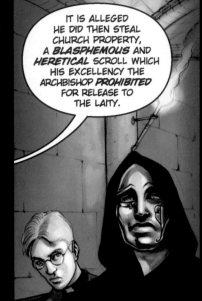

IT IS ALLEGED HE DID THEN STEAL CHURCH PROPERTY, A *BLASPHEMOUS* AND *HERETICAL* SCROLL WHICH HIS EXCELLENCY THE ARCHBISHOP *PROHIBITED* FOR RELEASE TO THE LAITY.

DR. SAUNIÈRE DID THEN PURSUE AN INVESTIGATION OF THE SCROLL, IN CONTRAVENTION TO THE EXPLICIT ORDERS OF HIS EXCELLENCY.

THAT'S A LIE!

ARCHBISHOP IRENEAUX KNEW *ALL ALONG* WHAT I WAS DOING, HE *APPROVED--*

AHEM. THE SUBJECT OF HIS INVESTIGATION, THE *HOLY GRAIL* AND ITS CONNECTION TO THE THE *DUKES OF LORRAINE,* A SUBJECT UTTERLY *FORBIDDEN* FROM DISCUSSION SAVE BY PERSONS SANCTIONED BY THE HOLY FATHER HIMSELF.

AGHK!

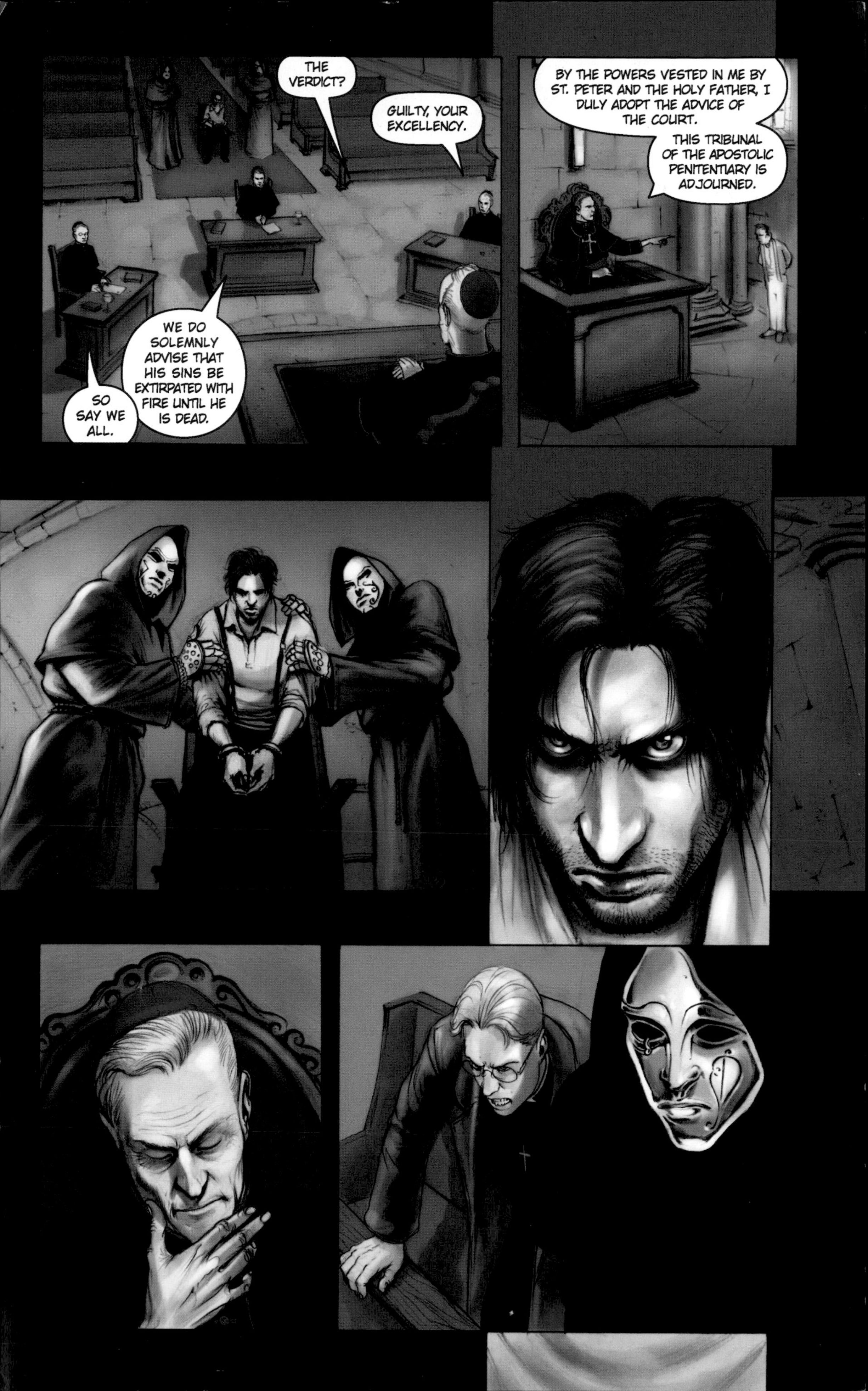
THE VERDICT?
GUILTY, YOUR EXCELLENCY.
WE DO SOLEMNLY ADVISE THAT HIS SINS BE EXTIRPATED WITH FIRE UNTIL HE IS DEAD.
SO SAY WE ALL.
BY THE POWERS VESTED IN ME BY ST. PETER AND THE HOLY FATHER, I DULY ADOPT THE ADVICE OF THE COURT.
THIS TRIBUNAL OF THE APOSTOLIC PENITENTIARY IS ADJOURNED.

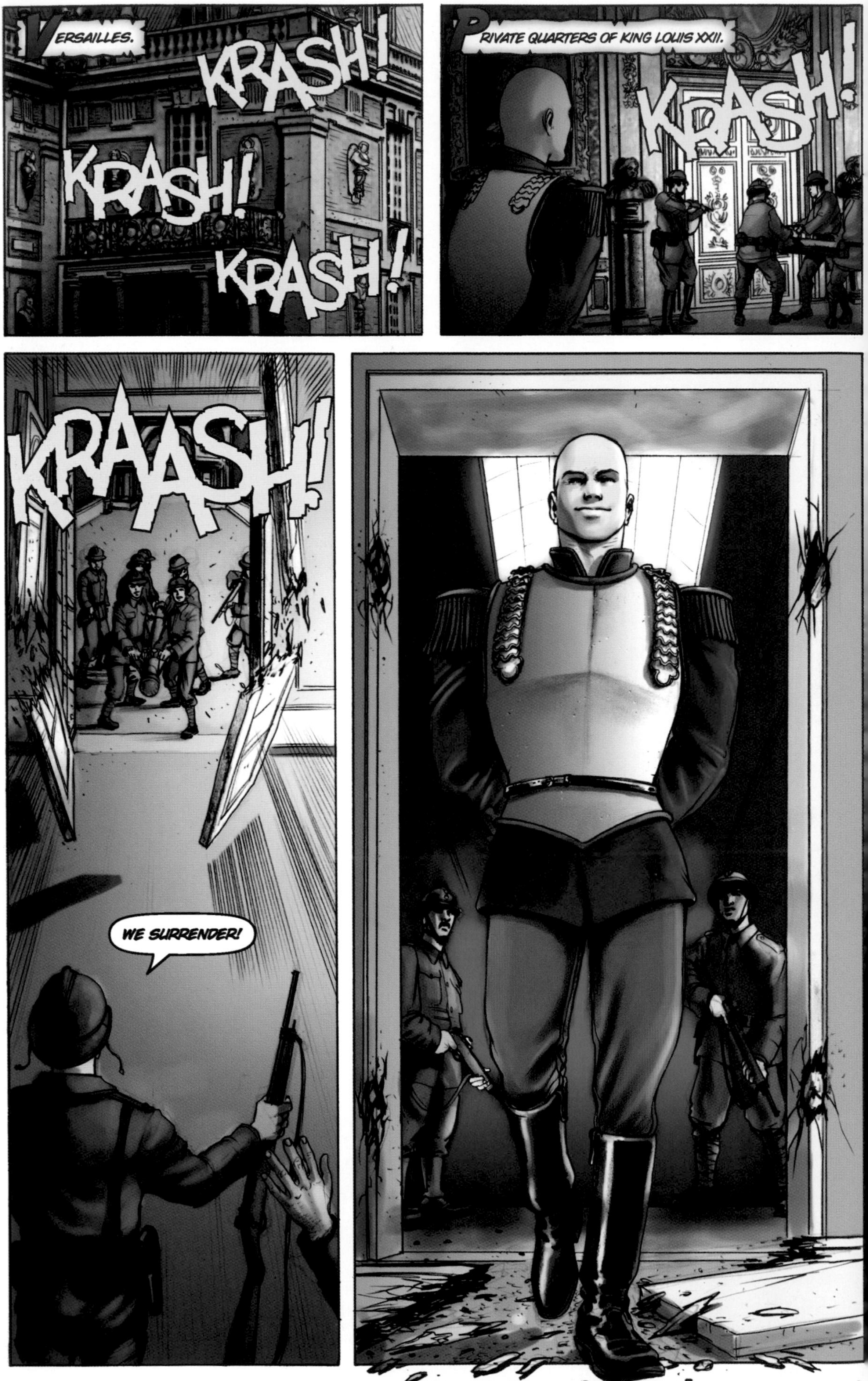
VERSAILLES.
KRASH!
KRASH!
KRASH!
PRIVATE QUARTERS OF KING LOUIS XXII.
KRASH!
KRAASH!
WE SURRENDER!

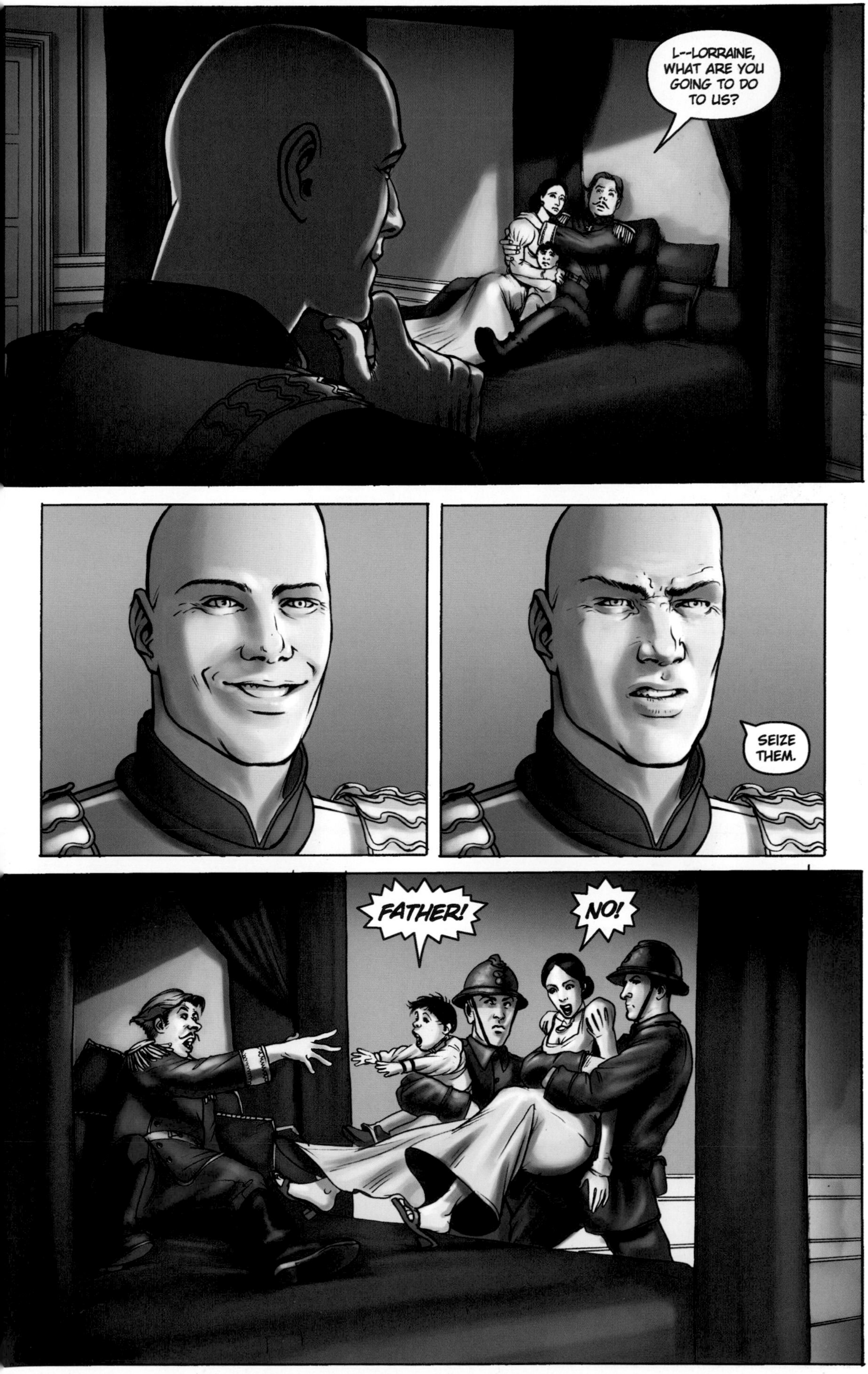
L--LORRAINE, WHAT ARE YOU GOING TO DO TO US?
SEIZE THEM.
FATHER!
NO!

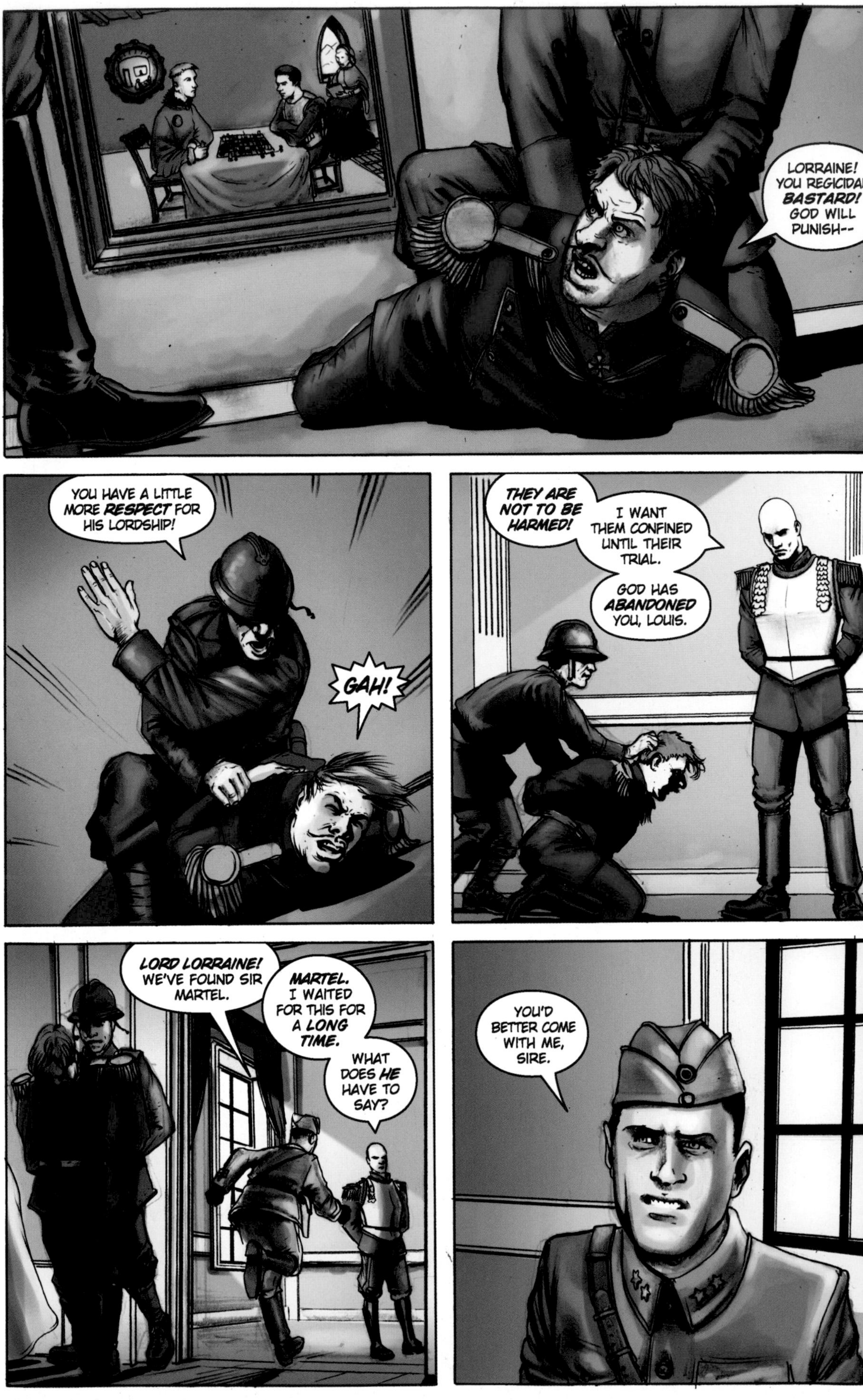
LORRAINE! YOU REGICIDAL BASTARD! GOD WILL PUNISH--
YOU HAVE A LITTLE MORE RESPECT FOR HIS LORDSHIP!
GAH!
THEY ARE NOT TO BE HARMED!
I WANT THEM CONFINED UNTIL THEIR TRIAL.
GOD HAS ABANDONED YOU, LOUIS.
LORD LORRAINE! WE'VE FOUND SIR MARTEL.
MARTEL. I WAITED FOR THIS FOR A LONG TIME.
WHAT DOES HE HAVE TO SAY?
YOU'D BETTER COME WITH ME, SIRE.

Sir Charles Martel, Mayor of the Court to King Louis XXII.

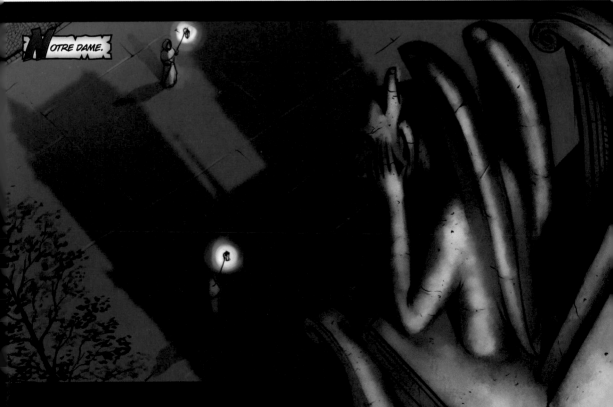

Notre Dame.

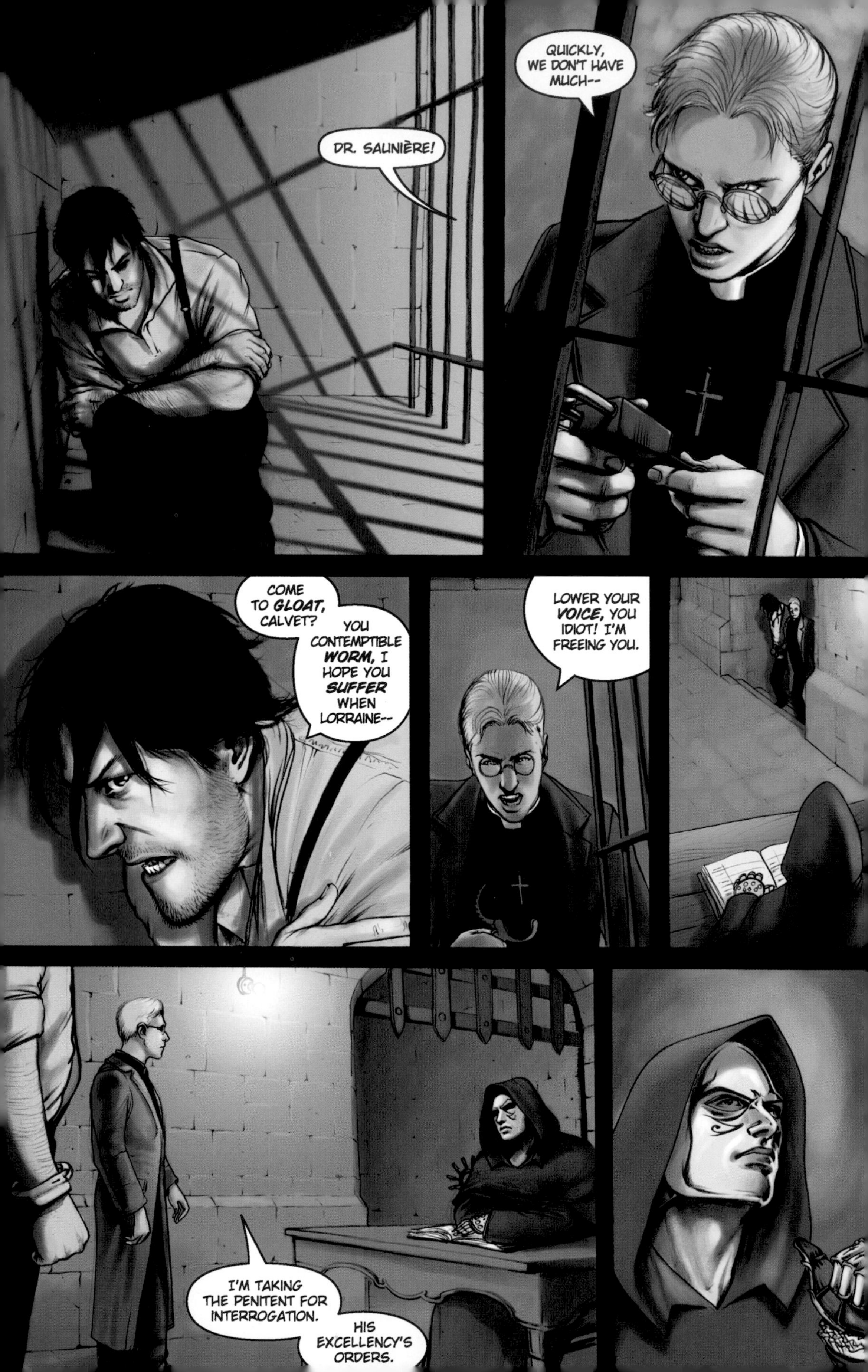
DR. SAUNIÈRE!
QUICKLY, WE DON'T HAVE MUCH--
COME TO GLOAT, CALVET?
YOU CONTEMPTIBLE WORM, I HOPE YOU SUFFER WHEN LORRAINE--
LOWER YOUR VOICE, YOU IDIOT! I'M FREEING YOU.
I'M TAKING THE PENITENT FOR INTERROGATION.
HIS EXCELLENCY'S ORDERS.

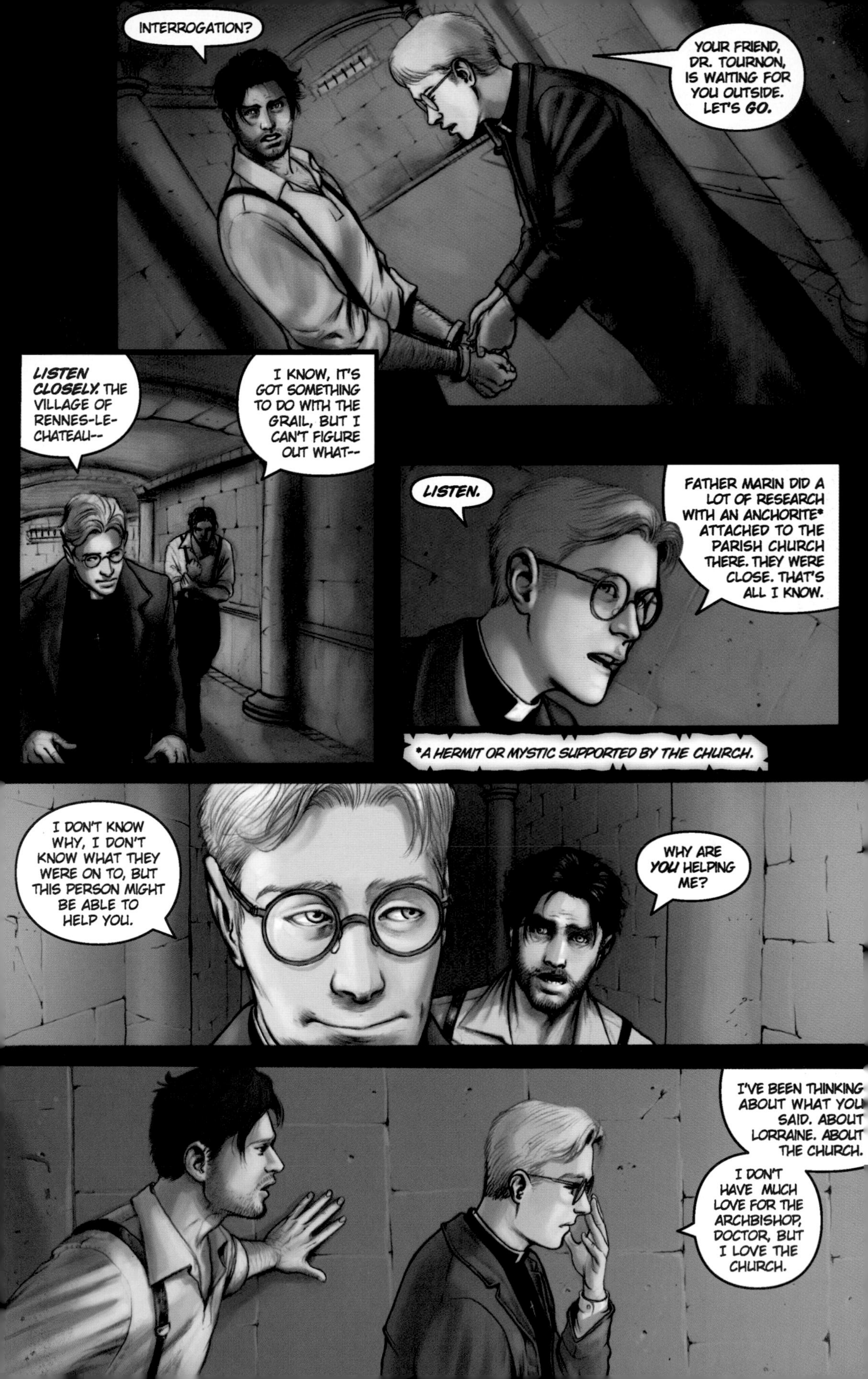
INTERROGATION?
YOUR FRIEND, DR. TOURNON, IS WAITING FOR YOU OUTSIDE. LET'S GO.
LISTEN CLOSELY. THE VILLAGE OF RENNES-LE-CHATEAU--
I KNOW, IT'S GOT SOMETHING TO DO WITH THE GRAIL, BUT I CAN'T FIGURE OUT WHAT--
LISTEN.
FATHER MARIN DID A LOT OF RESEARCH WITH AN ANCHORITE* ATTACHED TO THE PARISH CHURCH THERE. THEY WERE CLOSE. THAT'S ALL I KNOW.
*A HERMIT OR MYSTIC SUPPORTED BY THE CHURCH.
I DON'T KNOW WHY, I DON'T KNOW WHAT THEY WERE ON TO, BUT THIS PERSON MIGHT BE ABLE TO HELP YOU.
WHY ARE YOU HELPING ME?
I'VE BEEN THINKING ABOUT WHAT YOU SAID. ABOUT LORRAINE. ABOUT THE CHURCH.
I DON'T HAVE MUCH LOVE FOR THE ARCHBISHOP, DOCTOR, BUT I LOVE THE CHURCH.

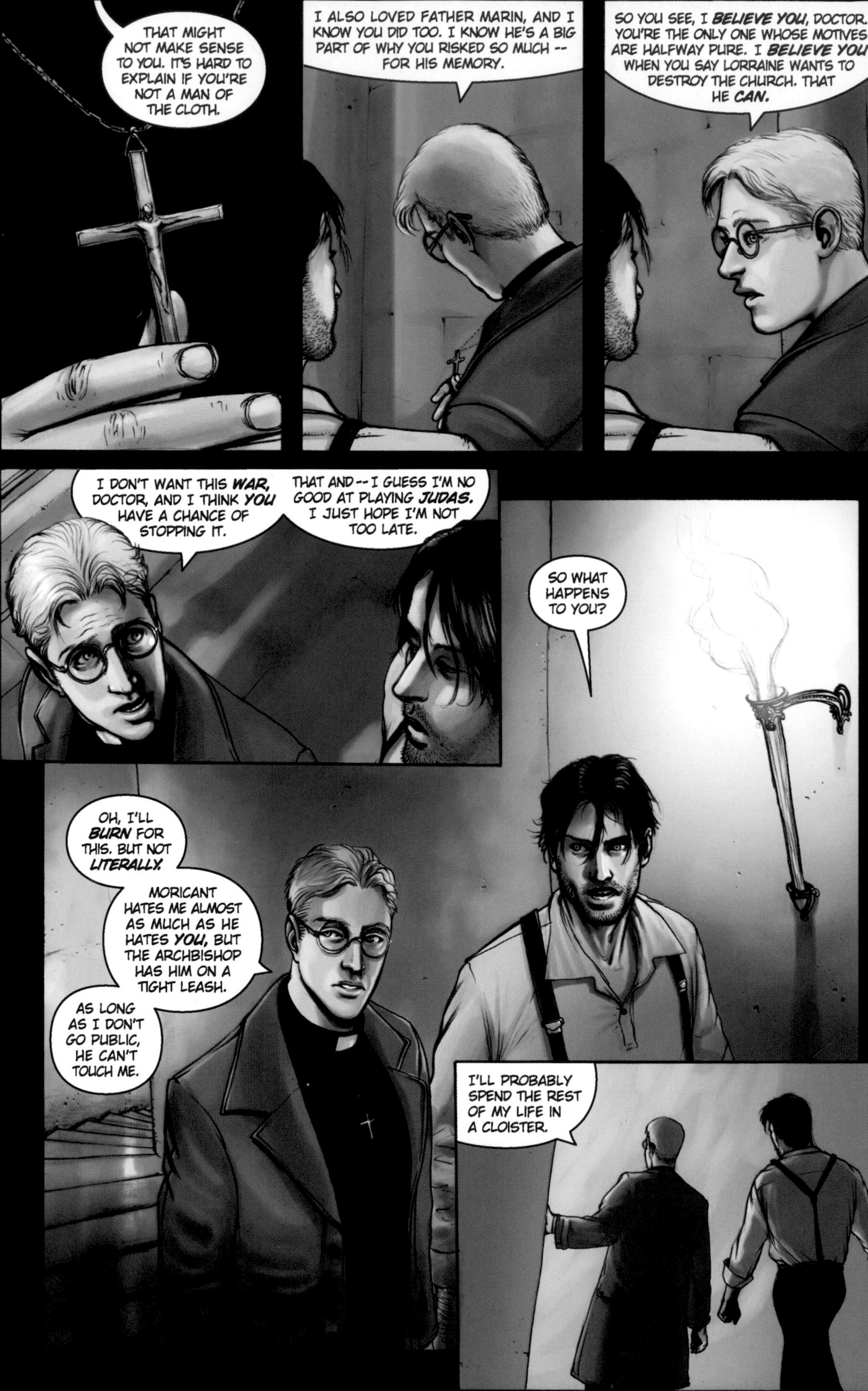
THAT MIGHT NOT MAKE SENSE TO YOU. IT'S HARD TO EXPLAIN IF YOU'RE NOT A MAN OF THE CLOTH.
I ALSO LOVED FATHER MARIN, AND I KNOW YOU DID TOO. I KNOW HE'S A BIG PART OF WHY YOU RISKED SO MUCH -- FOR HIS MEMORY.
SO YOU SEE, I BELIEVE YOU, DOCTOR. YOU'RE THE ONLY ONE WHOSE MOTIVES ARE HALFWAY PURE. I BELIEVE YOU WHEN YOU SAY LORRAINE WANTS TO DESTROY THE CHURCH. THAT HE CAN.
I DON'T WANT THIS WAR, DOCTOR, AND I THINK YOU HAVE A CHANCE OF STOPPING IT.
THAT AND -- I GUESS I'M NO GOOD AT PLAYING JUDAS. I JUST HOPE I'M NOT TOO LATE.
SO WHAT HAPPENS TO YOU?
OH, I'LL BURN FOR THIS. BUT NOT LITERALLY.
MORICANT HATES ME ALMOST AS MUCH AS HE HATES YOU, BUT THE ARCHBISHOP HAS HIM ON A TIGHT LEASH.
AS LONG AS I DON'T GO PUBLIC, HE CAN'T TOUCH ME.
I'LL PROBABLY SPEND THE REST OF MY LIFE IN A CLOISTER.

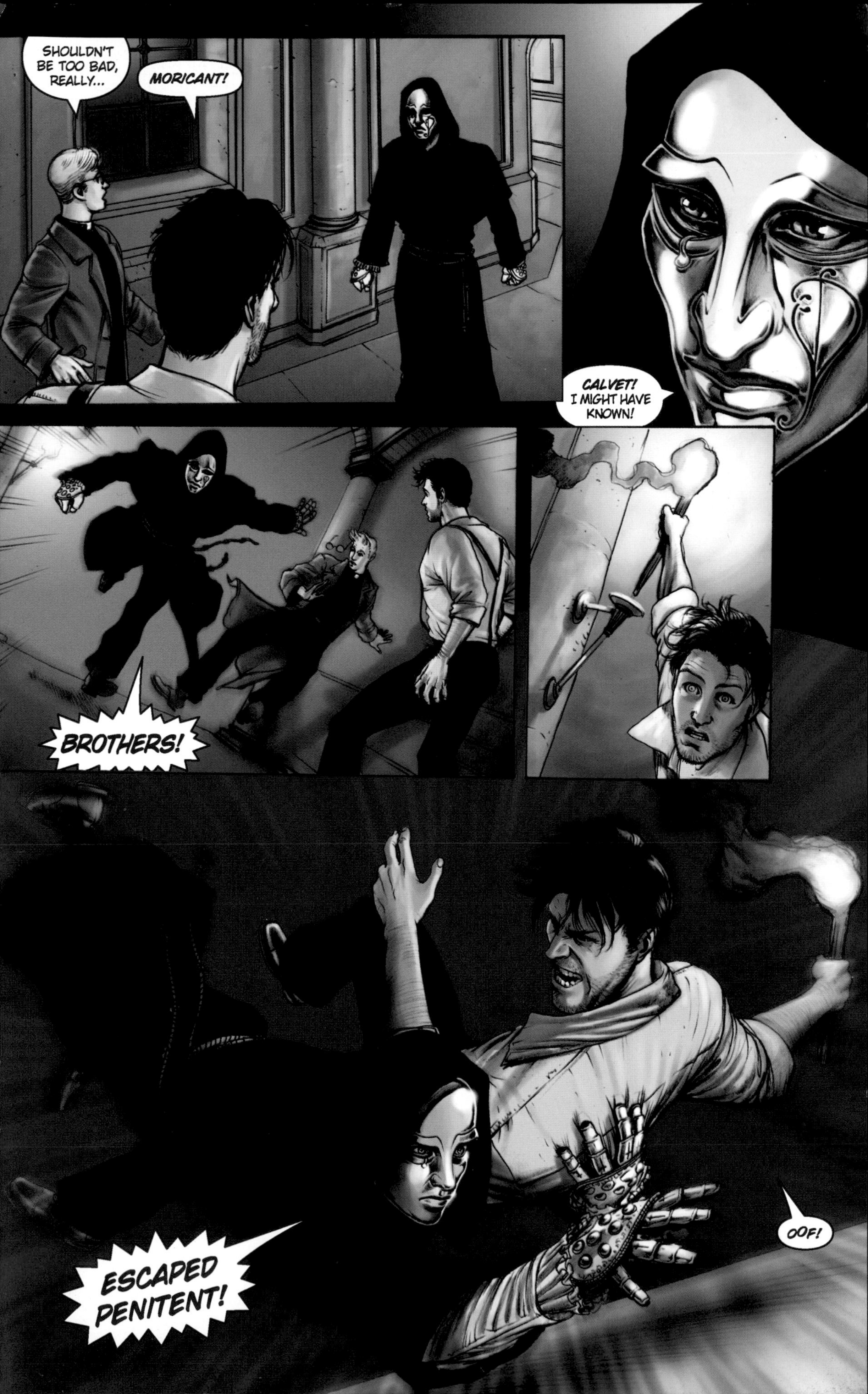
SHOULDN'T BE TOO BAD, REALLY...
MORICANT!
CALVET! I MIGHT HAVE KNOWN!
BROTHERS!
ESCAPED PENITENT!
OOF!

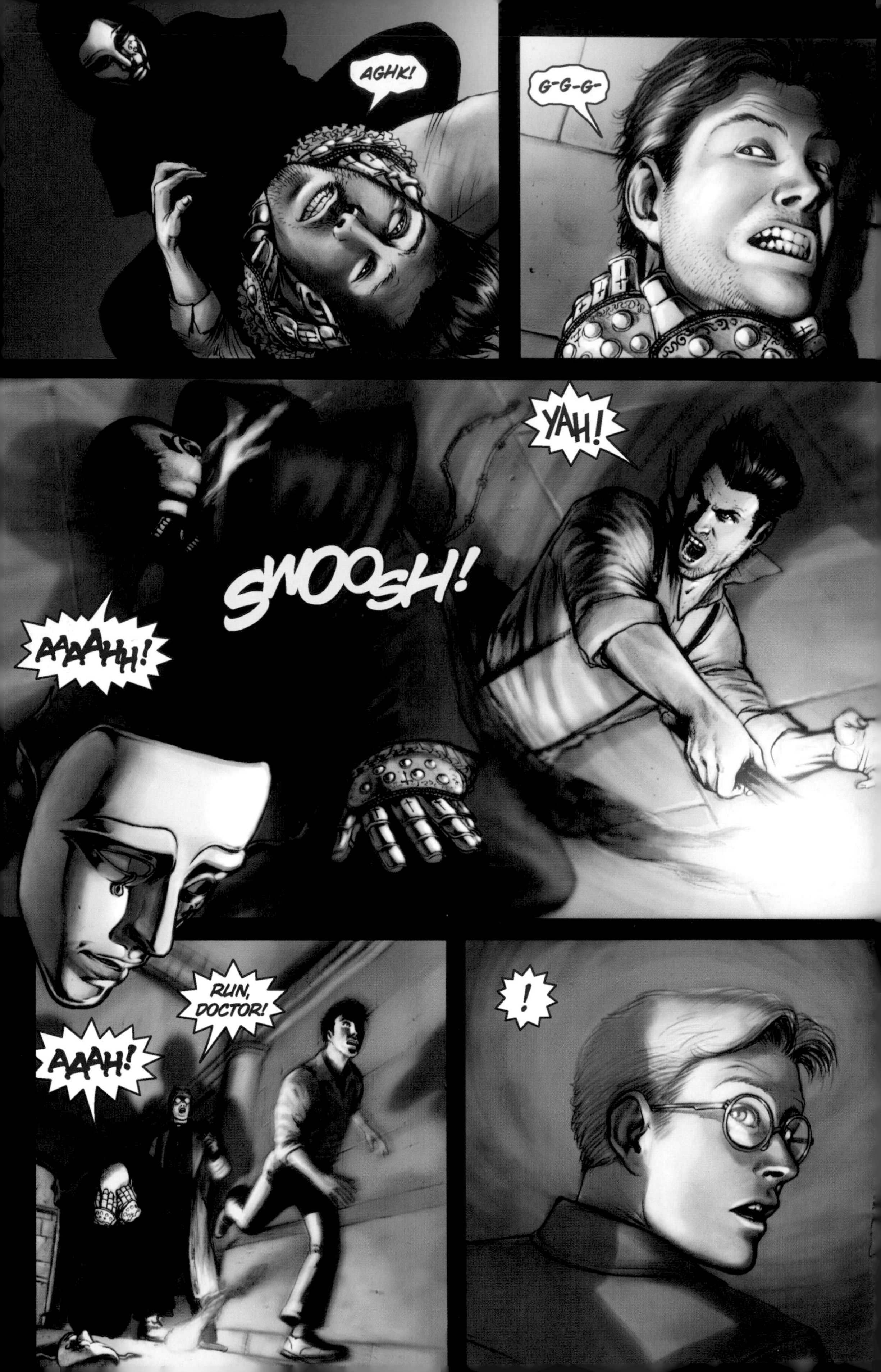
AGHK!
G-G-G-
YAH!
SWOOSH!
AAAAHH!
RUN, DOCTOR!
AAAH!
!

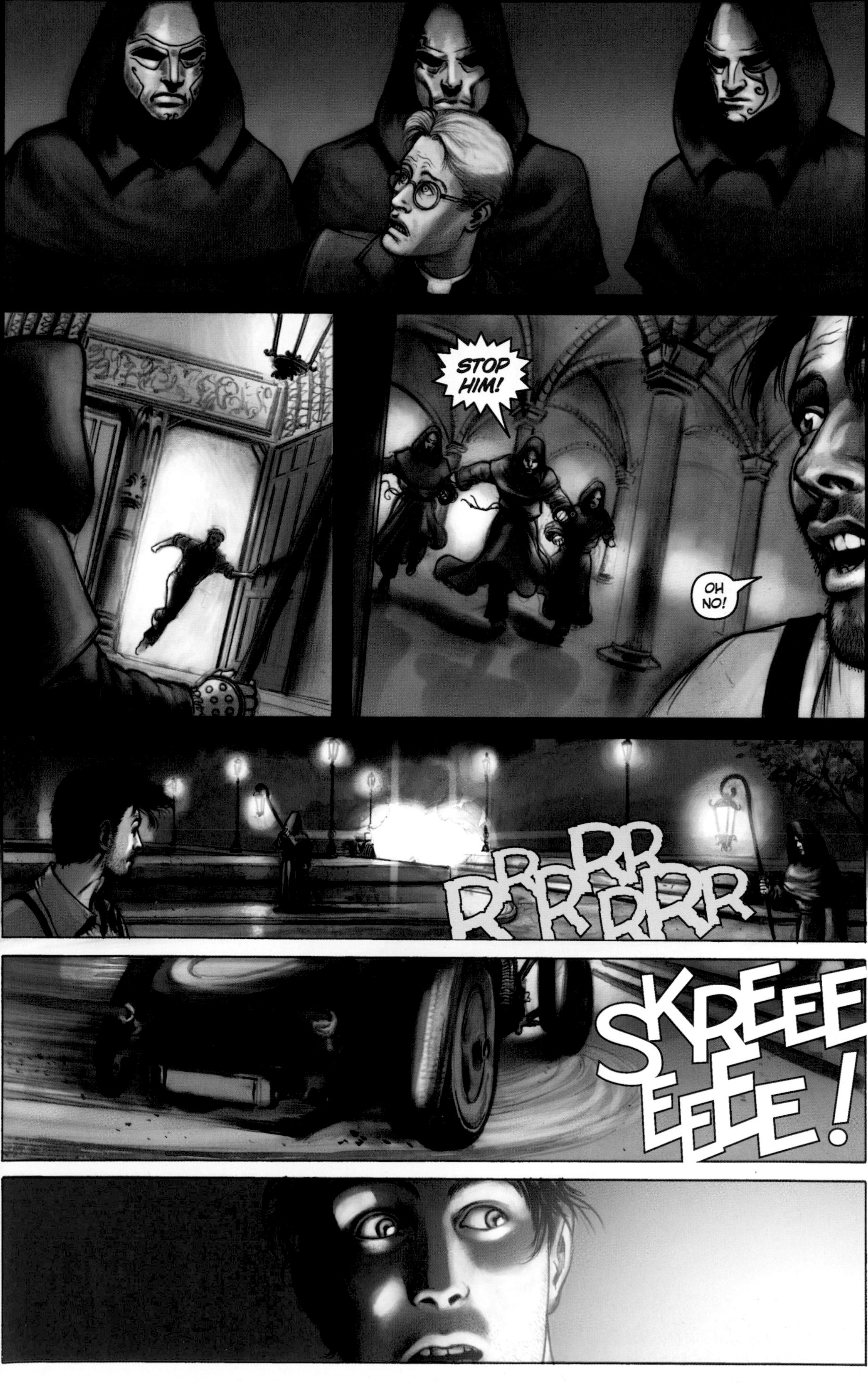
STOP HIM!
OH NO!
RRRRRRRRRRR
SKREEEEEEE!

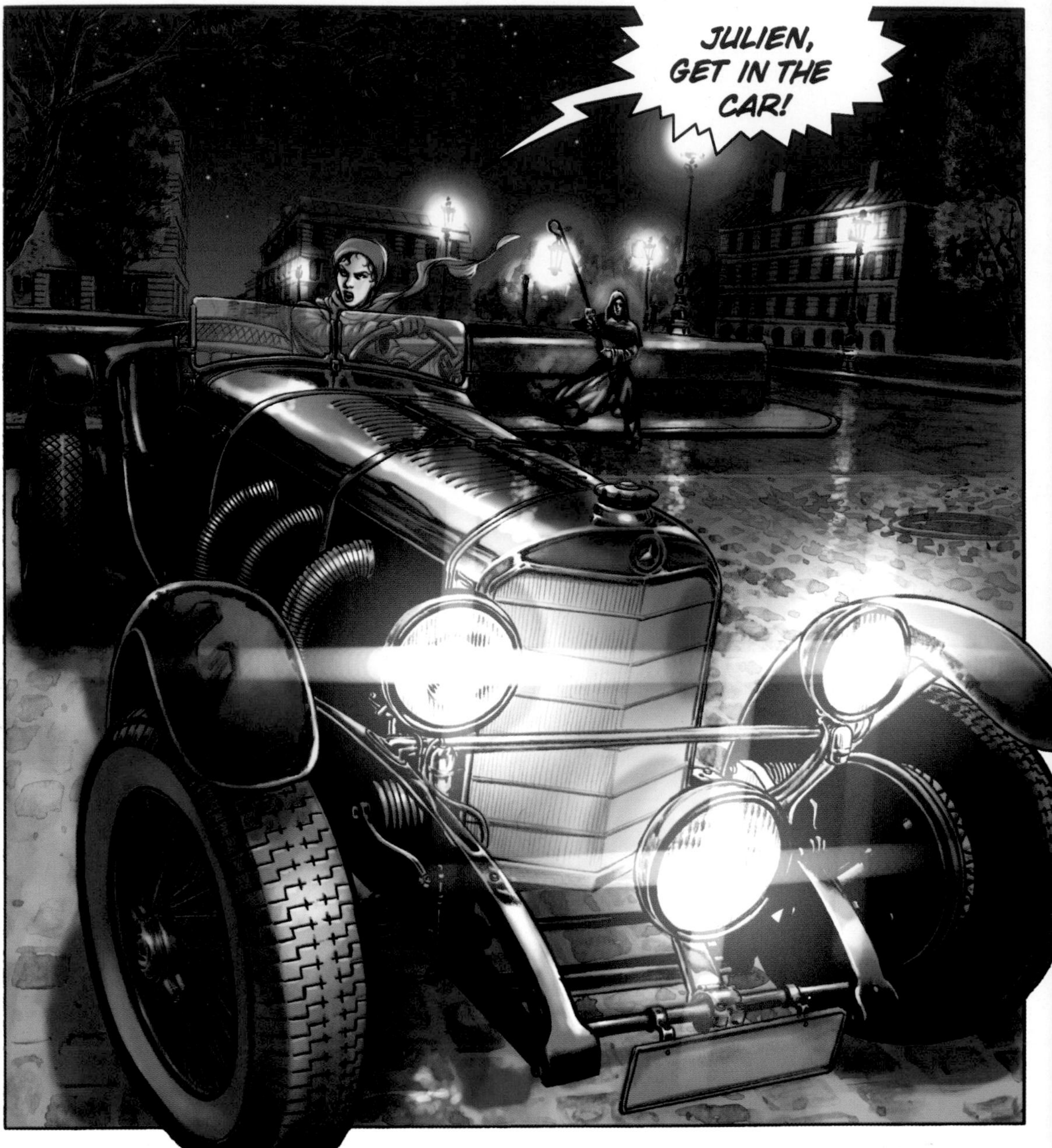
JULIEN, GET IN THE CAR!

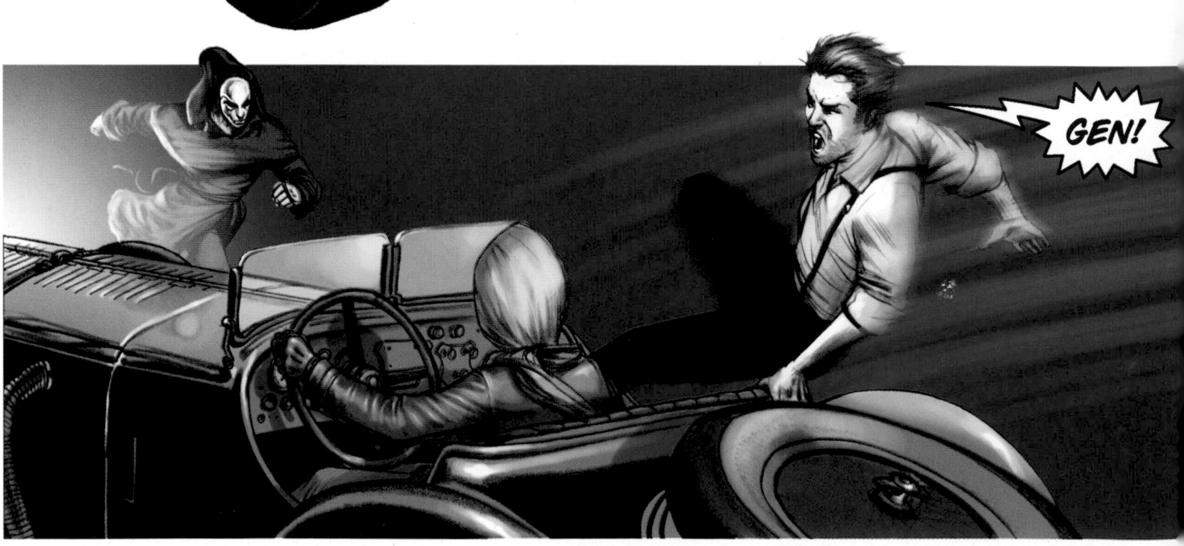
GEN!

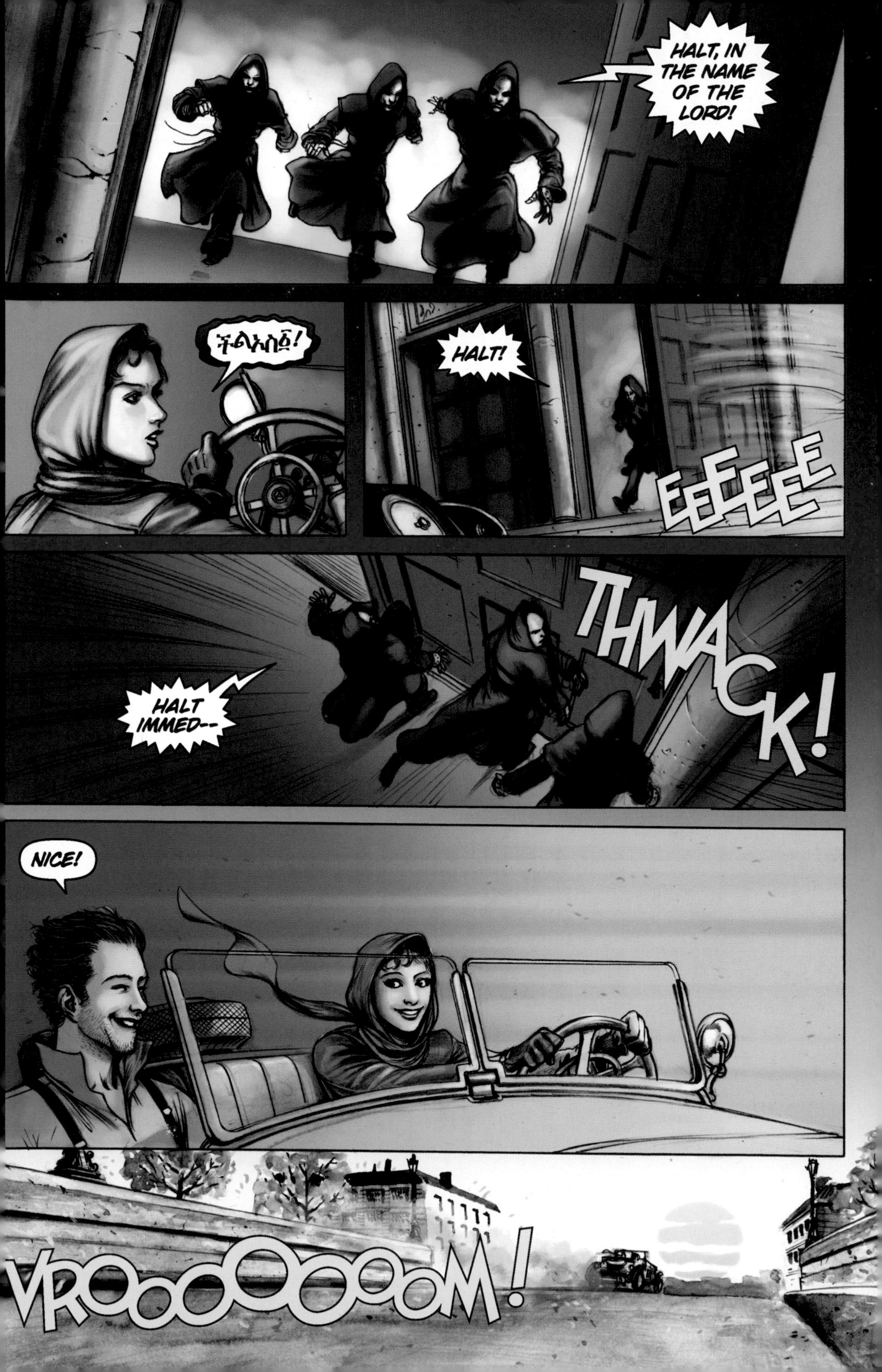
HALT, IN THE NAME OF THE LORD!
ቾልአስ፩!
HALT!
EEEEEE
THWACK!
HALT IMMED--
NICE!
VROOOOOOOOM!

Le Journal de la Liberté

Paris's leading anglophone newspaper • vol. 205, no. 102 • Nov. 14, MCMXXXIII

Papal seal

Editors in Chief: M. Tait Bergstrom, M. Matthew Pasteris. **Story Editor:** M. Arvid Nelson. **Art Editor:** M. Juan Ferreyra. **Photography Editor:** M. Alexander Waldman. **Layout Supervisor:** M. William Kartalopoulos. **Editors Emeritus:** M. Clark A. Smith, M. Howard P. Lovecraft, M. Robert E. Howard. Redacted by the Holy Inquisition under the direction of His Excellency Archbishop Emile-Jean Ireneaux. *Le Journal de la Liberté* is printed under the benign auspices of his most puissant majesty KING LOUIS XXII of FRANCE! GOD SAVE THE KING!

of Approval

LORRAINE SEIZES VERSAILLES; PRUSSIA DECLARES WAR

Germans Mass Troops on Northwestern Frontier; Lorraine Vows to Restore Order, Fight Invaders

Versailles – Outnumbered and heavily outgunned, the meager royalist force guarding King Louis in Versailles capitulated to the Duke of Lorraine yesterday, the latest in a series of devastating political upheavals that leaves the very future of France in question.

Some say the Duke of Lorraine is responsible for the chaos, while others blame the King himself.

King Louis caused a furor earlier this week by disbanding an increasingly unruly parliament and issuing arrest warrants for his political enemies, mainly France's ancient aristocracy.

The King made the move to shore up political support and crack down on dissidence, but it has had the opposite effect.

Lord Lorraine, one of those for whom King Louis issued an arrest warrant, is popular with the army and with the *ancien régime*.

That popularity surged in the wake of the King's actions.

Previously, Lorraine had become a symbol of defiance in a series of increasingly dramatic political showdowns with the King. He and the Crown were at odds on foreign policy, particularly regarding colonial expansion.

Lorraine favored an aggressive, imperialistic agenda, while the King called for restraint, to preserve peace.

The issue came to a head when the Marquis of Navarre unexpectedly died. In his will he left to France all his ancestral lands, located to the southeast of the Languedoc region. The marquises of Aragon and Catalonia followed with similar pledges.

The annexation of these lands, the Spanish Marches, became a political crisis for the King.

"King Louis saw the Spanish Marches as a sort of poison apple," a source close to the King said. "And he was exactly right. It only exacerbated tensions with our neighbors."

Despite the King's objections, the Hall of the Robe, the lower house of parliament and King Louis's traditional political base, shocked the world by doing what it had never done before: siding with the Hall of the Sword, Lorraine's power base, against the King.

The annexation went forward, exactly as Lorraine wanted.

The Marquis of Aragon was assassinated by Moslem extremists a few days after the "reunification," as Lorraine's supporters called it, fostering outrage in France. Lorraine once again led a majority in parliament to override the King's wishes and declare war on the Cordovan Emirate, where the assassins are thought to have originated.

It was the war declaration and parliament's decision to put the Duke of Lorraine in charge of the military campaign which prompted the King to call for Lorraine's arrest, and to dissolve parliament.

News of Lorraine's outlaw status caused outrage in the armed forces. Troops deserted the Crown en masse to side with Lorraine; exact numbers are not available at this time.

Lorraine outmaneuvered royalist generals expecting a straight fight. He cut straight to King Louis's residence at Versailles. Lorraine's daring move caught King Louis off guard.

After a short battle outside Versailles, royalist forces handed the palace and King Louis himself over to Lorraine.

An equally stunning development follows on the heels of Lorraine's meteoric rise from outlaw to apparent master of France.

The Prussian Kaiser declared war on France today, in response to France's declaration of war on Cordova.

Massive German troop formations are building in the Alsace for what could be an invasion of unprecedented scale.

"The Huns are using France's

INSIDE

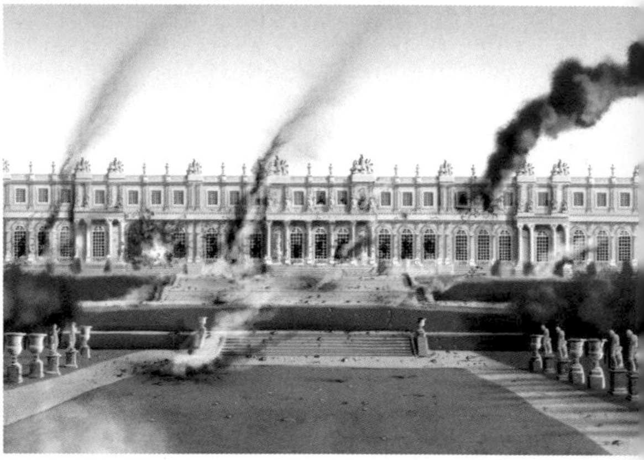

Versailles is pounded into submission by the Duke of Lorraine's artillery. A spokesman for Lorraine said the duke "regretted the damage but had no choice."

KING LOUIS CAPTURED, FATE UNCERTAIN

King Louis and the royal family have been unaccounted for since Lorraine stormed Versailles. There is widespread speculation the King may already be dead.

Lorraine has issued statements vigorously denying those claims.

"The King is in good health, in my custody and under my personal protection," Lorraine said. But he would not speculate as to King Louis's ultimate fate. His supporters had suggestions.

"I think King Louis should have a fair trial and then be shot," Baronet Guillaume de Bretagne said. "His list of crimes against the French people is long and well documented."

Others warned that reprisals might come to haunt Lorraine.

"Lorraine has no legitimacy, none whatsoever," a former member of the Hall of the Robe said. "The current situation is unacceptable. Regicide will lead to a protracted civil war, and

CHAPTER THREE
GOMORRAH IS BURNING

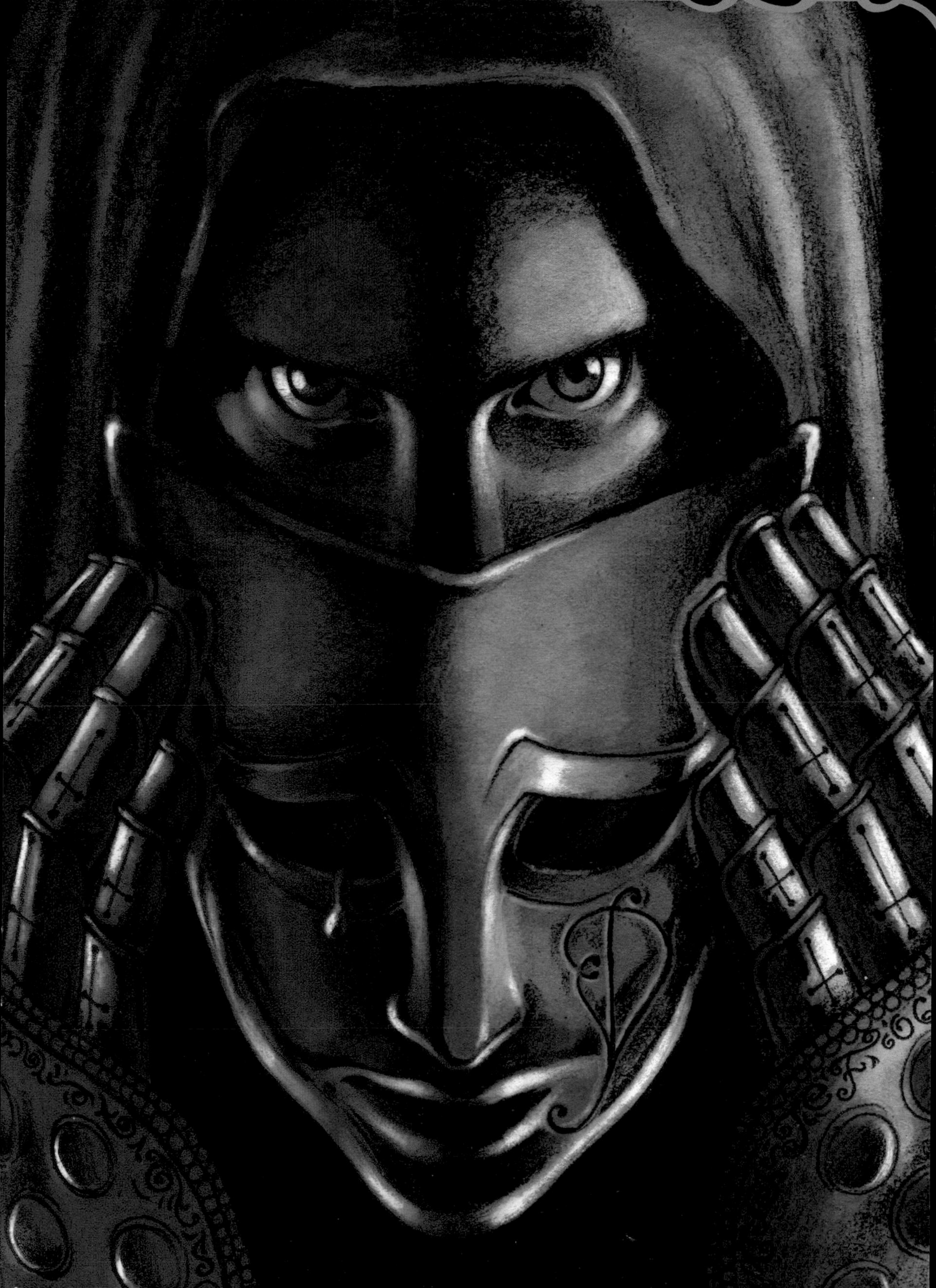

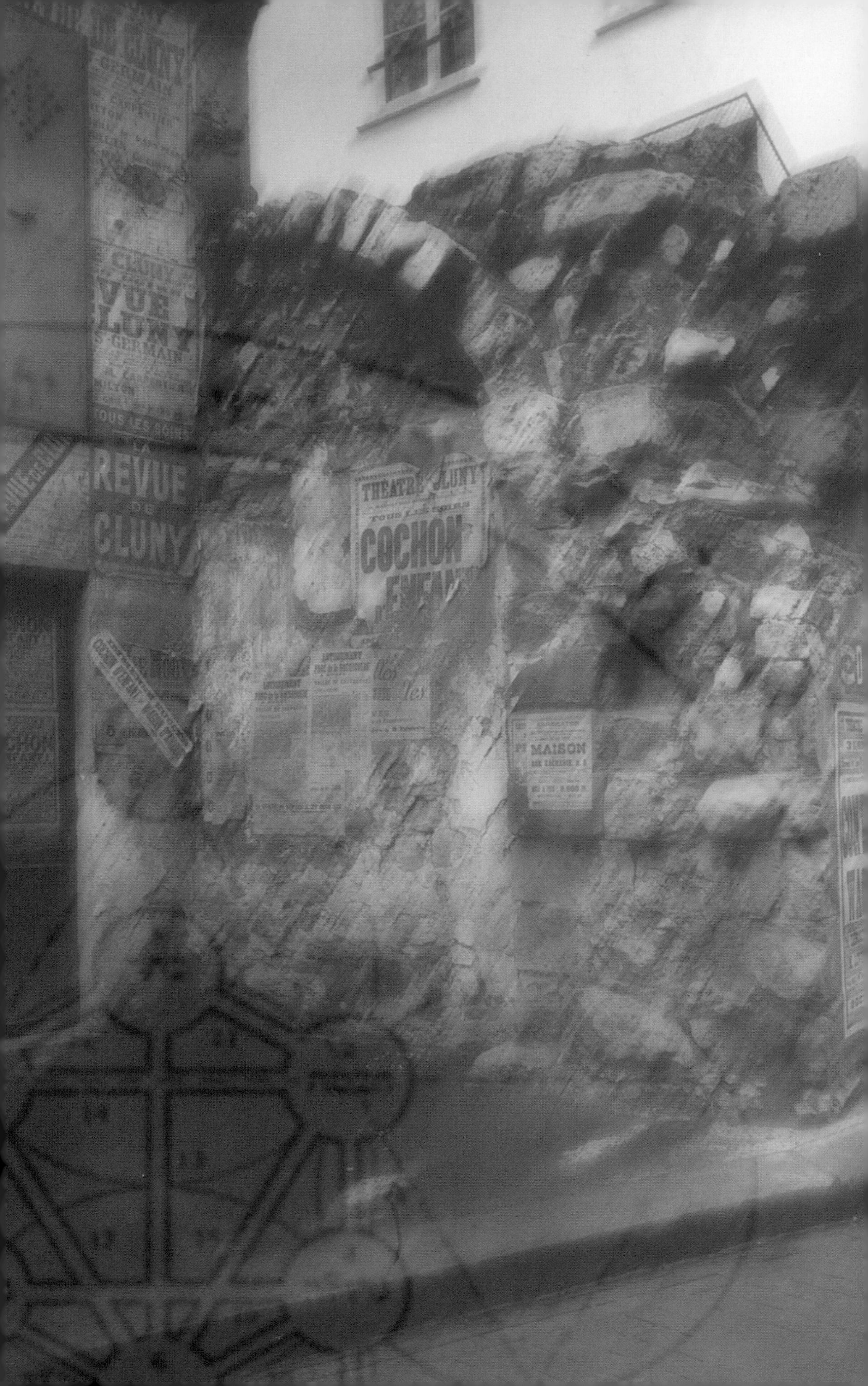
TOUS LES SOIRS
REVUE
DE
CLUNY
THEATRE CLUNY
COCHON
MAISON

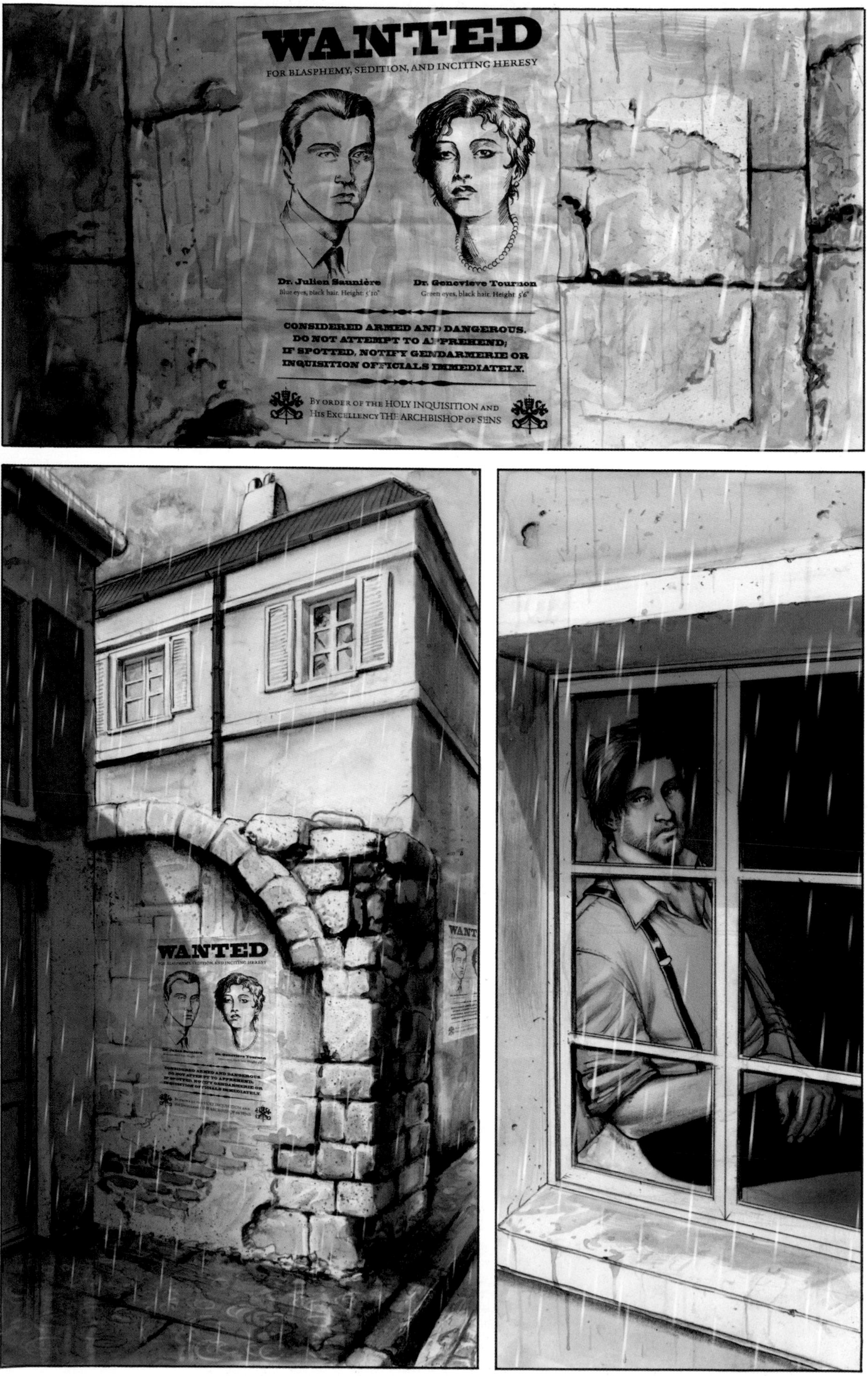
WANTED
FOR BLASPHEMY, SEDITION, AND INCITING HERESY
Dr. Julien Saunière
Blue eyes, black hair. Height: 5'10"
Dr. Genevieve Tournon
Green eyes, black hair. Height 5'6"
CONSIDERED ARMED AND DANGEROUS.
DO NOT ATTEMPT TO APPREHEND;
IF SPOTTED, NOTIFY GENDARMERIE OR
INQUISITION OFFICIALS IMMEDIATELY.
BY ORDER OF THE HOLY INQUISITION AND
HIS EXCELLENCY THE ARCHBISHOP OF SENS

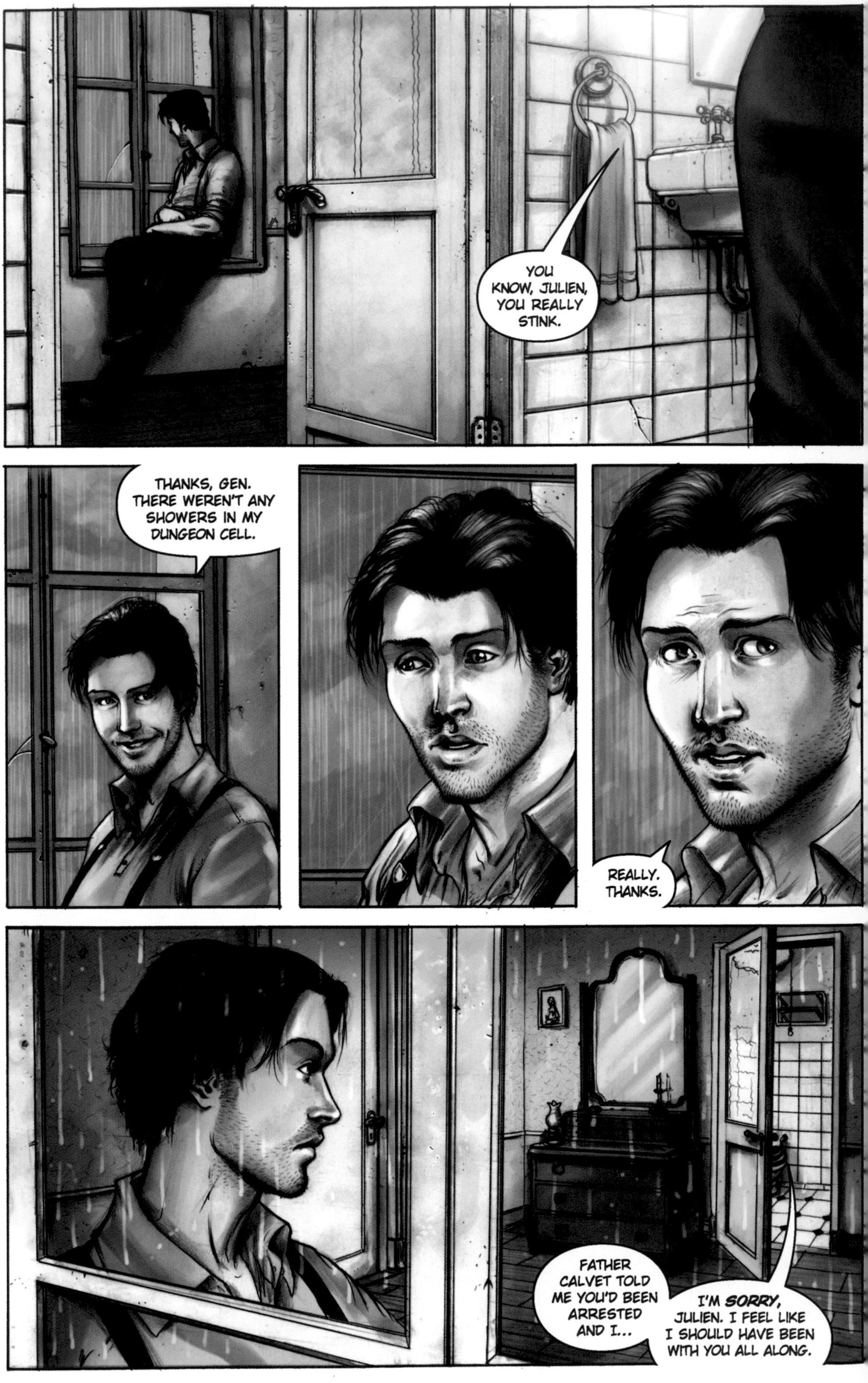
YOU KNOW, JULIEN, YOU REALLY STINK.
THANKS, GEN. THERE WEREN'T ANY SHOWERS IN MY DUNGEON CELL.
REALLY. THANKS.
FATHER CALVET TOLD ME YOU'D BEEN ARRESTED AND I...
I'M *SORRY,* JULIEN. I FEEL LIKE I SHOULD HAVE BEEN WITH YOU ALL ALONG.

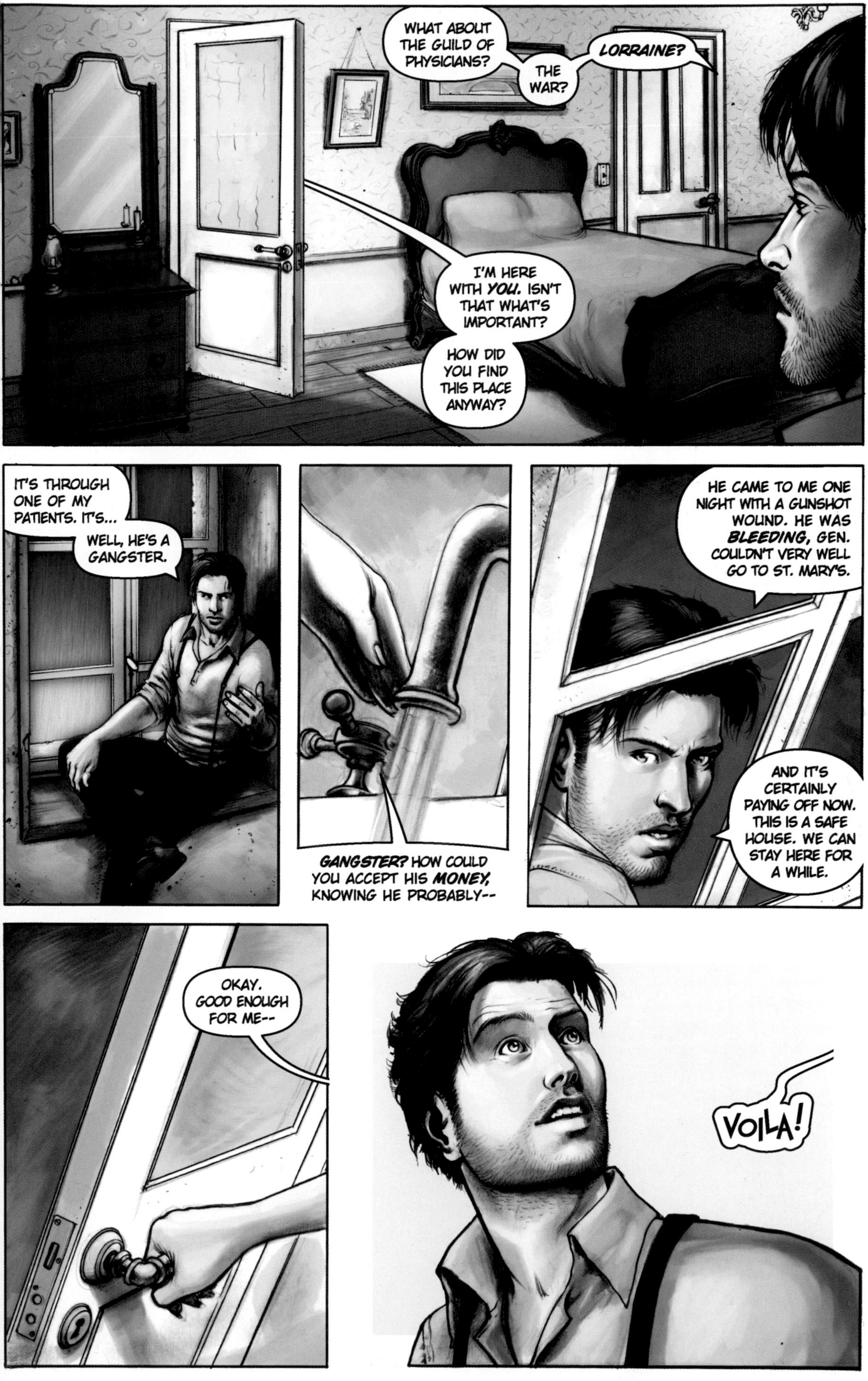
WHAT ABOUT THE GUILD OF PHYSICIANS?
THE WAR?
LORRAINE?
I'M HERE WITH YOU. ISN'T THAT WHAT'S IMPORTANT?
HOW DID YOU FIND THIS PLACE ANYWAY?
IT'S THROUGH ONE OF MY PATIENTS. IT'S...
WELL, HE'S A GANGSTER.
GANGSTER? HOW COULD YOU ACCEPT HIS MONEY, KNOWING HE PROBABLY--
HE CAME TO ME ONE NIGHT WITH A GUNSHOT WOUND. HE WAS BLEEDING, GEN. COULDN'T VERY WELL GO TO ST. MARY'S.
AND IT'S CERTAINLY PAYING OFF NOW. THIS IS A SAFE HOUSE. WE CAN STAY HERE FOR A WHILE.
OKAY. GOOD ENOUGH FOR ME--
VOILA!

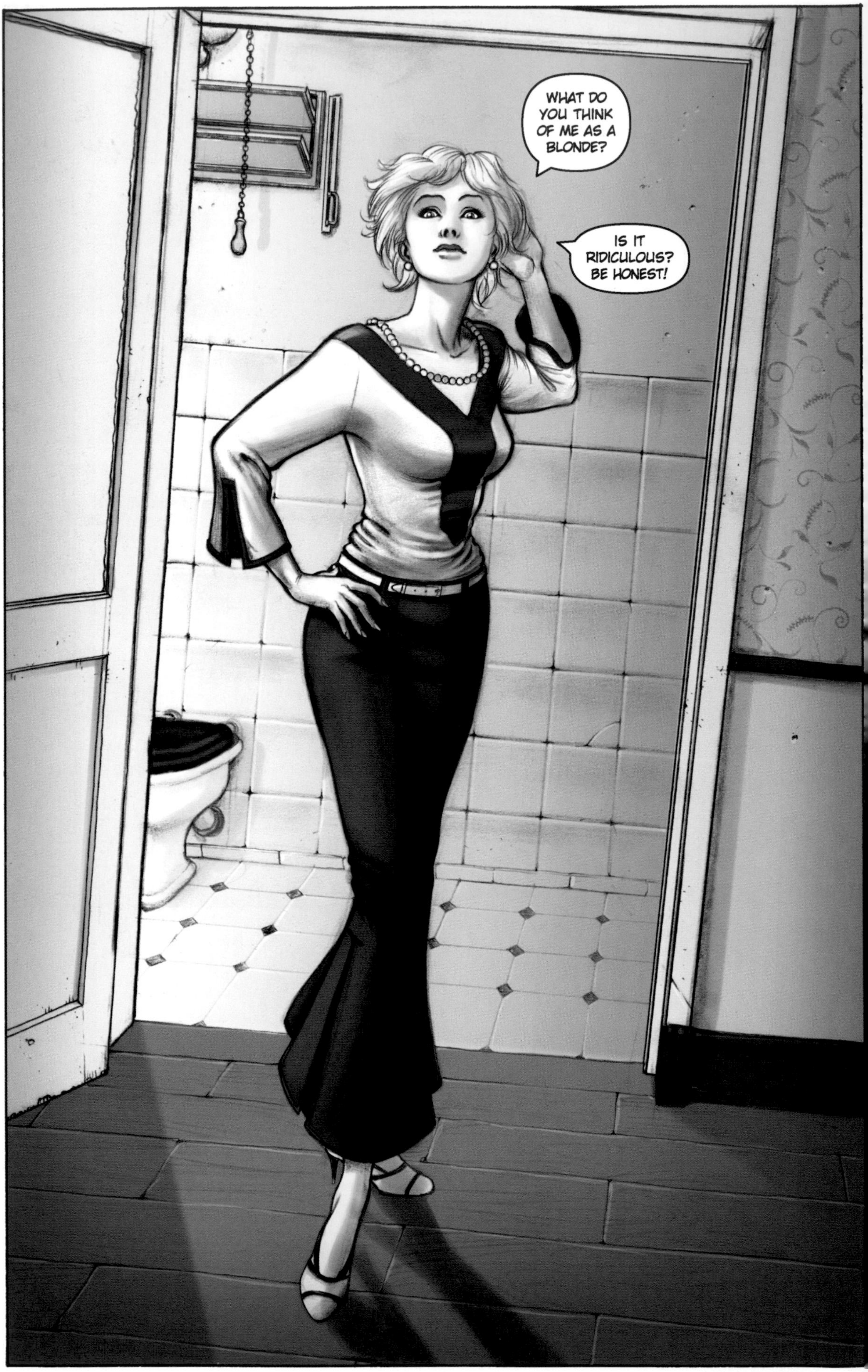
WHAT DO YOU THINK OF ME AS A BLONDE?
IS IT RIDICULOUS? BE HONEST!

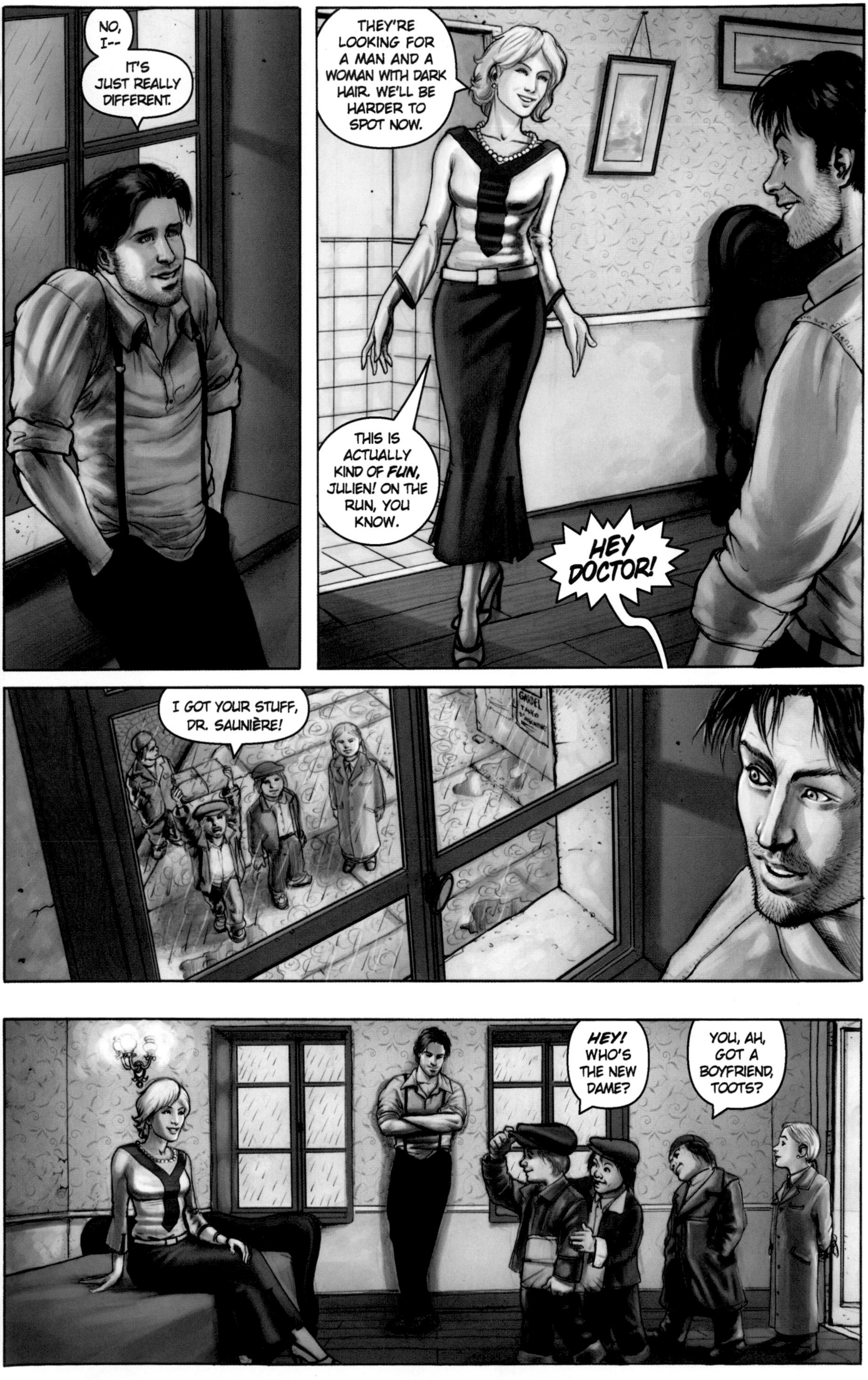
NO, I--
IT'S JUST REALLY DIFFERENT.
THEY'RE LOOKING FOR A MAN AND A WOMAN WITH DARK HAIR. WE'LL BE HARDER TO SPOT NOW.
THIS IS ACTUALLY KIND OF FUN, JULIEN! ON THE RUN, YOU KNOW.
HEY DOCTOR!
I GOT YOUR STUFF, DR. SAUNIÈRE!
HEY! WHO'S THE NEW DAME?
YOU, AH, GOT A BOYFRIEND, TOOTS?

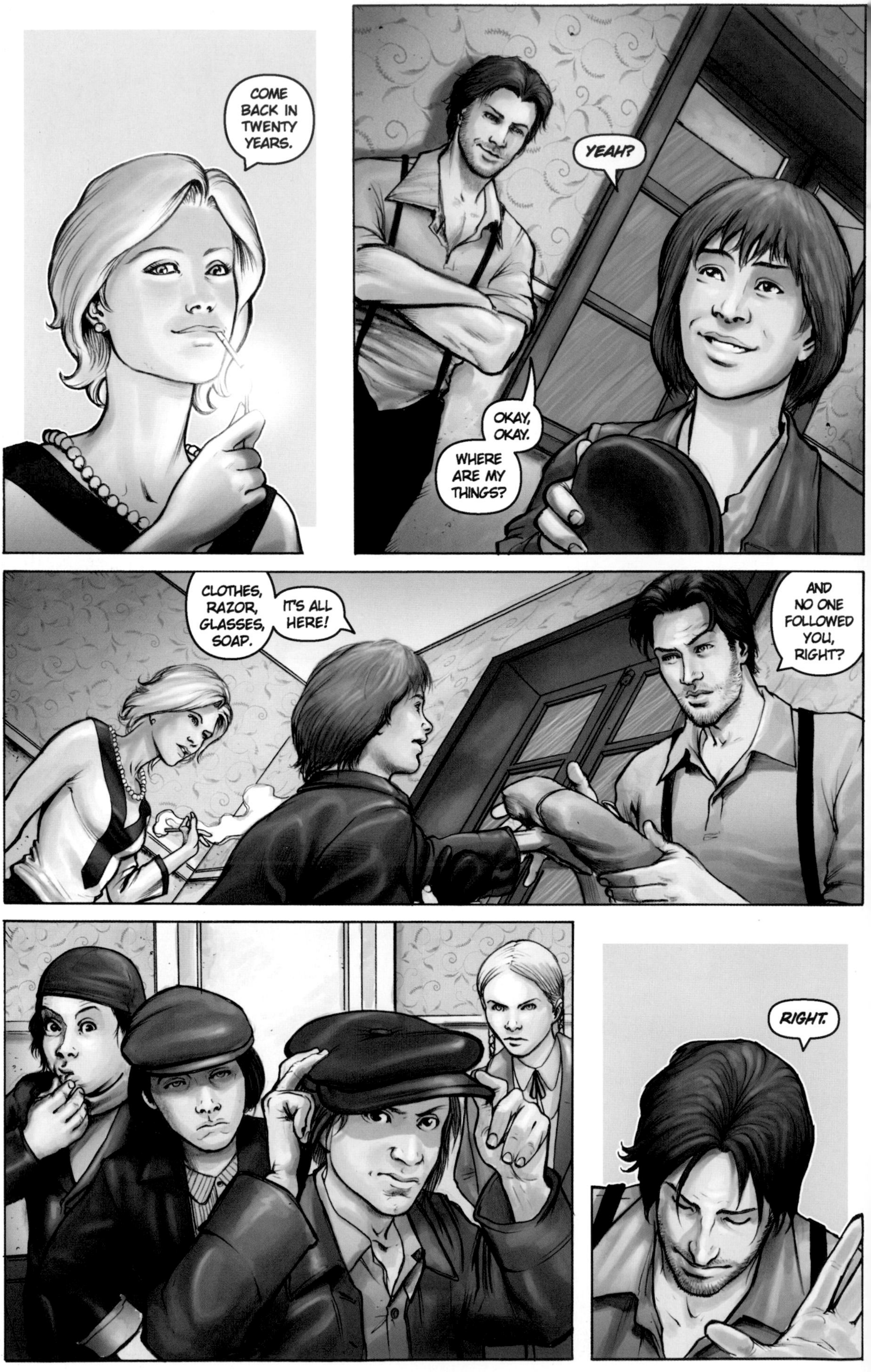
COME BACK IN TWENTY YEARS.
YEAH?
OKAY, OKAY.
WHERE ARE MY THINGS?
CLOTHES, RAZOR, GLASSES, SOAP.
IT'S ALL HERE!
AND NO ONE FOLLOWED YOU, RIGHT?
RIGHT.

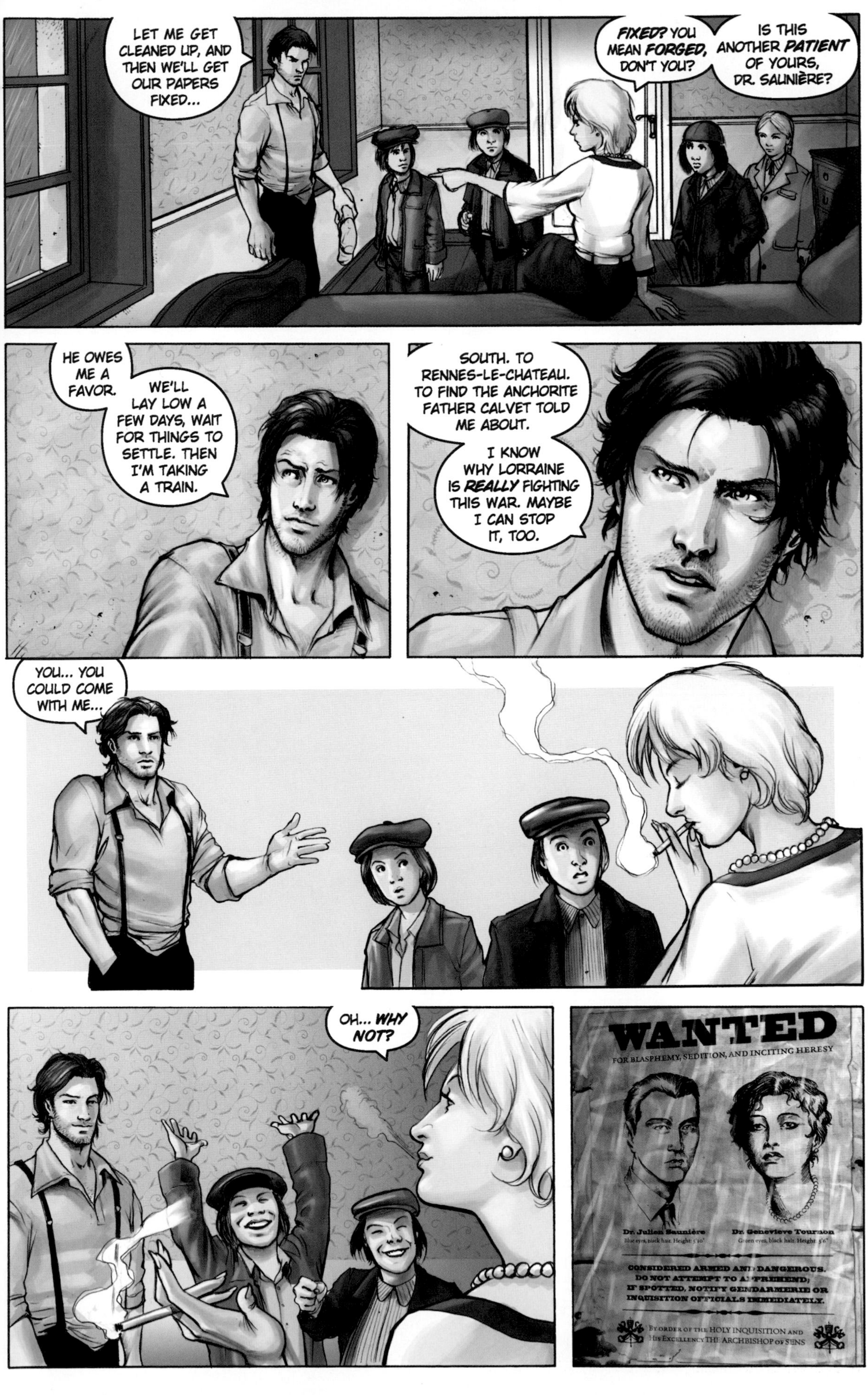
LET ME GET CLEANED UP, AND THEN WE'LL GET OUR PAPERS FIXED...
FIXED? YOU MEAN FORGED, DON'T YOU?
IS THIS ANOTHER PATIENT OF YOURS, DR. SAUNIÈRE?
HE OWES ME A FAVOR.
WE'LL LAY LOW A FEW DAYS, WAIT FOR THINGS TO SETTLE. THEN I'M TAKING A TRAIN.
SOUTH. TO RENNES-LE-CHATEAU. TO FIND THE ANCHORITE FATHER CALVET TOLD ME ABOUT.
I KNOW WHY LORRAINE IS REALLY FIGHTING THIS WAR. MAYBE I CAN STOP IT, TOO.
YOU... YOU COULD COME WITH ME...
OH... WHY NOT?
WANTED
FOR BLASPHEMY, SEDITION, AND INCITING HERESY
Dr. Julien Saunière
Blue eyes, black hair. Height: 5'10"
Dr. Genevieve Tournon
Green eyes, black hair. Height: 5'6"
CONSIDERED ARMED AND DANGEROUS.
DO NOT ATTEMPT TO APPREHEND;
IF SPOTTED, NOTIFY GENDARMERIE OR
INQUISITION OFFICIALS IMMEDIATELY.
BY ORDER OF THE HOLY INQUISITION AND
HIS EXCELLENCY THE ARCHBISHOP OF SENS

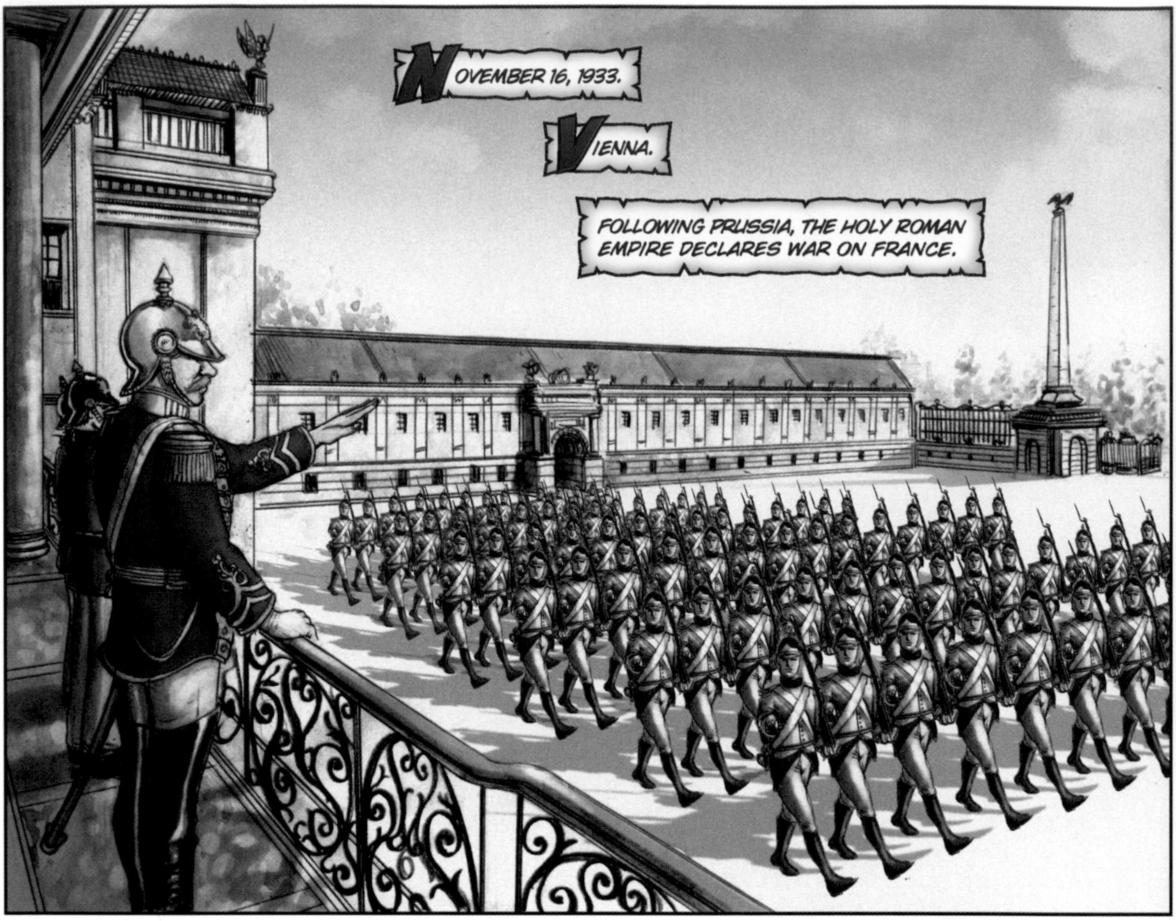
NOVEMBER 16, 1933.
VIENNA.
FOLLOWING PRUSSIA, THE HOLY ROMAN EMPIRE DECLARES WAR ON FRANCE.

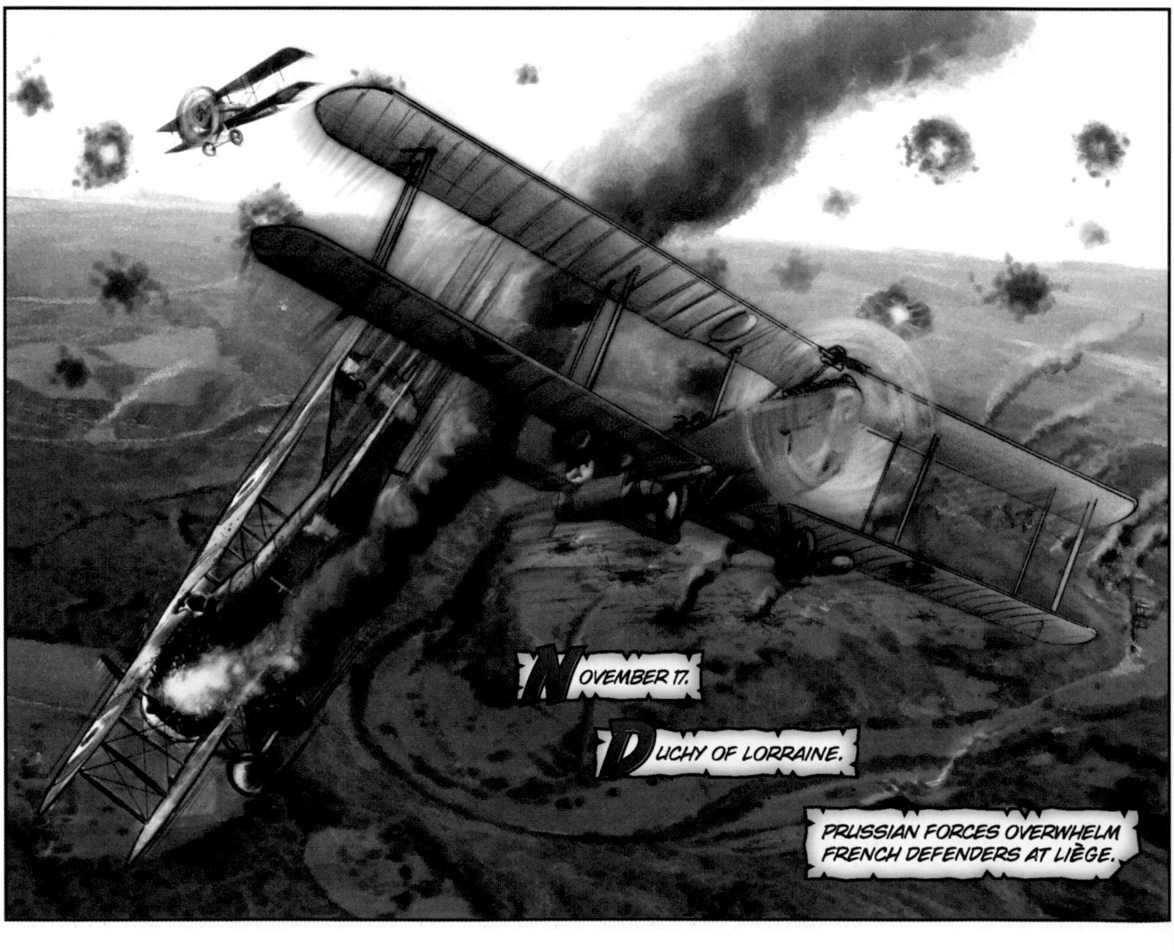
NOVEMBER 17.
DUCHY OF LORRAINE.
PRUSSIAN FORCES OVERWHELM FRENCH DEFENDERS AT LIÈGE.

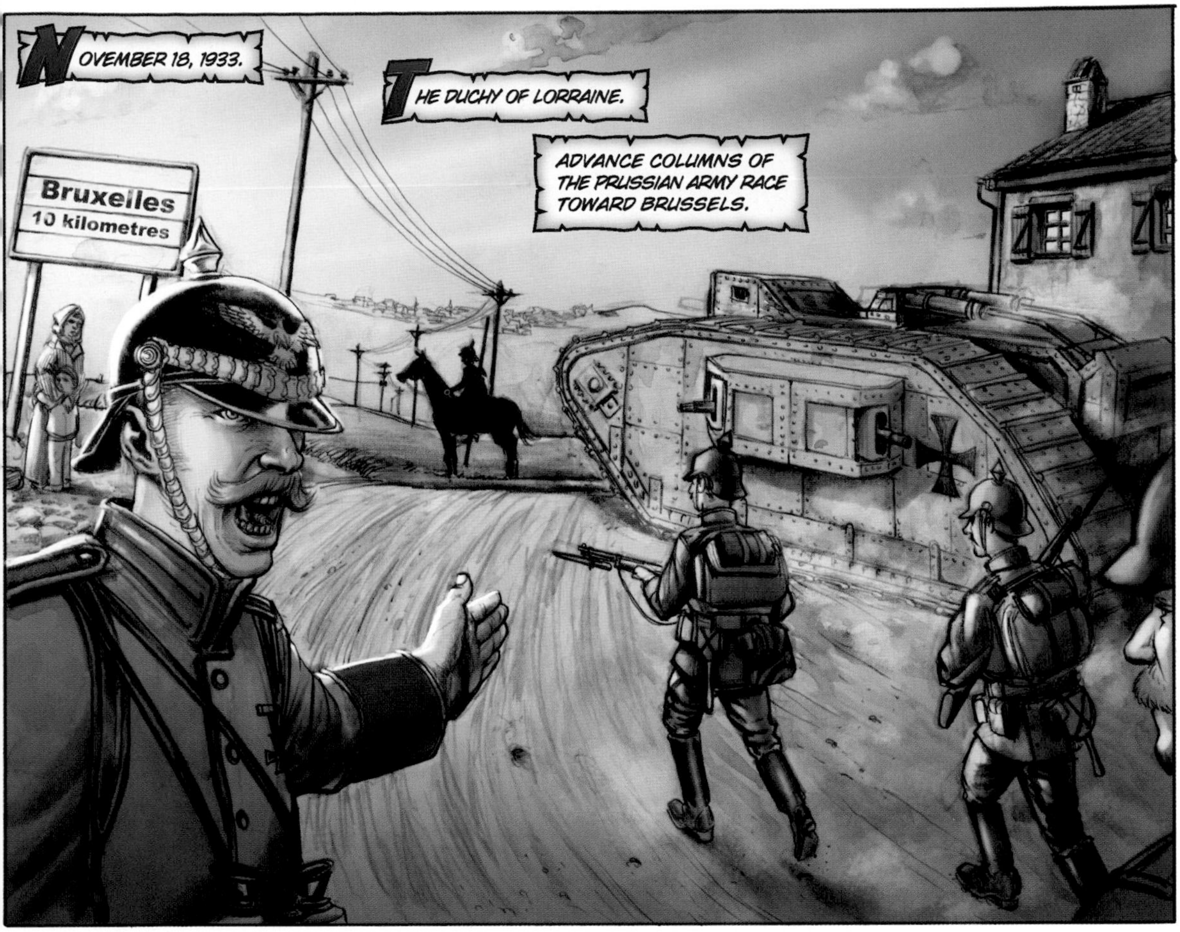
NOVEMBER 18, 1933.
THE DUCHY OF LORRAINE.
ADVANCE COLUMNS OF THE PRUSSIAN ARMY RACE TOWARD BRUSSELS.
Bruxelles
10 kilometres

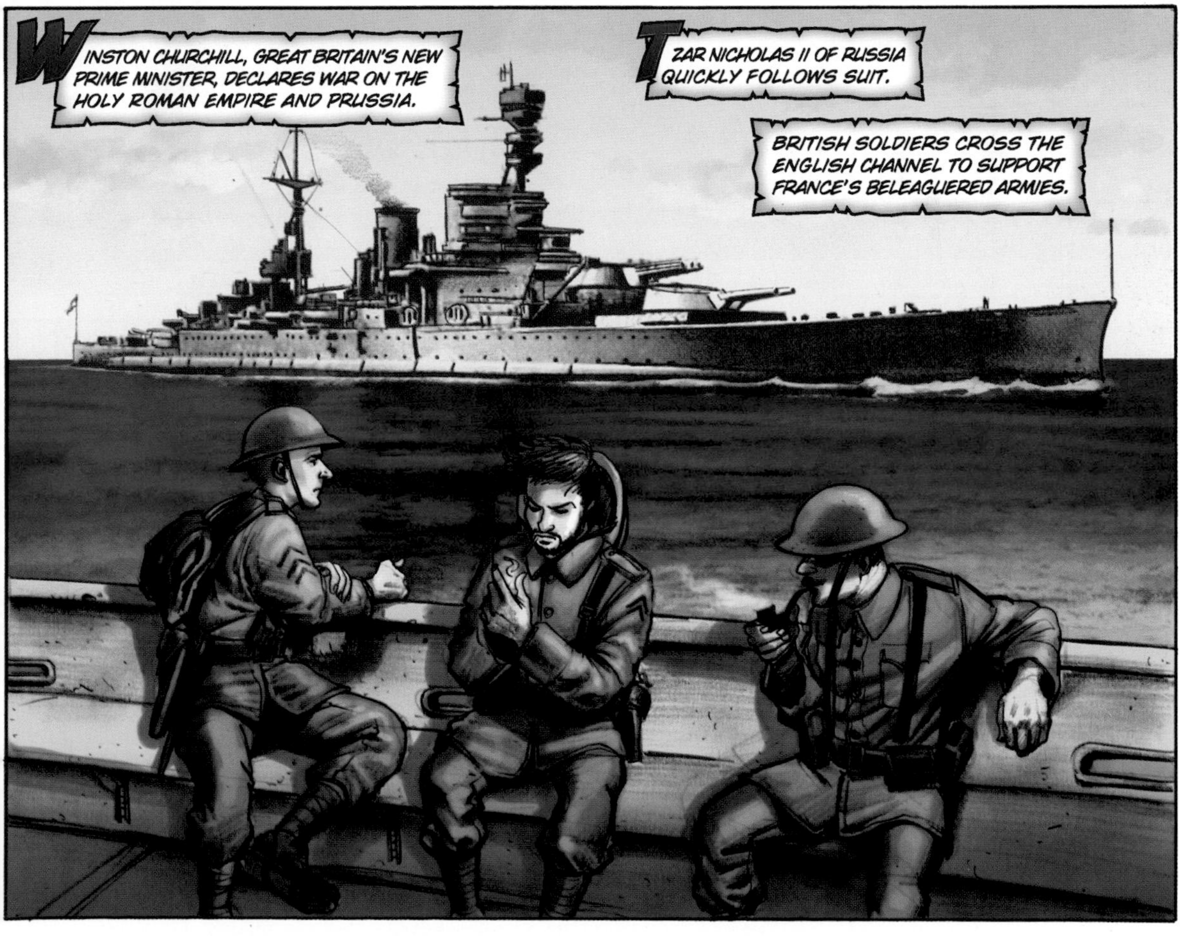
WINSTON CHURCHILL, GREAT BRITAIN'S NEW PRIME MINISTER, DECLARES WAR ON THE HOLY ROMAN EMPIRE AND PRUSSIA.
TZAR NICHOLAS II OF RUSSIA QUICKLY FOLLOWS SUIT.
BRITISH SOLDIERS CROSS THE ENGLISH CHANNEL TO SUPPORT FRANCE'S BELEAGUERED ARMIES.

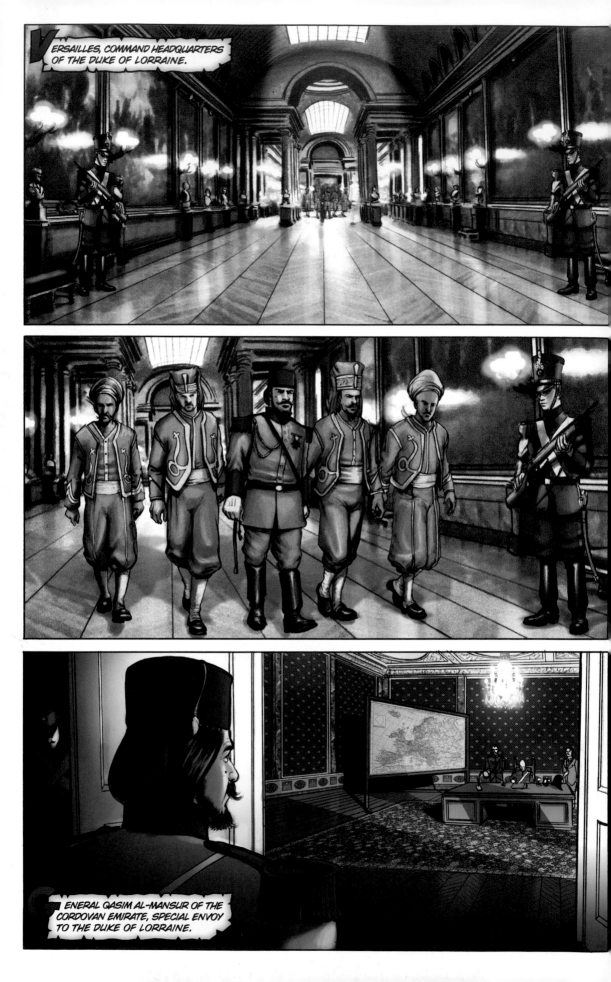

VERSAILLES, COMMAND HEADQUARTERS OF THE DUKE OF LORRAINE.

GENERAL QASIM AL-MANSUR OF THE CORDOVAN EMIRATE, SPECIAL ENVOY TO THE DUKE OF LORRAINE.

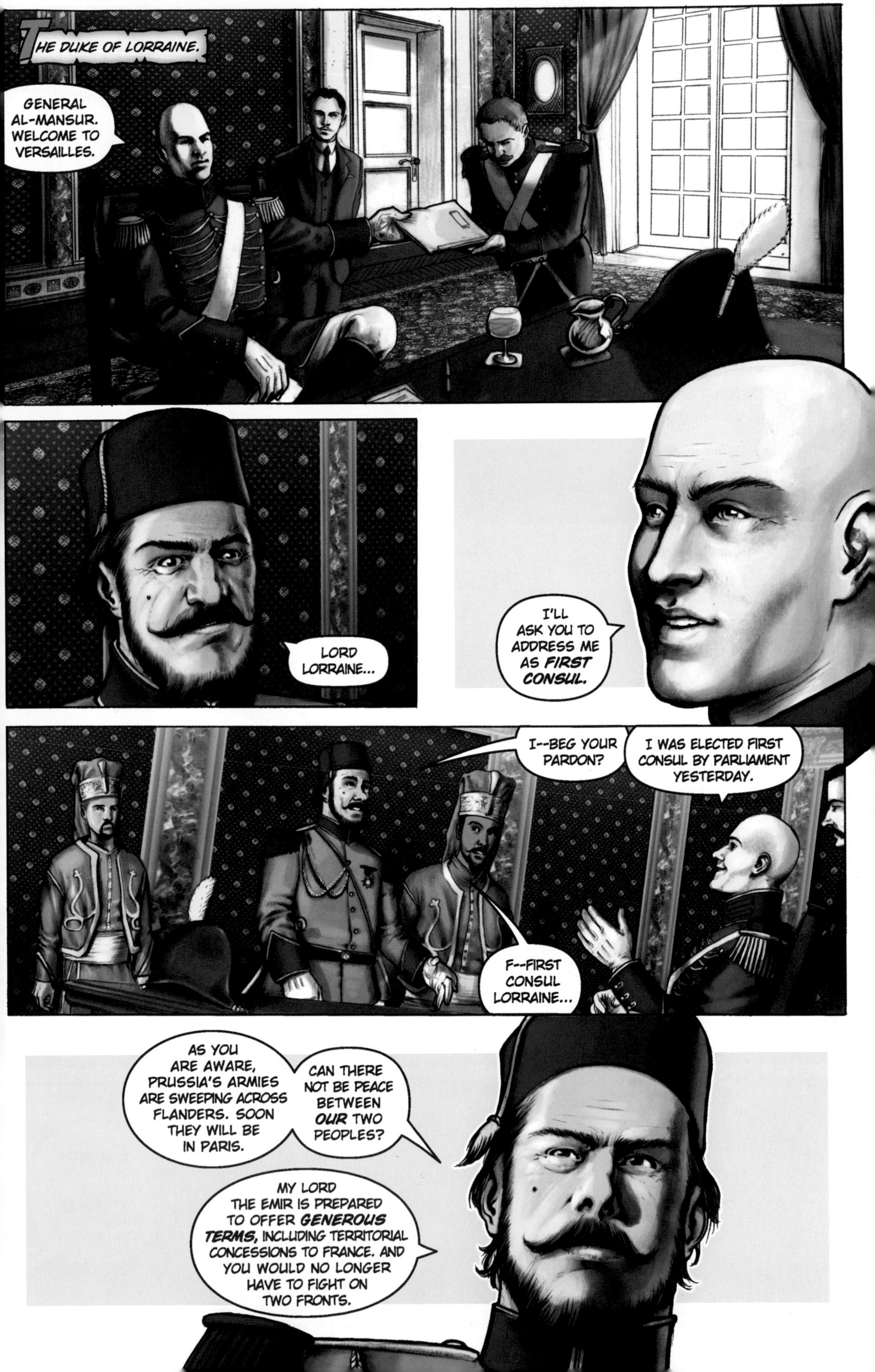
THE DUKE OF LORRAINE.
GENERAL AL-MANSUR. WELCOME TO VERSAILLES.
LORD LORRAINE...
I'LL ASK YOU TO ADDRESS ME AS FIRST CONSUL.
I--BEG YOUR PARDON?
I WAS ELECTED FIRST CONSUL BY PARLIAMENT YESTERDAY.
F--FIRST CONSUL LORRAINE...
AS YOU ARE AWARE, PRUSSIA'S ARMIES ARE SWEEPING ACROSS FLANDERS. SOON THEY WILL BE IN PARIS.
CAN THERE NOT BE PEACE BETWEEN OUR TWO PEOPLES?
MY LORD THE EMIR IS PREPARED TO OFFER GENEROUS TERMS, INCLUDING TERRITORIAL CONCESSIONS TO FRANCE. AND YOU WOULD NO LONGER HAVE TO FIGHT ON TWO FRONTS.

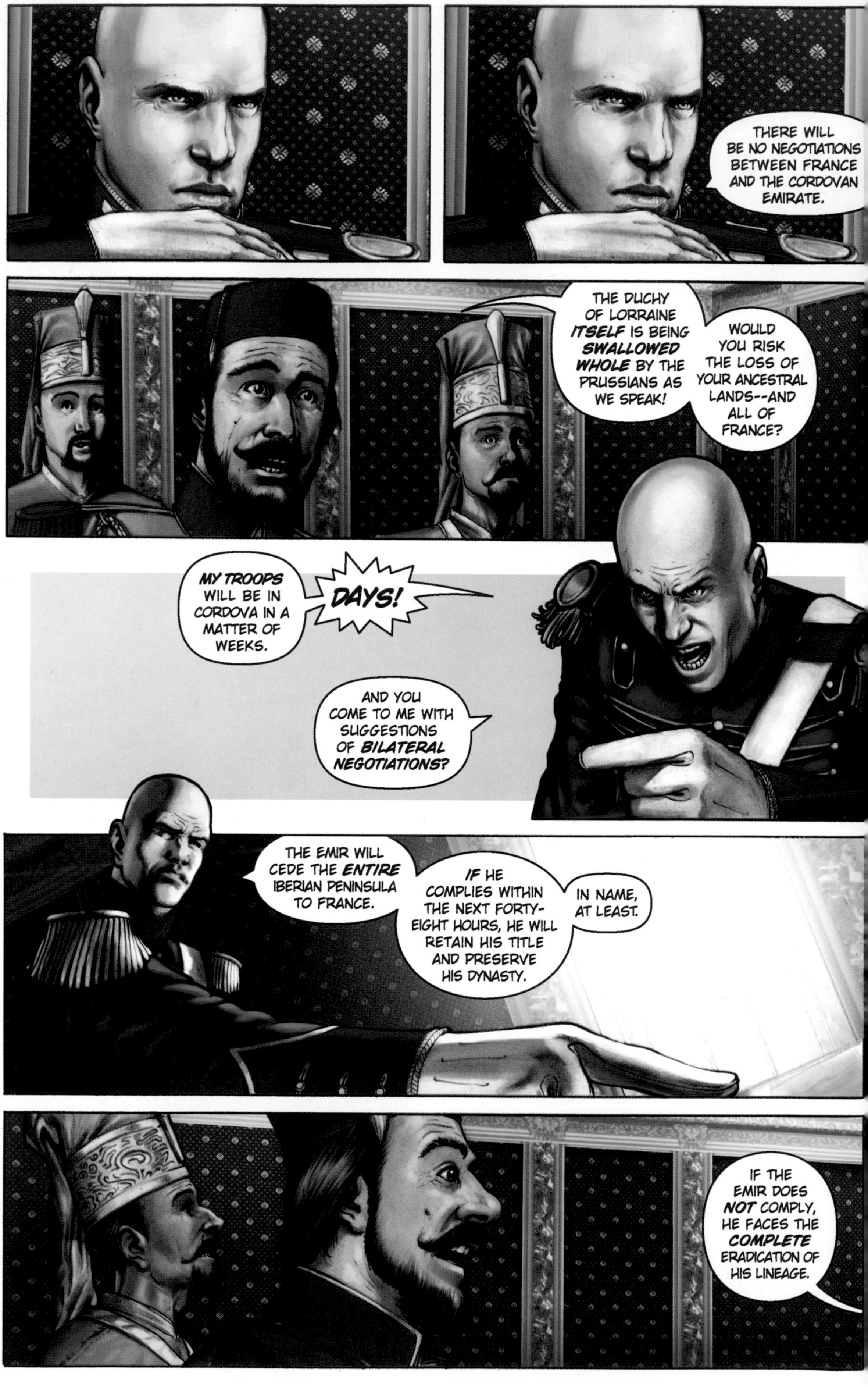
THERE WILL BE NO NEGOTIATIONS BETWEEN FRANCE AND THE CORDOVAN EMIRATE.
THE DUCHY OF LORRAINE *ITSELF* IS BEING *SWALLOWED WHOLE* BY THE PRUSSIANS AS WE SPEAK!
WOULD YOU RISK THE LOSS OF YOUR ANCESTRAL LANDS--AND ALL OF FRANCE?
MY TROOPS WILL BE IN CORDOVA IN A MATTER OF WEEKS.
DAYS!
AND YOU COME TO ME WITH SUGGESTIONS OF *BILATERAL NEGOTIATIONS?*
THE EMIR WILL CEDE THE *ENTIRE* IBERIAN PENINSULA TO FRANCE.
IF HE COMPLIES WITHIN THE NEXT FORTY-EIGHT HOURS, HE WILL RETAIN HIS TITLE AND PRESERVE HIS DYNASTY.
IN NAME, AT LEAST.
IF THE EMIR DOES *NOT* COMPLY, HE FACES THE *COMPLETE* ERADICATION OF HIS LINEAGE.

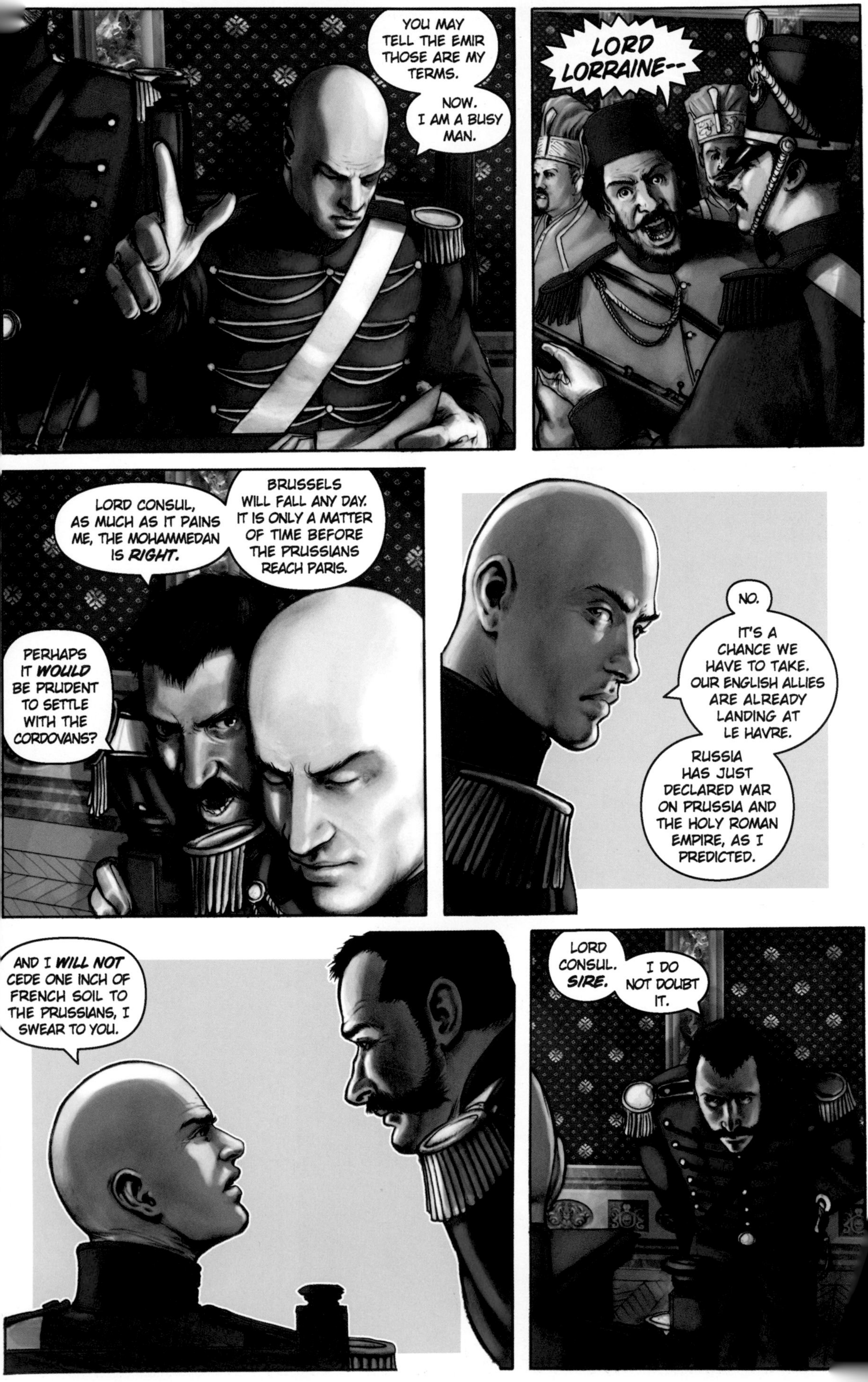
YOU MAY TELL THE EMIR THOSE ARE MY TERMS.
NOW. I AM A BUSY MAN.
LORD LORRAINE--
LORD CONSUL, AS MUCH AS IT PAINS ME, THE MOHAMMEDAN IS *RIGHT.*
BRUSSELS WILL FALL ANY DAY. IT IS ONLY A MATTER OF TIME BEFORE THE PRUSSIANS REACH PARIS.
PERHAPS IT *WOULD* BE PRUDENT TO SETTLE WITH THE CORDOVANS?
NO.
IT'S A CHANCE WE HAVE TO TAKE. OUR ENGLISH ALLIES ARE ALREADY LANDING AT LE HAVRE.
RUSSIA HAS JUST DECLARED WAR ON PRUSSIA AND THE HOLY ROMAN EMPIRE, AS I PREDICTED.
AND I *WILL NOT* CEDE ONE INCH OF FRENCH SOIL TO THE PRUSSIANS, I SWEAR TO YOU.
LORD CONSUL. *SIRE.*
I DO NOT DOUBT IT.

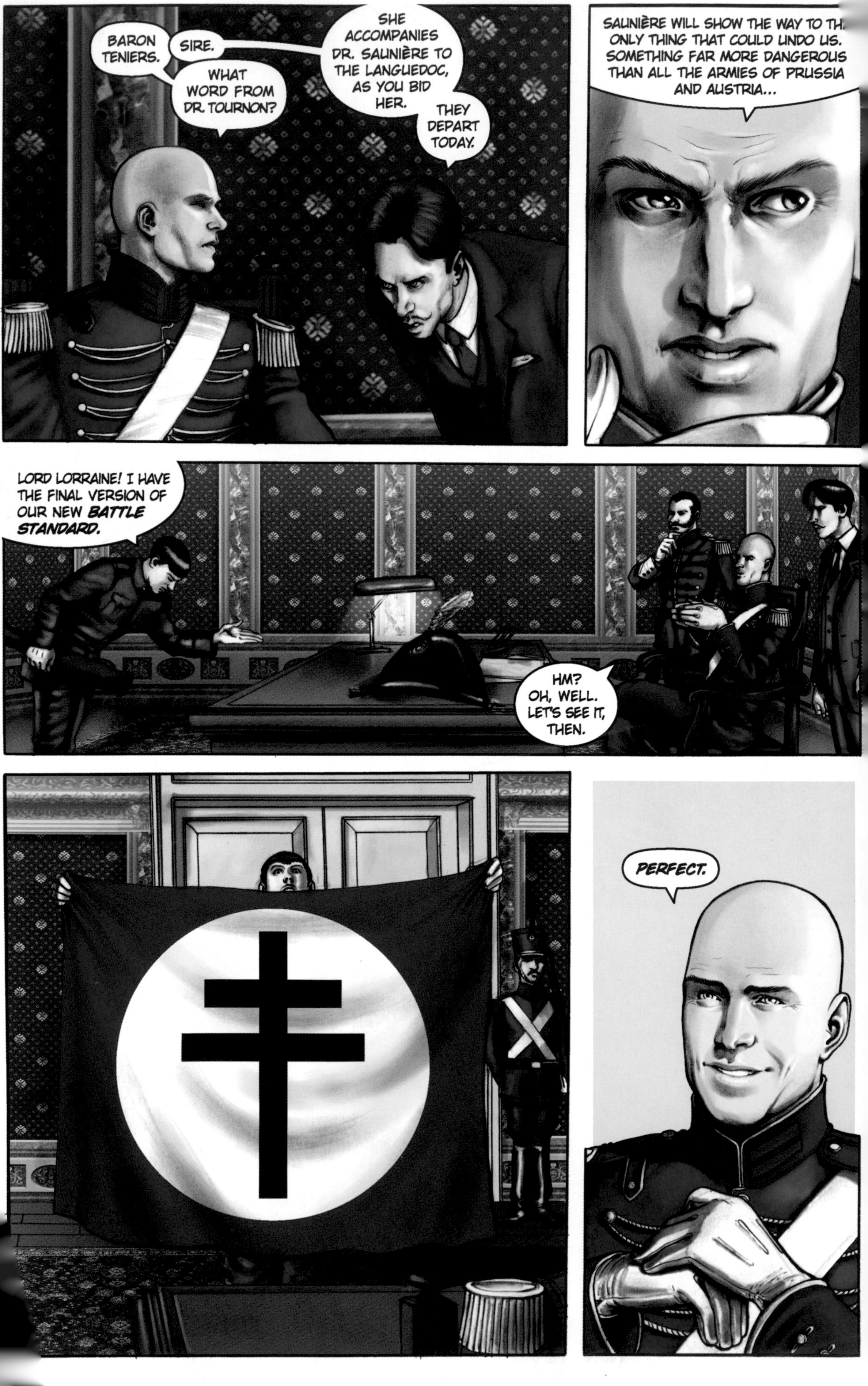
BARON TENIERS.
SIRE.
WHAT WORD FROM DR. TOURNON?
SHE ACCOMPANIES DR. SAUNIÈRE TO THE LANGUEDOC, AS YOU BID HER.
THEY DEPART TODAY.
SAUNIÈRE WILL SHOW THE WAY TO TH ONLY THING THAT COULD UNDO US. SOMETHING FAR MORE DANGEROUS THAN ALL THE ARMIES OF PRUSSIA AND AUSTRIA...
LORD LORRAINE! I HAVE THE FINAL VERSION OF OUR NEW BATTLE STANDARD.
HM? OH, WELL. LET'S SEE IT, THEN.
PERFECT.

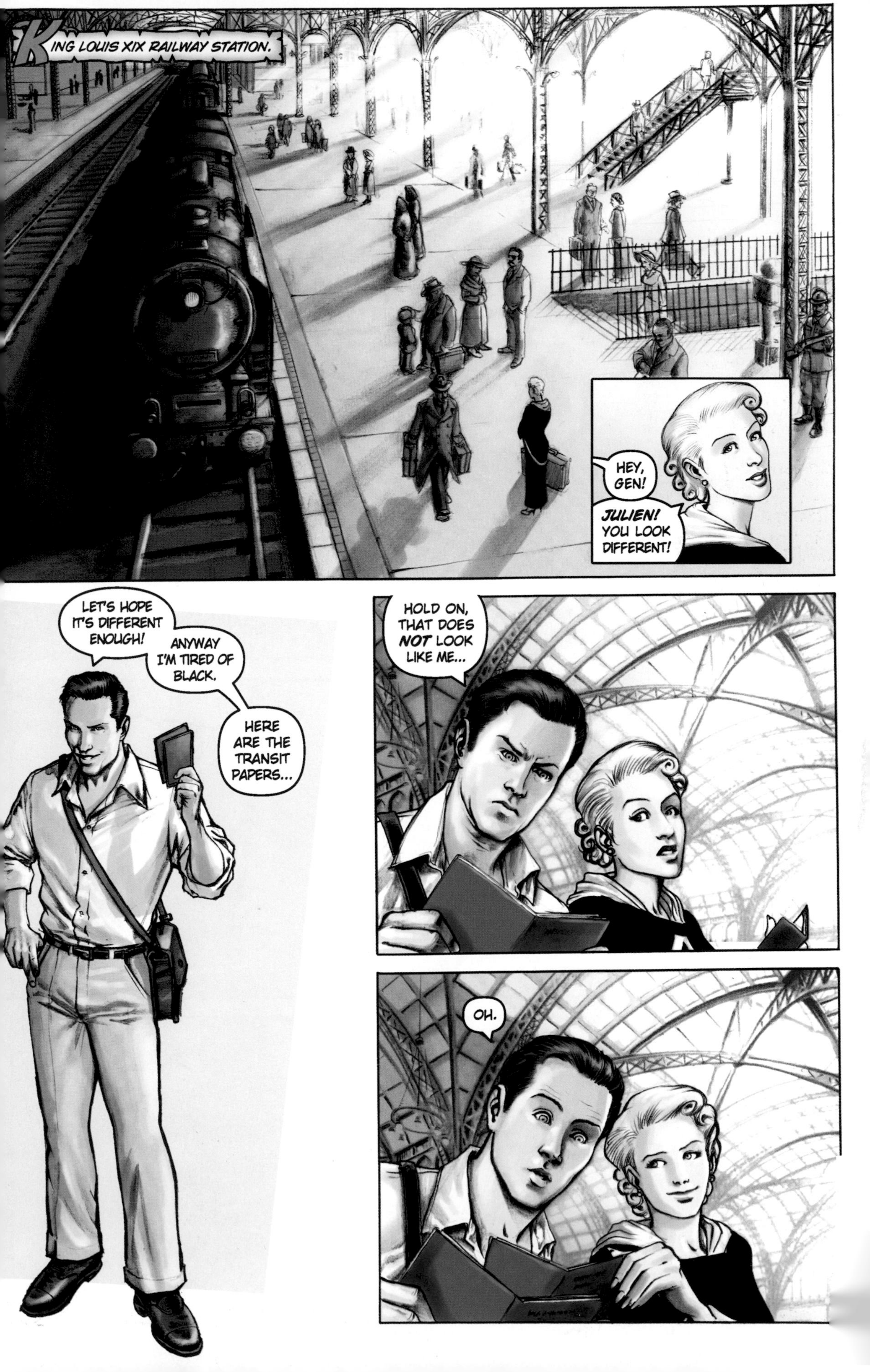
KING LOUIS XIX RAILWAY STATION.
HEY, GEN!
JULIEN! YOU LOOK DIFFERENT!
LET'S HOPE IT'S DIFFERENT ENOUGH!
ANYWAY I'M TIRED OF BLACK.
HERE ARE THE TRANSIT PAPERS...
HOLD ON, THAT DOES NOT LOOK LIKE ME...
OH.

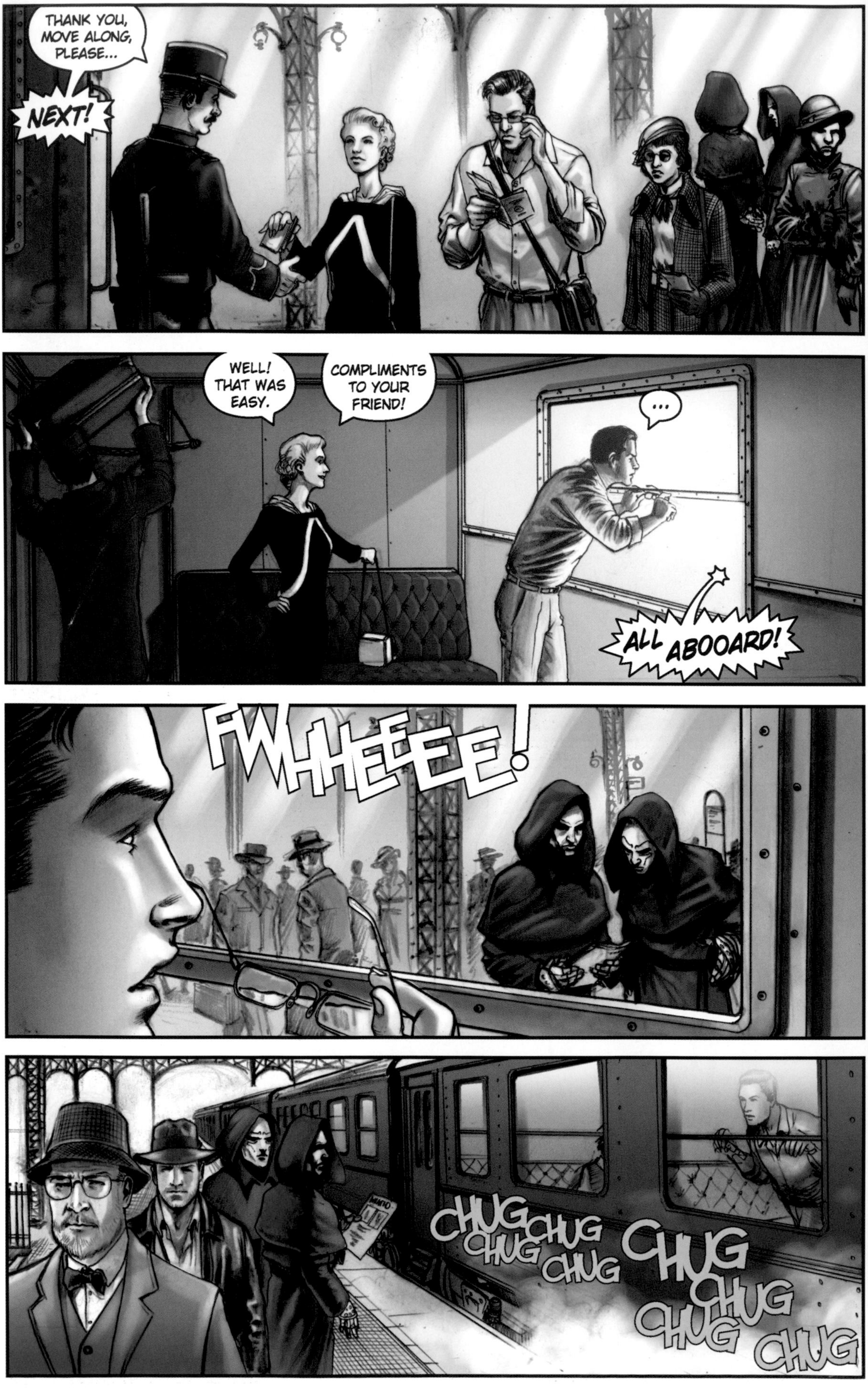
THANK YOU, MOVE ALONG, PLEASE...
NEXT!
WELL! THAT WAS EASY.
COMPLIMENTS TO YOUR FRIEND!
...
ALL ABOOARD!
FWHHEEEEE!
CHUG CHUG CHUG CHUG CHUG CHUG CHUG CHUG

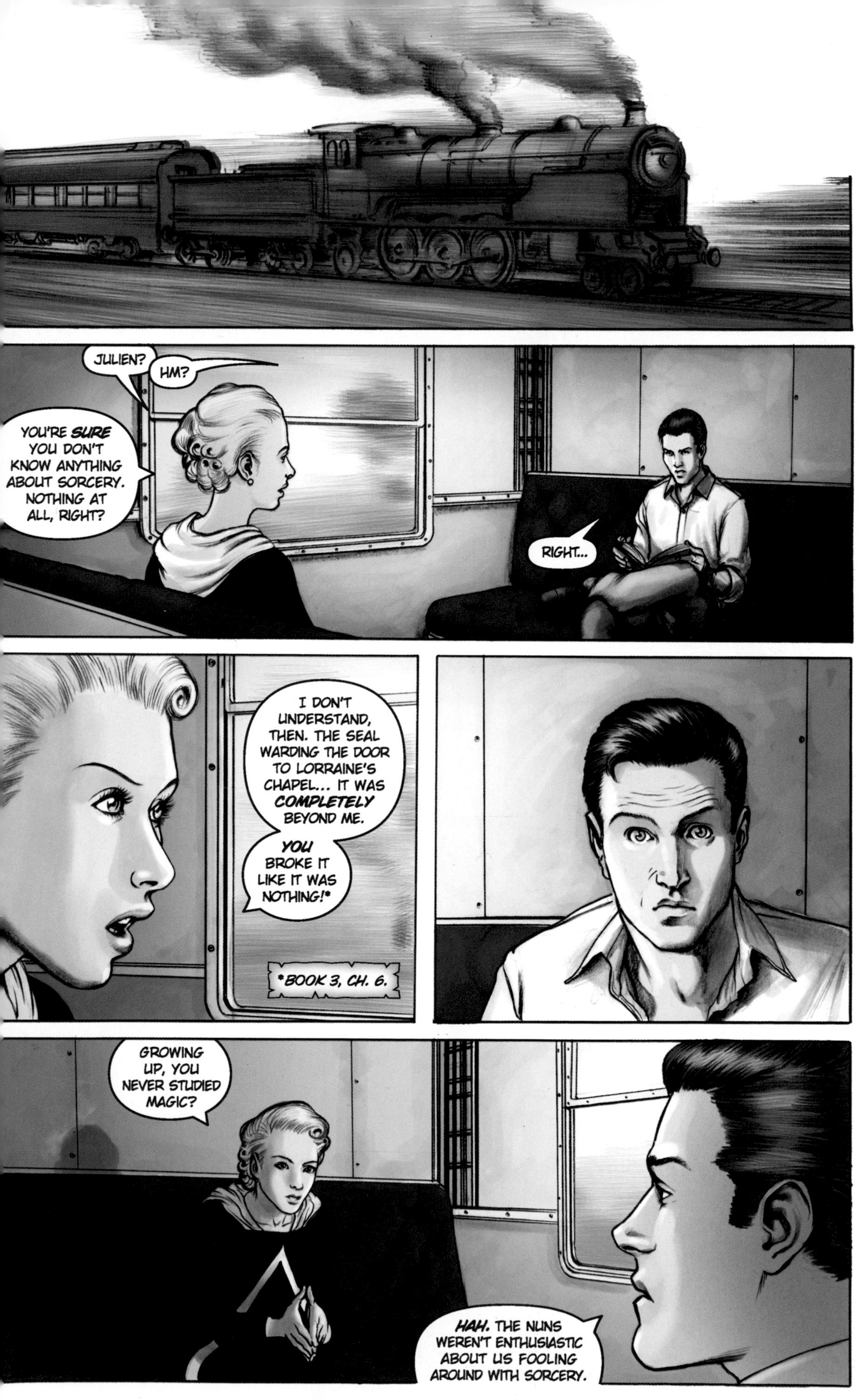
JULIEN?
HM?
YOU'RE SURE YOU DON'T KNOW ANYTHING ABOUT SORCERY. NOTHING AT ALL, RIGHT?
RIGHT...
I DON'T UNDERSTAND, THEN. THE SEAL WARDING THE DOOR TO LORRAINE'S CHAPEL... IT WAS COMPLETELY BEYOND ME.
YOU BROKE IT LIKE IT WAS NOTHING!*
*BOOK 3, CH. 6.
GROWING UP, YOU NEVER STUDIED MAGIC?
HAH. THE NUNS WEREN'T ENTHUSIASTIC ABOUT US FOOLING AROUND WITH SORCERY.

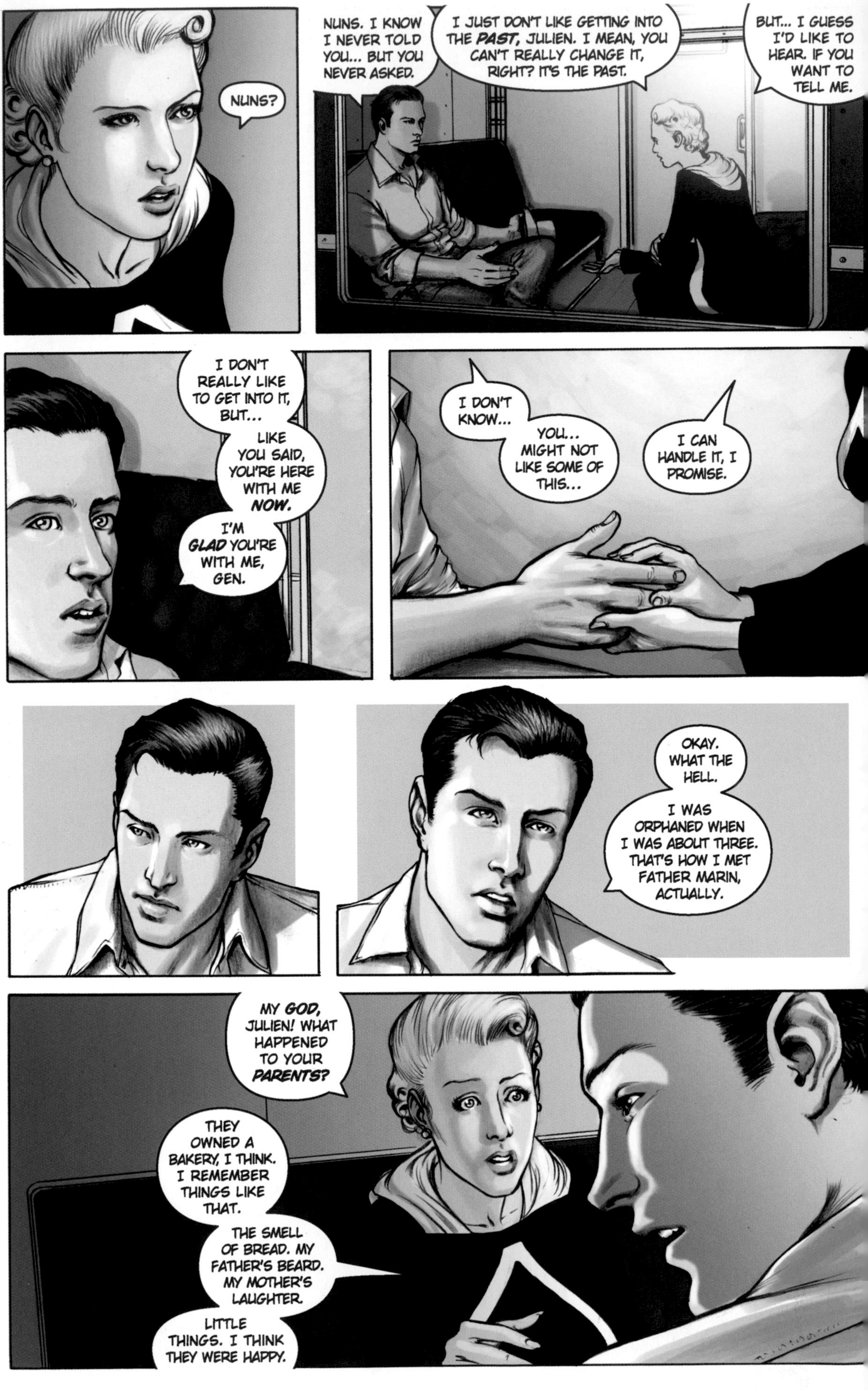
NUNS?
NUNS. I KNOW I NEVER TOLD YOU... BUT YOU NEVER ASKED.
I JUST DON'T LIKE GETTING INTO THE PAST, JULIEN. I MEAN, YOU CAN'T REALLY CHANGE IT, RIGHT? IT'S THE PAST.
BUT... I GUESS I'D LIKE TO HEAR. IF YOU WANT TO TELL ME.
I DON'T REALLY LIKE TO GET INTO IT, BUT...
LIKE YOU SAID, YOU'RE HERE WITH ME NOW.
I'M GLAD YOU'RE WITH ME, GEN.
I DON'T KNOW...
YOU... MIGHT NOT LIKE SOME OF THIS...
I CAN HANDLE IT, I PROMISE.
OKAY. WHAT THE HELL.
I WAS ORPHANED WHEN I WAS ABOUT THREE. THAT'S HOW I MET FATHER MARIN, ACTUALLY.
MY GOD, JULIEN! WHAT HAPPENED TO YOUR PARENTS?
THEY OWNED A BAKERY, I THINK. I REMEMBER THINGS LIKE THAT.
THE SMELL OF BREAD. MY FATHER'S BEARD. MY MOTHER'S LAUGHTER.
LITTLE THINGS. I THINK THEY WERE HAPPY.

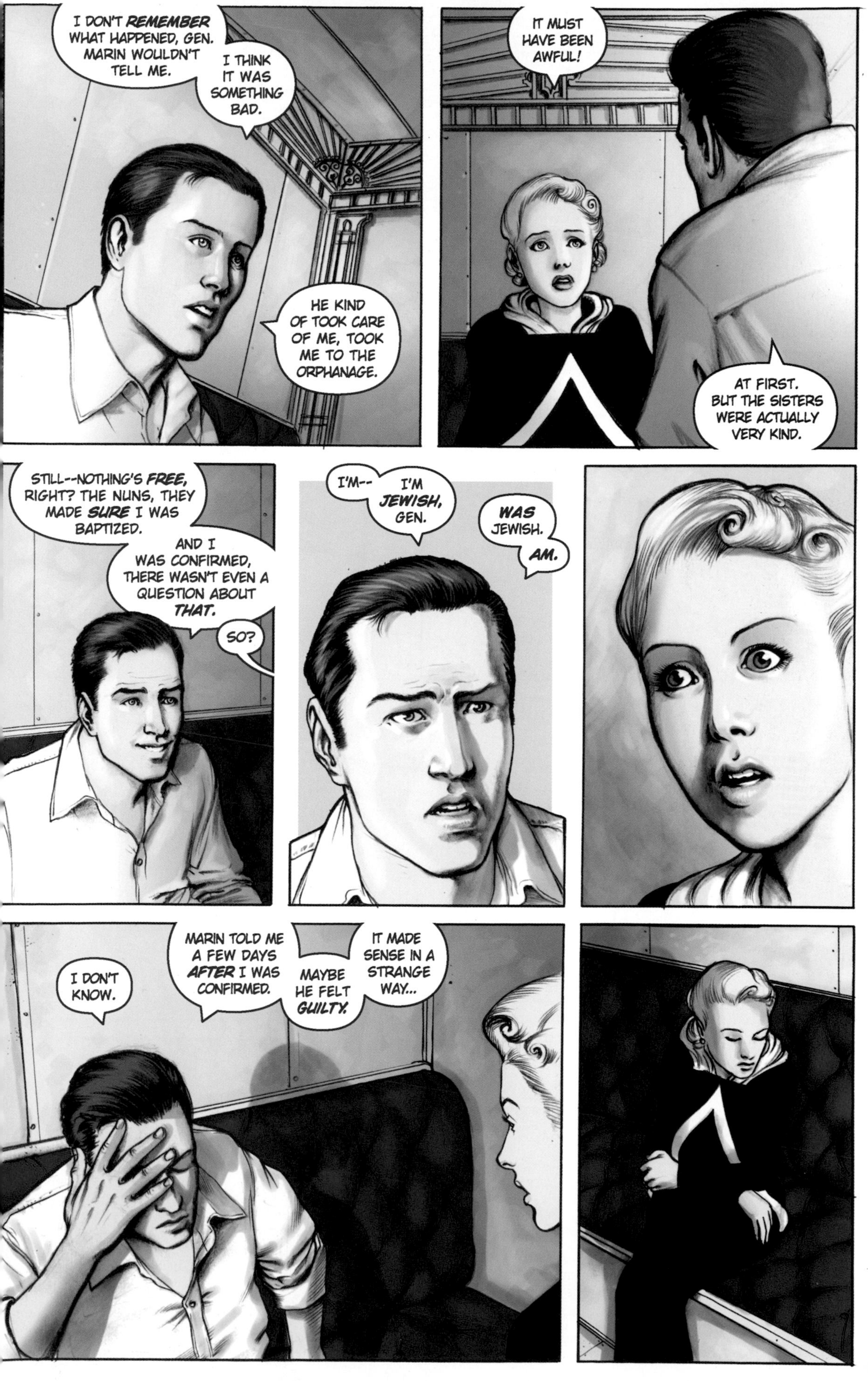
I DON'T REMEMBER WHAT HAPPENED, GEN. MARIN WOULDN'T TELL ME.
I THINK IT WAS SOMETHING BAD.
HE KIND OF TOOK CARE OF ME, TOOK ME TO THE ORPHANAGE.
IT MUST HAVE BEEN AWFUL!
AT FIRST. BUT THE SISTERS WERE ACTUALLY VERY KIND.
STILL--NOTHING'S FREE, RIGHT? THE NUNS, THEY MADE SURE I WAS BAPTIZED.
AND I WAS CONFIRMED, THERE WASN'T EVEN A QUESTION ABOUT THAT.
SO?
I'M--
I'M JEWISH, GEN.
WAS JEWISH.
AM.
I DON'T KNOW.
MARIN TOLD ME A FEW DAYS AFTER I WAS CONFIRMED.
MAYBE HE FELT GUILTY.
IT MADE SENSE IN A STRANGE WAY...

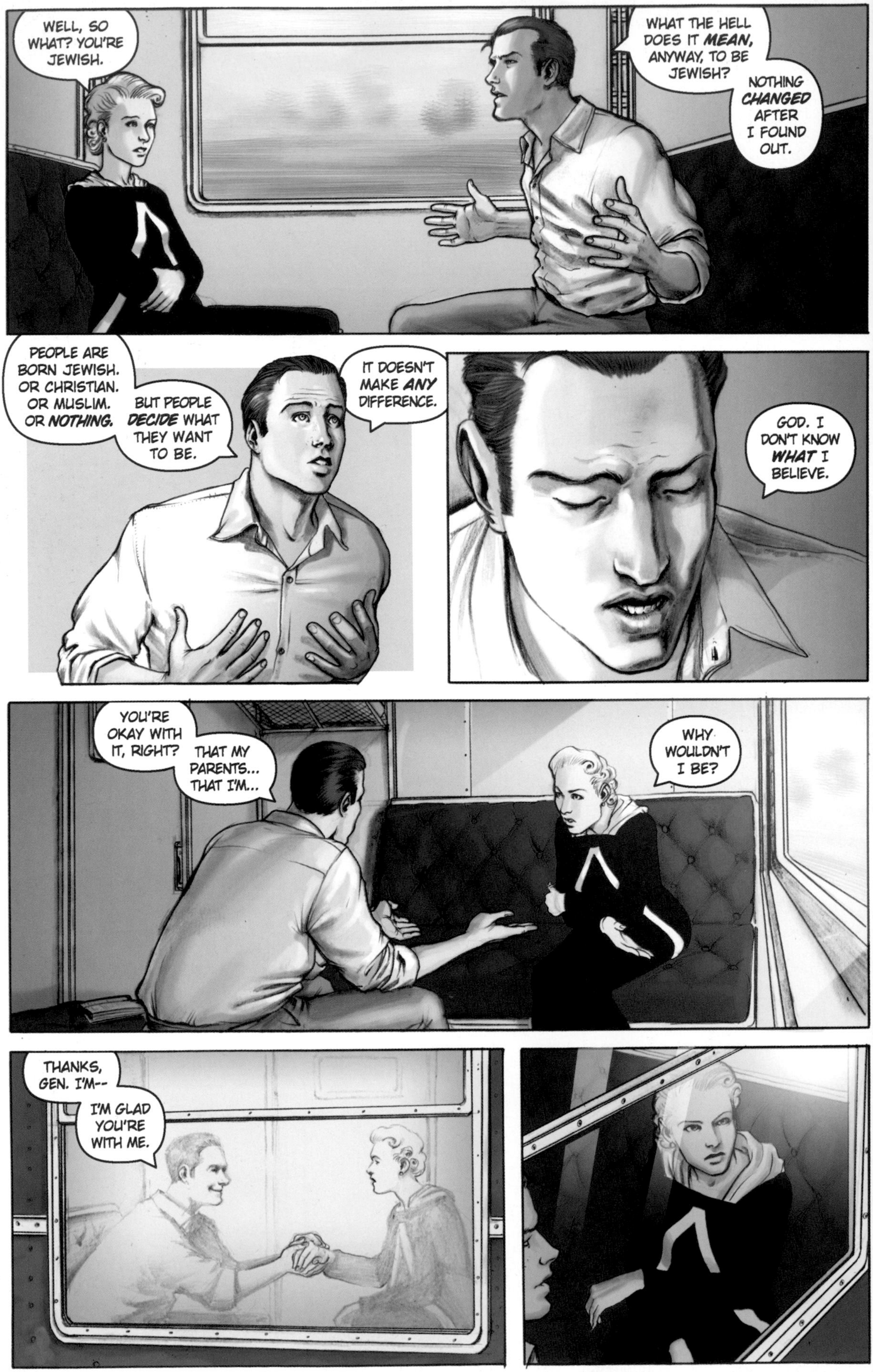
WELL, SO WHAT? YOU'RE JEWISH.
WHAT THE HELL DOES IT MEAN, ANYWAY, TO BE JEWISH?
NOTHING CHANGED AFTER I FOUND OUT.
PEOPLE ARE BORN JEWISH. OR CHRISTIAN. OR MUSLIM. OR NOTHING.
BUT PEOPLE DECIDE WHAT THEY WANT TO BE.
IT DOESN'T MAKE ANY DIFFERENCE.
GOD. I DON'T KNOW WHAT I BELIEVE.
YOU'RE OKAY WITH IT, RIGHT?
THAT MY PARENTS... THAT I'M...
WHY WOULDN'T I BE?
THANKS, GEN. I'M--
I'M GLAD YOU'RE WITH ME.

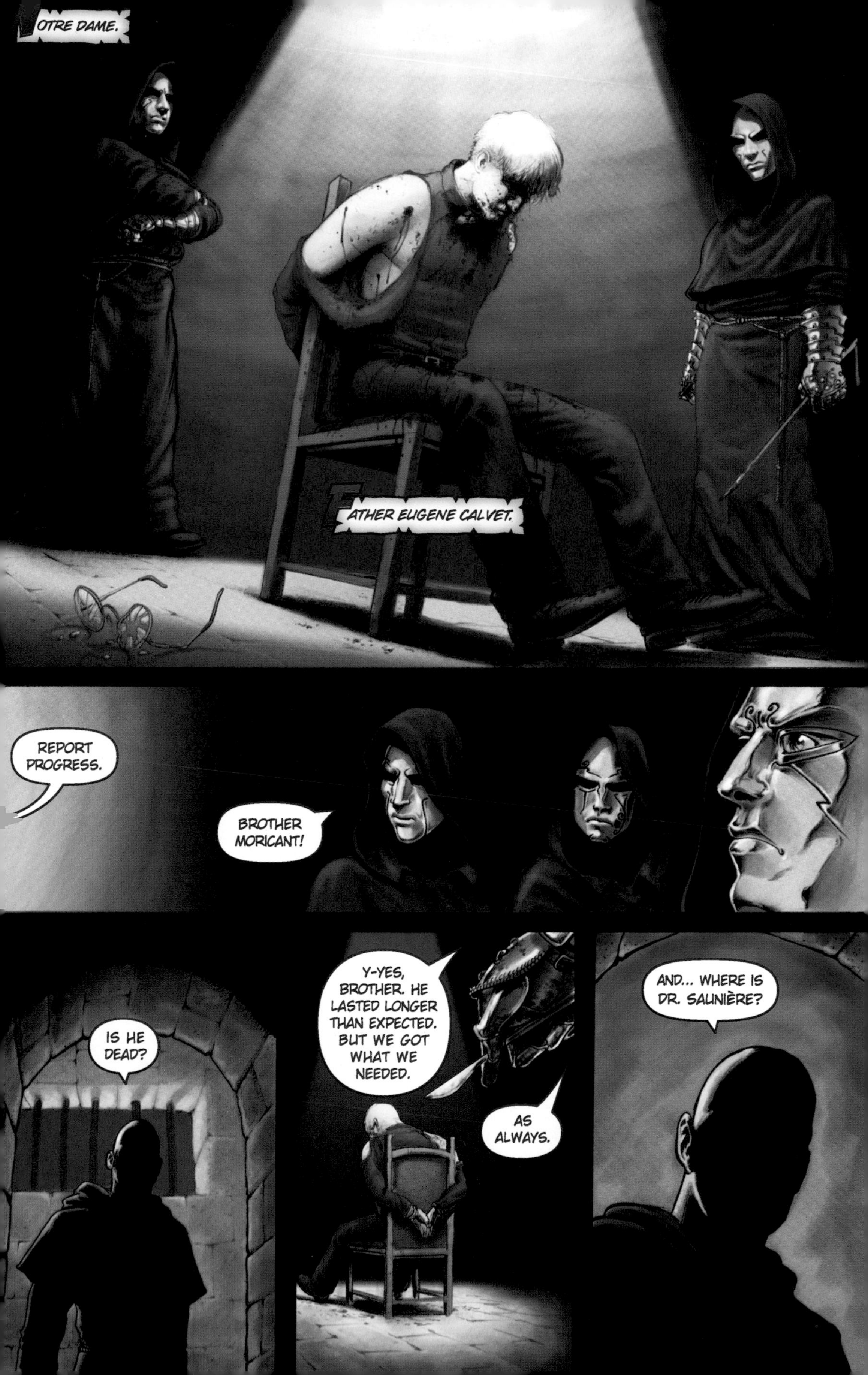
NOTRE DAME.
FATHER EUGENE CALVET.
REPORT PROGRESS.
BROTHER MORICANT!
IS HE DEAD?
Y-YES, BROTHER. HE LASTED LONGER THAN EXPECTED. BUT WE GOT WHAT WE NEEDED.
AS ALWAYS.
AND... WHERE IS DR. SAUNIÈRE?

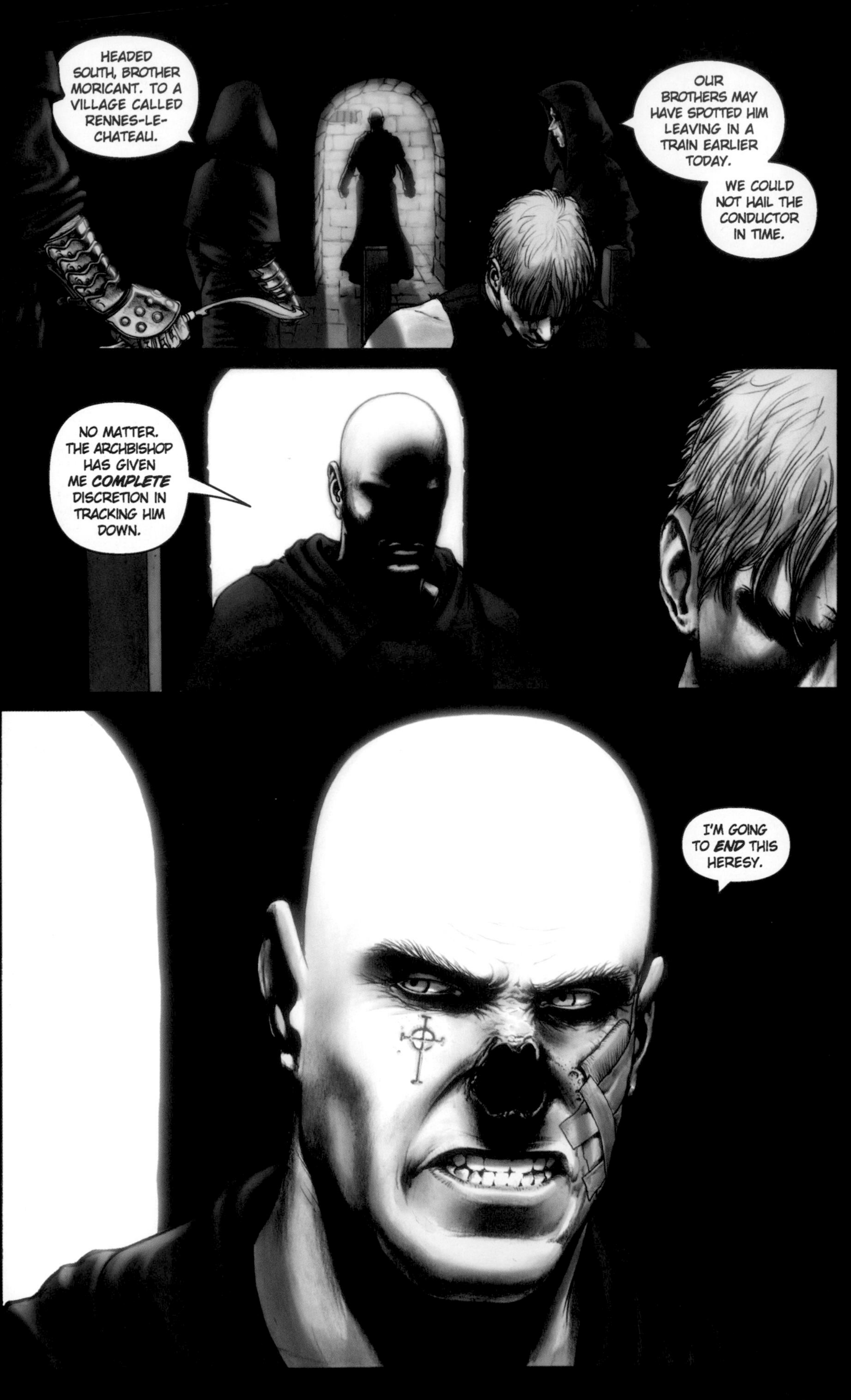
HEADED SOUTH, BROTHER MORICANT. TO A VILLAGE CALLED RENNES-LE-CHATEAU.
OUR BROTHERS MAY HAVE SPOTTED HIM LEAVING IN A TRAIN EARLIER TODAY.
WE COULD NOT HAIL THE CONDUCTOR IN TIME.
NO MATTER. THE ARCHBISHOP HAS GIVEN ME ***COMPLETE*** DISCRETION IN TRACKING HIM DOWN.
I'M GOING TO ***END*** THIS HERESY.

Le Journal de la Liberté

Paris's leading anglophone newspaper • vol. 205, no. 102 • Nov. 18, MCMXXXIII

Editors in Chief: M. Tait Bergstrom, M. Matthew Pasteris. **Story Editor:** M. Arvid Nelson.
Art Editor: M. Juan Ferreyra. **Photography Editor:** M. Alexander Waldman.
Layout Supervisor: M. William Kartalopoulos. **Editors Emeritus:** M. Clark A. Smith,
M. Howard P. Lovecraft, M. Robert E. Howard. Redacted under the direction of His Excellency
Archbishop Emile-Jean Ireneaux. *Le Journal de la Liberté* is printed under the benign auspices of his
eminence David Louis Plantard de St. Clair, Duke of Lorraine and First Consul of the Empire of France.

Papal seal of Approval

WAR INTENSIFIES; PARLIAMENT NAMES LORRAINE FIRST CONSUL

Lorrainer troops hastily fall back, disheartened by the voracity of the Prussian advance through the duchy of Lorraine.

Paris – The Hall of the Sword and Robe made a unanimous pledge of support to the Duke of Lorraine yesterday, naming him "First Consul of the Empire of France," despite dire news on the Eastern Front.

"Lorraine is the right man to lead this war," the Count of Razès, a member of the Hall of the Sword, said.

Despite the enthusiastic support, even his staunchest supporters admit "difficulty" in checking the Prussian advance in the duke's own duchy of Lorraine.

"So far we have been unable to halt the Prussians. The lay of the land is against us, but we're regrouping," the Duke of Orleans, commander of operations in the east, said.

He refused to comment on whether the town of Liège had been left to the Prussians, or whether Brussels was in danger.

If Prussian forces occupy the duchy of Lorraine, Paris itself would be in striking distance.

British troops have already embarked for Le Havre to aid the beleaguered defenders.

"We will lend our blood and sweat to France," British Prime Minister Winston Churchill said. British forces are expected to join the fight within days.

Holy Roman Empire Declares War on France, Serbia in Open Revolt

Vienna – Yesterday the Holy Roman Empire (HRE) declared war on France. Austrian troops are moving through Bavaria to join their Prussian allies in the offensive in northeastern France.

But Emperor Rudolf of the HRE might find his forces spread thinly. Serbian nationalists took advantage of the chaos to declare independence from the Habsburg emperor.

Unconfirmed reports that Serb rebels have massacred Austrian garrisons in Belgrade and Sarajevo have reached Paris.

Russia Declares War on Prussia, HRE, Opening a New Front

Moscow – Russia declared war jointly on Prussia and the HRE early today, stoking French hopes that a second front on the east could alleviate pressure on French forces defending Paris.

Russia's entrance into the war follows the HRE's promise to "eradicate" Serbian nationalists struggling for independence.

Yuri Zolotukin, a spokesman for Tzar Nicholas, denied reports Serbian revolutionaries had been in contact with Russian officials prior to the uprising.

Russia's fighting capabilities are unknown, but the Tzar commands massive reserves of troops.

Offensive Against Cordovans Proceeds Better for France

Zaragoza – The armies of the Cordovan Emirate are in full retreat across the Iberian Peninsula, withering under the advance of French troops.

"At this rate we'll be in Cordova itself within a fortnight," the Duke of Nevers, in charge of French forces in the west, said.

All this is in accordance with the Duke of Lorraine's plans. Lorraine was named supreme commander of the French armed forces by parliament late last month. But off record, some are questioning his strategy.

"Lorraine put our best-trained units in the west, when he knows fully well the Prussians are much more dangerous," a high-ranking army officer said.

"Lorraine's strategy is to knock out the Cordovans quickly, then focus on the Prussians," an aide to the Duke of Nevers said. "It's a risky strategy, but wars are won by taking risks."

Lorraine remains confident in
continued on page A3

DARING NIGHTTIME ESCAPE FROM NOTRE DAME

Paris – Dr. Julien Saunière, a licensed member of the Guild of Physicians, escaped the custody of the Holy Inquisition yesterday. He had at least two accomplices.

Dr. Saunière was being held on charges of blasphemy, sedition and inciting heresy. He was no stranger to Church authorities prior to his arrest.

"Dr. Saunière exhibited a profound contempt for authority and the Church," High Inquisitor Gervase Moricant said.

According to Inquisitor Moricant, Saunière lied to Inquisition officials on numerous occasions and was involved in "heretical undertakings explicitly banned by the Church." He refused to comment further.

The escape took place early last night, when Dr. Saunière's accomplices freed him from his cell and spirited him away by automobile.

Dr. Saunière was abetted by a fellow member of the Physician's Guild, Genevieve Tournon, also on the run from the Inquisition.

Inquisition officials did not release the identity of Dr. Saunière's second accomplice, saying only that the "individual in question is in custody and won't be causing any more trouble."

Inquisitor Moricant was personally injured by Dr. S... in his escape but insists ... no personal animosit... the doctor.

"Christ bids us to ... who have wronged ... pray for Dr. Sauni...

As to what ... a man of lear... from the C... Moricant said ...

"It's sad ... gence and ...

Latest Wartime Developments

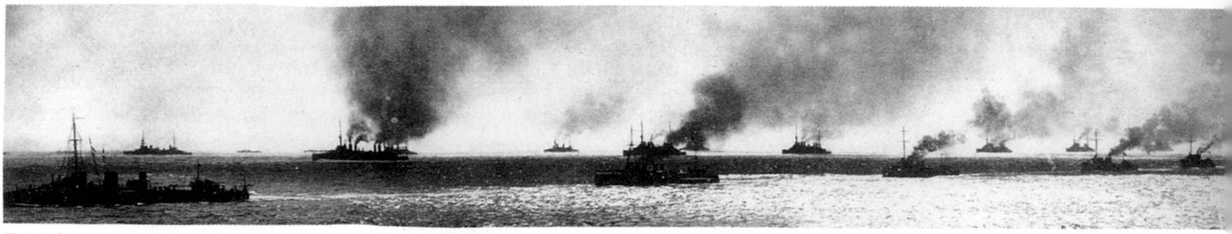

British troop transports set out across the English Channel for Le Havre yesterday to support France against Prussian invaders.

The war which began when the Duke of Lorraine was forced to invade Cordova has quickly escalated into a pan-European conflict. On one side are the Axis powers of France and her supporters. They struggle against the Allied aggressors of the German empires and the Mohammedan regimes of Europe.

The Axis Powers

Greater France

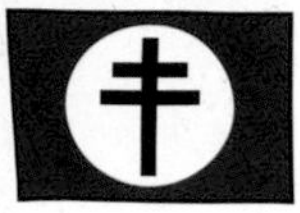

France is at the center of the ever-expanding war. She is determined to defend herself against German aggression and drive Islam from Europe. The Duke of Lorraine changed the French flag from the "tricolor" to the Cross of Lorraine after seizing power from the Bourbon king Louis XXII.

United Kingdom

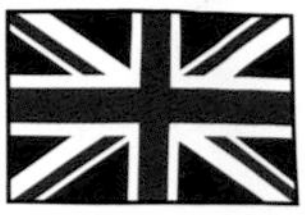

British Prime Minister Winston Churchill and the Duke of Lorraine devised private treaties prior to the outbreak of hostilities, including a mutual defense pact and a plan to divide conquered lands in the event of war. Although France's strongest ally, Britain's colonial ambitions might prove dangerous in the long term.

Russia

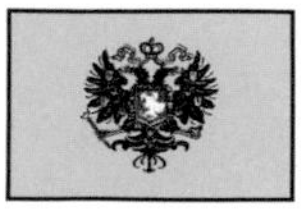

Russia joined the Axis when the Holy Roman Empire declared war on France, provoking its Serb subjects to open rebellion. Russia has long-standing cultural ties with Serbian minorities oppressed by Habsburg autocracy.

The Allies

The Prussian Empire

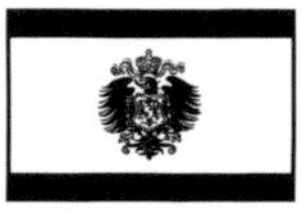

Crown Prince Wilhelm III declared war on France following the aftermath of the Marquis of Aragon's assassination. Prussia's army is considered the most advanced and highly motivated in the world. Their objective is to seize Paris as quickly as possible.

The Holy Roman Empire

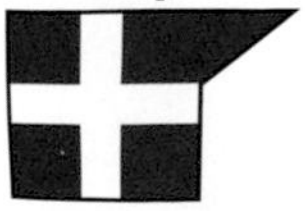

The Habsburg dynasty has ruled the Austrian empire for over eight hundred years. Although they vie for legitimacy as the rightful heirs of Charlemagne, the Austrians and Prussians made secret pledges of mutual assistance before the outbreak of war. Austria-Hungary is plagued by chronic internal unrest among its diverse subjects.

The Emirate of Cordova

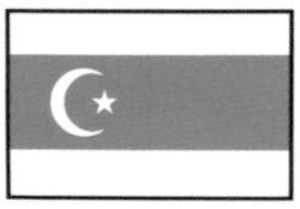

The old Arab proverb "an enemy of an enemy is a friend" applies to the alliance among the German and Islamic powers. The Iberian Muslims have so far proved even weaker than anticipated by French military planners.

The Ottoman Empire

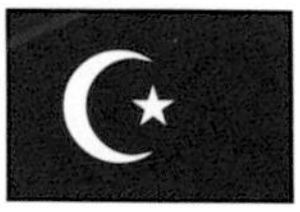

Rivalry with Russia and ties to Prussia make it likely the Turks will declare war on the Axis in the coming days. Already their fleets are poised outside Russian ports.

⚜

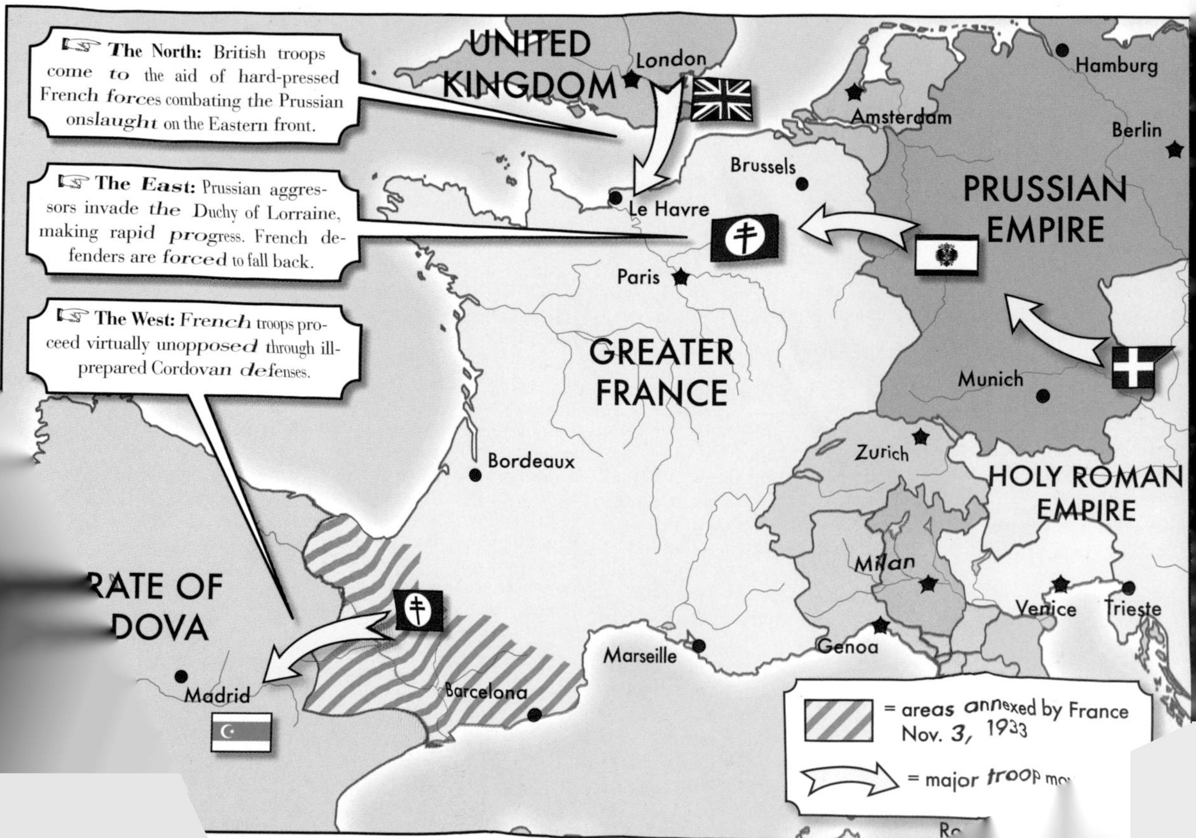
The North: British troops come to the aid of hard-pressed French forces combating the Prussian onslaught on the Eastern front.
The East: Prussian aggressors invade the Duchy of Lorraine, making rapid progress. French defenders are forced to fall back.
The West: French troops proceed virtually unopposed through ill-prepared Cordovan defenses.
UNITED KINGDOM
London
Hamburg
Amsterdam
Berlin
Brussels
Le Havre
PRUSSIAN EMPIRE
Paris
GREATER FRANCE
Munich
Bordeaux
Zurich
HOLY ROMAN EMPIRE
RATE OF
DOVA
Milan
Venice
Trieste
Marseille
Genoa
Madrid
Barcelona
= areas annexed by France Nov. 3, 1933
= major troop mo

CHAPTER FOUR
ET IN ARCADIA EGO

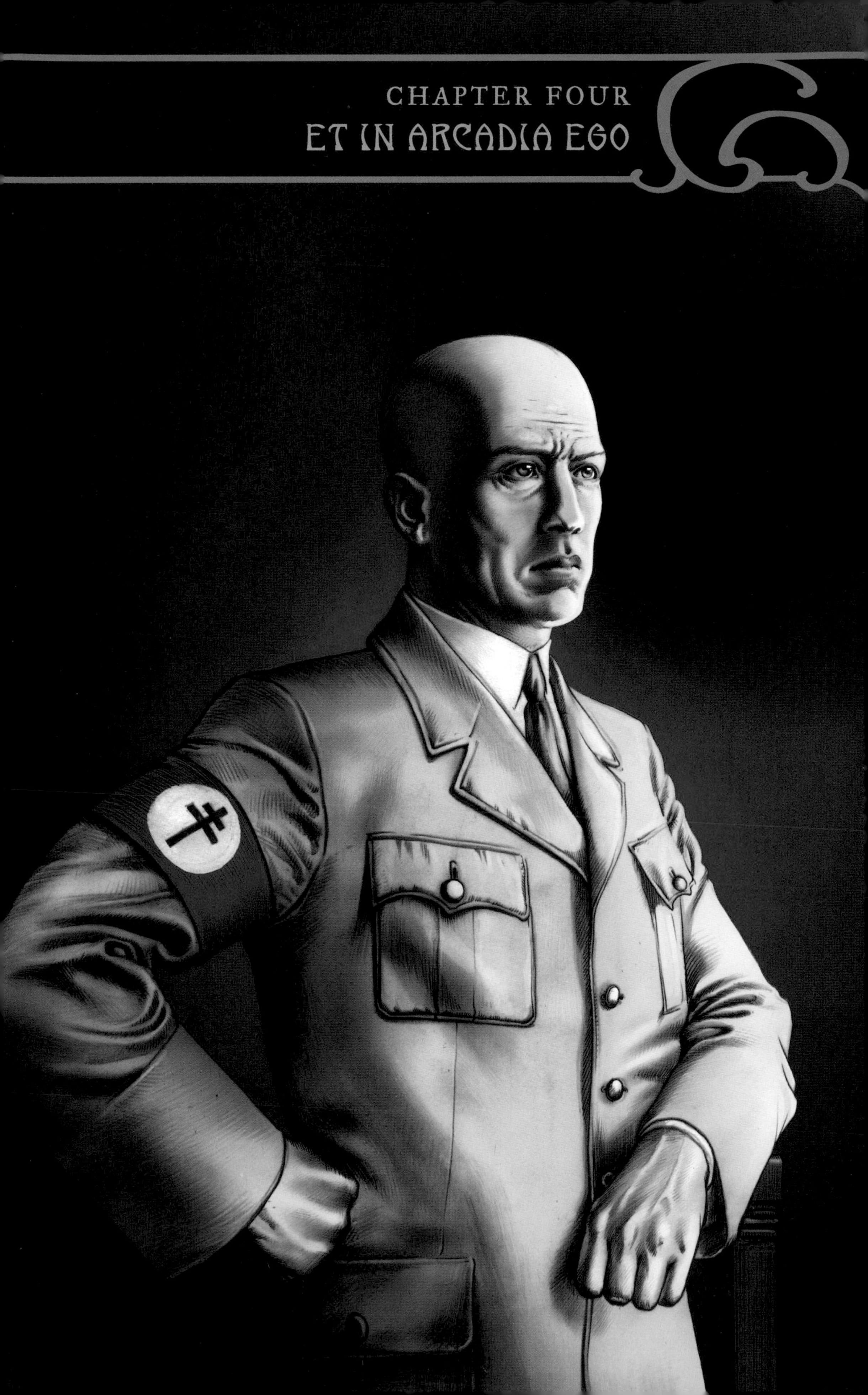

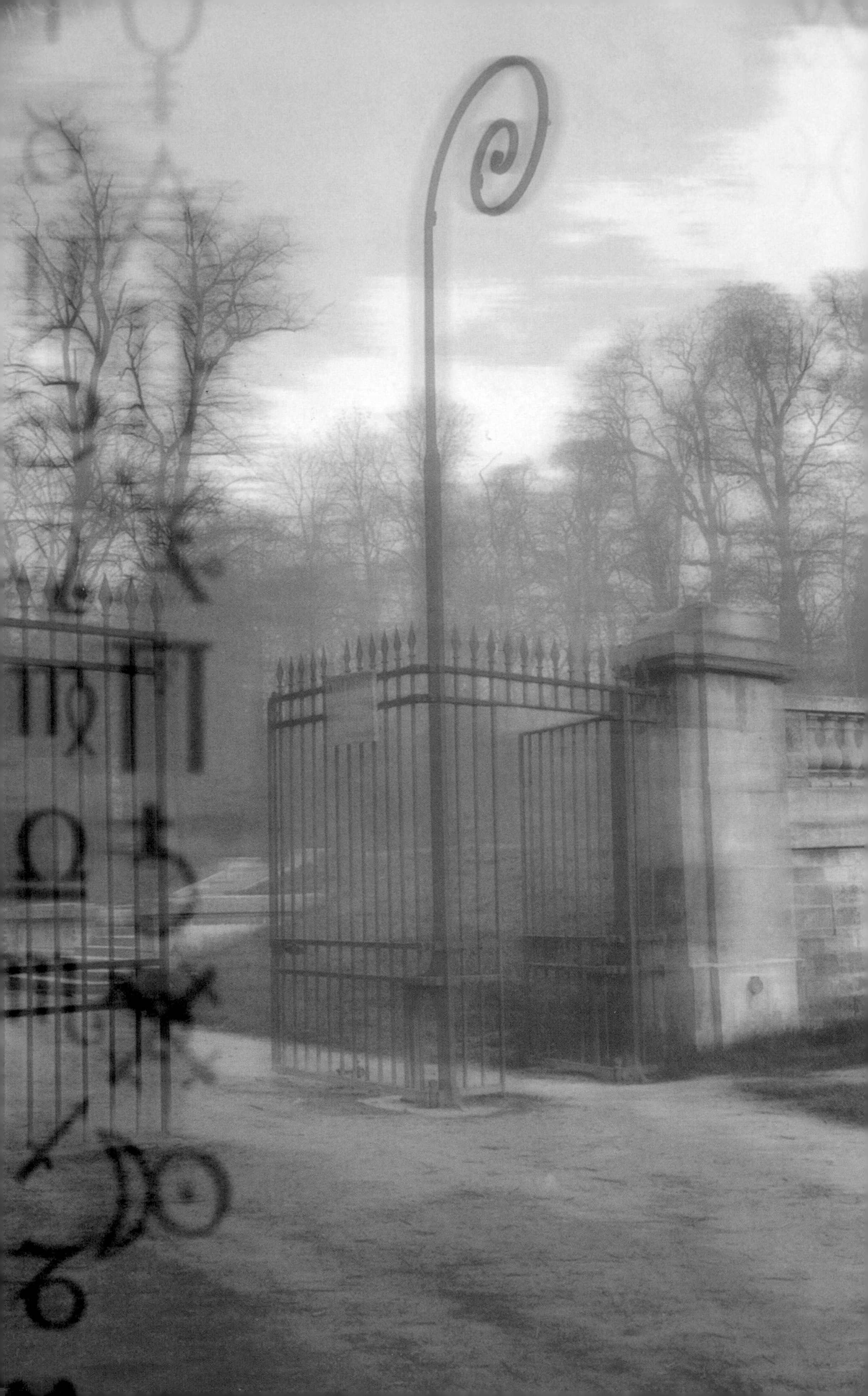

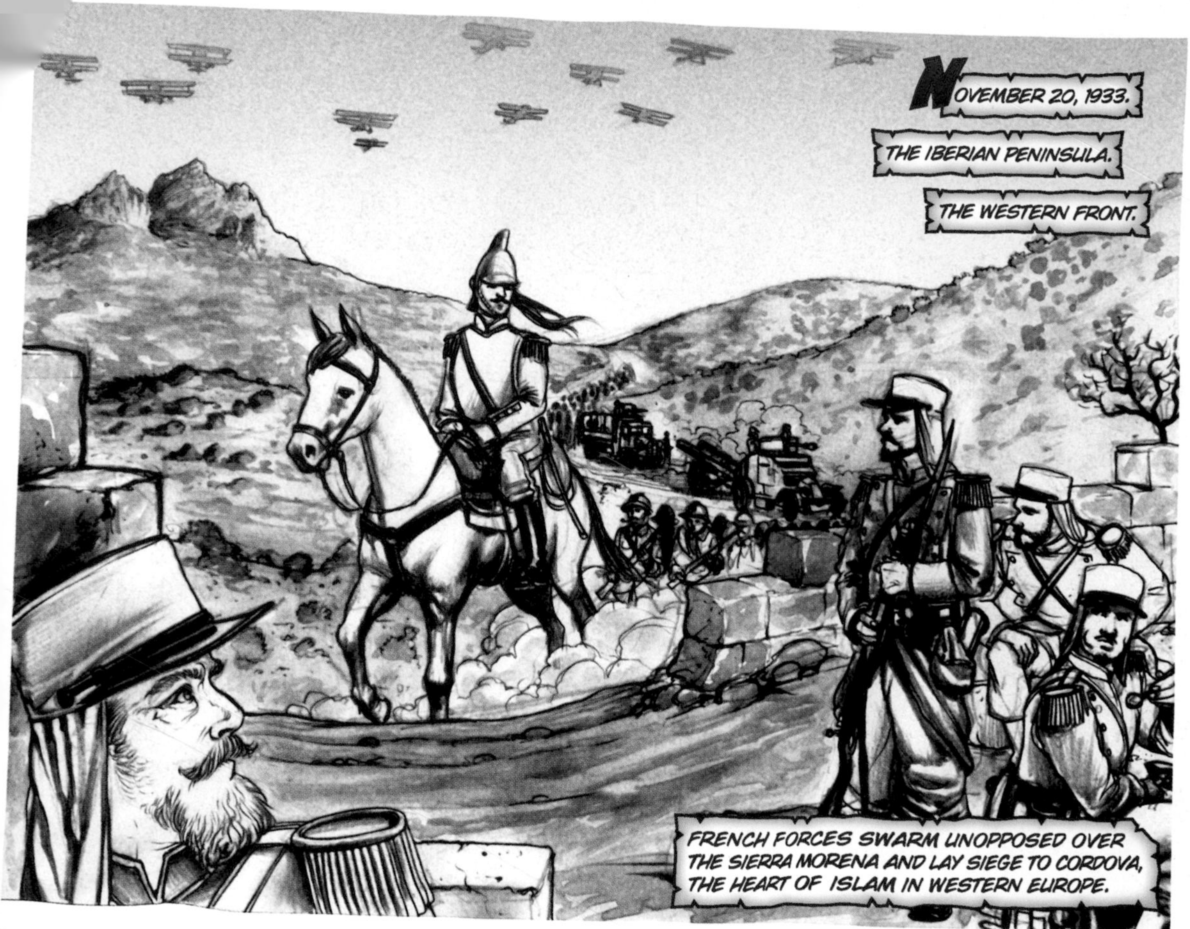
NOVEMBER 20, 1933.
THE IBERIAN PENINSULA.
THE WESTERN FRONT.
FRENCH FORCES SWARM UNOPPOSED OVER THE SIERRA MORENA AND LAY SIEGE TO CORDOVA, THE HEART OF ISLAM IN WESTERN EUROPE.

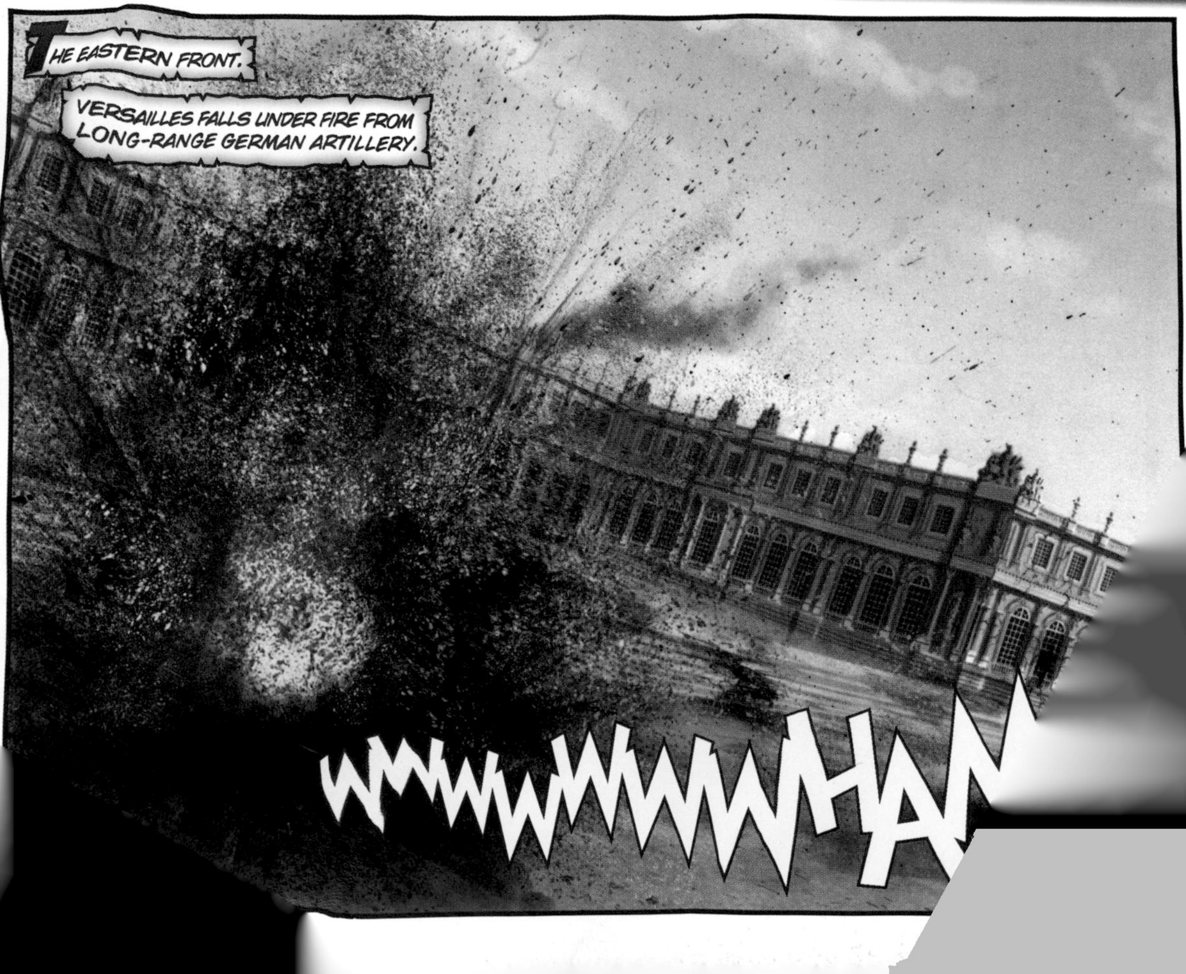
THE EASTERN FRONT.
VERSAILLES FALLS UNDER FIRE FROM LONG-RANGE GERMAN ARTILLERY.
WHWHWHWHWHAM

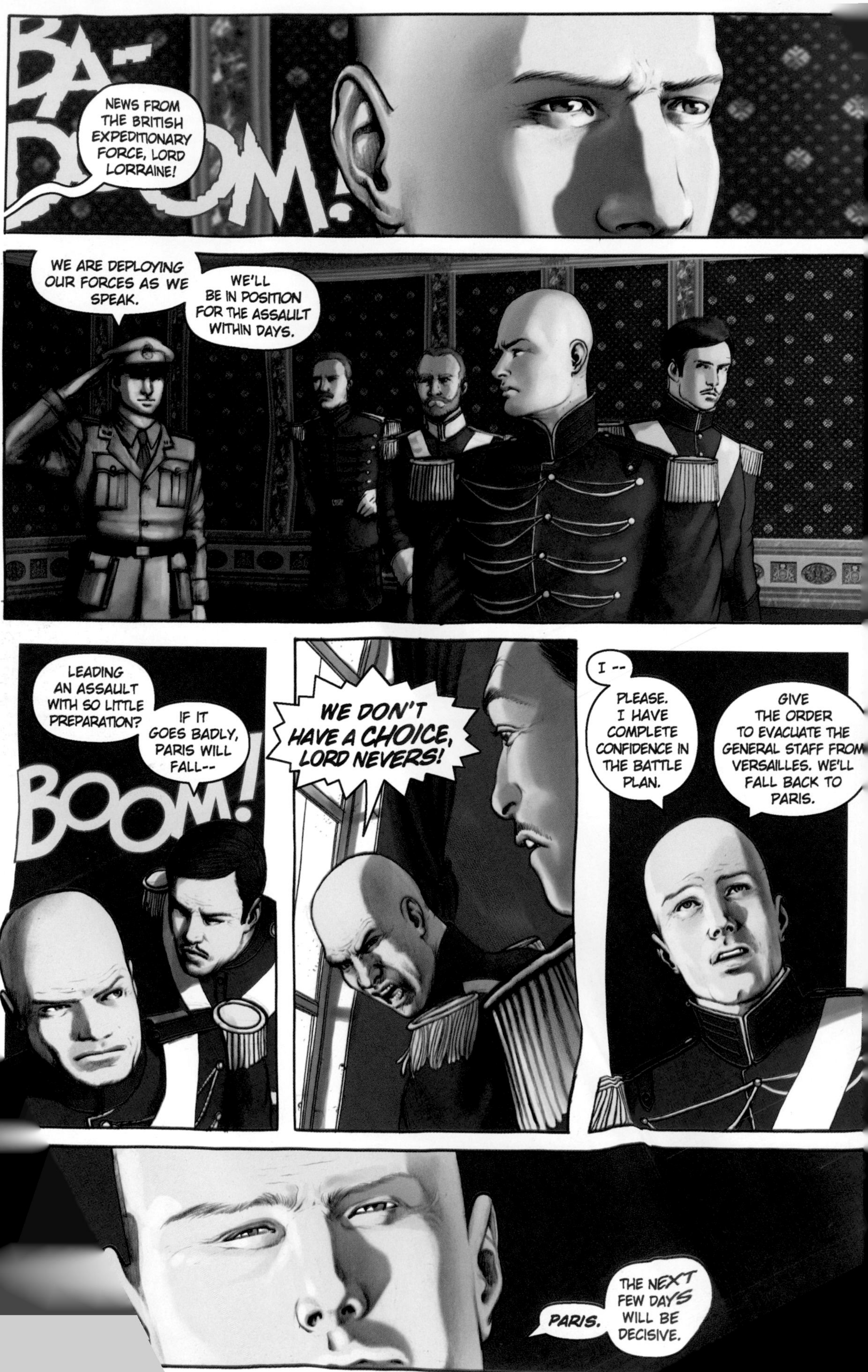
BA-DOOM!
NEWS FROM THE BRITISH EXPEDITIONARY FORCE, LORD LORRAINE!
WE ARE DEPLOYING OUR FORCES AS WE SPEAK.
WE'LL BE IN POSITION FOR THE ASSAULT WITHIN DAYS.
LEADING AN ASSAULT WITH SO LITTLE PREPARATION?
IF IT GOES BADLY, PARIS WILL FALL--
BOOM!
WE DON'T HAVE A CHOICE, LORD NEVERS!
I --
PLEASE. I HAVE COMPLETE CONFIDENCE IN THE BATTLE PLAN.
GIVE THE ORDER TO EVACUATE THE GENERAL STAFF FROM VERSAILLES. WE'LL FALL BACK TO PARIS.
PARIS.
THE NEXT FEW DAYS WILL BE DECISIVE.

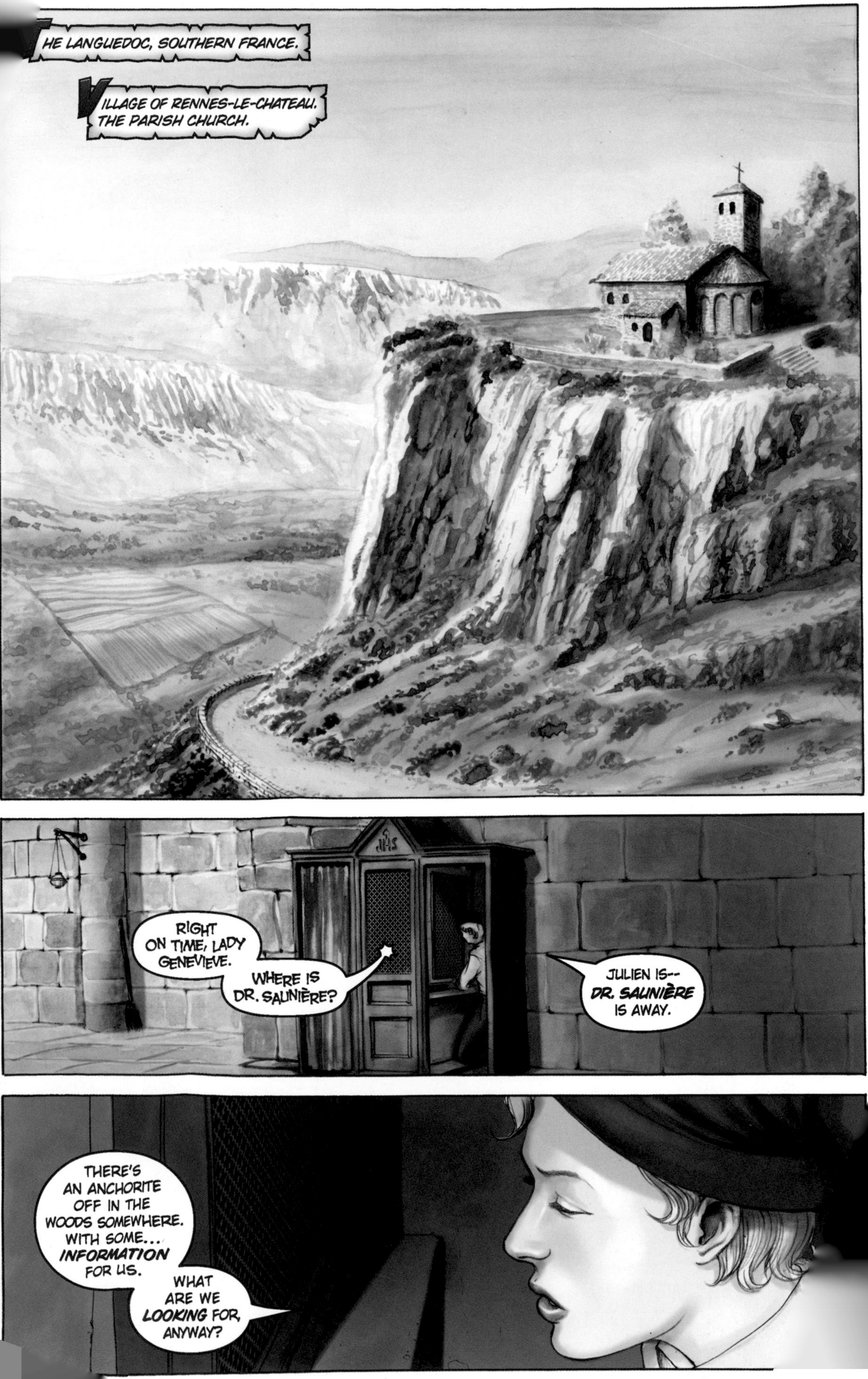
THE LANGUEDOC, SOUTHERN FRANCE.
VILLAGE OF RENNES-LE-CHATEAU. THE PARISH CHURCH.
RIGHT ON TIME, LADY GENEVIEVE.
WHERE IS DR. SAUNIÈRE?
JULIEN IS-- DR. SAUNIÈRE IS AWAY.
THERE'S AN ANCHORITE OFF IN THE WOODS SOMEWHERE. WITH SOME... INFORMATION FOR US.
WHAT ARE WE LOOKING FOR, ANYWAY?

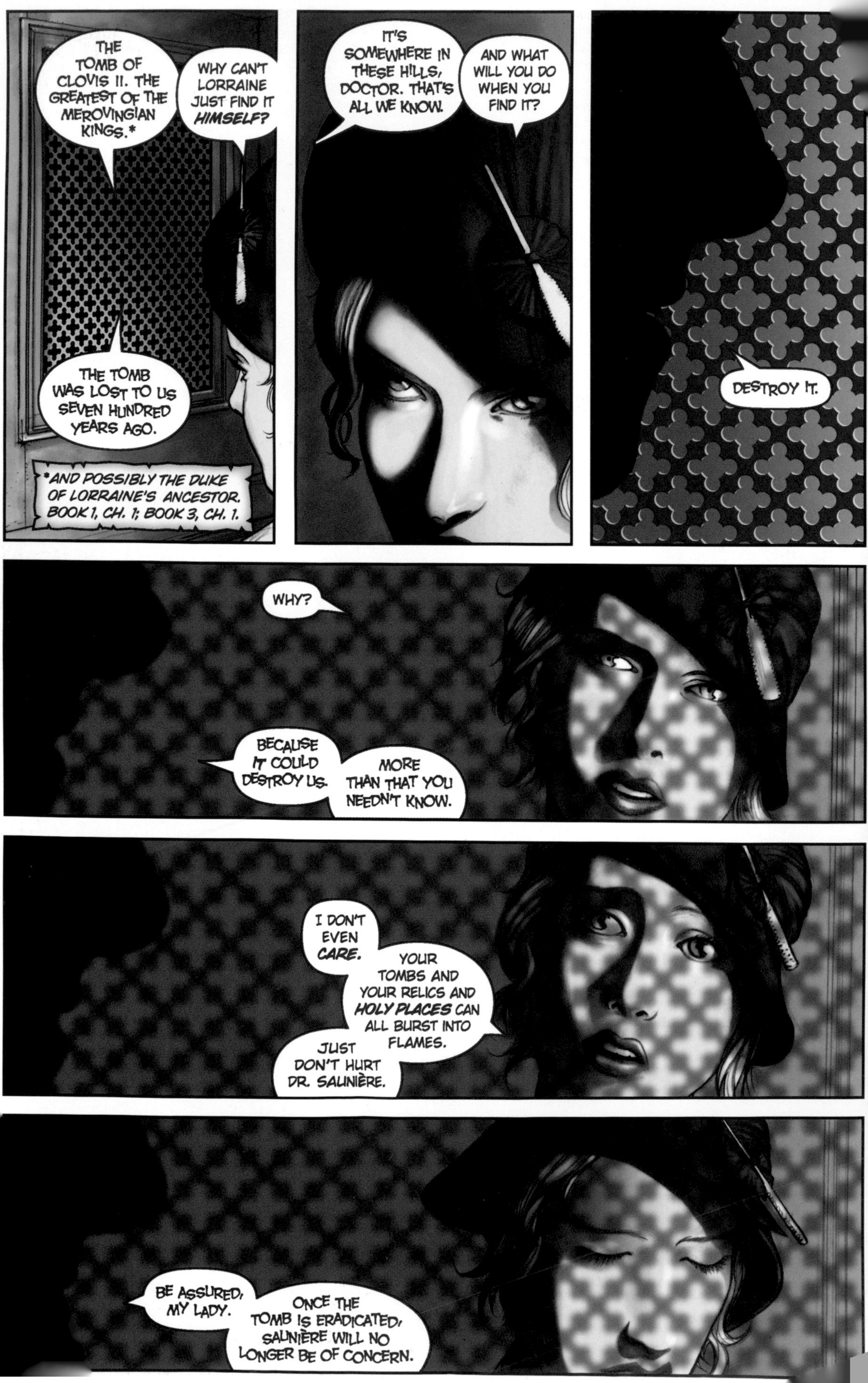
THE TOMB OF CLOVIS II. THE GREATEST OF THE MEROVINGIAN KINGS.*
WHY CAN'T LORRAINE JUST FIND IT HIMSELF?
THE TOMB WAS LOST TO US SEVEN HUNDRED YEARS AGO.
*AND POSSIBLY THE DUKE OF LORRAINE'S ANCESTOR. BOOK 1, CH. 1; BOOK 3, CH. 1.
IT'S SOMEWHERE IN THESE HILLS, DOCTOR. THAT'S ALL WE KNOW.
AND WHAT WILL YOU DO WHEN YOU FIND IT?
DESTROY IT.
WHY?
BECAUSE IT COULD DESTROY US.
MORE THAN THAT YOU NEEDN'T KNOW.
I DON'T EVEN CARE.
YOUR TOMBS AND YOUR RELICS AND HOLY PLACES CAN ALL BURST INTO FLAMES.
JUST DON'T HURT DR. SAUNIÈRE.
BE ASSURED, MY LADY.
ONCE THE TOMB IS ERADICATED, SAUNIÈRE WILL NO LONGER BE OF CONCERN.

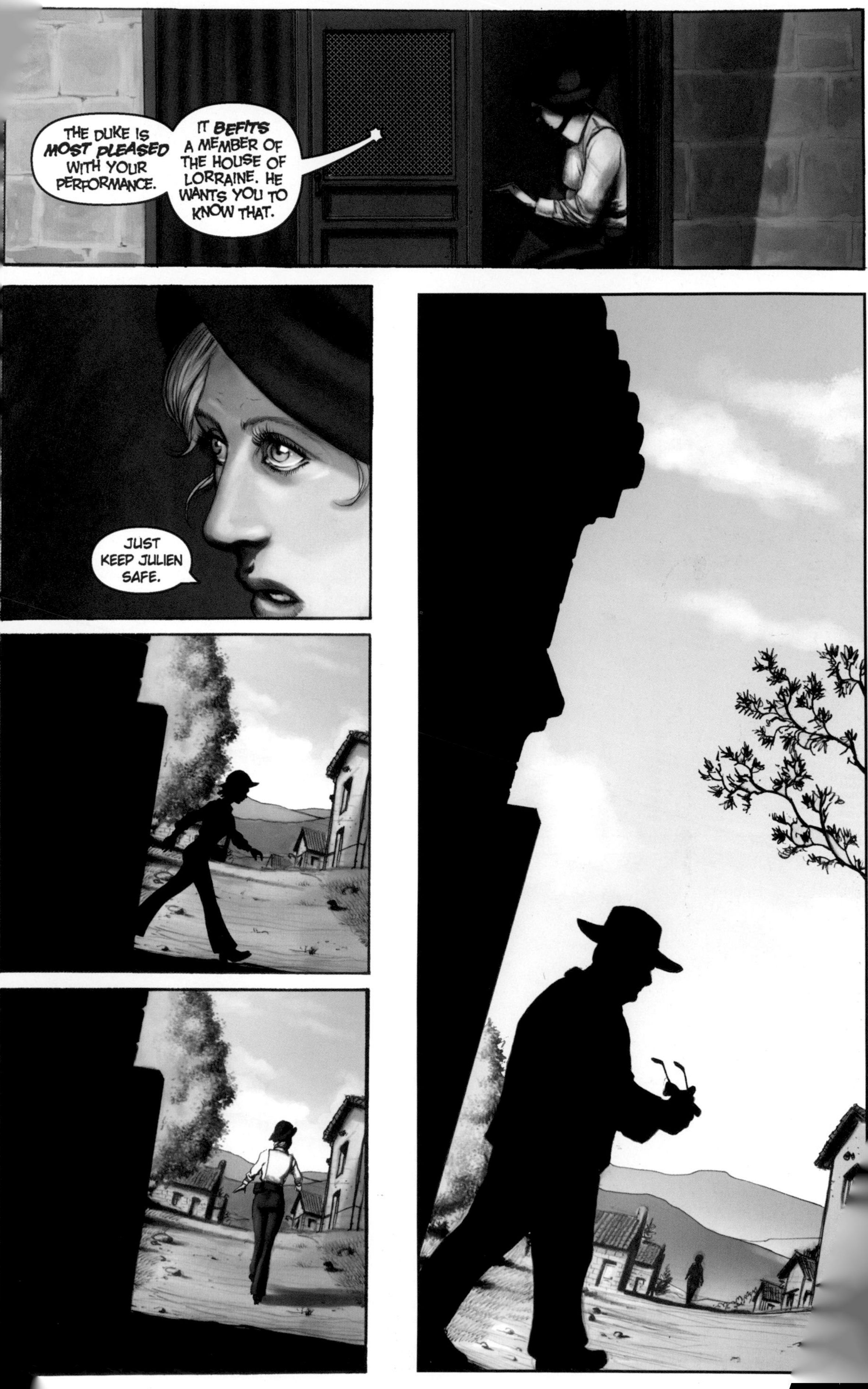
THE DUKE IS MOST PLEASED WITH YOUR PERFORMANCE.
IT BEFITS A MEMBER OF THE HOUSE OF LORRAINE. HE WANTS YOU TO KNOW THAT.
JUST KEEP JULIEN SAFE.

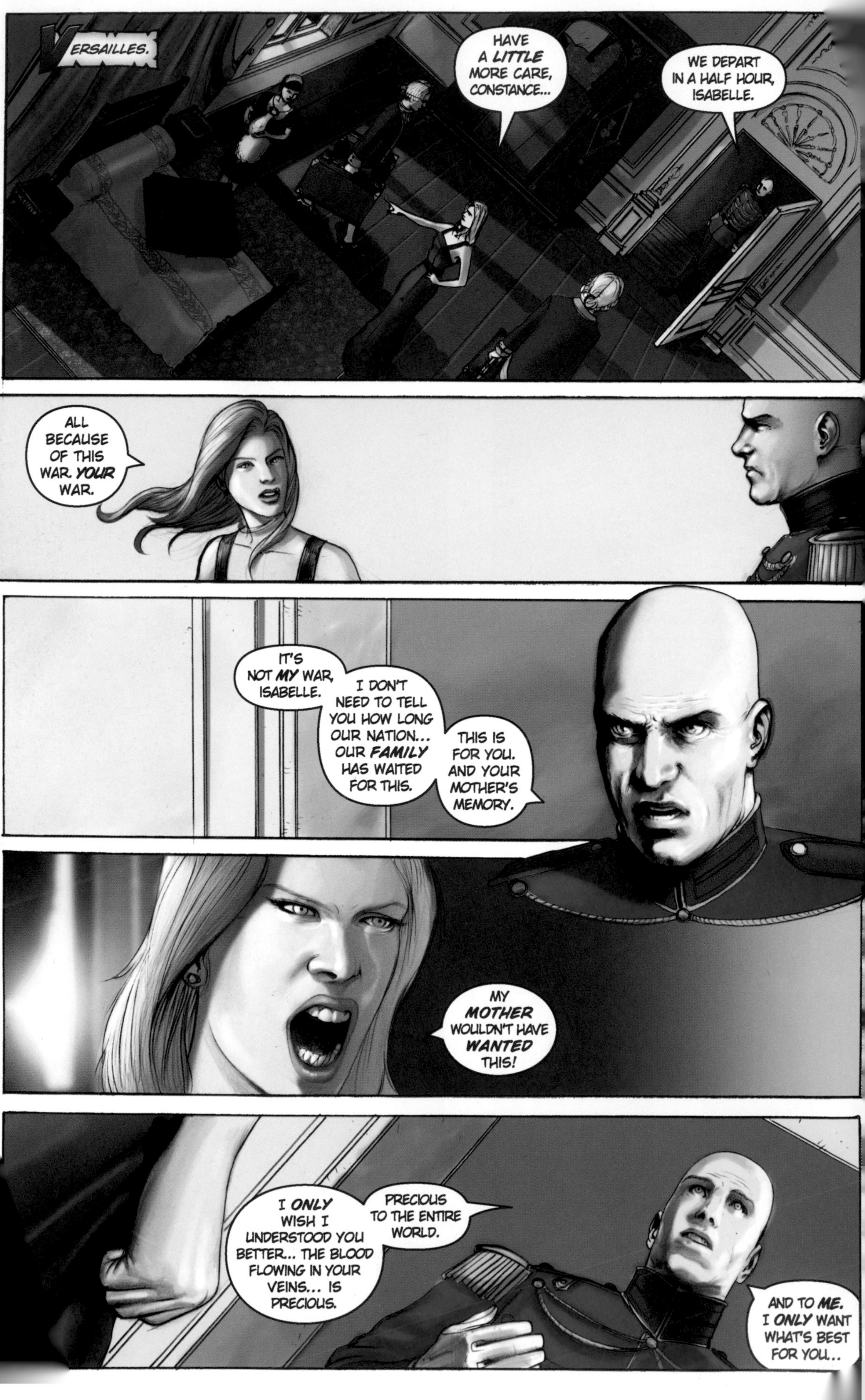
VERSAILLES.
HAVE A LITTLE MORE CARE, CONSTANCE...
WE DEPART IN A HALF HOUR, ISABELLE.
ALL BECAUSE OF THIS WAR. YOUR WAR.
IT'S NOT MY WAR, ISABELLE.
I DON'T NEED TO TELL YOU HOW LONG OUR NATION... OUR FAMILY HAS WAITED FOR THIS.
THIS IS FOR YOU. AND YOUR MOTHER'S MEMORY.
MY MOTHER WOULDN'T HAVE WANTED THIS!
I ONLY WISH I UNDERSTOOD YOU BETTER... THE BLOOD FLOWING IN YOUR VEINS... IS PRECIOUS.
PRECIOUS TO THE ENTIRE WORLD.
AND TO ME. I ONLY WANT WHAT'S BEST FOR YOU...

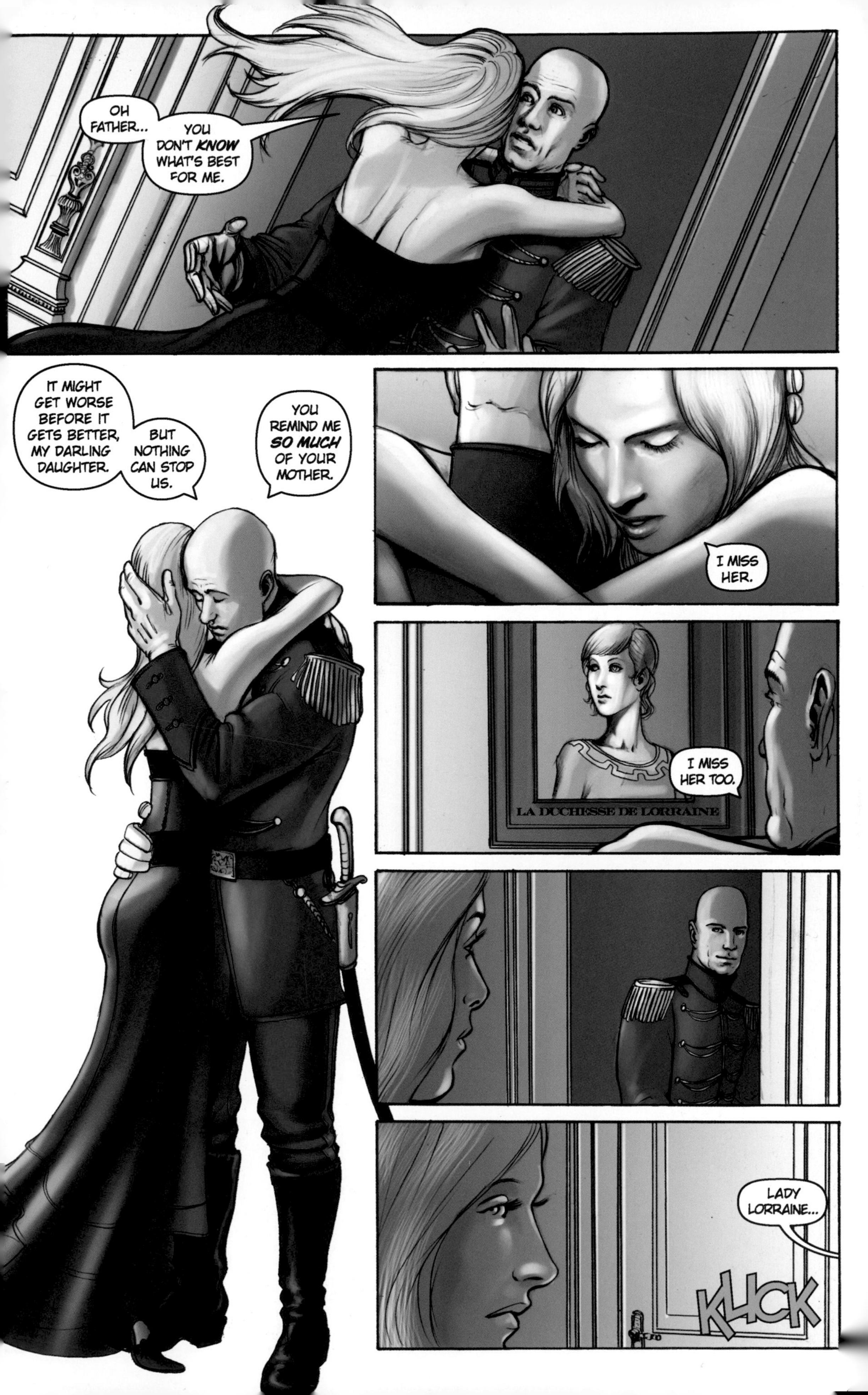
OH FATHER...
YOU DON'T KNOW WHAT'S BEST FOR ME.
IT MIGHT GET WORSE BEFORE IT GETS BETTER, MY DARLING DAUGHTER.
BUT NOTHING CAN STOP US.
YOU REMIND ME SO MUCH OF YOUR MOTHER.
I MISS HER.
LA DUCHESSE DE LORRAINE
I MISS HER TOO.
LADY LORRAINE...
KLICK

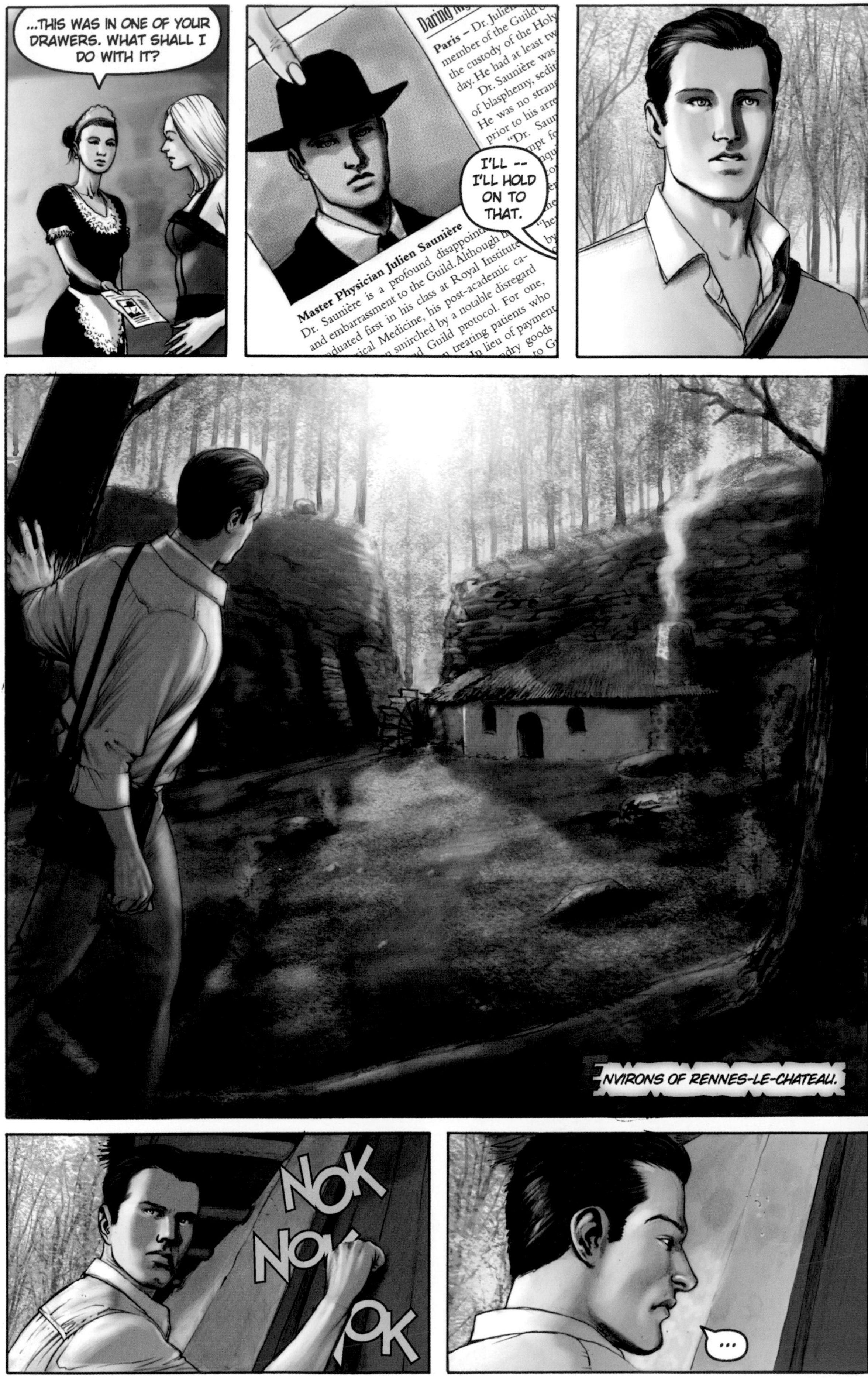
...THIS WAS IN ONE OF YOUR DRAWERS. WHAT SHALL I DO WITH IT?
Master Physician Julien Saunière
I'LL -- I'LL HOLD ON TO THAT.
NVIRONS OF RENNES-LE-CHATEAU.
NOK
NO
OK
...

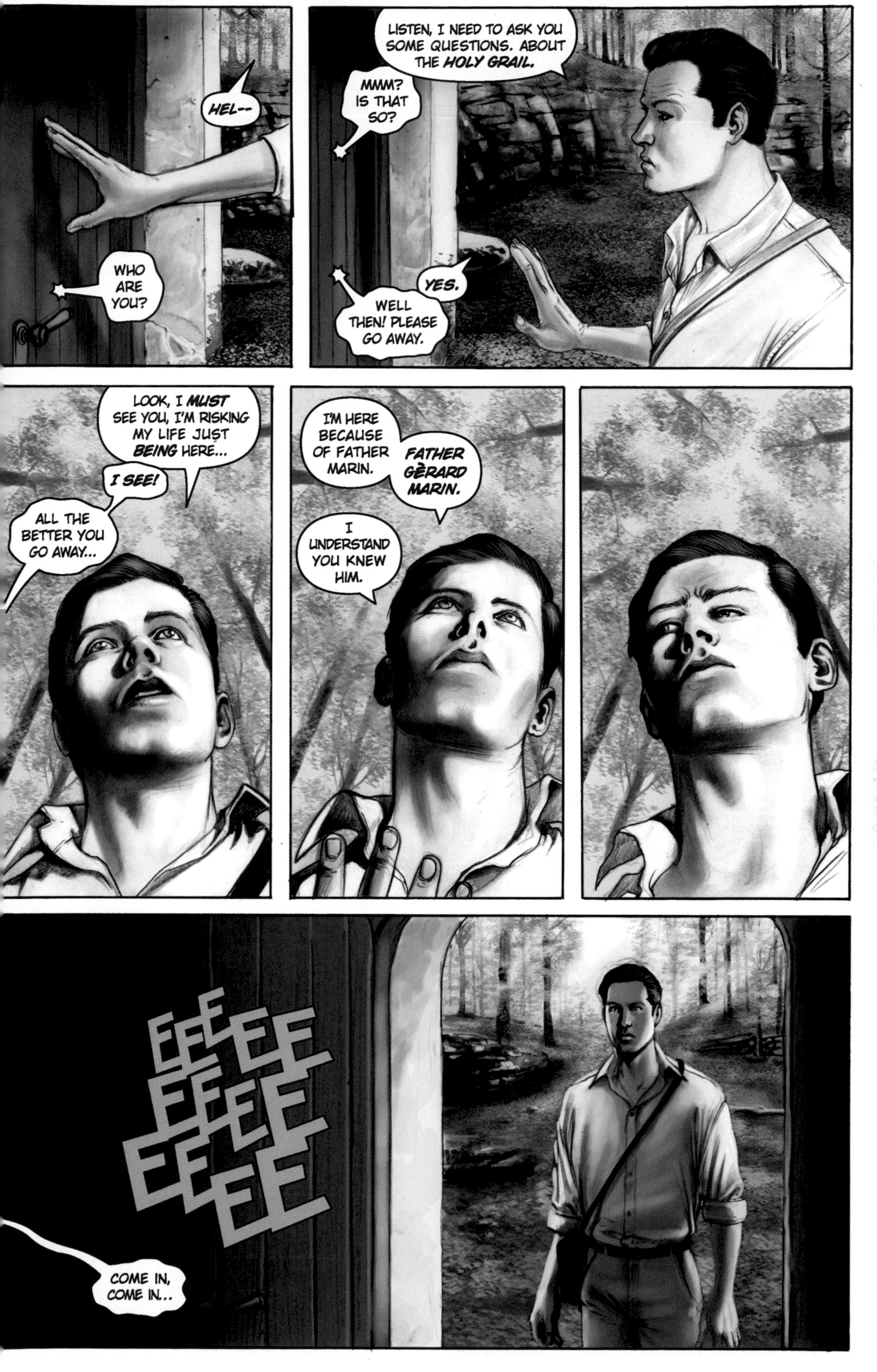
HEL--
WHO ARE YOU?
LISTEN, I NEED TO ASK YOU SOME QUESTIONS. ABOUT THE HOLY GRAIL.
MMM? IS THAT SO?
YES.
WELL THEN! PLEASE GO AWAY.
LOOK, I MUST SEE YOU, I'M RISKING MY LIFE JUST BEING HERE...
I SEE!
ALL THE BETTER YOU GO AWAY...
I'M HERE BECAUSE OF FATHER MARIN.
FATHER GÈRARD MARIN.
I UNDERSTAND YOU KNEW HIM.
EEEEEEEEEEEEE
COME IN, COME IN...

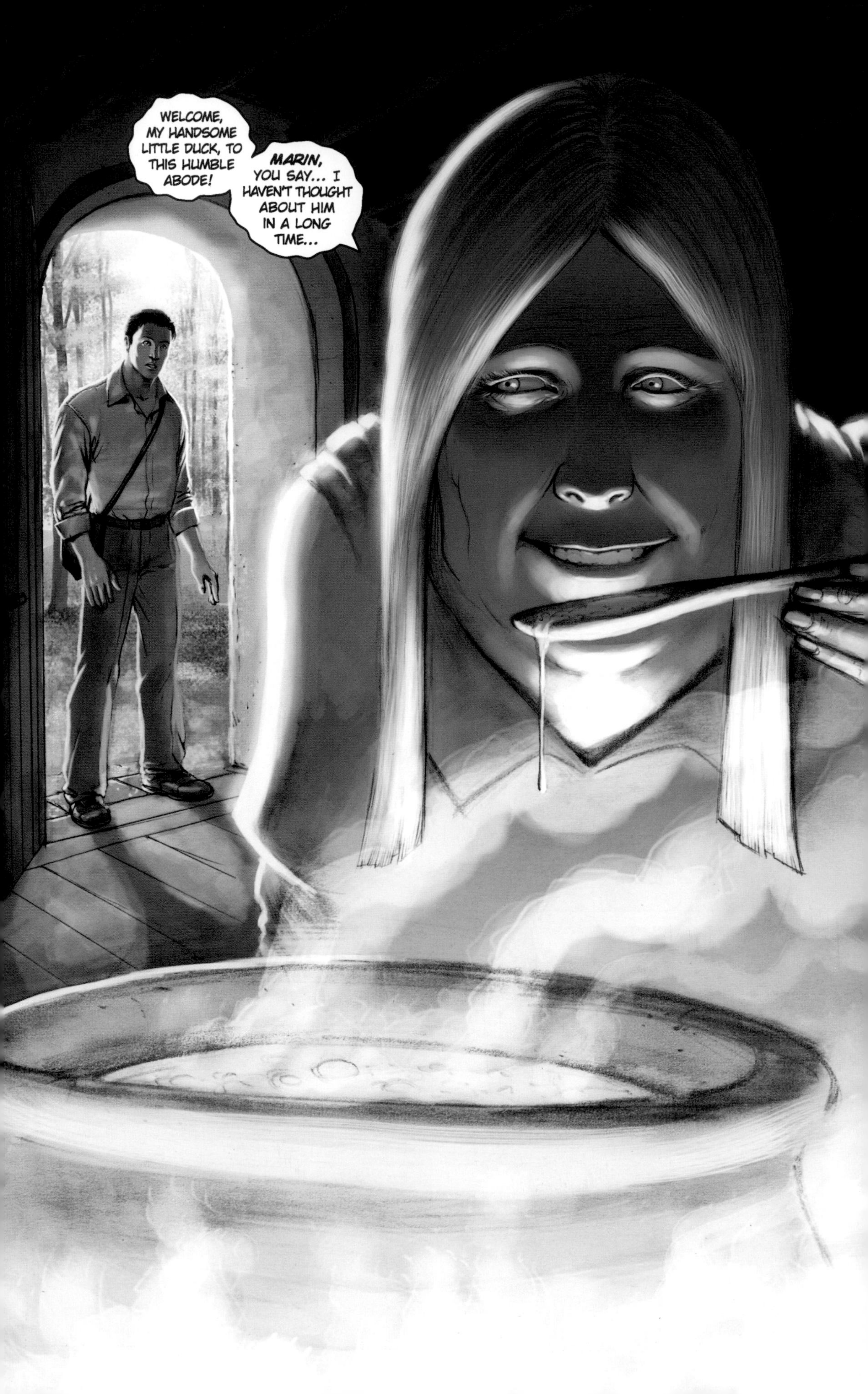
WELCOME, MY HANDSOME LITTLE DUCK, TO THIS HUMBLE ABODE!
MARIN, YOU SAY... I HAVEN'T THOUGHT ABOUT HIM IN A LONG TIME...

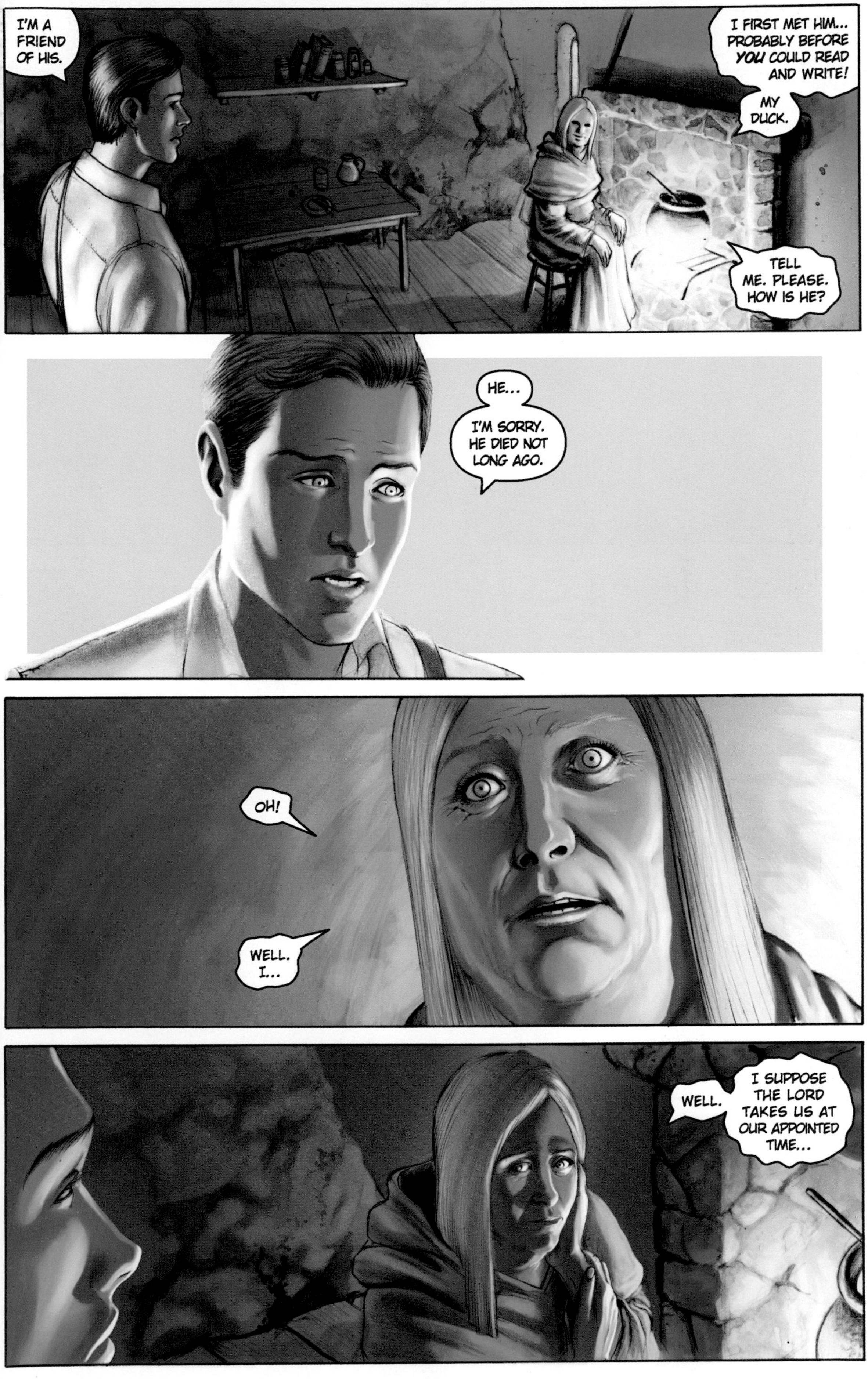
I'M A FRIEND OF HIS.
I FIRST MET HIM... PROBABLY BEFORE YOU COULD READ AND WRITE!
MY DUCK.
TELL ME. PLEASE. HOW IS HE?
HE...
I'M SORRY. HE DIED NOT LONG AGO.
OH!
WELL. I...
WELL.
I SUPPOSE THE LORD TAKES US AT OUR APPOINTED TIME...

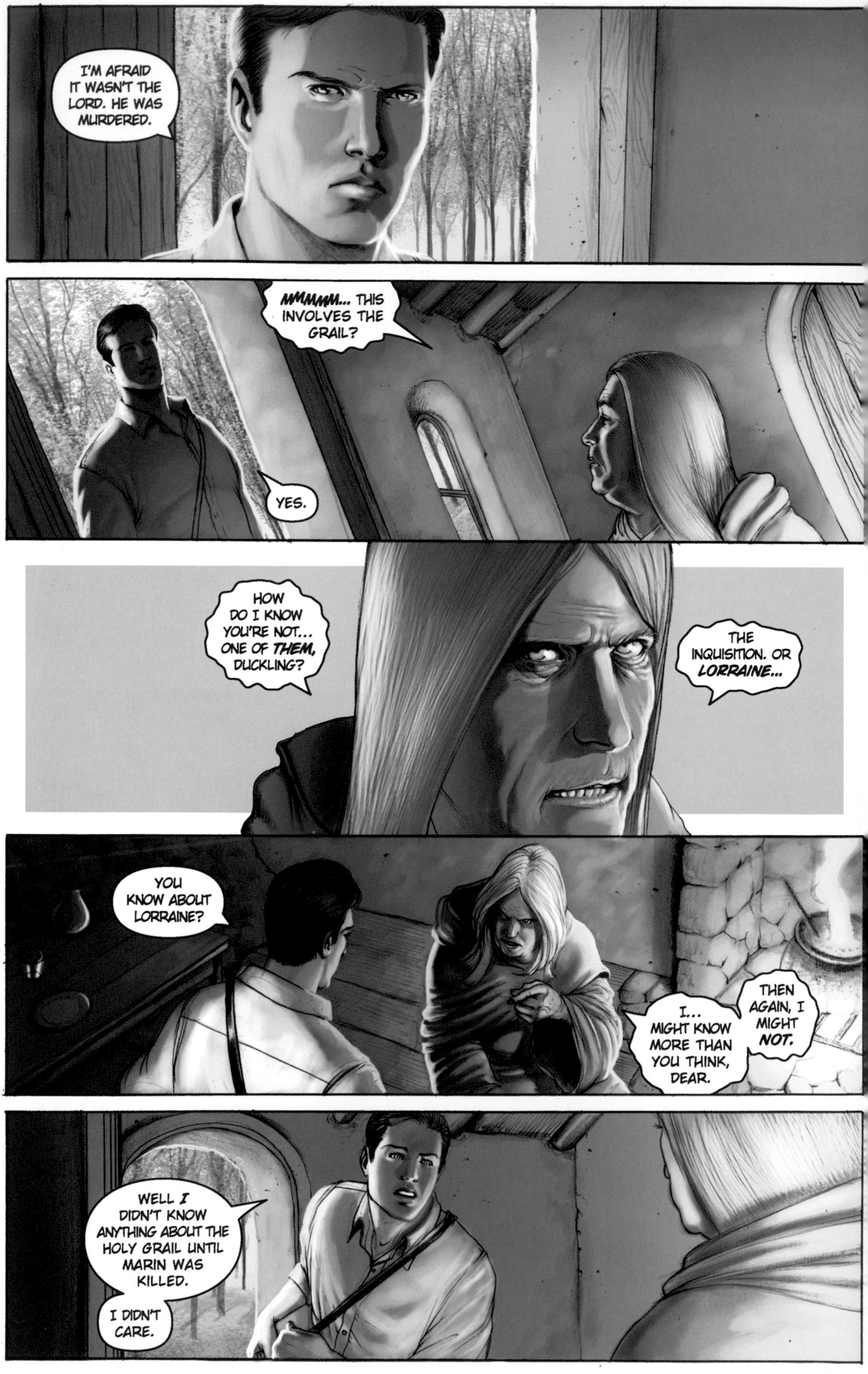
I'M AFRAID IT WASN'T THE LORD. HE WAS MURDERED.
MMMMM... THIS INVOLVES THE GRAIL?
YES.
HOW DO I KNOW YOU'RE NOT... ONE OF THEM, DUCKLING?
THE INQUISITION. OR LORRAINE...
YOU KNOW ABOUT LORRAINE?
I... MIGHT KNOW MORE THAN YOU THINK, DEAR.
THEN AGAIN, I MIGHT NOT.
WELL I DIDN'T KNOW ANYTHING ABOUT THE HOLY GRAIL UNTIL MARIN WAS KILLED.
I DIDN'T CARE.

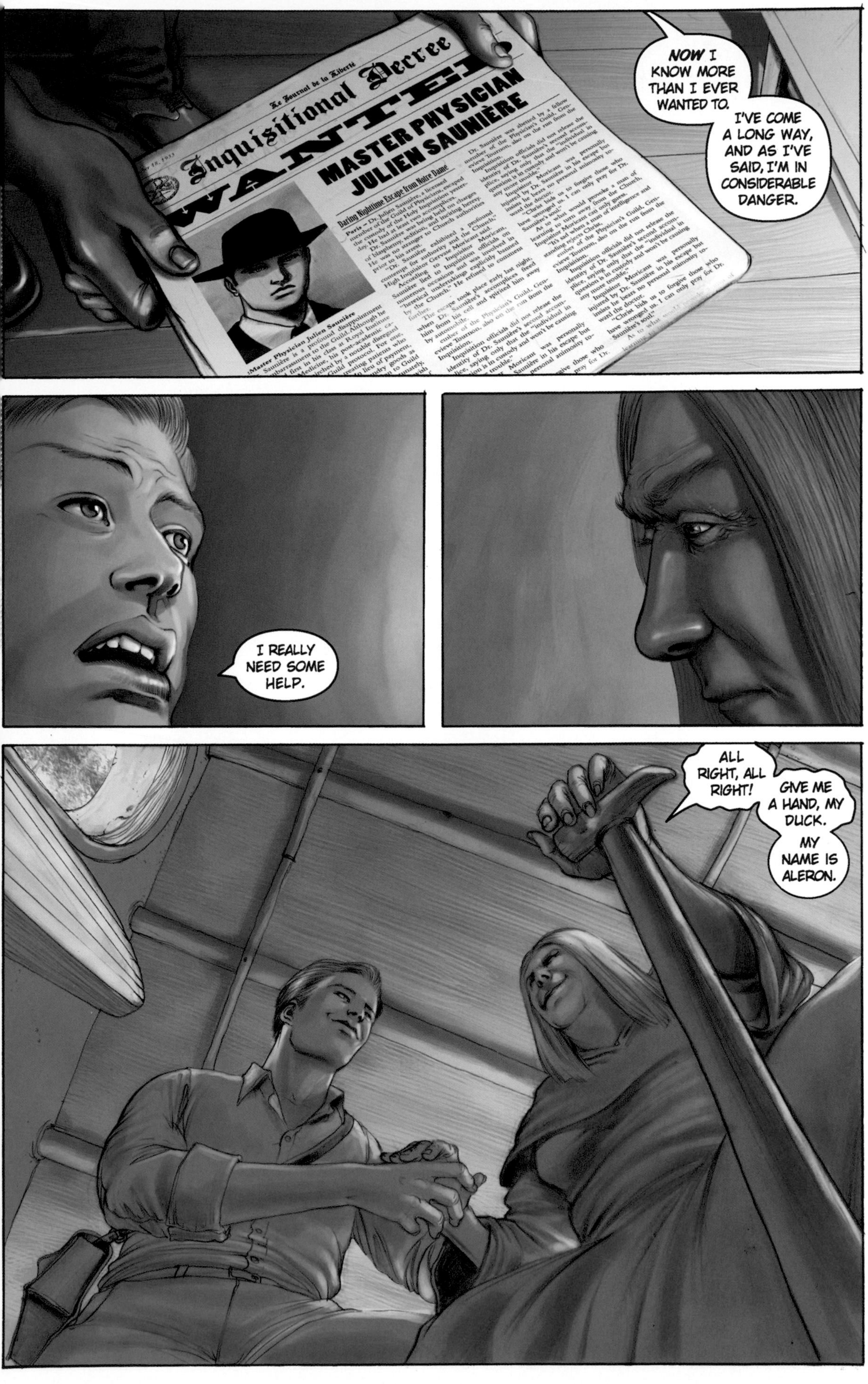
Le Journal de la Liberté
Inquisitional Decree
WANTED
MASTER PHYSICIAN JULIEN SAUNIÈRE
Daring Nighttime Escape from Notre Dame
NOW I KNOW MORE THAN I EVER WANTED TO.
I'VE COME A LONG WAY, AND AS I'VE SAID, I'M IN CONSIDERABLE DANGER.
I REALLY NEED SOME HELP.
ALL RIGHT, ALL RIGHT!
GIVE ME A HAND, MY DUCK.
MY NAME IS ALERON.

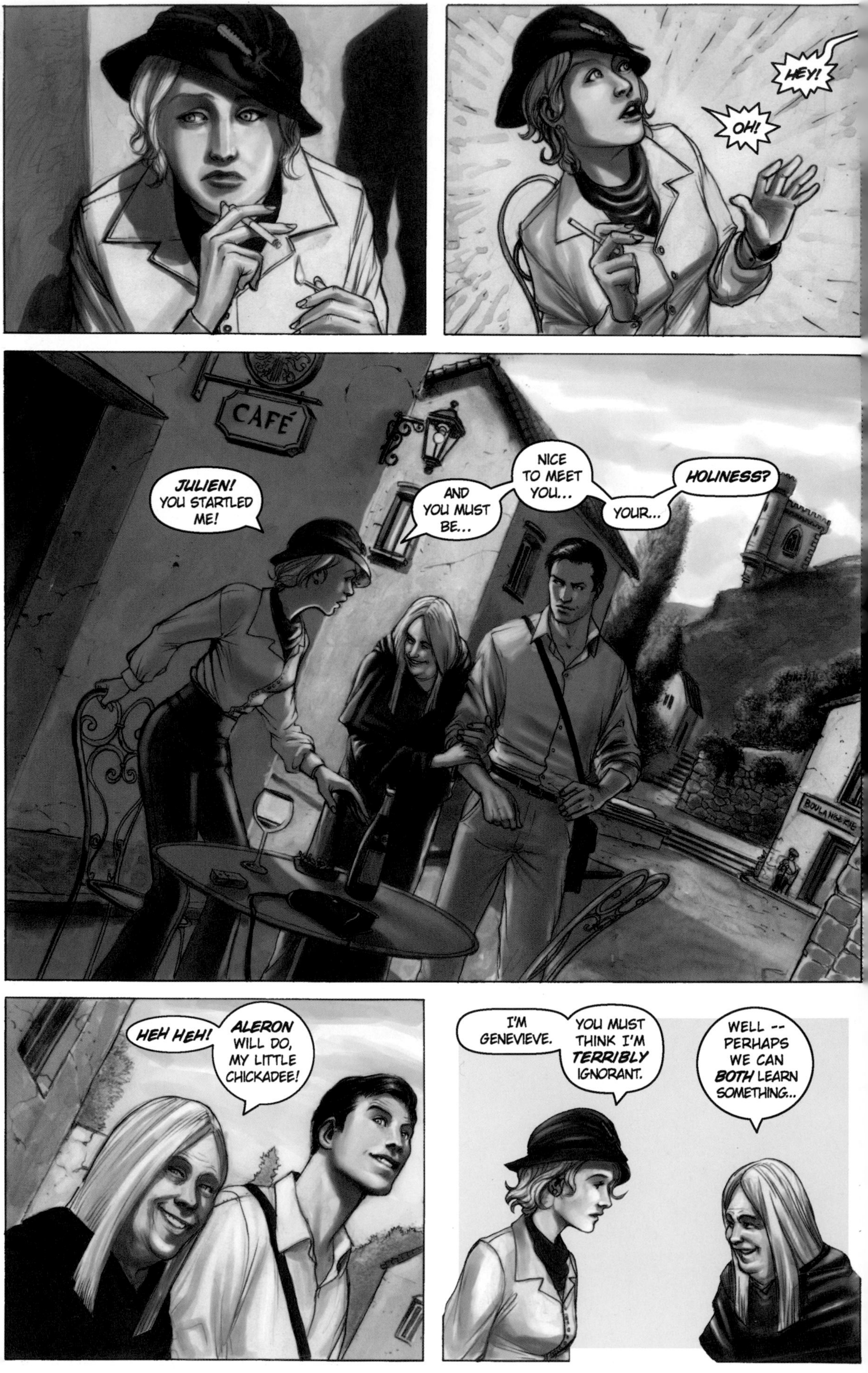
HEY!
OH!
CAFÉ
JULIEN! YOU STARTLED ME!
AND YOU MUST BE...
NICE TO MEET YOU...
YOUR...
HOLINESS?
BOULANGERIE
HEH HEH!
ALERON WILL DO, MY LITTLE CHICKADEE!
I'M GENEVIEVE.
YOU MUST THINK I'M TERRIBLY IGNORANT.
WELL -- PERHAPS WE CAN BOTH LEARN SOMETHING...

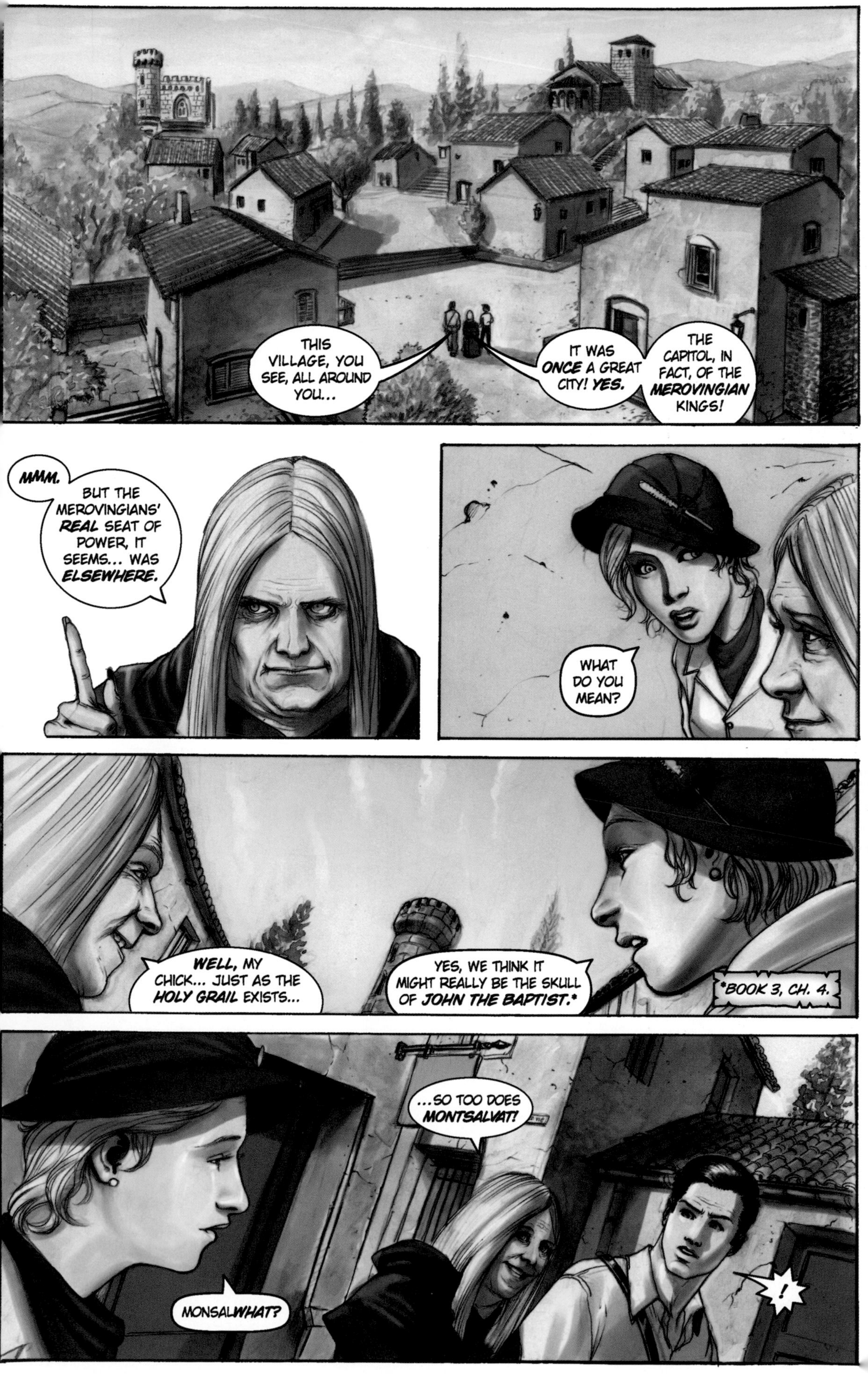
THIS VILLAGE, YOU SEE, ALL AROUND YOU...
IT WAS ONCE A GREAT CITY! YES.
THE CAPITOL, IN FACT, OF THE MEROVINGIAN KINGS!
MMM.
BUT THE MEROVINGIANS' REAL SEAT OF POWER, IT SEEMS... WAS ELSEWHERE.
WHAT DO YOU MEAN?
WELL, MY CHICK... JUST AS THE HOLY GRAIL EXISTS...
YES, WE THINK IT MIGHT REALLY BE THE SKULL OF JOHN THE BAPTIST.*
*BOOK 3, CH. 4.
...SO TOO DOES MONTSALVAT!
MONSALWHAT?
!

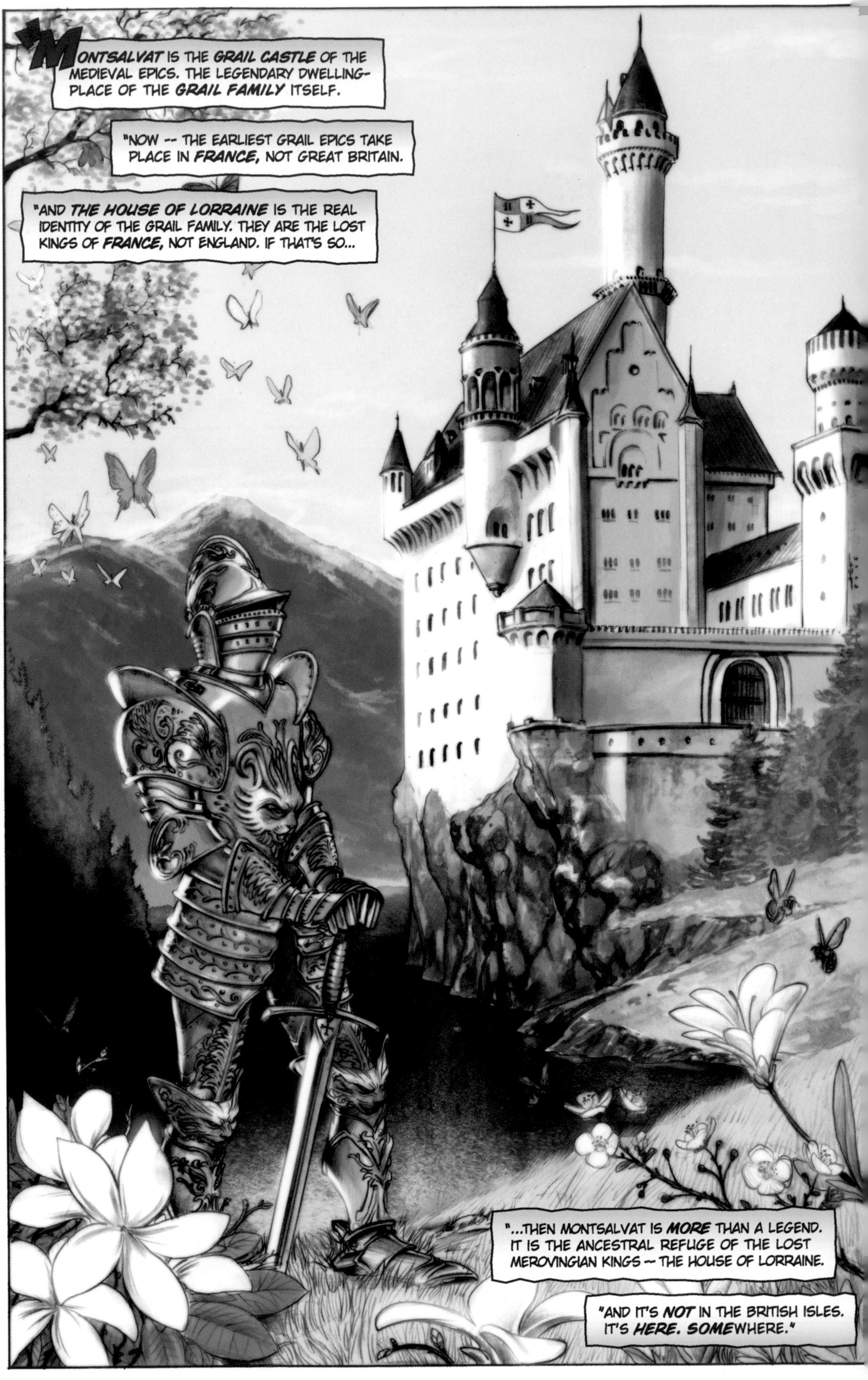
"MONTSALVAT IS THE GRAIL CASTLE OF THE MEDIEVAL EPICS. THE LEGENDARY DWELLING-PLACE OF THE GRAIL FAMILY ITSELF.
"NOW -- THE EARLIEST GRAIL EPICS TAKE PLACE IN FRANCE, NOT GREAT BRITAIN.
"AND THE HOUSE OF LORRAINE IS THE REAL IDENTITY OF THE GRAIL FAMILY. THEY ARE THE LOST KINGS OF FRANCE, NOT ENGLAND. IF THAT'S SO...
"...THEN MONTSALVAT IS MORE THAN A LEGEND. IT IS THE ANCESTRAL REFUGE OF THE LOST MEROVINGIAN KINGS -- THE HOUSE OF LORRAINE.
"AND IT'S NOT IN THE BRITISH ISLES. IT'S HERE. SOMEWHERE."

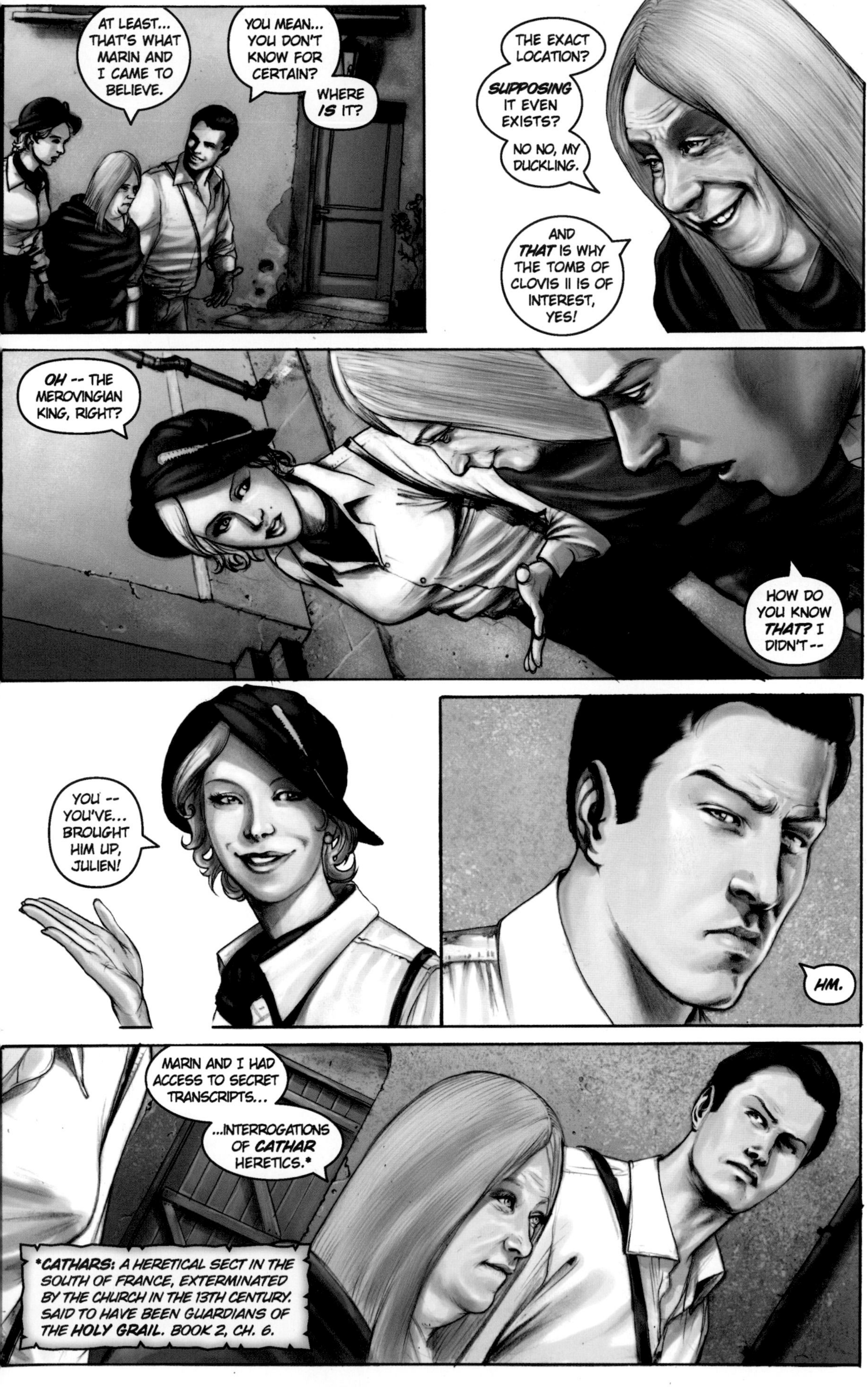
AT LEAST... THAT'S WHAT MARIN AND I CAME TO BELIEVE.
YOU MEAN... YOU DON'T KNOW FOR CERTAIN?
WHERE *IS* IT?
THE EXACT LOCATION?
SUPPOSING IT EVEN EXISTS?
NO NO, MY DUCKLING.
AND *THAT* IS WHY THE TOMB OF CLOVIS II IS OF INTEREST, YES!
OH -- THE MEROVINGIAN KING, RIGHT?
HOW DO YOU KNOW *THAT?* I DIDN'T --
YOU -- YOU'VE... BROUGHT HIM UP, JULIEN!
HM.
MARIN AND I HAD ACCESS TO SECRET TRANSCRIPTS...
...INTERROGATIONS OF *CATHAR* HERETICS.*
**CATHARS:* A HERETICAL SECT IN THE SOUTH OF FRANCE, EXTERMINATED BY THE CHURCH IN THE 13TH CENTURY. SAID TO HAVE BEEN GUARDIANS OF THE *HOLY GRAIL*. BOOK 2, CH. 6.

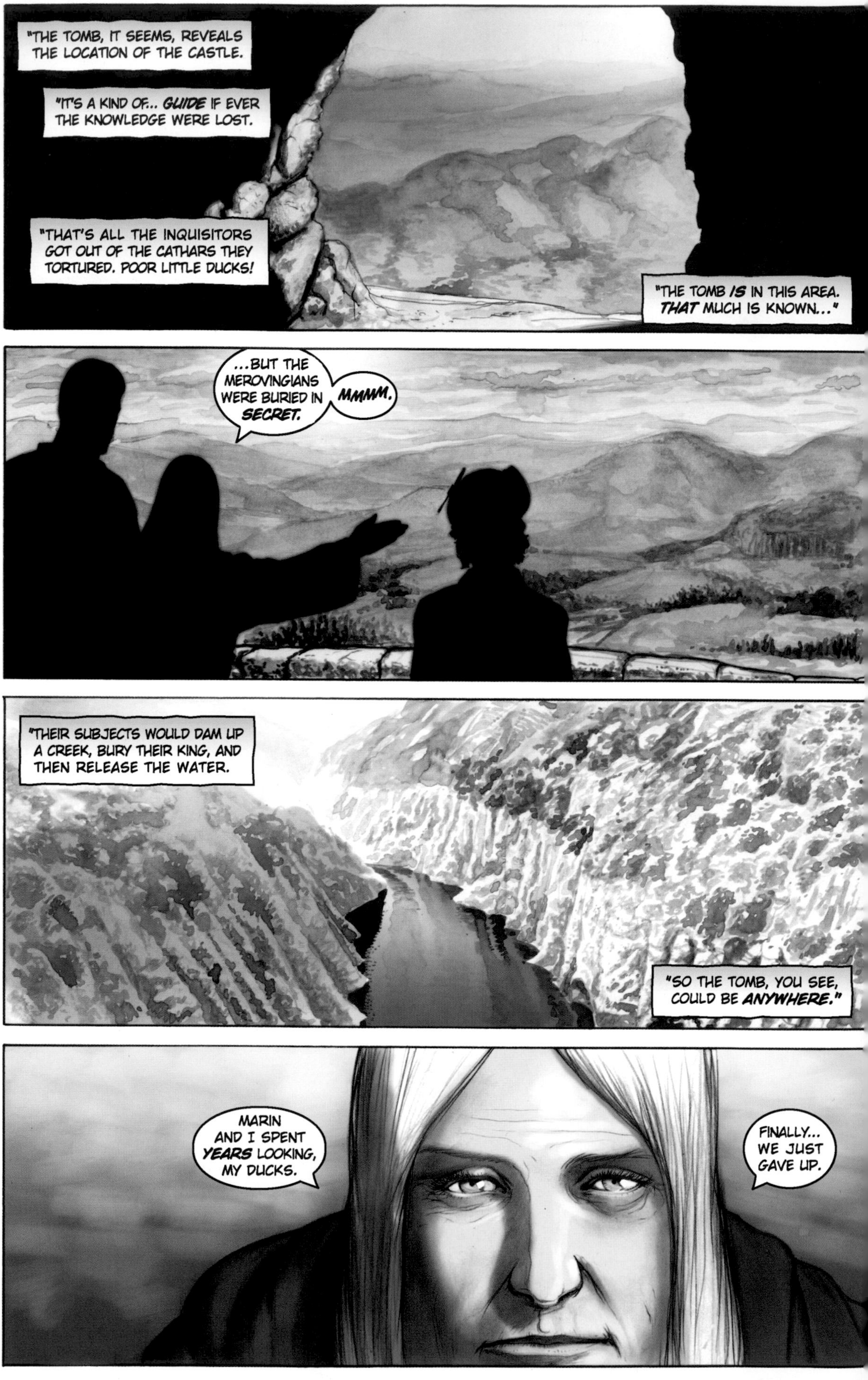
"THE TOMB, IT SEEMS, REVEALS THE LOCATION OF THE CASTLE.
"IT'S A KIND OF... GUIDE IF EVER THE KNOWLEDGE WERE LOST.
"THAT'S ALL THE INQUISITORS GOT OUT OF THE CATHARS THEY TORTURED. POOR LITTLE DUCKS!
"THE TOMB IS IN THIS AREA. THAT MUCH IS KNOWN..."
...BUT THE MEROVINGIANS WERE BURIED IN SECRET.
MMMM.
"THEIR SUBJECTS WOULD DAM UP A CREEK, BURY THEIR KING, AND THEN RELEASE THE WATER.
"SO THE TOMB, YOU SEE, COULD BE ANYWHERE."
MARIN AND I SPENT YEARS LOOKING, MY DUCKS.
FINALLY... WE JUST GAVE UP.

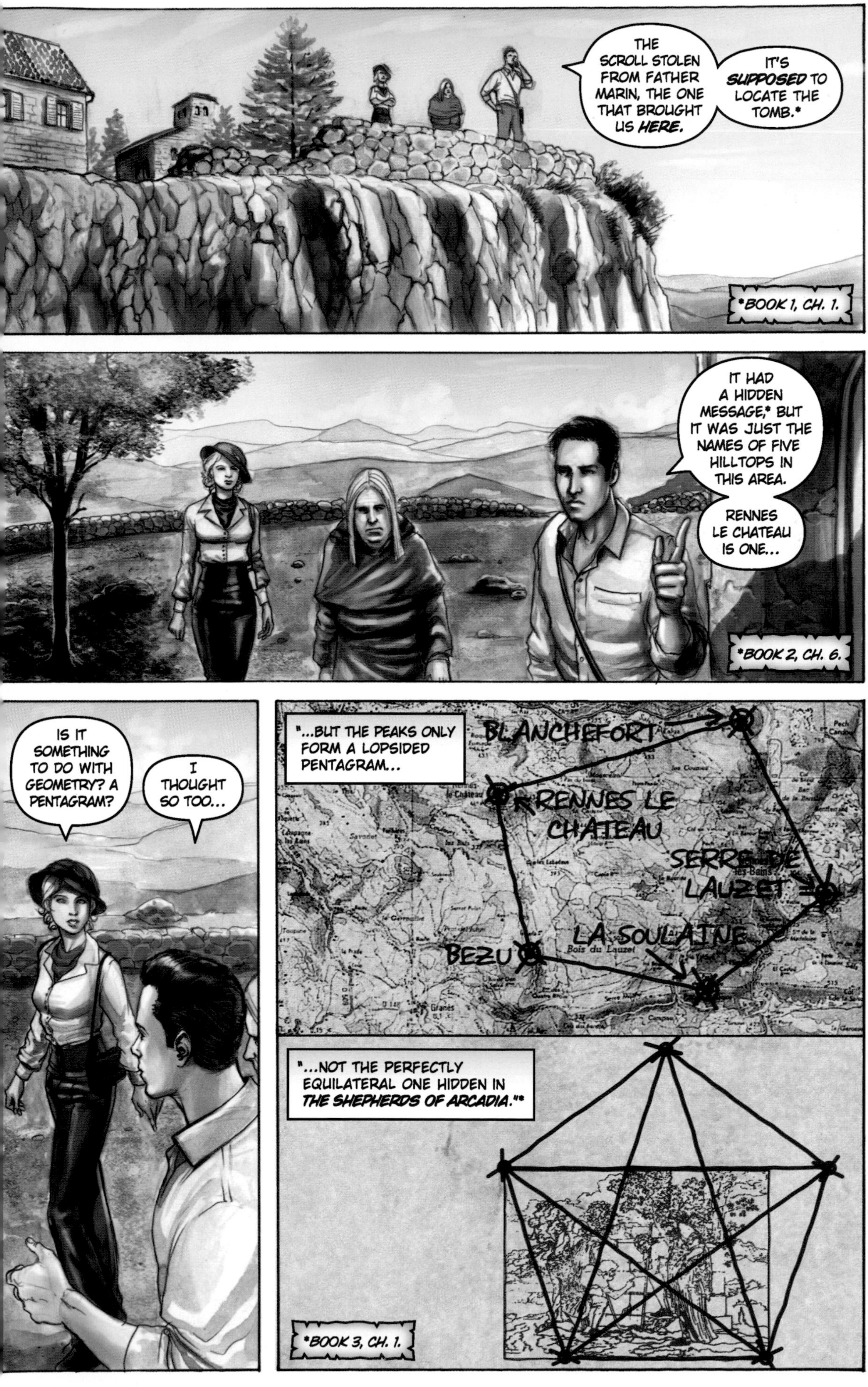
THE SCROLL STOLEN FROM FATHER MARIN, THE ONE THAT BROUGHT US HERE.
IT'S SUPPOSED TO LOCATE THE TOMB.*
*BOOK 1, CH. 1.
IT HAD A HIDDEN MESSAGE,* BUT IT WAS JUST THE NAMES OF FIVE HILLTOPS IN THIS AREA.
RENNES LE CHATEAU IS ONE...
*BOOK 2, CH. 6.
IS IT SOMETHING TO DO WITH GEOMETRY? A PENTAGRAM?
I THOUGHT SO TOO...
"...BUT THE PEAKS ONLY FORM A LOPSIDED PENTAGRAM...
BLANCHEFORT
RENNES LE CHATEAU
SERRE DE LAUZET
LA SOULAINE
BEZU
"...NOT THE PERFECTLY EQUILATERAL ONE HIDDEN IN THE SHEPHERDS OF ARCADIA."*
*BOOK 3, CH. 1.

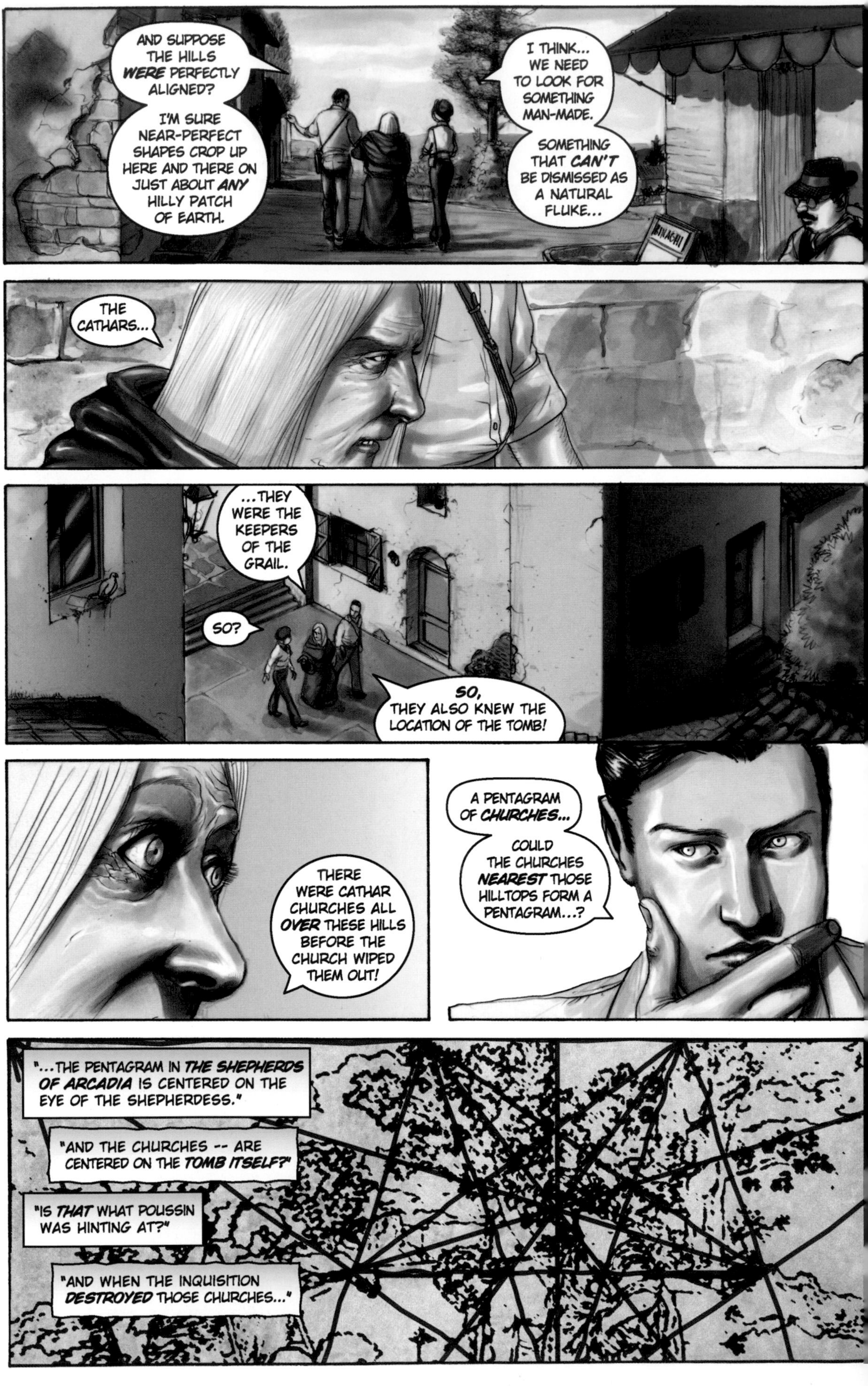
AND SUPPOSE THE HILLS WERE PERFECTLY ALIGNED?
I'M SURE NEAR-PERFECT SHAPES CROP UP HERE AND THERE ON JUST ABOUT ANY HILLY PATCH OF EARTH.
I THINK... WE NEED TO LOOK FOR SOMETHING MAN-MADE.
SOMETHING THAT CAN'T BE DISMISSED AS A NATURAL FLUKE...
BINAGHI
THE CATHARS...
...THEY WERE THE KEEPERS OF THE GRAIL.
SO?
SO, THEY ALSO KNEW THE LOCATION OF THE TOMB!
THERE WERE CATHAR CHURCHES ALL OVER THESE HILLS BEFORE THE CHURCH WIPED THEM OUT!
A PENTAGRAM OF CHURCHES...
COULD THE CHURCHES NEAREST THOSE HILLTOPS FORM A PENTAGRAM...?
"...THE PENTAGRAM IN THE SHEPHERDS OF ARCADIA IS CENTERED ON THE EYE OF THE SHEPHERDESS."
"AND THE CHURCHES -- ARE CENTERED ON THE TOMB ITSELF?"
"IS THAT WHAT POUSSIN WAS HINTING AT?"
"AND WHEN THE INQUISITION DESTROYED THOSE CHURCHES..."

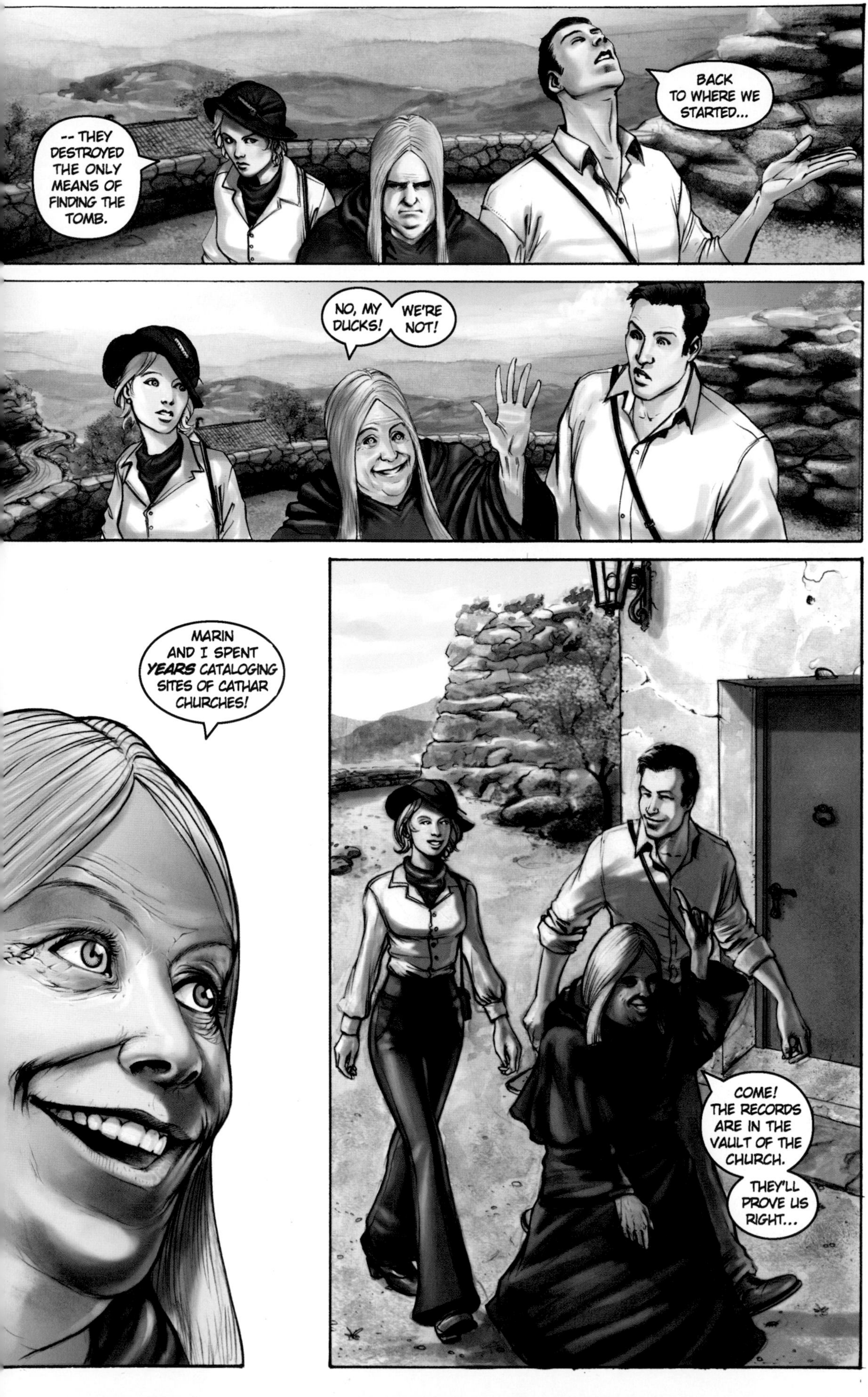
-- THEY DESTROYED THE ONLY MEANS OF FINDING THE TOMB.
BACK TO WHERE WE STARTED...
NO, MY DUCKS!
WE'RE NOT!
MARIN AND I SPENT *YEARS* CATALOGING SITES OF CATHAR CHURCHES!
COME! THE RECORDS ARE IN THE VAULT OF THE CHURCH.
THEY'LL PROVE US RIGHT...

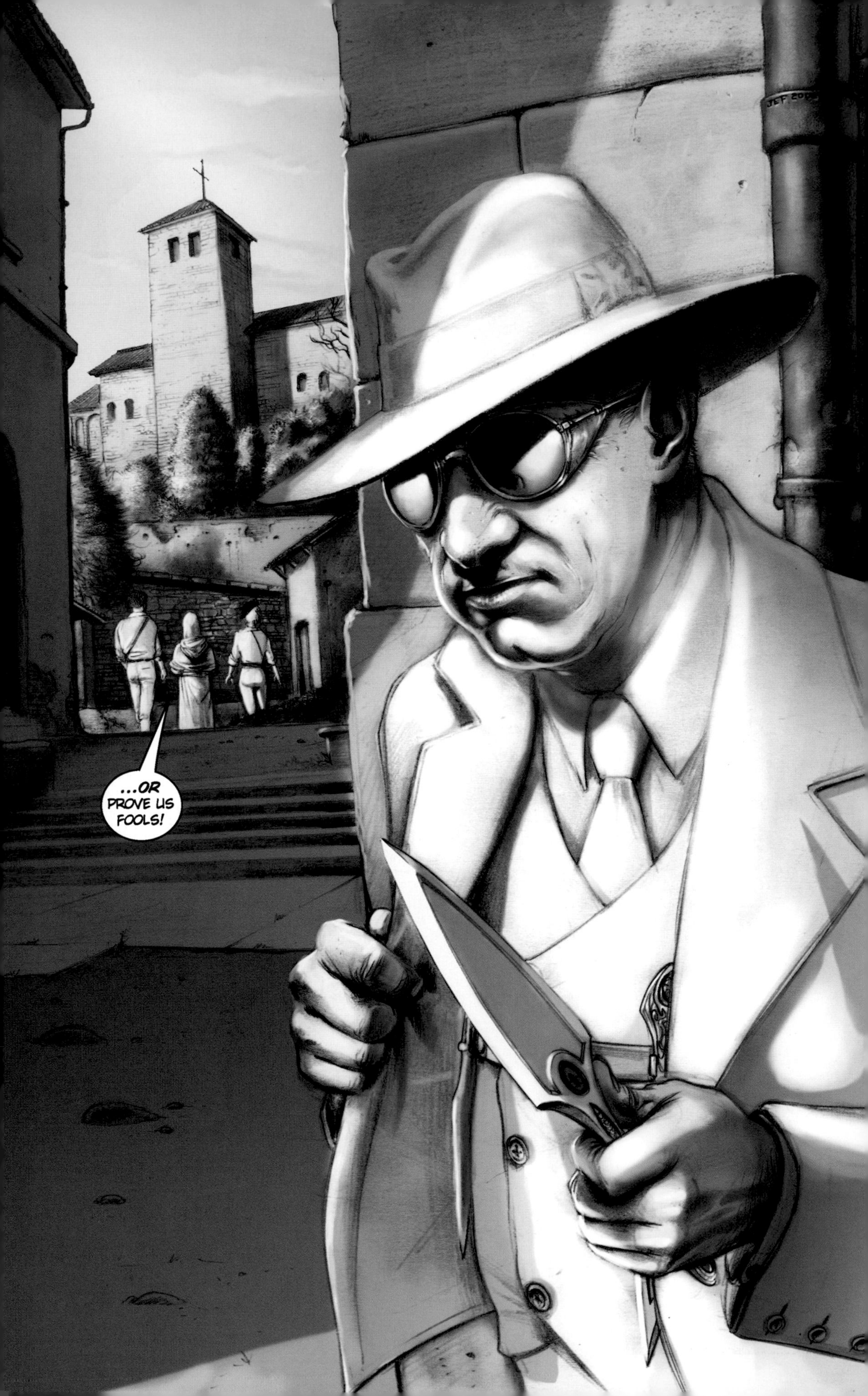
...OR PROVE US FOOLS!

Le Journal de la Liberté

Paris's leading anglophone newspaper • vol. 205, no. 104 • Nov. 20, MCMXXXIII

Papal seal

Editors in Chief: M. Tait Bergstrom, M. Matthew Pasteris. **Story Editor:** M. Arvid Nelson. **Art Editor:** M. Juan Ferreyra. **Photography Editor:** M. Alexander Waldman. **Layout Supervisor:** M. William Kartalopoulos. **Editors Emeritus:** M. Clark A. Smith, M. Howard P. Lovecraft, M. Robert E. Howard. Redacted under the direction of His Excellency Archbishop Emile-Jean Ireneaux. *Le Journal de la Liberté* is printed under the benign auspices of his eminence David Louis Plantard de St. Clair, Duke of Lorraine and First Consul of the Empire of France.

of Approval

FRENCH CAPTURE MADRID, GERMANS ADVANCE ON PARIS

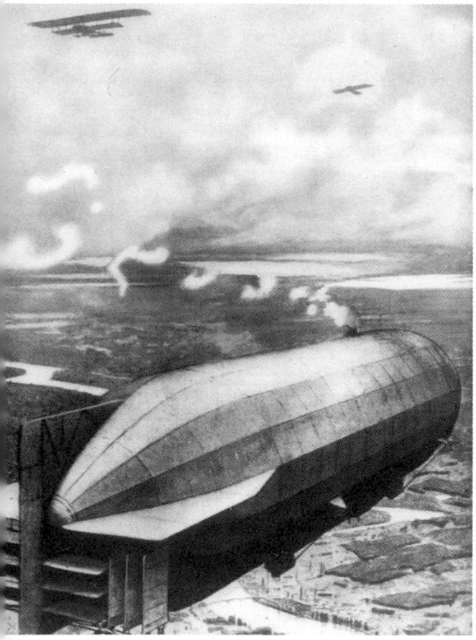

massive Prussian dirigible gunship lumbers inexorably ross the Duchy of Lorraine.

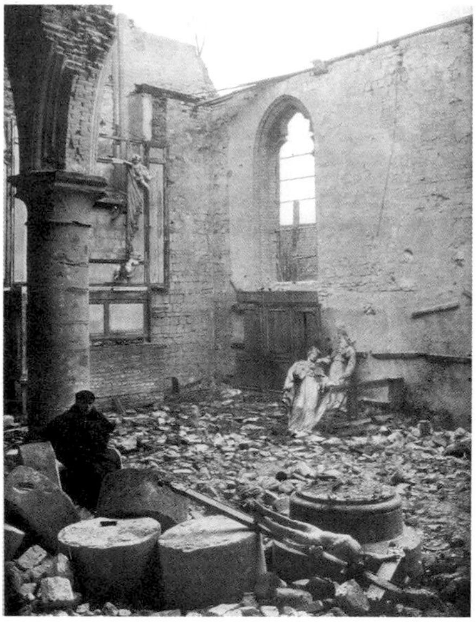

The ruins of a church at Liège. The Prussians have not spared consecrated ground from their artillery onslaught.

aris – The advance of French roops into the Iberian peninsula eems unstoppable. But so too does ne Prussian march toward Paris.

Most military experts agree nat, for the time being, the advantage lies with the Prussians, vho fight on a single front.

However, that might be bout to change. A second front opening up for the Prussians, n the eastern hinterlands of the ierman Reich.

Several days ago the Rusan Tzar declared war on her longtime rival, the Holy Roman Empire, and Prussia. Whether or not Russian troops can mobilize in time to affect the struggle for Paris remains to be seen.

Russia's entry into the war means a potential for three fronts: one in the west, where French troops are trying to seize control of the Iberian Peninsula from the Cordovan Emirate; one in the east, where the French are struggling to turn back the advance of the Prussians on Paris; and potentially one to the far east, where the Prussians and Austrians will themselves be forced into the role of defender against Russia.

Despite this potential complication, German optimism remains high.

"Prussia did not start this war, but she is going to end it," the Prussian Kaiser said in a speech in Berlin yesterday. "Responsibility for this conflict, and for France's eventual dissolution, rests solely on the shoulders of the Duke of Lorraine."

The relentless Prussian offensive shows no sign of slowing, and Paris itself could already be in striking distance.

The United Kingdom has come to aid French troops defending Paris. British forces began landing at Le Havre four days ago.

"Know that you are entering into a holy struggle against the Germans and the Mohammedans. Christ, Great Britain and her allies shall prevail," Queen Elizabeth II of Great Britain said in a address to troops bound to cross the English Channel yesterday.

There is widespread speculation about an imminent Anglo-French counter-attack.

The Duke of Nevers, who commands the French forces in the east, refused to comment on the possibility of such an operation.

In the south, French forces continue to make rapid progress against the ill-prepared troops of the Cordovan Emirate. "We've caught them off balance, and we're pushing forward aggressively," the Duke of Orleans, commander of the French forces in the south, said. "We'll be in Cordova, the capital, in days."

But some question the decision to commit the majority of French troops to the offensive against Cordova, leaving, detractors argue, Paris "open for the taking."

The Duke of Lorraine was elected Supreme Commander of the French armed forces by Parliament on the eve of the conflict. He is responsible for overall French strategy.

A spokesman for Lorraine vehemently denied claims the Duke was acting "irresponsibly."

"The Germans are laying waste to the Duchy of Lorraine, the Duke's ancestral homeland. Any suggestion he would deliberately expose his own lands to occupation is nothing short of calumny."

Lorraine seems to be counting on a quick knock-out victory over the Cordovans, which will allow him to re-deploy troops to turn back the Germans.

Although French forces are rapidly gaining ground in Iberia, it remains an open question whether they will capture Cordova in time to concentrate on the Prussians.

"Wars are won by attacking and taking risks," Lorraine said. "The only sure way to lose is not to try to win."

Lorraine's stated goal is to "drive Islam across the pillars of Hercules forever." Parliament recently elected him First Consul of France.

The current, ever-widening conflict began when Islamic militants assassinated the Marquis of Aragon. France then declared war on the Cordovan Emirate, and Prussia declared war on France soon thereafter. ⚜

INSIDE

Latest Wartime Developments

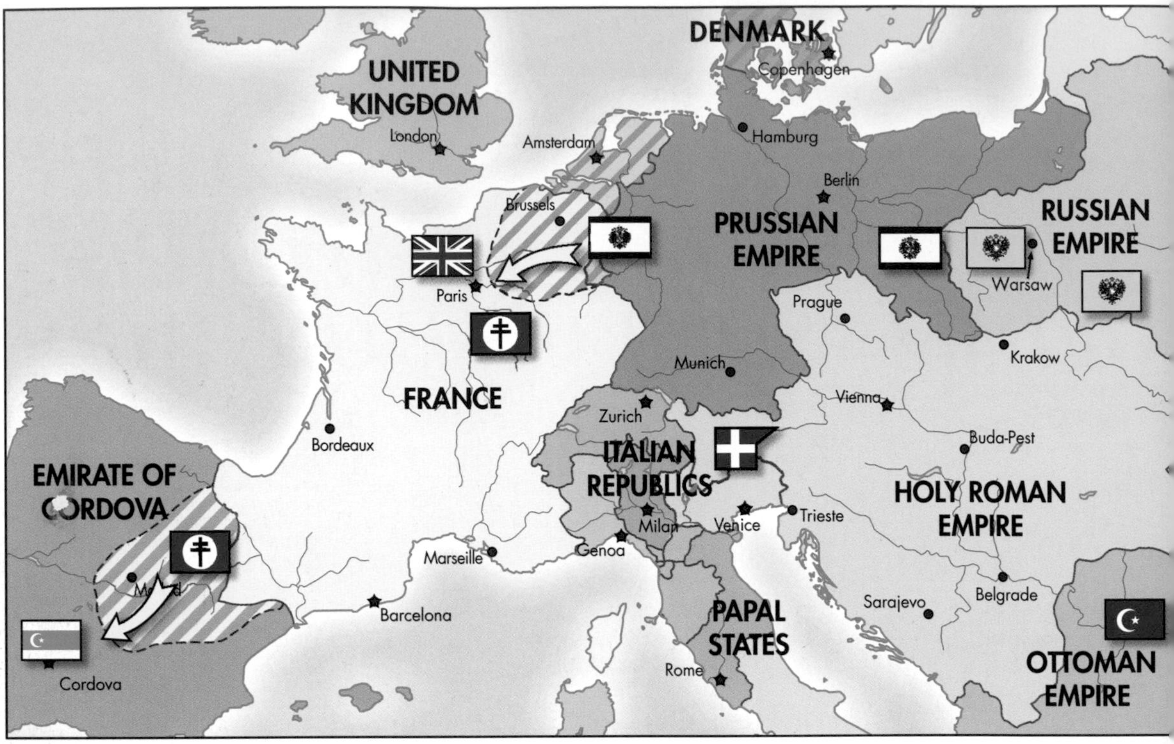
DENMARK
Copenhagen
UNITED KINGDOM
London
Amsterdam
Hamburg
Berlin
Brussels
PRUSSIAN EMPIRE
RUSSIAN EMPIRE
Paris
Warsaw
Prague
Krakow
Munich
FRANCE
Zurich
Vienna
Bordeaux
Buda-Pest
ITALIAN REPUBLICS
EMIRATE OF CORDOVA
HOLY ROMAN EMPIRE
Milan
Venice
Trieste
Genoa
Marseille
Madrid
Belgrade
Sarajevo
PAPAL STATES
Barcelona
Rome
Cordova
OTTOMAN EMPIRE

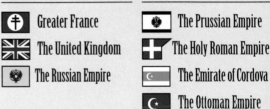

THE AXIS:

- Greater France
- The United Kingdom
- The Russian Empire

THE ALLIES:

- The Prussian Empire
- The Holy Roman Empire
- The Emirate of Cordova
- The Ottoman Empire

The Western Front

French troops are advancing "like a pistol shot" through Cordova, according to top military officials taking part in the campaign.

"Madrid fell in just one day," Commandant Jules Sabaret of the XII Imperial Hussars said. "The Cordovans are in complete disarray, I dare say panic."

French troops are relentlessly pursuing the Emir's demoralized soldiers to Cordova, the capital.

"If Cordova falls, so does the Emir. The Mohammedans will make a last stand there," Colonel Robert Grasset said. "Expect a decisive battle soon."

"Speed is an absolute imperative. We cannot allow the Islamists time to gain poise." The speed of the advance could also determine the outcome in the East.

The Eastern Front

Cordova is buried deep within the interior of the Iberian Peninsula. This fact of geography means French forces have much further to travel than the Prussian army fighting its way to Paris.

"Even though we're proceeding far more swiftly against the Cordovans than the Germans on Paris, they simply have less ground to cover," a spokesman for the Duke of Lorraine said.

"The question now is whether we can finish off Cordova swiftly enough to divert forces to Paris."

In its pursuit of Paris the Prussian army trampled over the Netherlands and Luxembourg without contest.

"They were poised on our doorstep, bristling with weapons. What could we do but acquiesce to their demand for passage?" a prominent member of Dutch parliament said.

The Far East

The entrance of the Russians and Ottoman Turks into the conflict in recent days further complicates the unfolding war.

Reports on Russian troop movements are sporadic and unconfirmed; the Tzar is an uneas ally of the French and British.

"It's a case of common er emies, but it remains to be see if we have anything in commo beyond that," a source said.

"This war will be fought ov the entire globe," the Duke Lorraine said. "It will be a cruc ble for a new world order, a ne France."

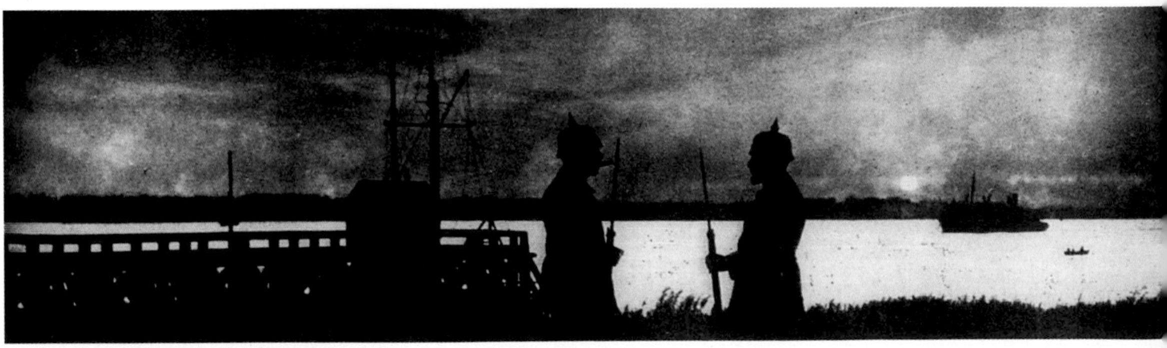

German sentries stand watch on the Somme River.

CHAPTER FIVE
THE EYE OF THE SHEPHERDESS

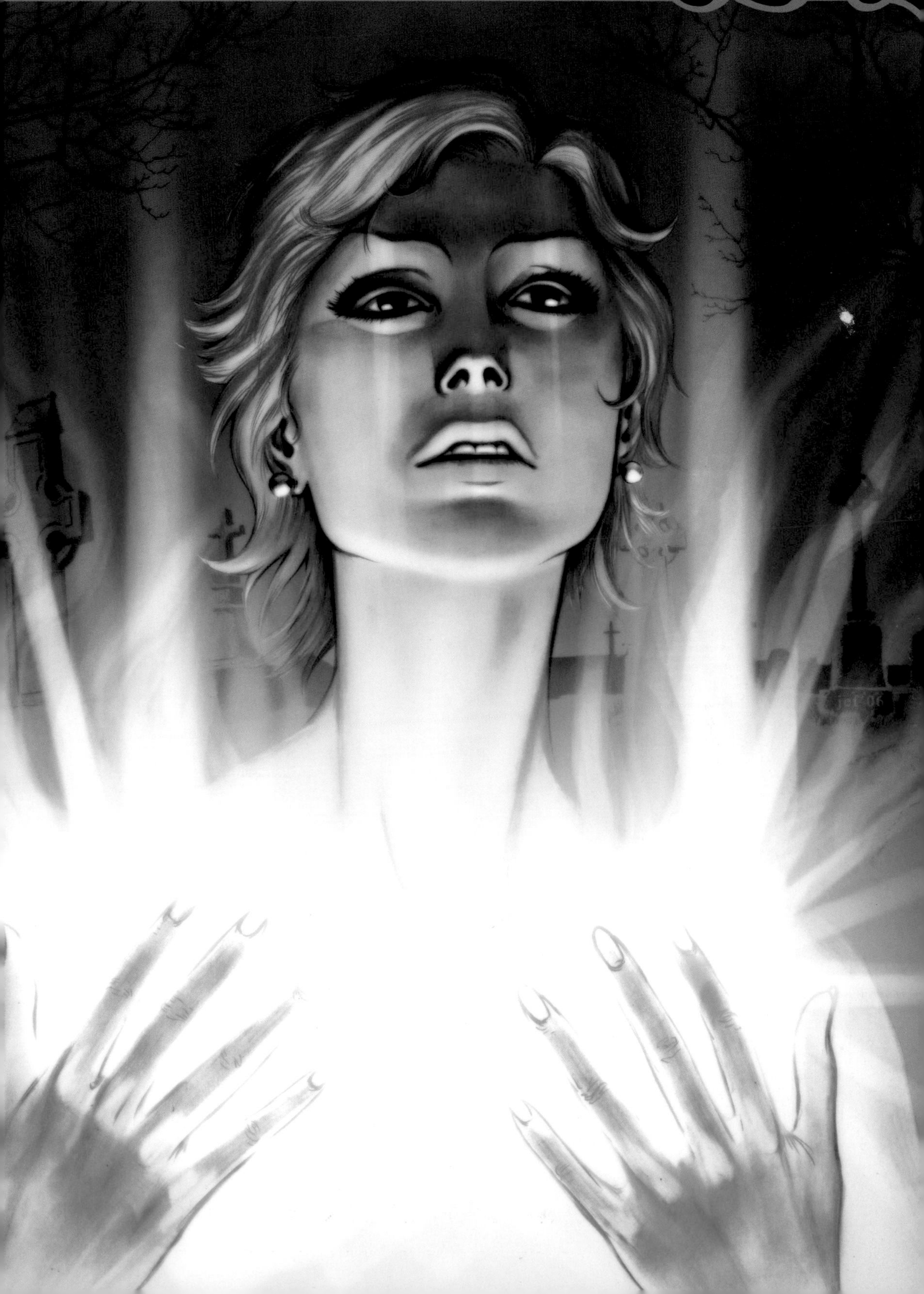

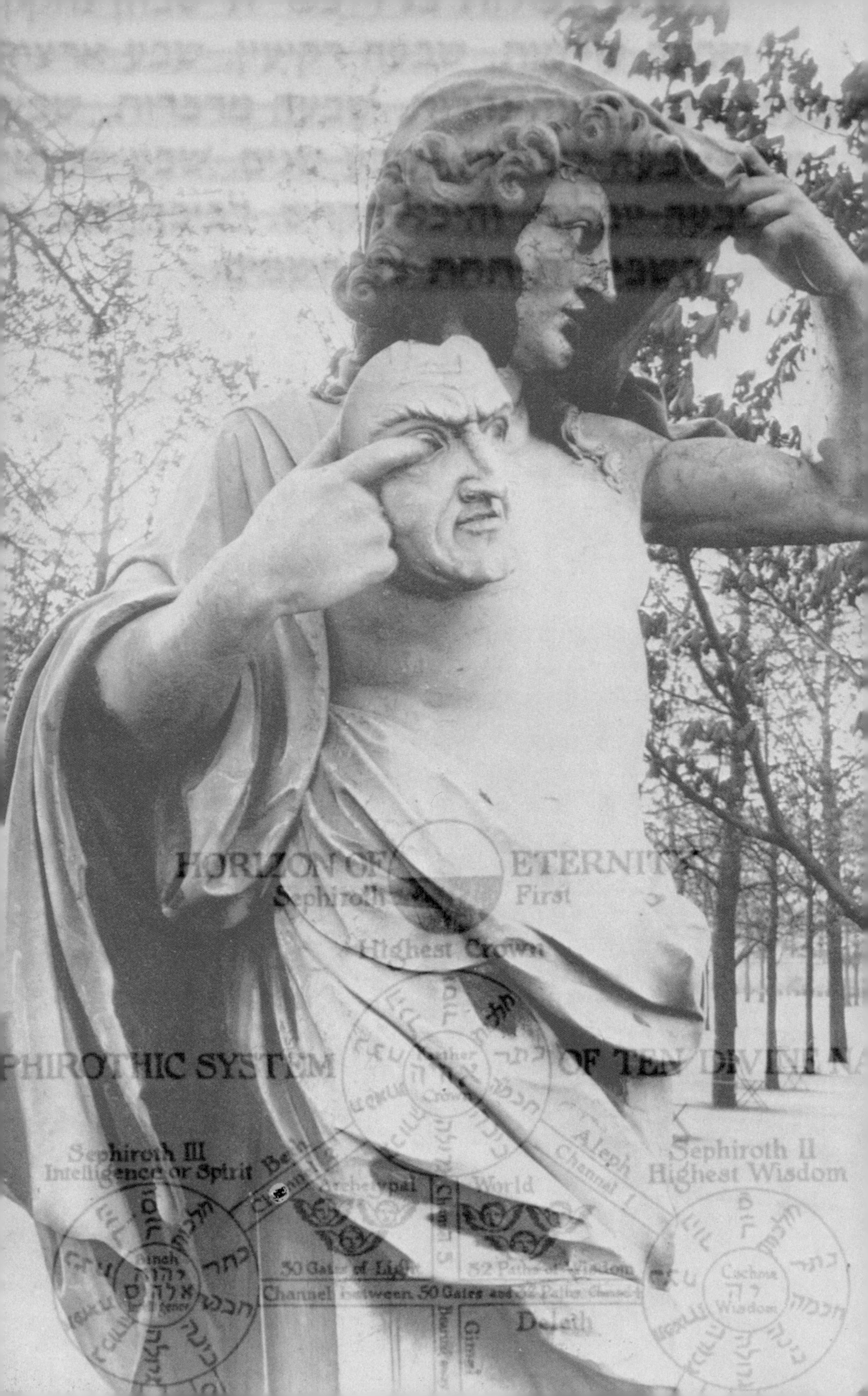
First
Highest Crown
Sephiroth III
Sephiroth II
Highest Wisdom
Aleph
Channel 1
World
50 Gates of Light
Daleth
Wisdom

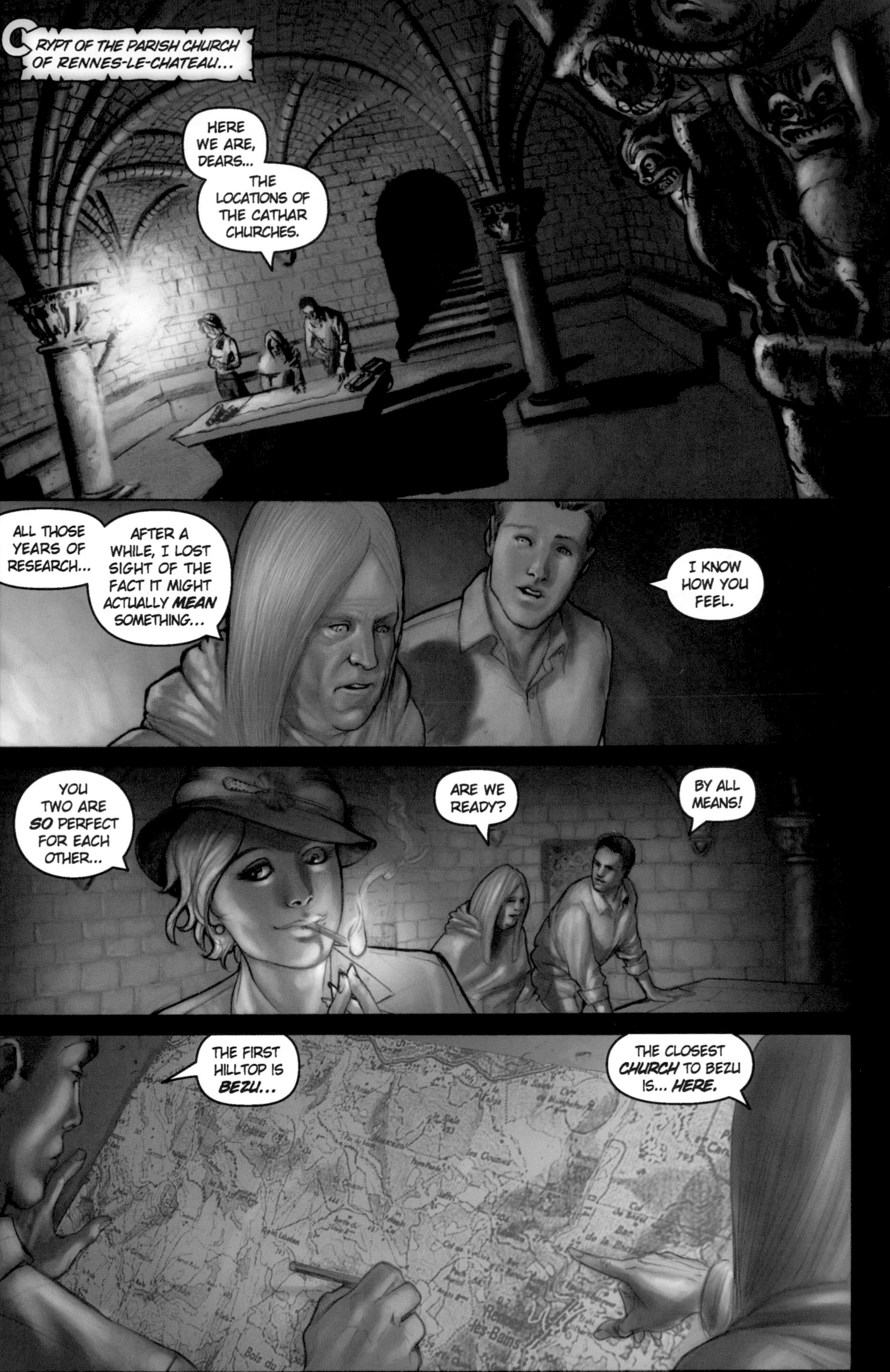
CRYPT OF THE PARISH CHURCH OF RENNES-LE-CHATEAU...
HERE WE ARE, DEARS...
THE LOCATIONS OF THE CATHAR CHURCHES.
ALL THOSE YEARS OF RESEARCH...
AFTER A WHILE, I LOST SIGHT OF THE FACT IT MIGHT ACTUALLY MEAN SOMETHING...
I KNOW HOW YOU FEEL.
YOU TWO ARE SO PERFECT FOR EACH OTHER...
ARE WE READY?
BY ALL MEANS!
THE FIRST HILLTOP IS BEZU...
THE CLOSEST CHURCH TO BEZU IS... HERE.

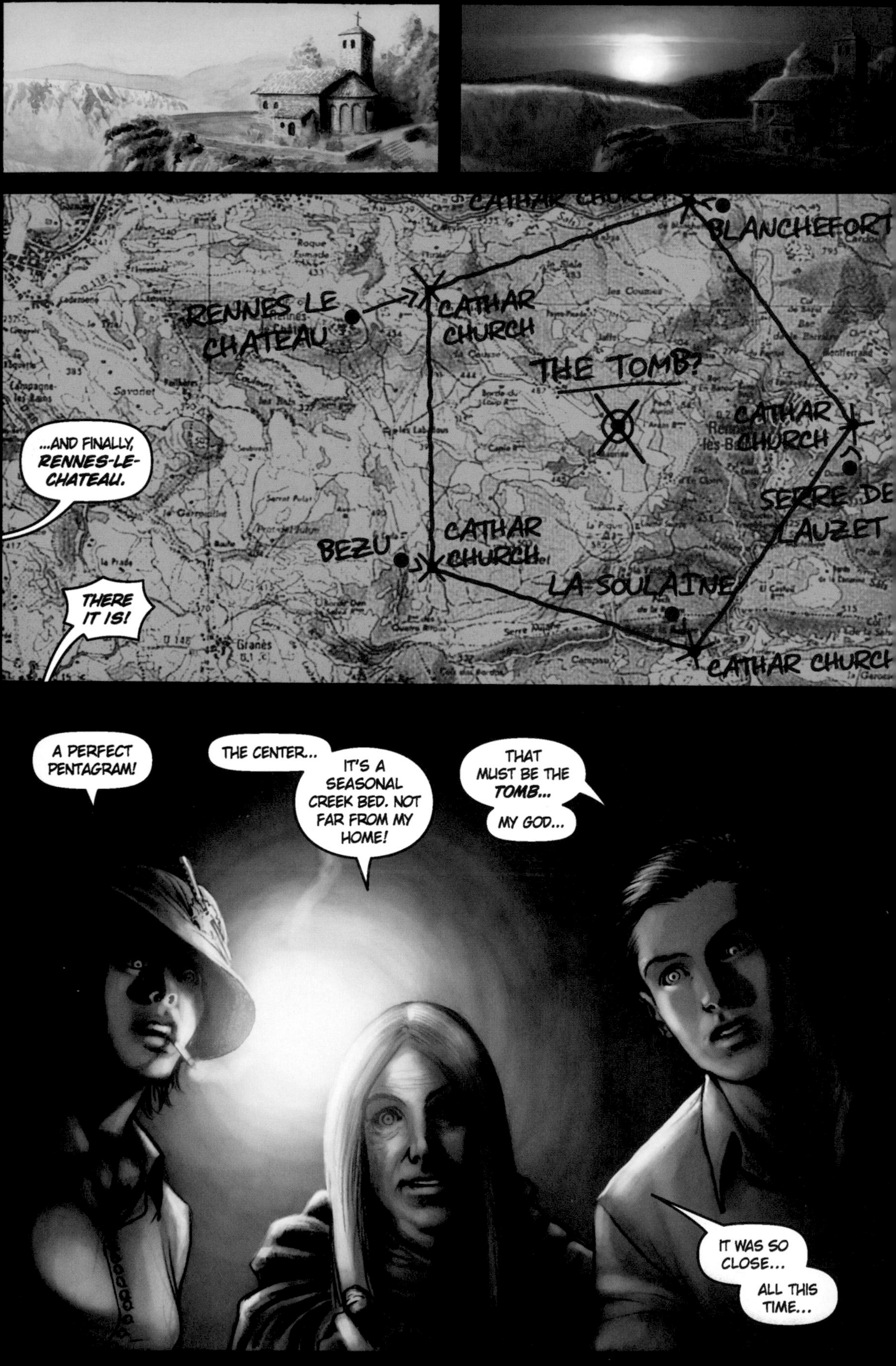

BLANCHEFORT
RENNES LE CHATEAU
CATHAR CHURCH
THE TOMB?
CATHAR CHURCH
SERRE DE LAUZET
BEZU
CATHAR CHURCH
LA SOULAINE
...AND FINALLY, RENNES-LE-CHATEAU.
THERE IT IS!
A PERFECT PENTAGRAM!
THE CENTER...
IT'S A SEASONAL CREEK BED. NOT FAR FROM MY HOME!
THAT MUST BE THE TOMB...
MY GOD...
IT WAS SO CLOSE...
ALL THIS TIME...

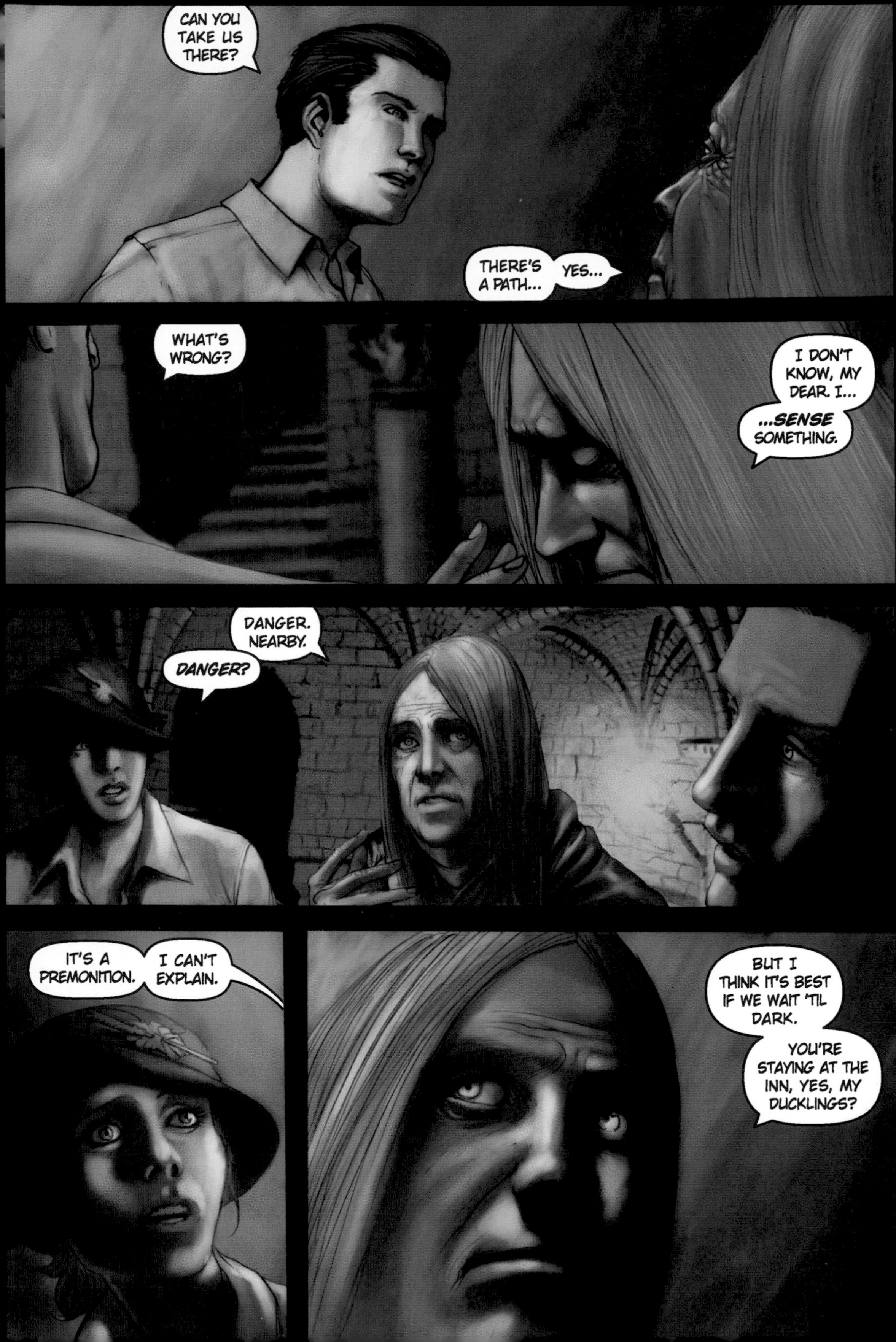
CAN YOU TAKE US THERE?
THERE'S A PATH...
YES...
WHAT'S WRONG?
I DON'T KNOW, MY DEAR. I...
...SENSE SOMETHING.
DANGER. NEARBY.
DANGER?
IT'S A PREMONITION.
I CAN'T EXPLAIN.
BUT I THINK IT'S BEST IF WE WAIT 'TIL DARK.
YOU'RE STAYING AT THE INN, YES, MY DUCKLINGS?

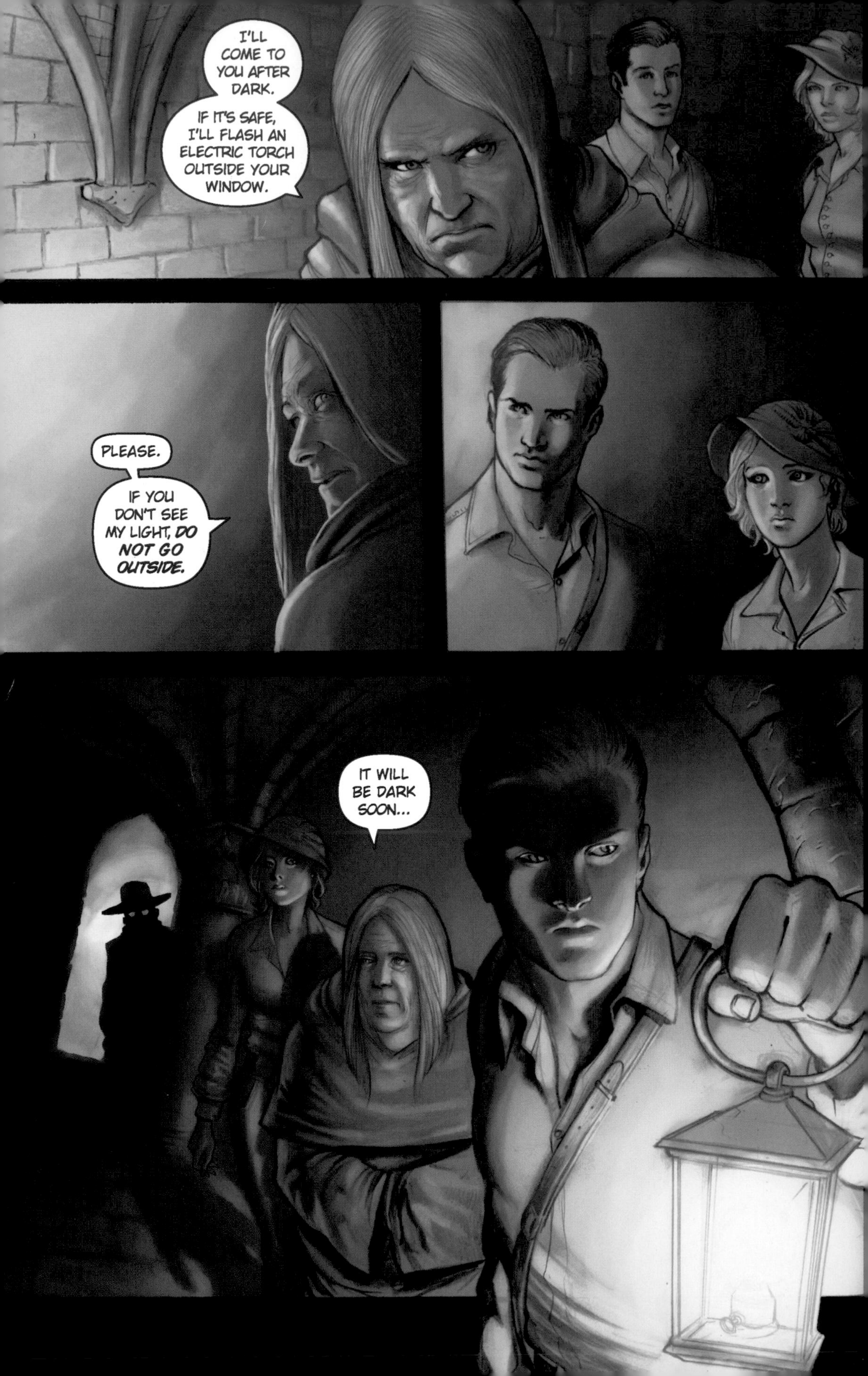
I'LL COME TO YOU AFTER DARK.
IF IT'S SAFE, I'LL FLASH AN ELECTRIC TORCH OUTSIDE YOUR WINDOW.
PLEASE.
IF YOU DON'T SEE MY LIGHT, *DO NOT GO OUTSIDE.*
IT WILL BE DARK SOON...

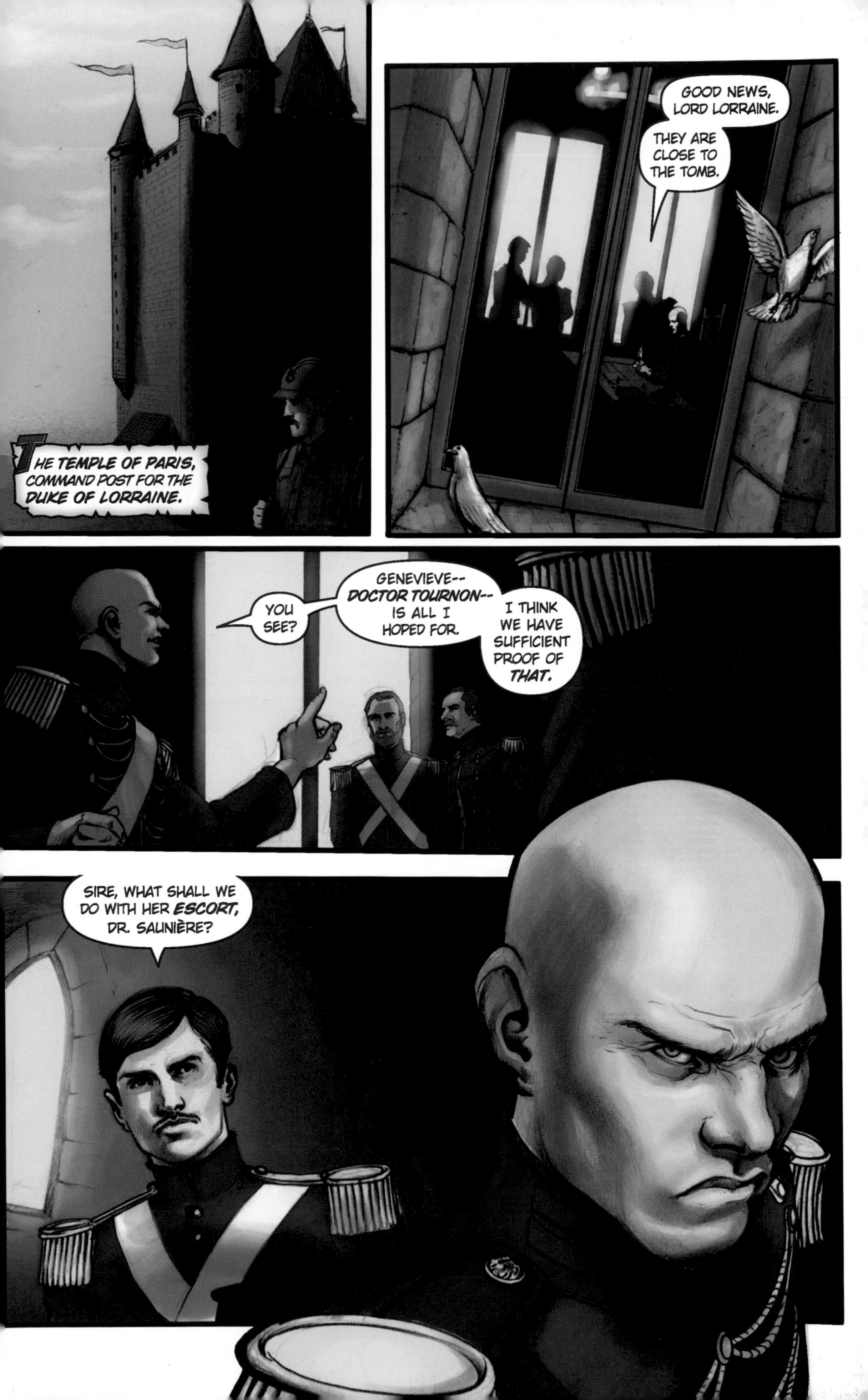
THE TEMPLE OF PARIS, COMMAND POST FOR THE DUKE OF LORRAINE.
GOOD NEWS, LORD LORRAINE.
THEY ARE CLOSE TO THE TOMB.
YOU SEE?
GENEVIEVE-- DOCTOR TOURNON-- IS ALL I HOPED FOR.
I THINK WE HAVE SUFFICIENT PROOF OF THAT.
SIRE, WHAT SHALL WE DO WITH HER ESCORT, DR. SAUNIÈRE?

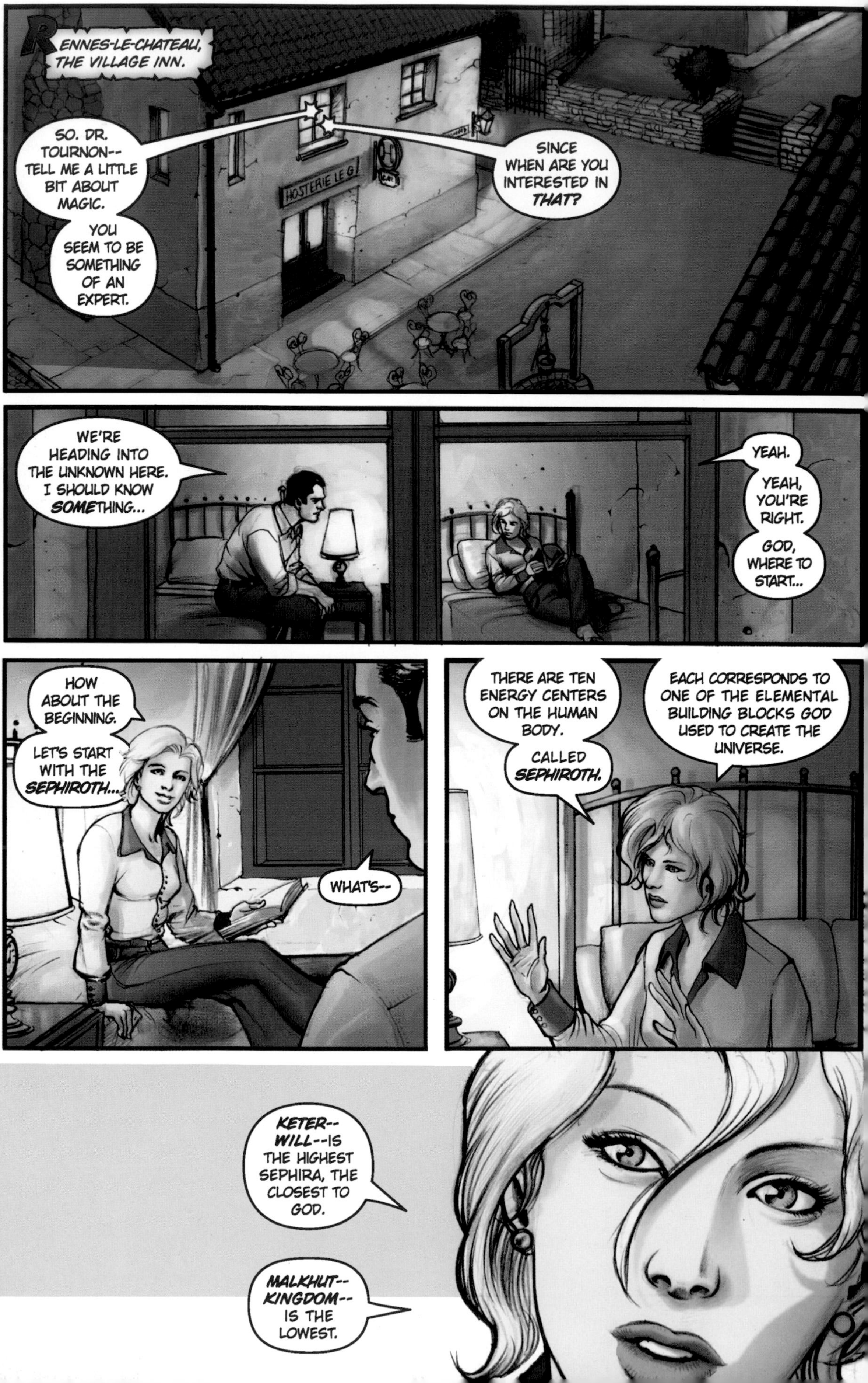
RENNES-LE-CHATEAU, THE VILLAGE INN.
SO. DR. TOURNON-- TELL ME A LITTLE BIT ABOUT MAGIC.
YOU SEEM TO BE SOMETHING OF AN EXPERT.
SINCE WHEN ARE YOU INTERESTED IN *THAT?*
HOSTERIE LE G
WE'RE HEADING INTO THE UNKNOWN HERE. I SHOULD KNOW *SOME*THING...
YEAH.
YEAH, YOU'RE RIGHT.
GOD, WHERE TO START...
HOW ABOUT THE BEGINNING.
LET'S START WITH THE *SEPHIROTH...*
WHAT'S--
THERE ARE TEN ENERGY CENTERS ON THE HUMAN BODY.
CALLED *SEPHIROTH.*
EACH CORRESPONDS TO ONE OF THE ELEMENTAL BUILDING BLOCKS GOD USED TO CREATE THE UNIVERSE.
KETER--
*WILL--*IS THE HIGHEST SEPHIRA, THE CLOSEST TO GOD.
MALKHUT--
KINGDOM-- IS THE LOWEST.

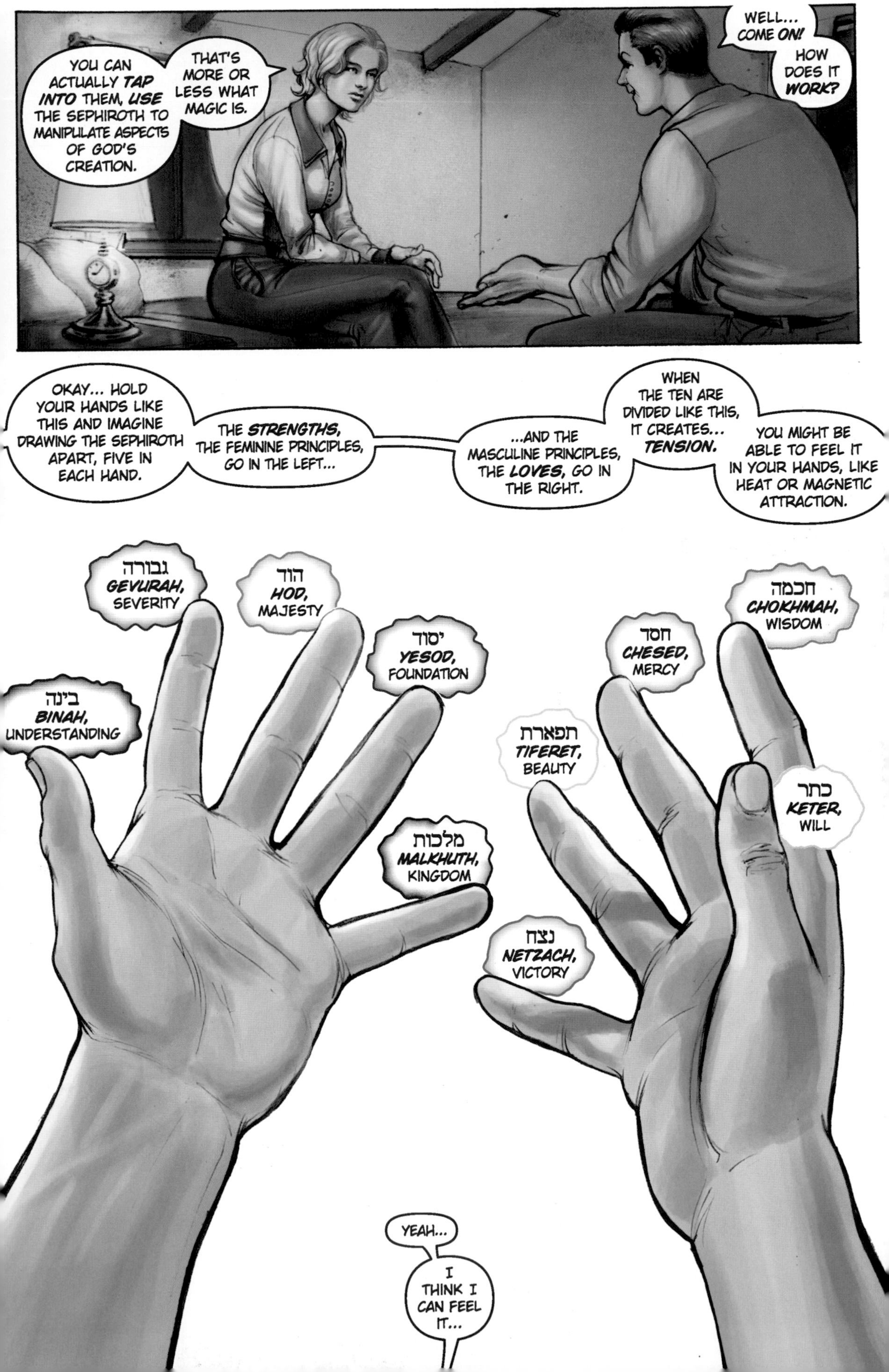

YOU CAN ACTUALLY TAP INTO THEM, USE THE SEPHIROTH TO MANIPULATE ASPECTS OF GOD'S CREATION.
THAT'S MORE OR LESS WHAT MAGIC IS.
WELL... COME ON!
HOW DOES IT WORK?
OKAY... HOLD YOUR HANDS LIKE THIS AND IMAGINE DRAWING THE SEPHIROTH APART, FIVE IN EACH HAND.
THE STRENGTHS, THE FEMININE PRINCIPLES, GO IN THE LEFT...
...AND THE MASCULINE PRINCIPLES, THE LOVES, GO IN THE RIGHT.
WHEN THE TEN ARE DIVIDED LIKE THIS, IT CREATES... TENSION.
YOU MIGHT BE ABLE TO FEEL IT IN YOUR HANDS, LIKE HEAT OR MAGNETIC ATTRACTION.
בינה BINAH, UNDERSTANDING
גבורה GEVURAH, SEVERITY
הוד HOD, MAJESTY
יסוד YESOD, FOUNDATION
מלכות MALKHUTH, KINGDOM
חכמה CHOKHMAH, WISDOM
חסד CHESED, MERCY
תפארת TIFERET, BEAUTY
כתר KETER, WILL
נצח NETZACH, VICTORY
YEAH...
I THINK I CAN FEEL IT...

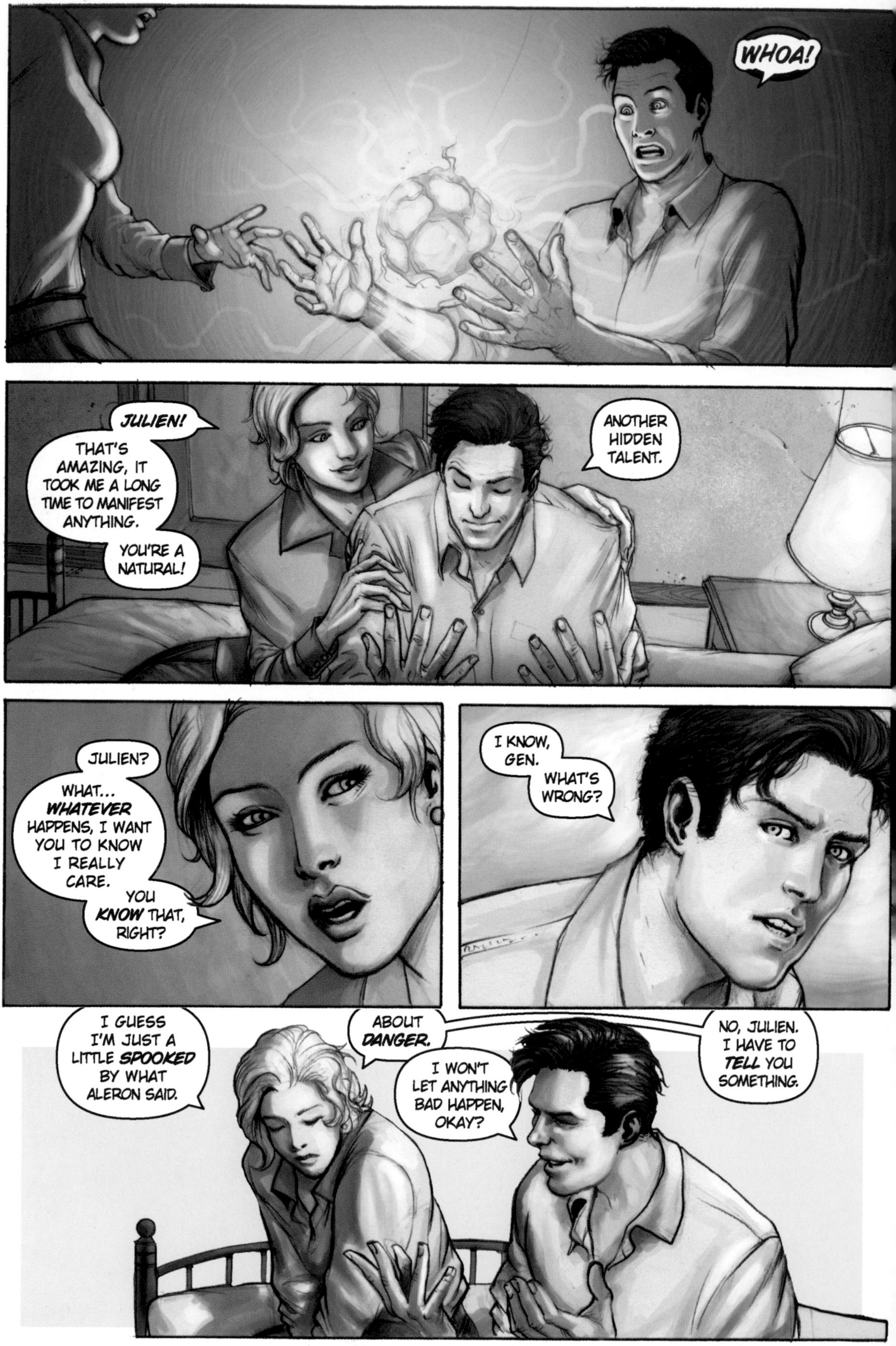
WHOA!
JULIEN!
THAT'S AMAZING, IT TOOK ME A LONG TIME TO MANIFEST ANYTHING.
YOU'RE A NATURAL!
ANOTHER HIDDEN TALENT.
JULIEN?
WHAT... WHATEVER HAPPENS, I WANT YOU TO KNOW I REALLY CARE.
YOU KNOW THAT, RIGHT?
I KNOW, GEN.
WHAT'S WRONG?
I GUESS I'M JUST A LITTLE SPOOKED BY WHAT ALERON SAID.
ABOUT DANGER.
I WON'T LET ANYTHING BAD HAPPEN, OKAY?
NO, JULIEN. I HAVE TO TELL YOU SOMETHING.

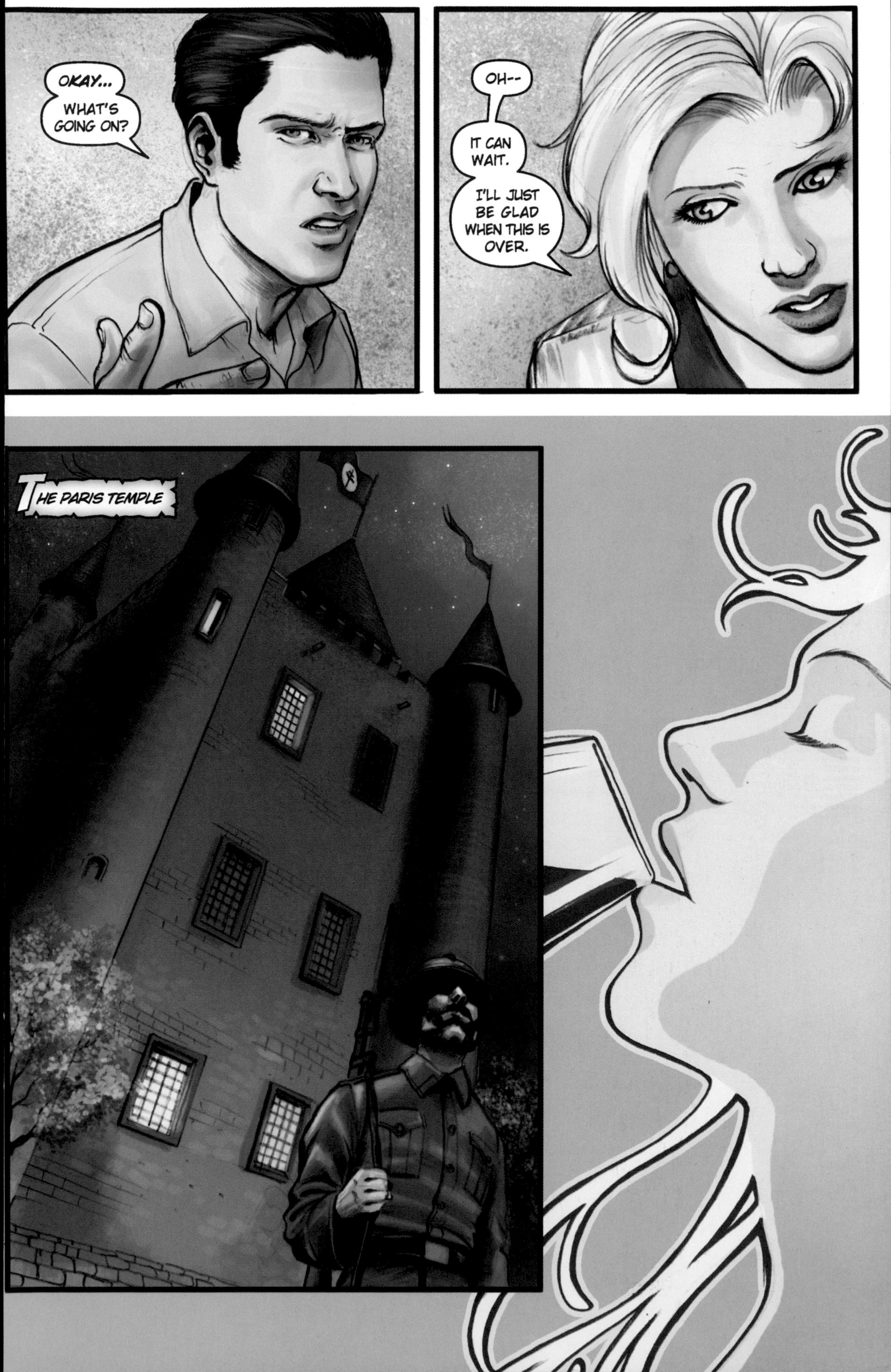
OKAY... WHAT'S GOING ON?
OH--
IT CAN WAIT.
I'LL JUST BE GLAD WHEN THIS IS OVER.
THE PARIS TEMPLE

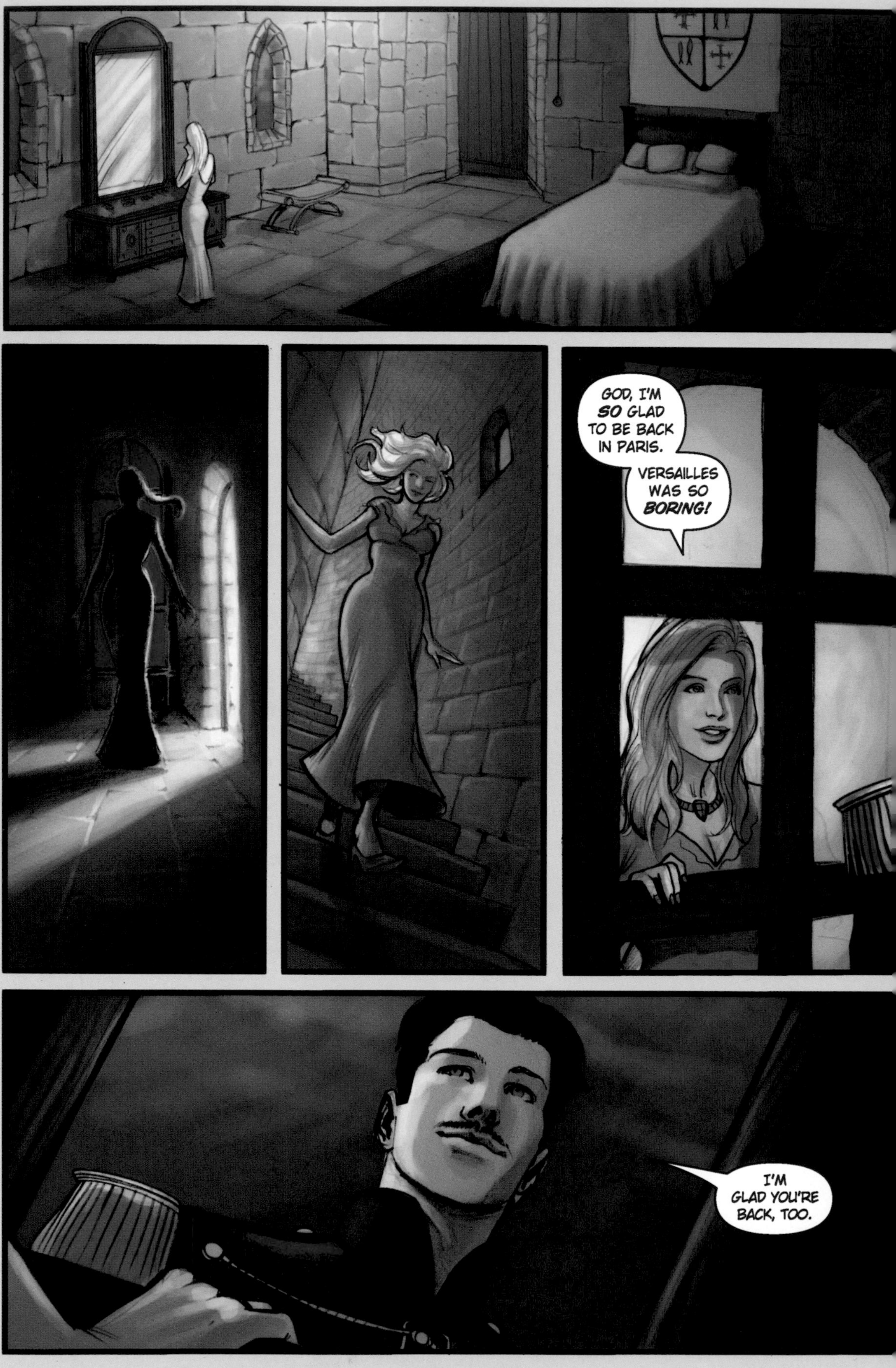
GOD, I'M SO GLAD TO BE BACK IN PARIS.
VERSAILLES WAS SO BORING!
I'M GLAD YOU'RE BACK, TOO.

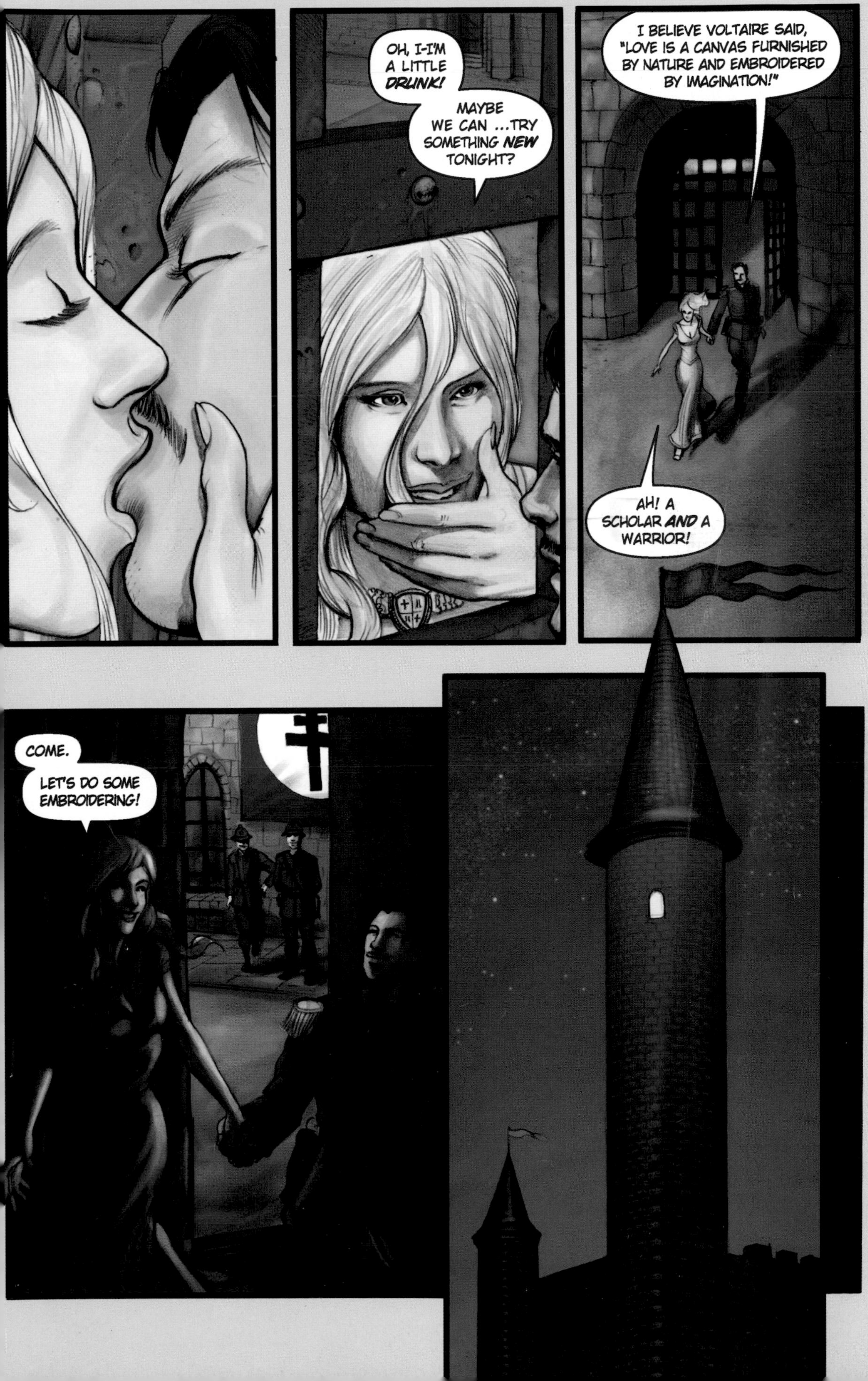
OH, I-I'M A LITTLE DRUNK!
MAYBE WE CAN ...TRY SOMETHING NEW TONIGHT?
I BELIEVE VOLTAIRE SAID, "LOVE IS A CANVAS FURNISHED BY NATURE AND EMBROIDERED BY IMAGINATION!"
AH! A SCHOLAR AND A WARRIOR!
COME.
LET'S DO SOME EMBROIDERING!

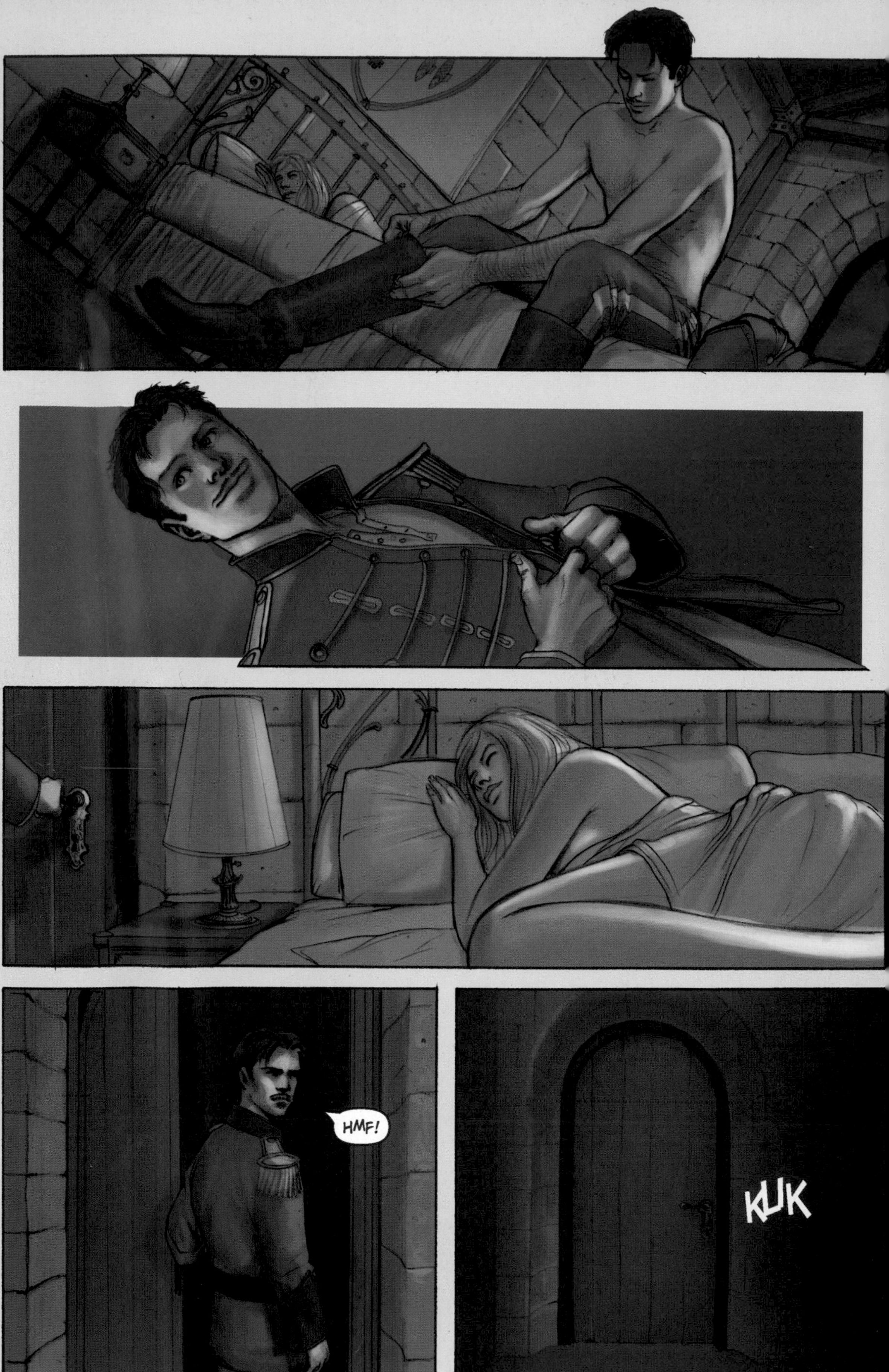
HMF!
KLIK

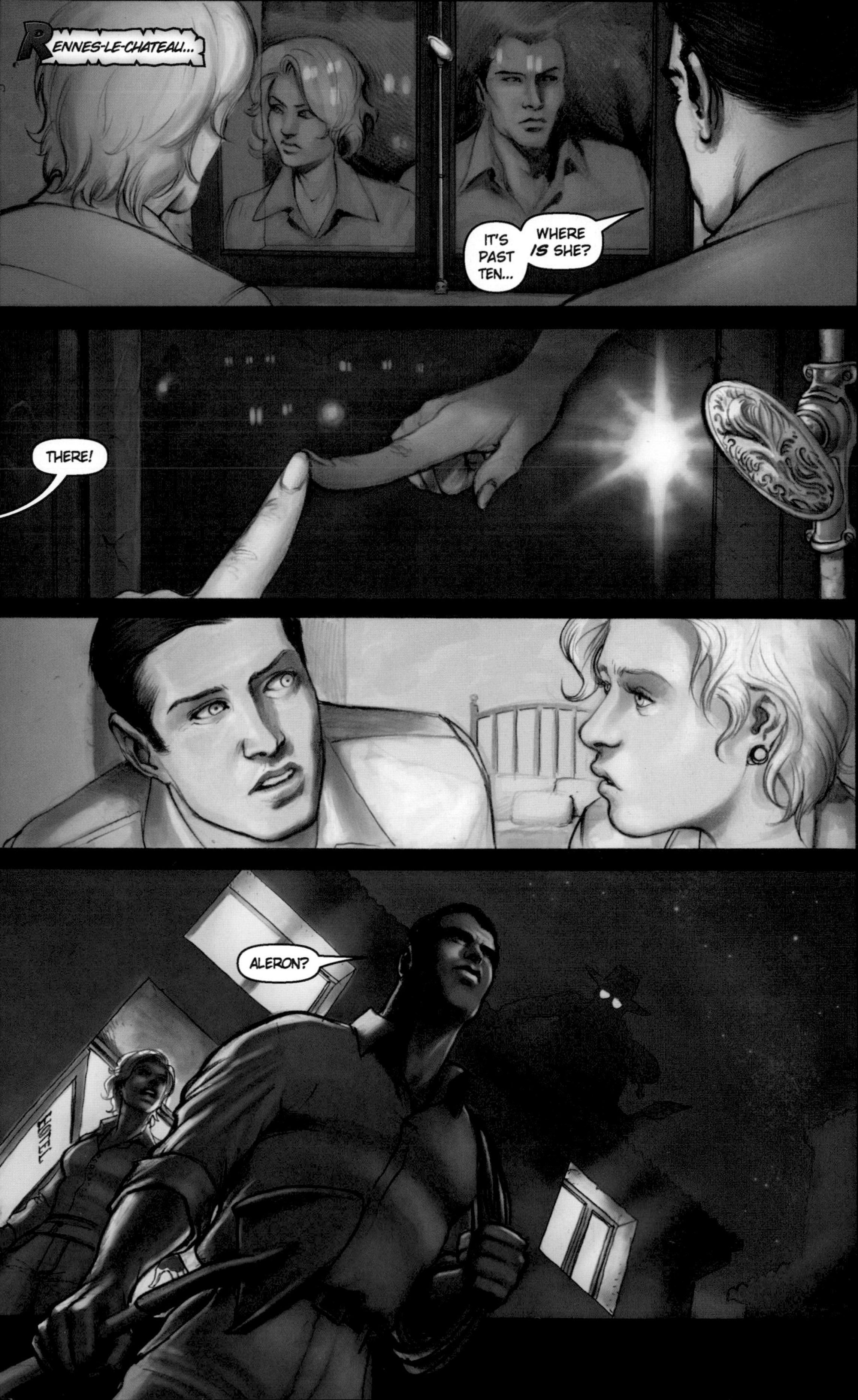
RENNES-LE-CHATEAU...
WHERE IS SHE?
IT'S PAST TEN...
THERE!
ALERON?
HOTEL

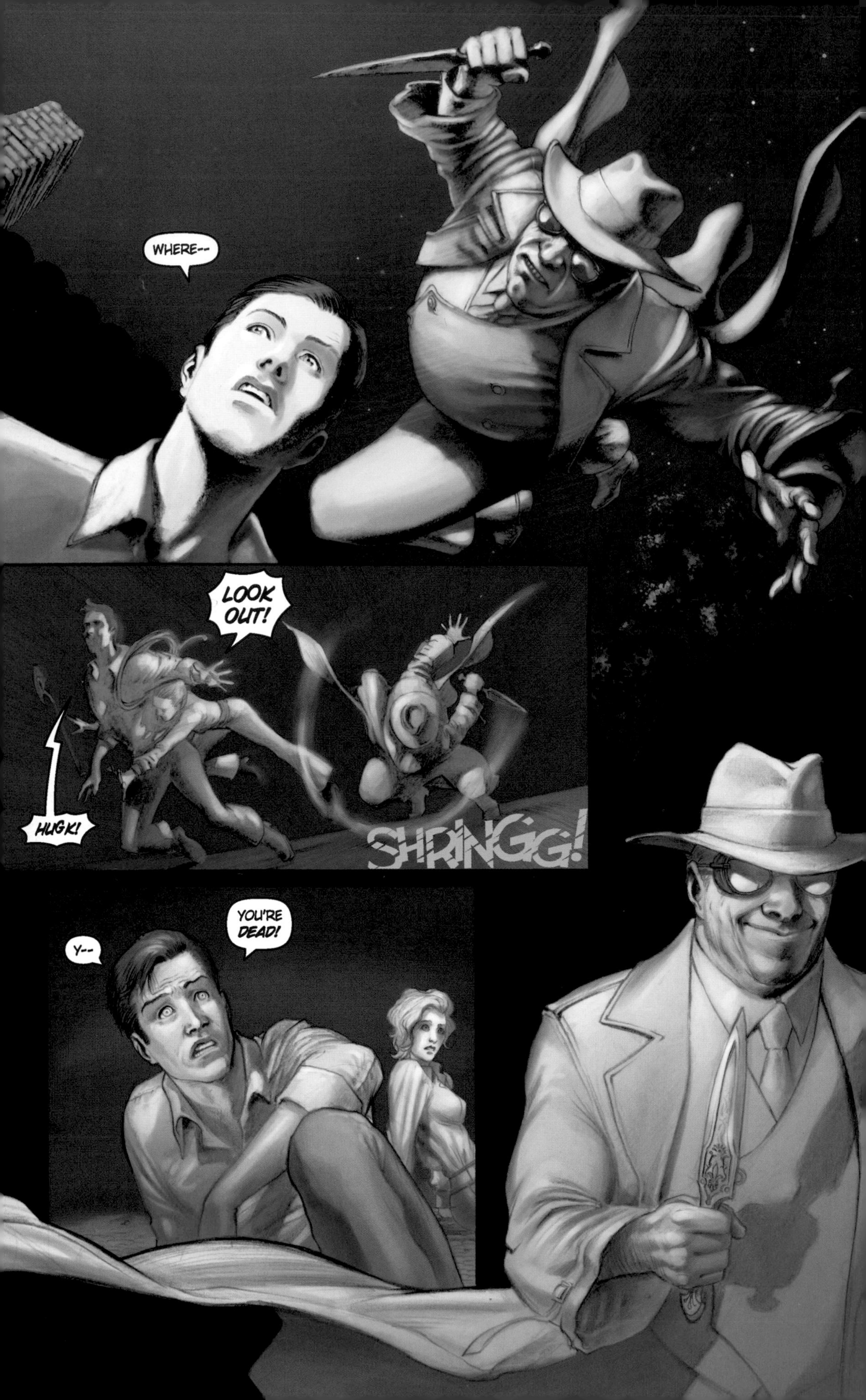
WHERE--
LOOK OUT!
HUGK!
SHRINGG!
Y--
YOU'RE DEAD!

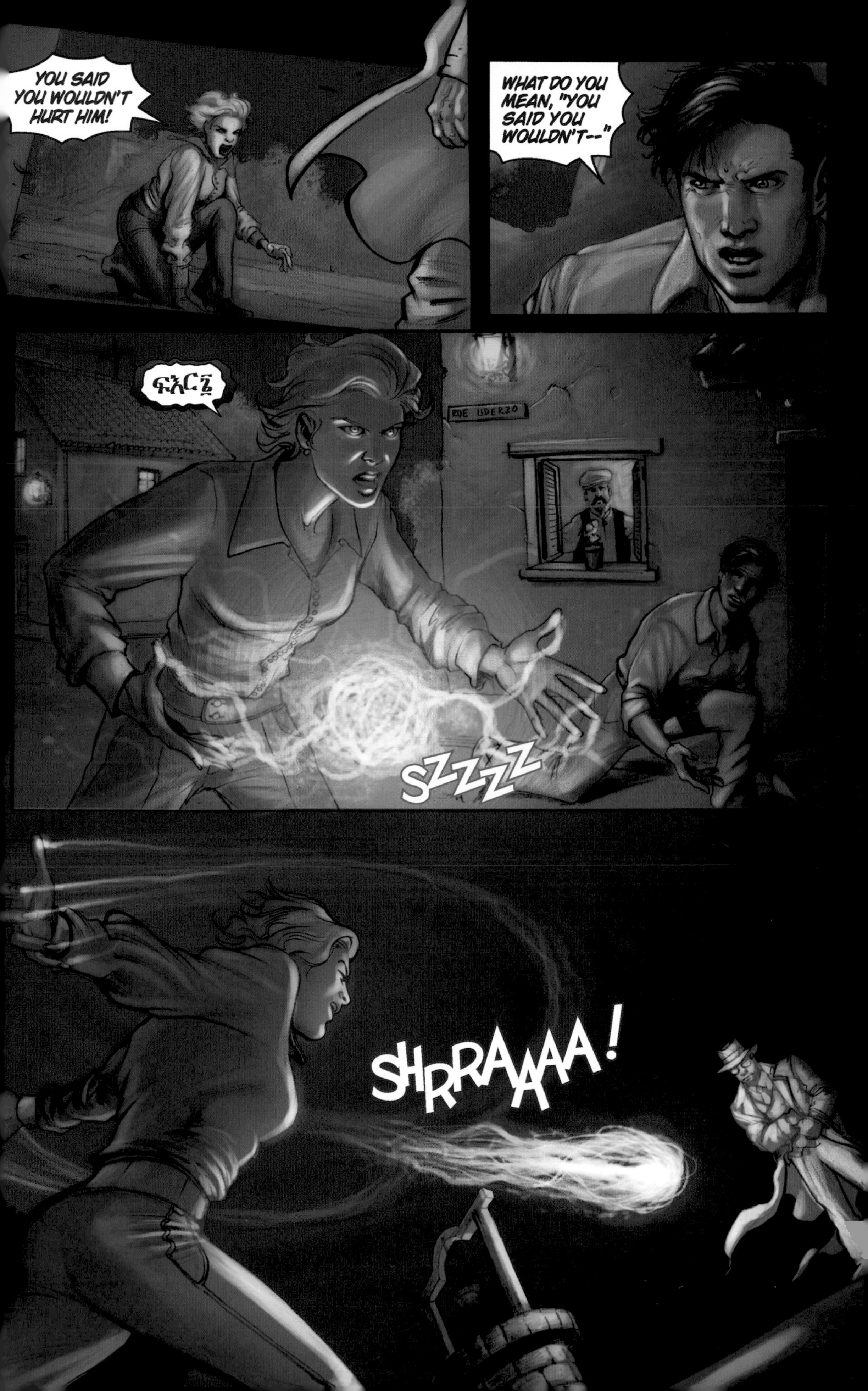
YOU SAID YOU WOULDN'T HURT HIM!
WHAT DO YOU MEAN, "YOU SAID YOU WOULDN'T--"
ፍእርቜ
RUE UDERZO
SZZZZZ
SHRRAAAA!

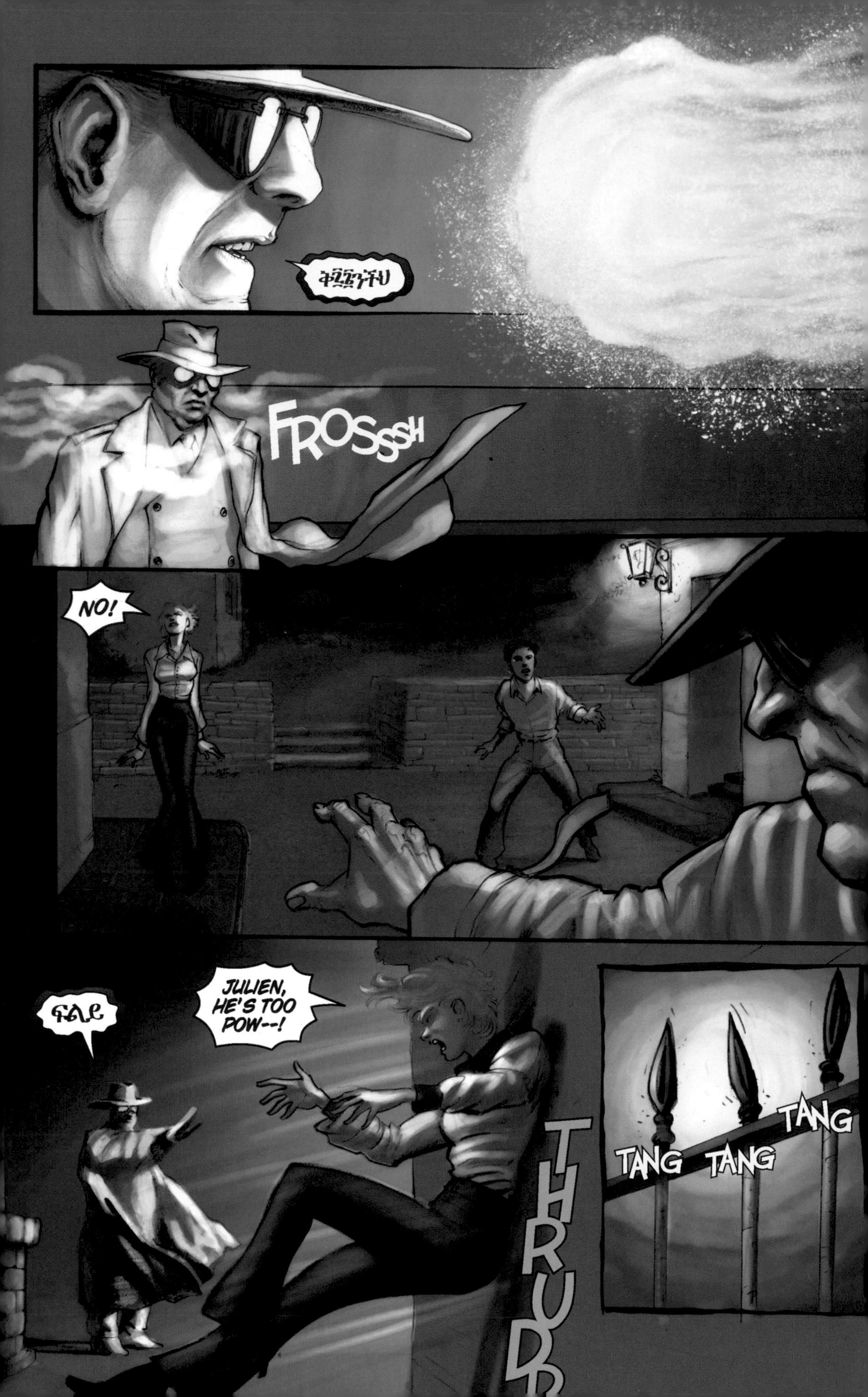
FROSSSH
NO!
JULIEN, HE'S TOO POW--!
THRUD
TANG TANG TANG

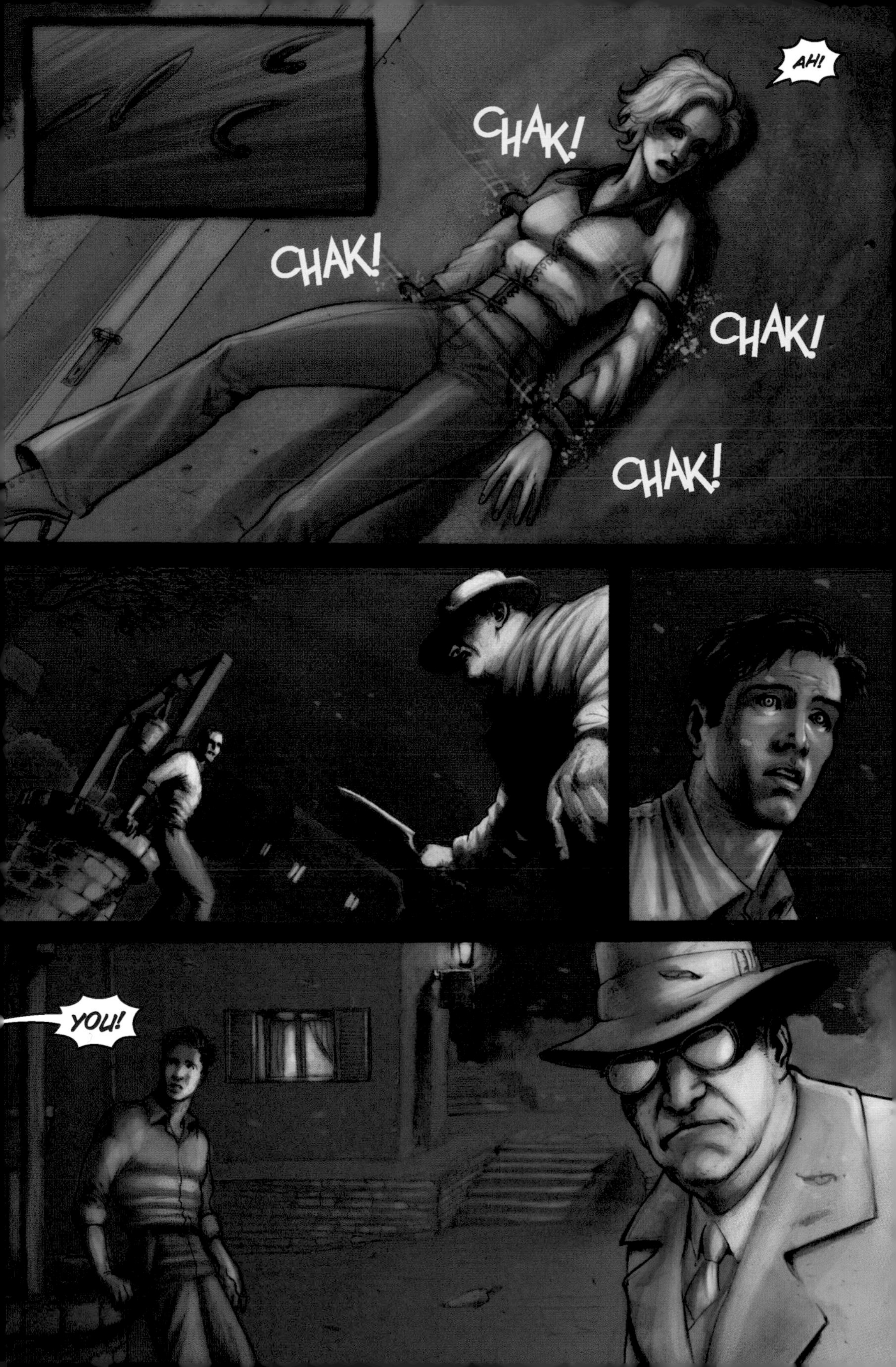
AH!
CHAK!
CHAK!
CHAK!
CHAK!
YOU!

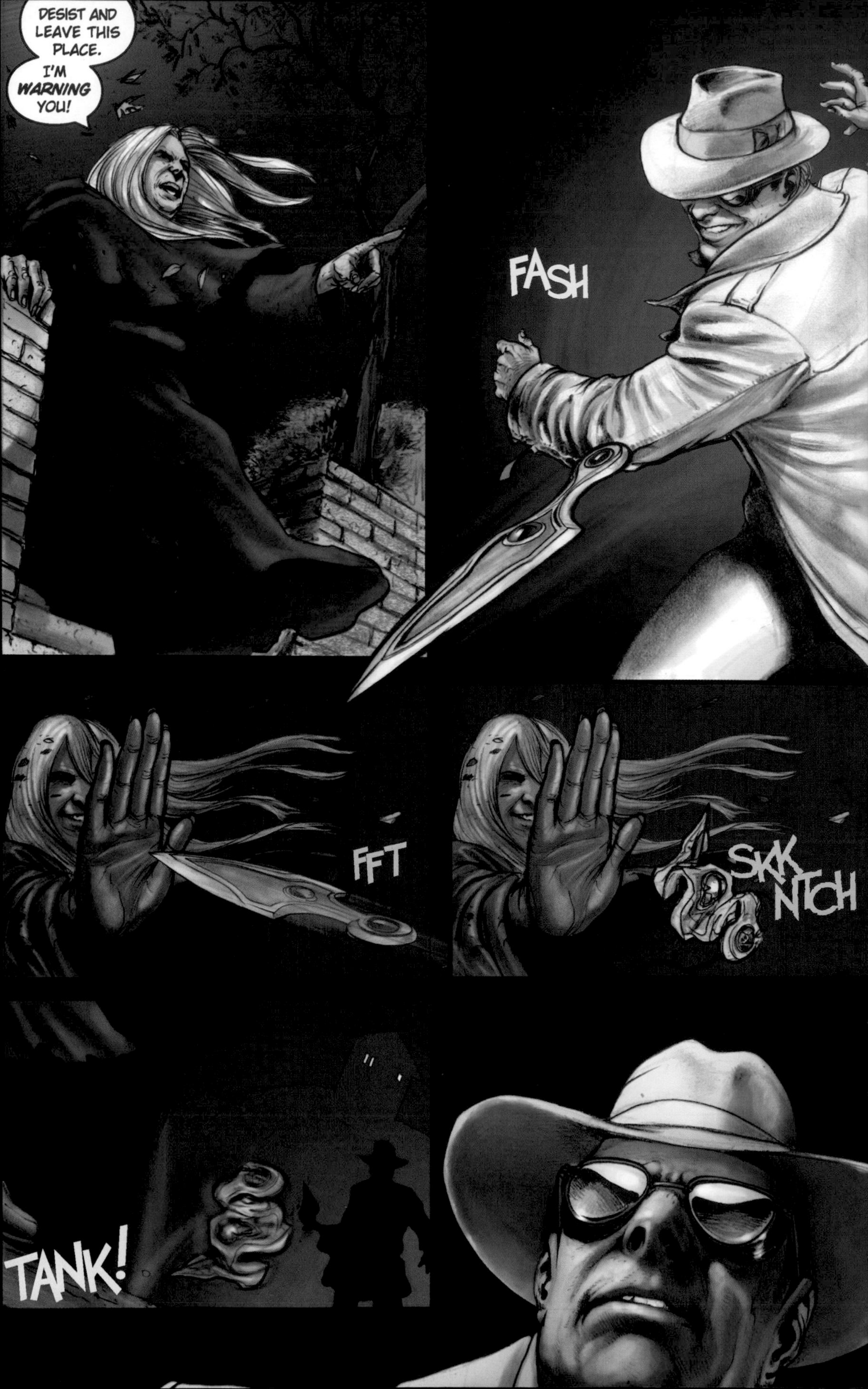
DESIST AND LEAVE THIS PLACE. I'M *WARNING* YOU!
FASH
FFT
SKK NTCH
TANK!

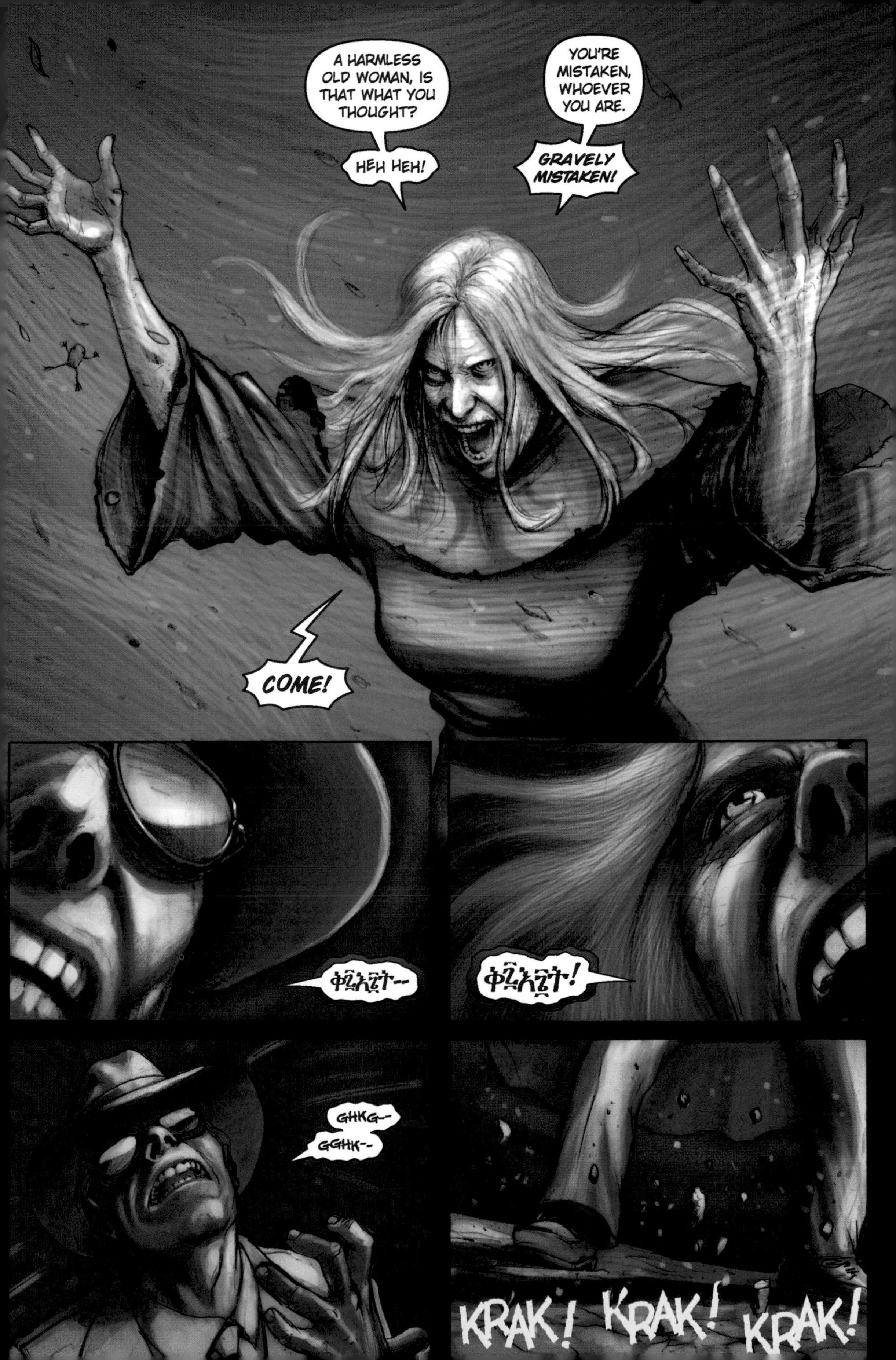
A HARMLESS OLD WOMAN, IS THAT WHAT YOU THOUGHT?
HEH HEH!
YOU'RE MISTAKEN, WHOEVER YOU ARE.
GRAVELY MISTAKEN!
COME!
GHKG--
GGHK--
KRAK! KRAK! KRAK!

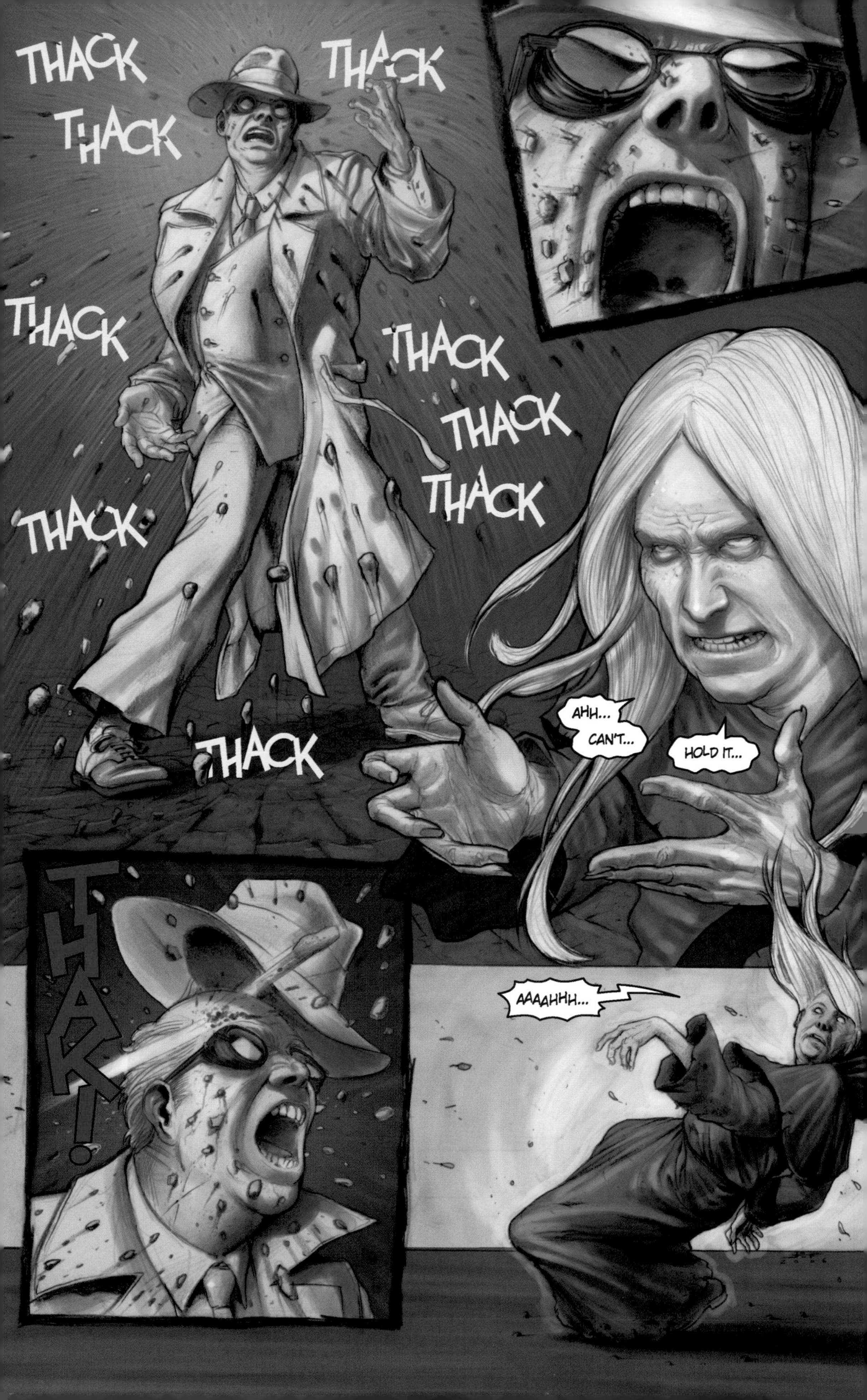
THACK
THACK
THACK
THACK
THACK
THACK
THACK
THACK
THACK
AHH...
CAN'T...
HOLD IT...
THAK!
AAAAHHH...

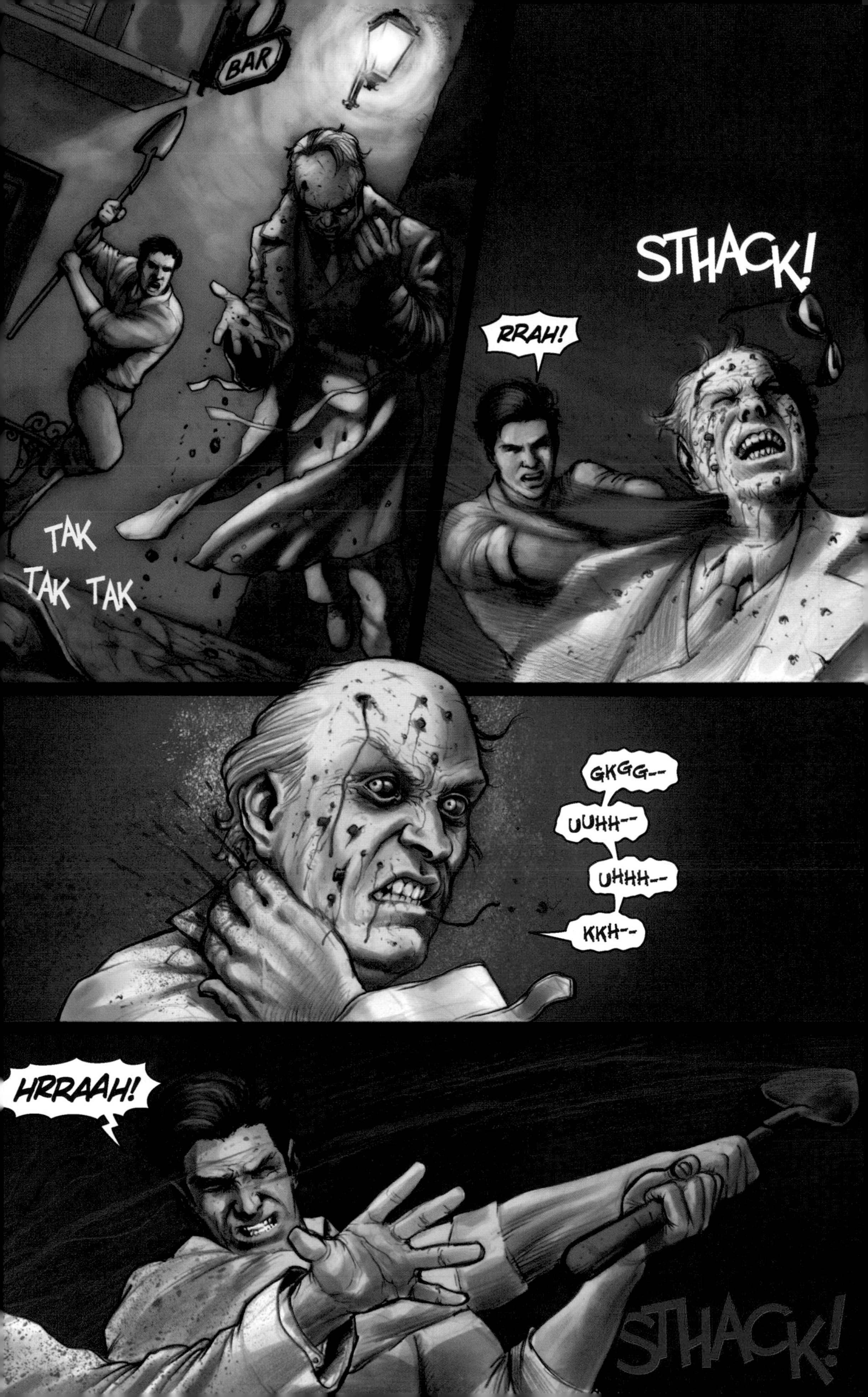
BAR
TAK
TAK TAK
STHACK!
RRAH!
GKGG--
UUHH--
UHHH--
KKH--
HRRAAH!
STHACK!

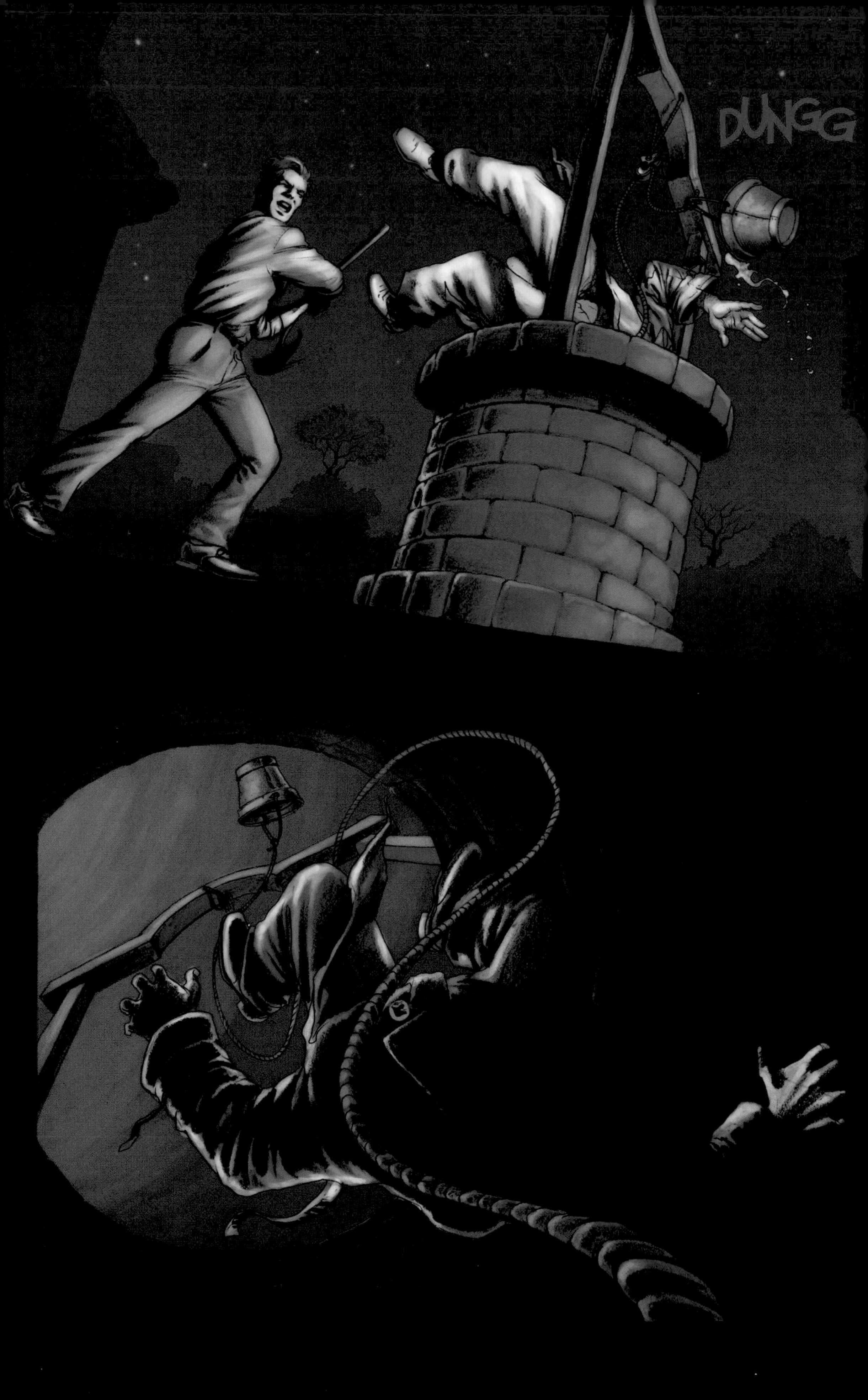
DUNGG

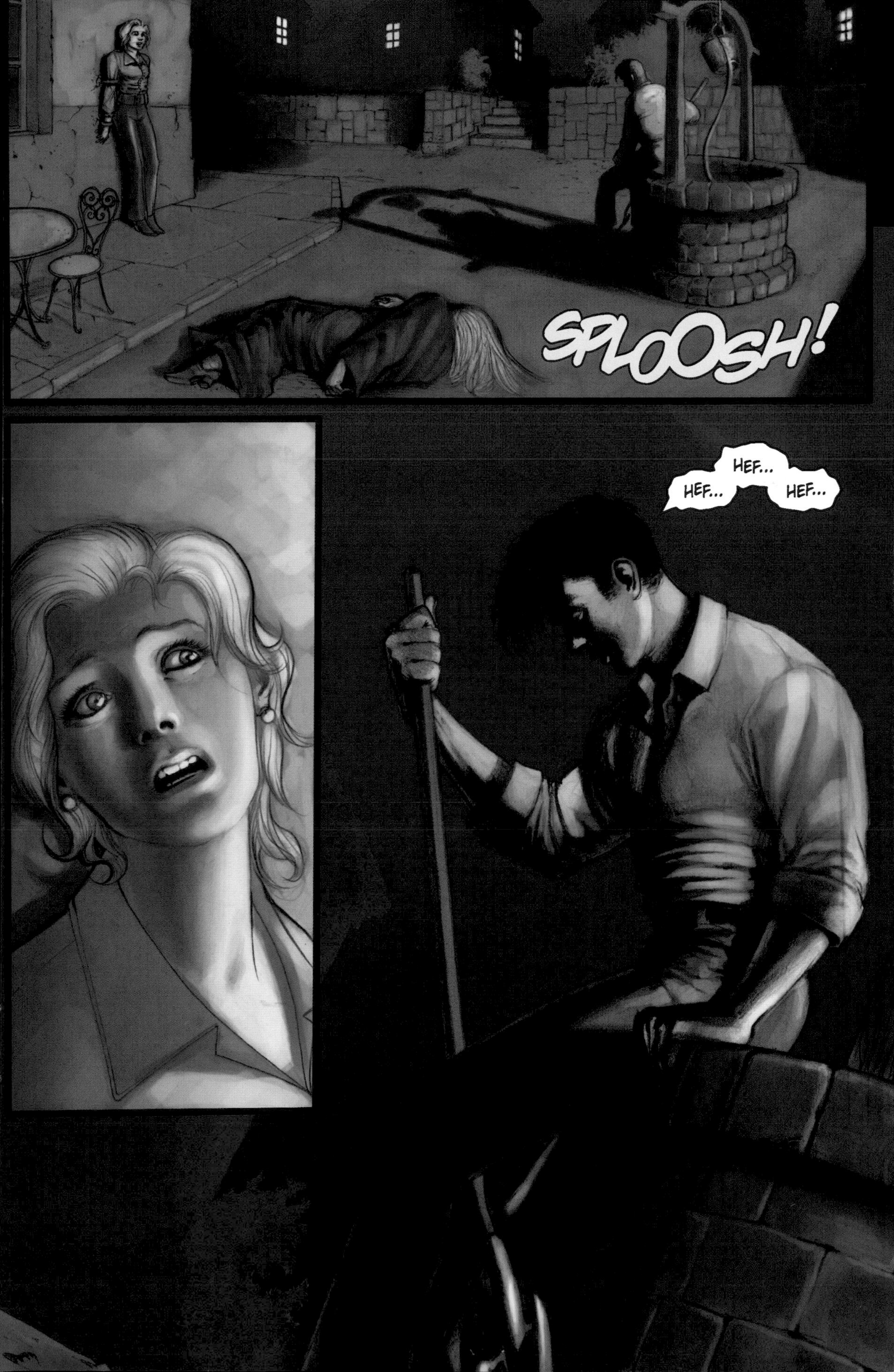
SPLOOSH!
HEF... HEF... HEF...

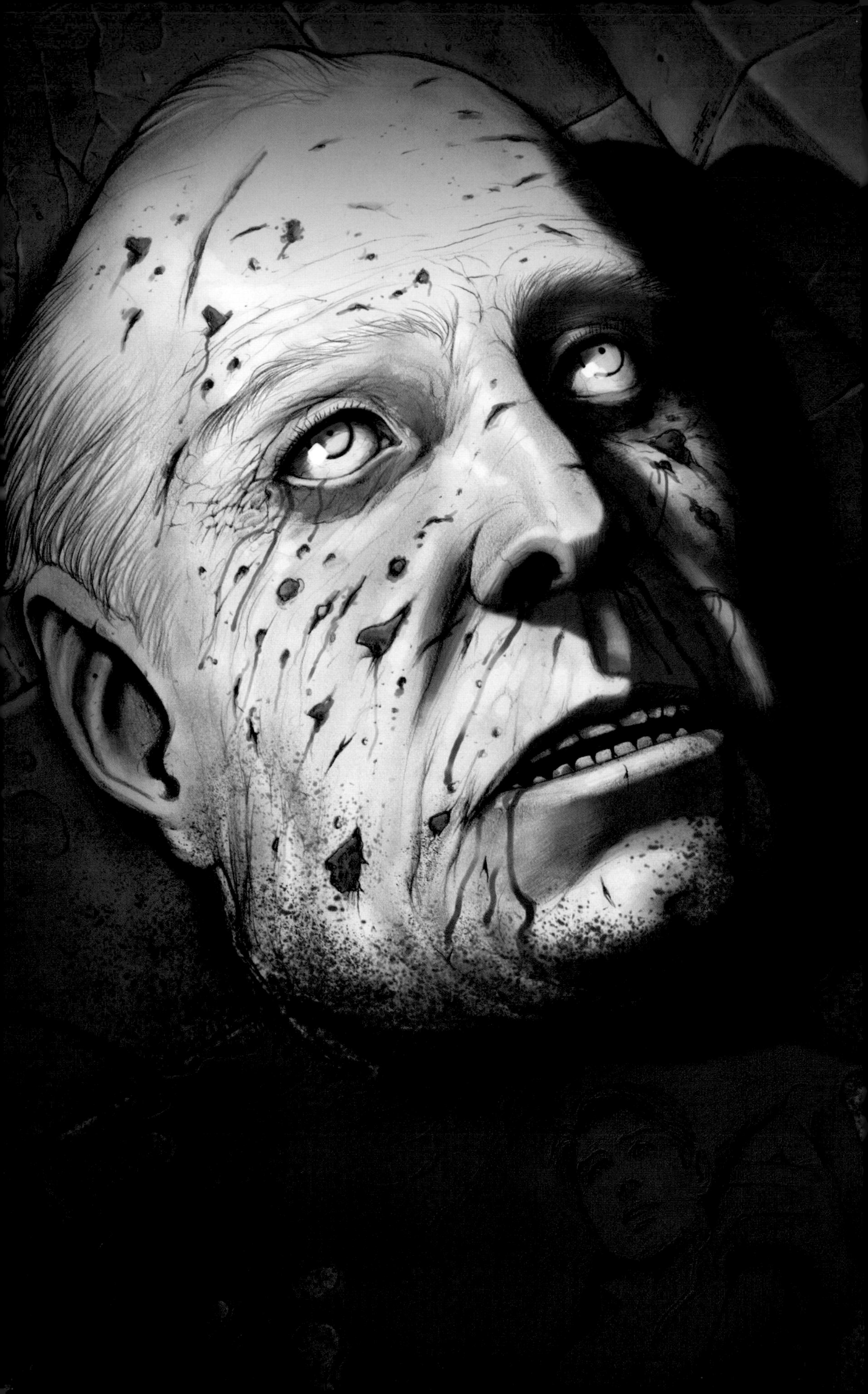

CHAPTER SIX
THE DESOLATION

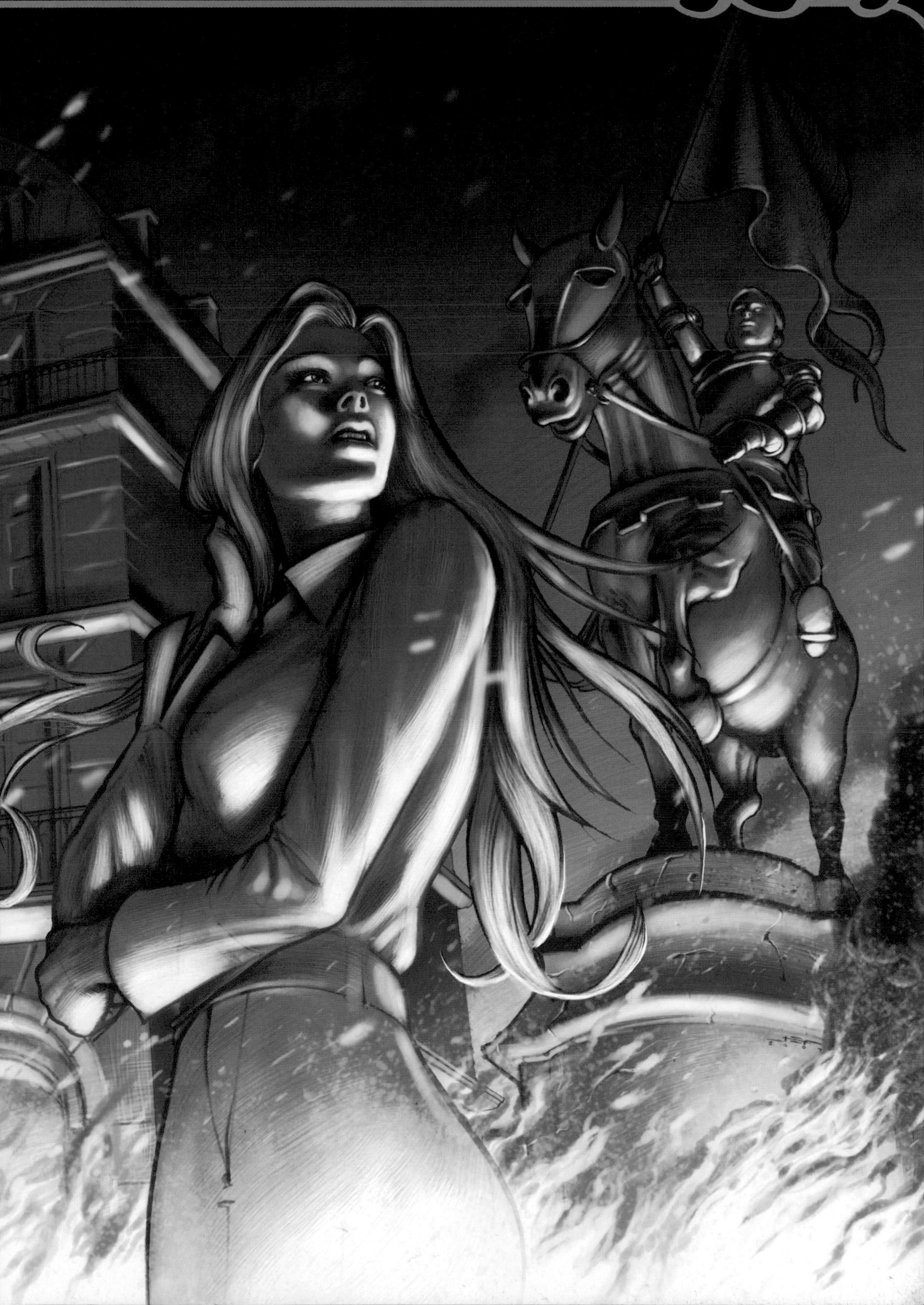

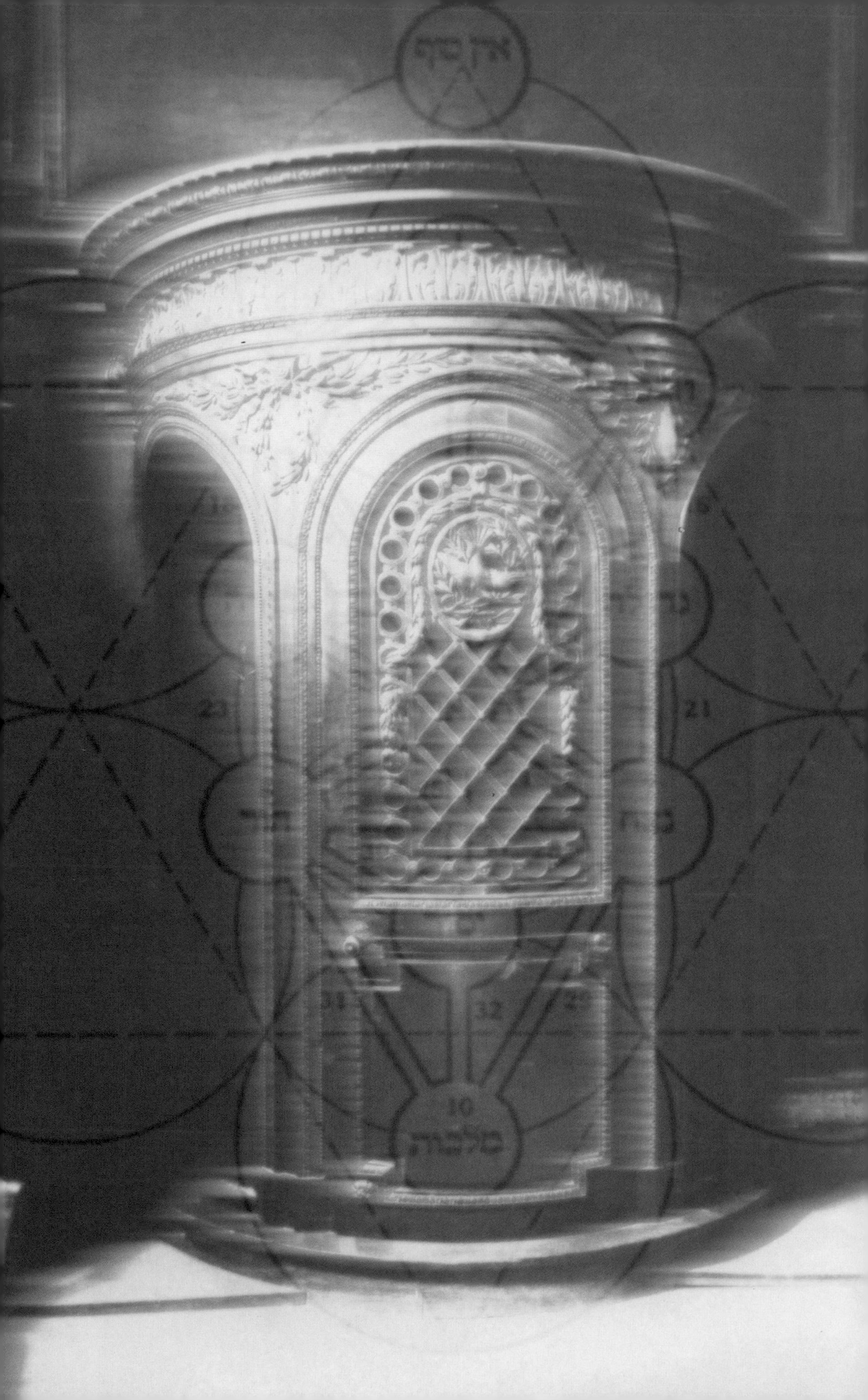
21
10
מלכות

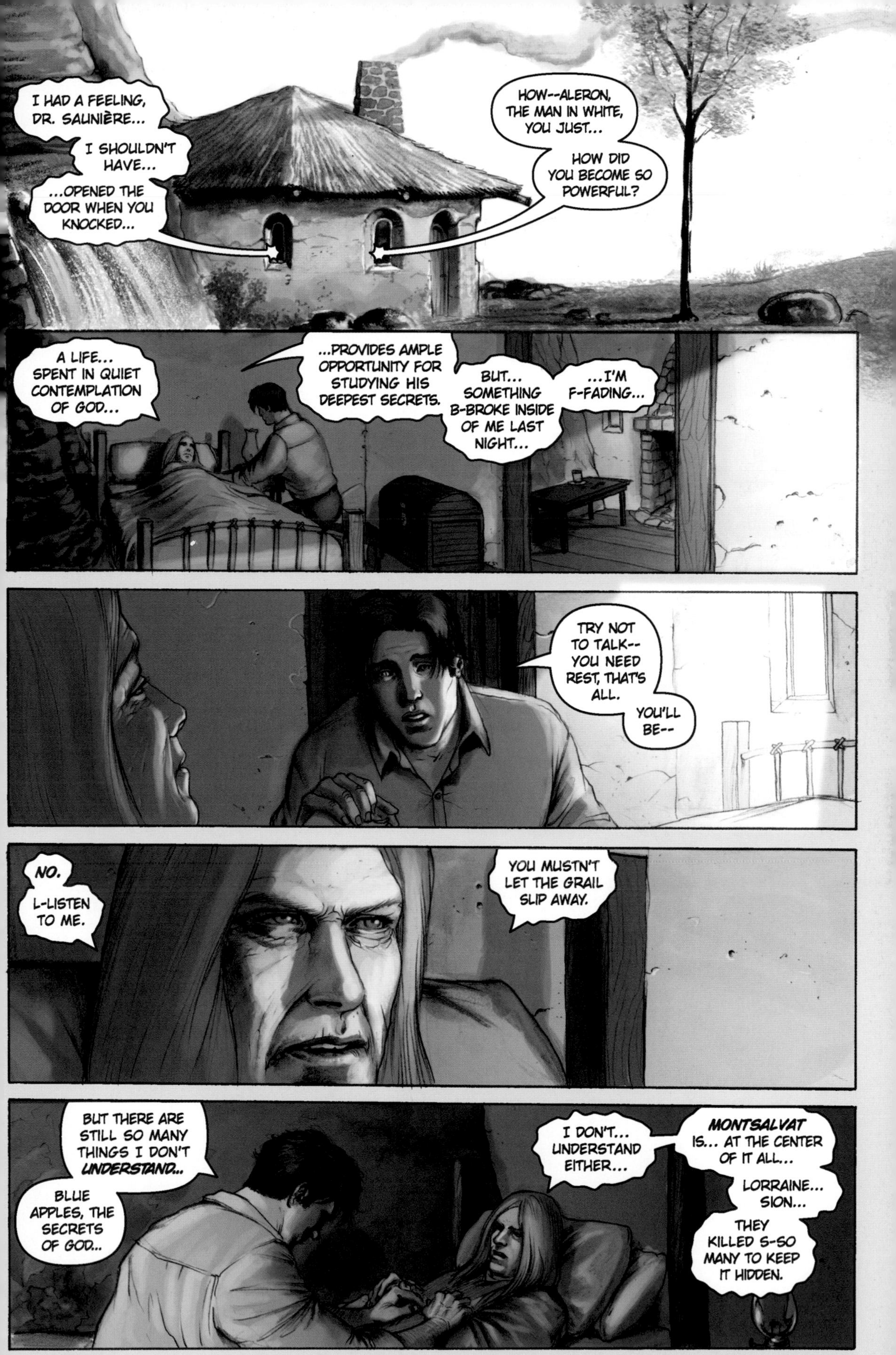
I HAD A FEELING, DR. SAUNIÈRE...
I SHOULDN'T HAVE...
...OPENED THE DOOR WHEN YOU KNOCKED...
HOW--ALERON, THE MAN IN WHITE, YOU JUST...
HOW DID YOU BECOME SO POWERFUL?
A LIFE... SPENT IN QUIET CONTEMPLATION OF GOD...
...PROVIDES AMPLE OPPORTUNITY FOR STUDYING HIS DEEPEST SECRETS.
BUT... SOMETHING B-BROKE INSIDE OF ME LAST NIGHT...
...I'M F-FADING...
TRY NOT TO TALK--YOU NEED REST, THAT'S ALL.
YOU'LL BE--
NO.
L-LISTEN TO ME.
YOU MUSTN'T LET THE GRAIL SLIP AWAY.
BUT THERE ARE STILL SO MANY THINGS I DON'T UNDERSTAND...
BLUE APPLES, THE SECRETS OF GOD...
I DON'T... UNDERSTAND EITHER...
MONTSALVAT IS... AT THE CENTER OF IT ALL...
LORRAINE... SION...
THEY KILLED S-SO MANY TO KEEP IT HIDDEN.

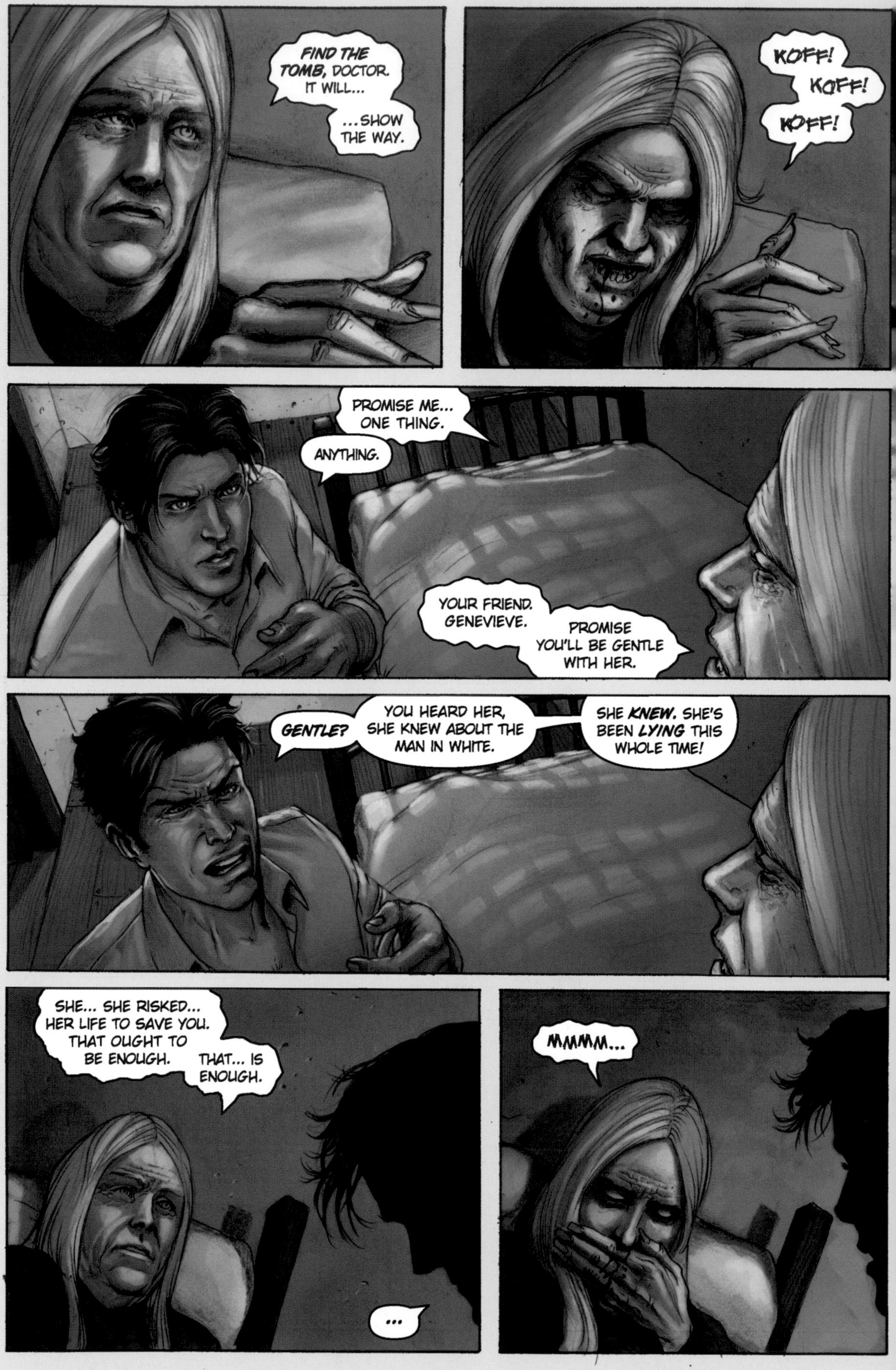
FIND THE TOMB, DOCTOR. IT WILL...
...SHOW THE WAY.
KOFF! KOFF! KOFF!
PROMISE ME... ONE THING.
ANYTHING.
YOUR FRIEND. GENEVIEVE.
PROMISE YOU'LL BE GENTLE WITH HER.
GENTLE?
YOU HEARD HER, SHE KNEW ABOUT THE MAN IN WHITE.
SHE KNEW. SHE'S BEEN LYING THIS WHOLE TIME!
SHE... SHE RISKED... HER LIFE TO SAVE YOU. THAT OUGHT TO BE ENOUGH.
THAT... IS ENOUGH.
...
MMMM...

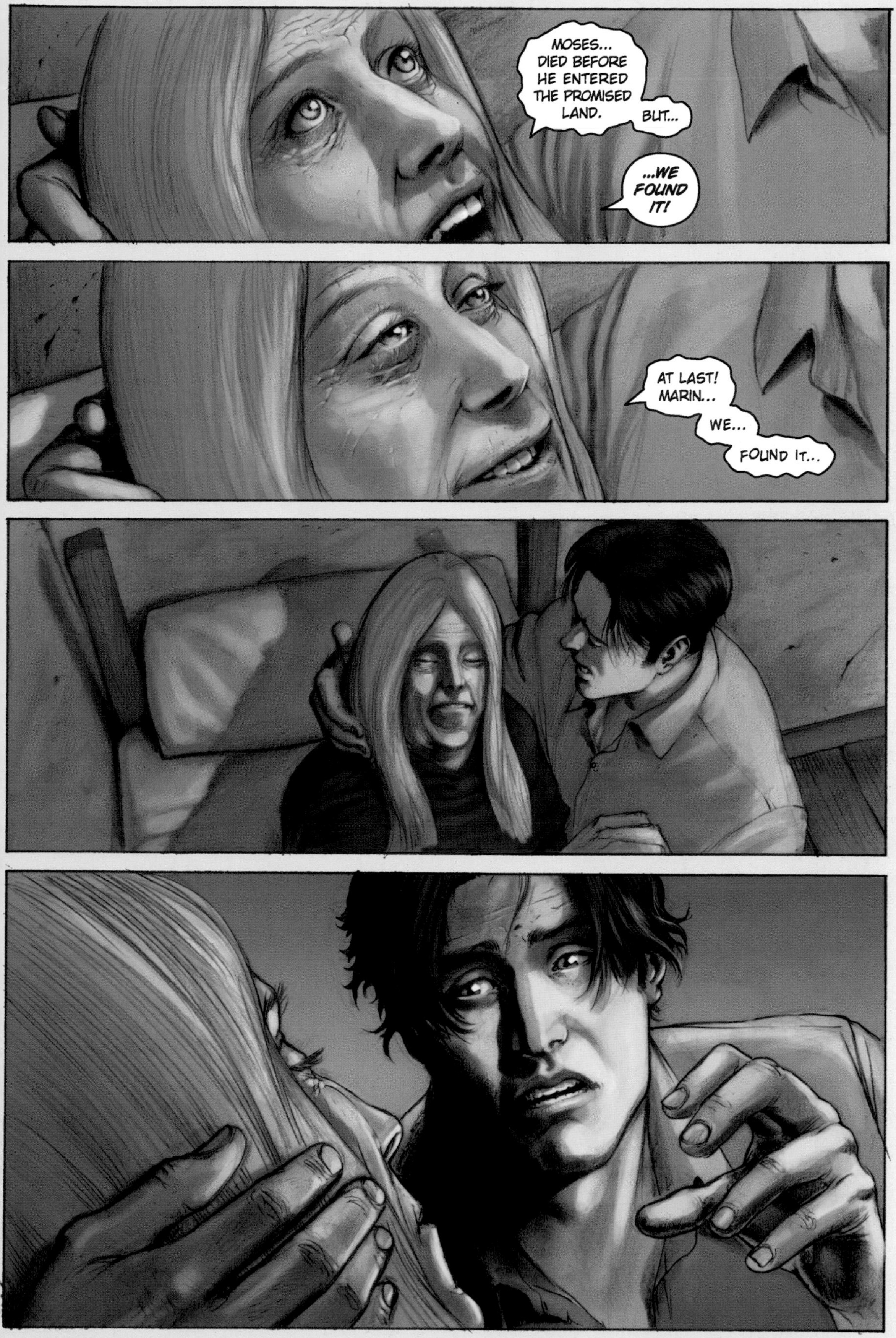
MOSES... DIED BEFORE HE ENTERED THE PROMISED LAND.
BUT...
...WE FOUND IT!
AT LAST! MARIN...
WE...
FOUND IT...

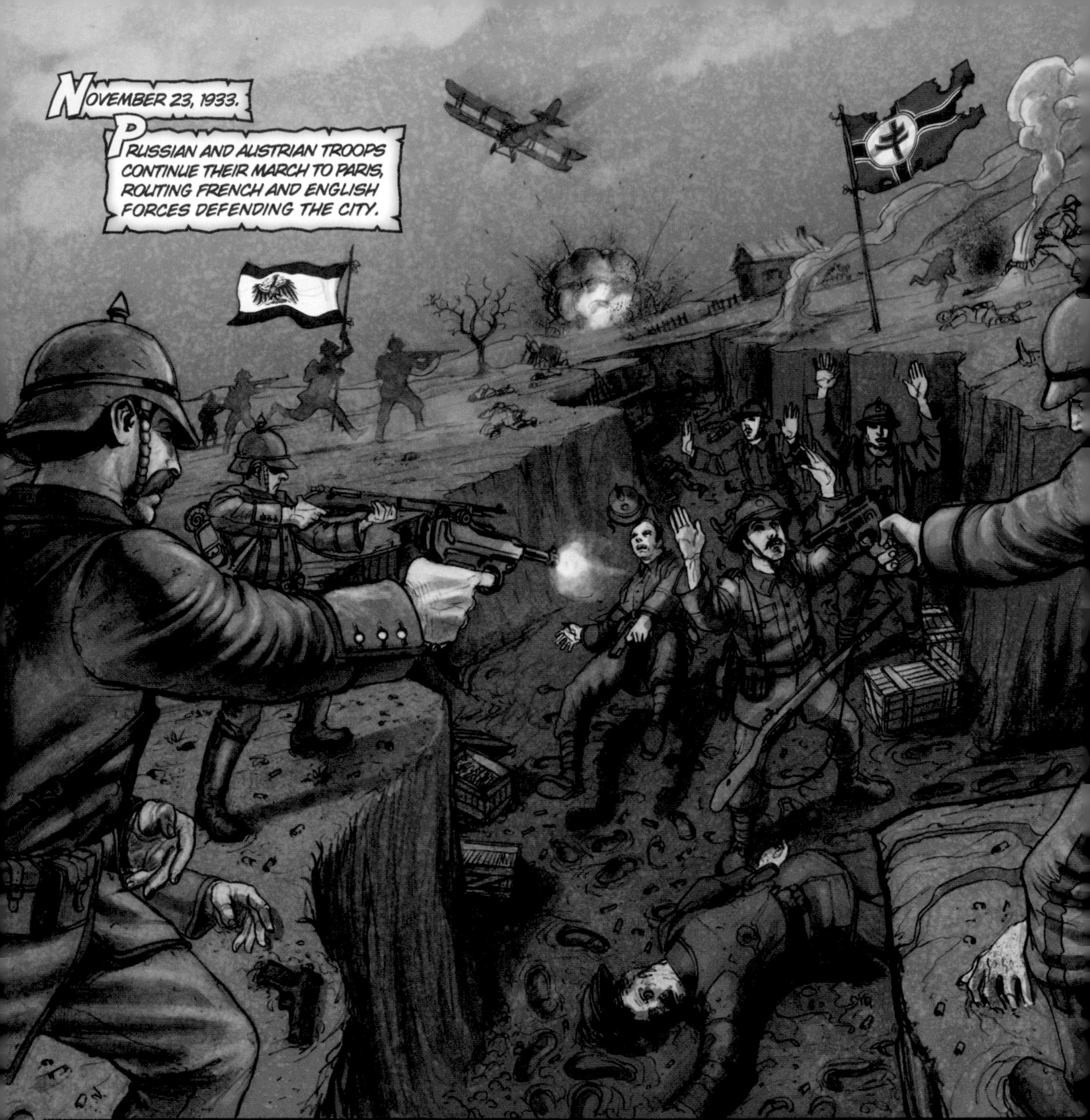
NOVEMBER 23, 1933.
PRUSSIAN AND AUSTRIAN TROOPS CONTINUE THEIR MARCH TO PARIS, ROUTING FRENCH AND ENGLISH FORCES DEFENDING THE CITY.

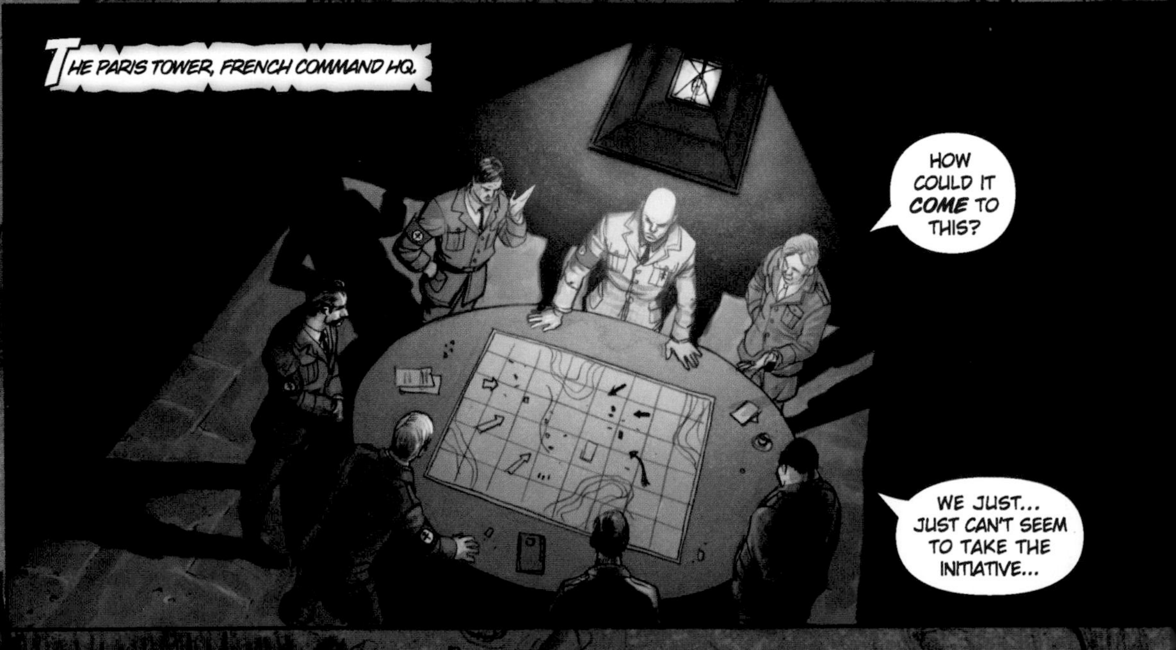
THE PARIS TOWER, FRENCH COMMAND HQ.
HOW COULD IT COME TO THIS?
WE JUST... JUST CAN'T SEEM TO TAKE THE INITIATIVE...

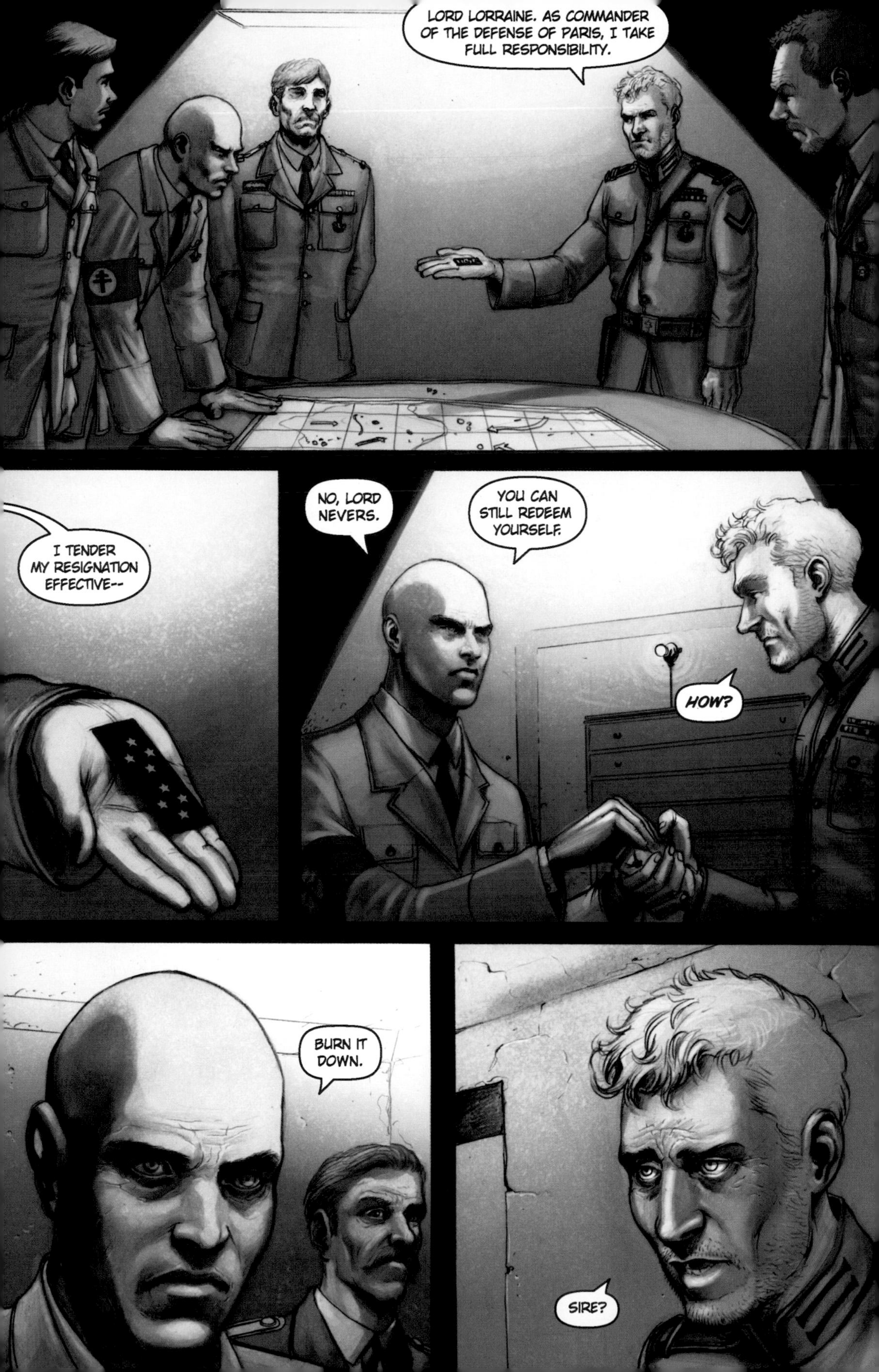

LORD LORRAINE. AS COMMANDER OF THE DEFENSE OF PARIS, I TAKE FULL RESPONSIBILITY.
I TENDER MY RESIGNATION EFFECTIVE--
NO, LORD NEVERS.
YOU CAN STILL REDEEM YOURSELF.
HOW?
BURN IT DOWN.
SIRE?

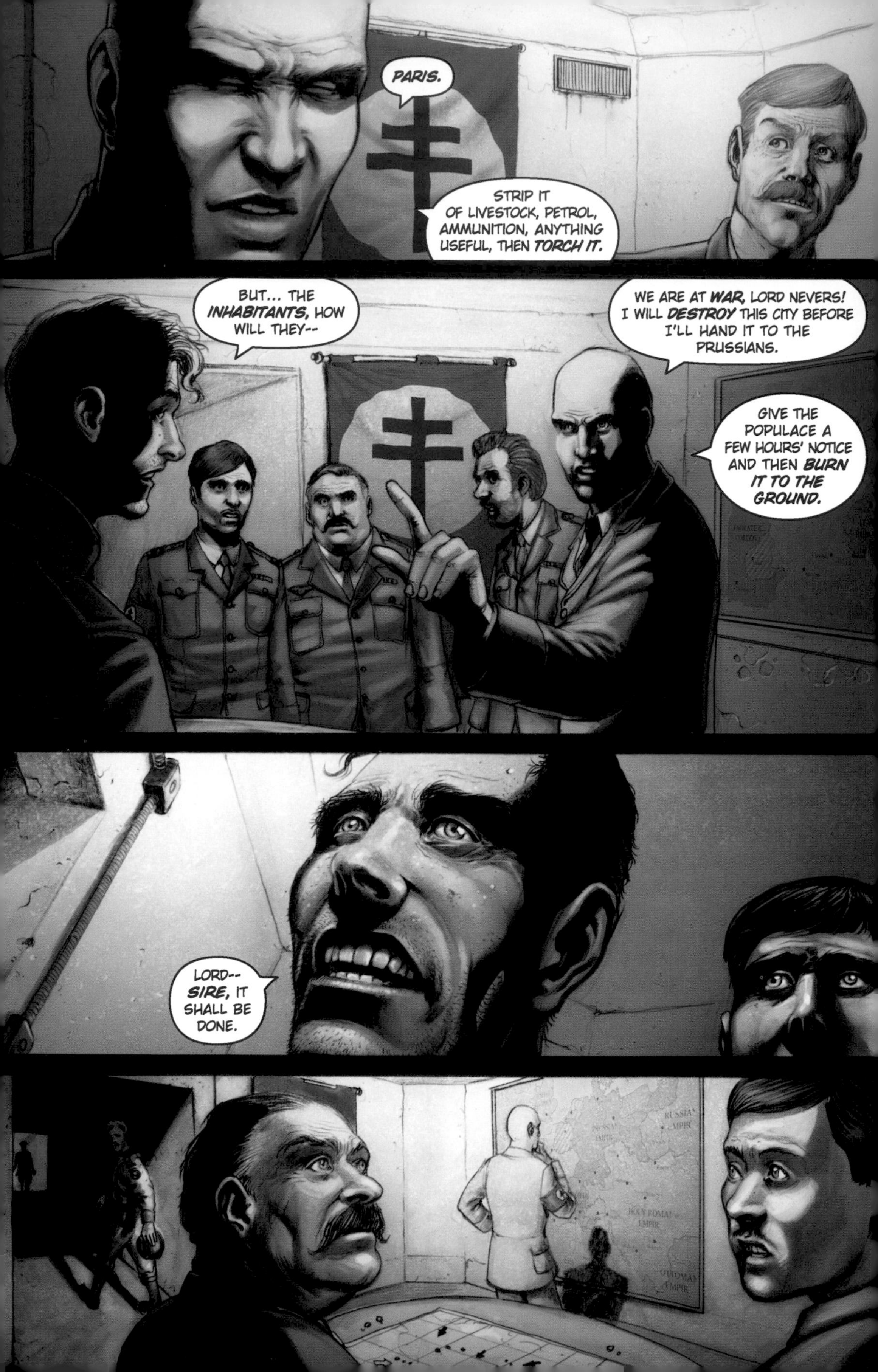
PARIS.
STRIP IT OF LIVESTOCK, PETROL, AMMUNITION, ANYTHING USEFUL, THEN TORCH IT.
BUT... THE INHABITANTS, HOW WILL THEY--
WE ARE AT WAR, LORD NEVERS! I WILL DESTROY THIS CITY BEFORE I'LL HAND IT TO THE PRUSSIANS.
GIVE THE POPULACE A FEW HOURS' NOTICE AND THEN BURN IT TO THE GROUND.
LORD-- SIRE, IT SHALL BE DONE.
RUSSIAN EMPIRE
PRUSSIAN EMPIRE
HOLY ROMAN EMPIRE
OTTOMAN EMPIRE

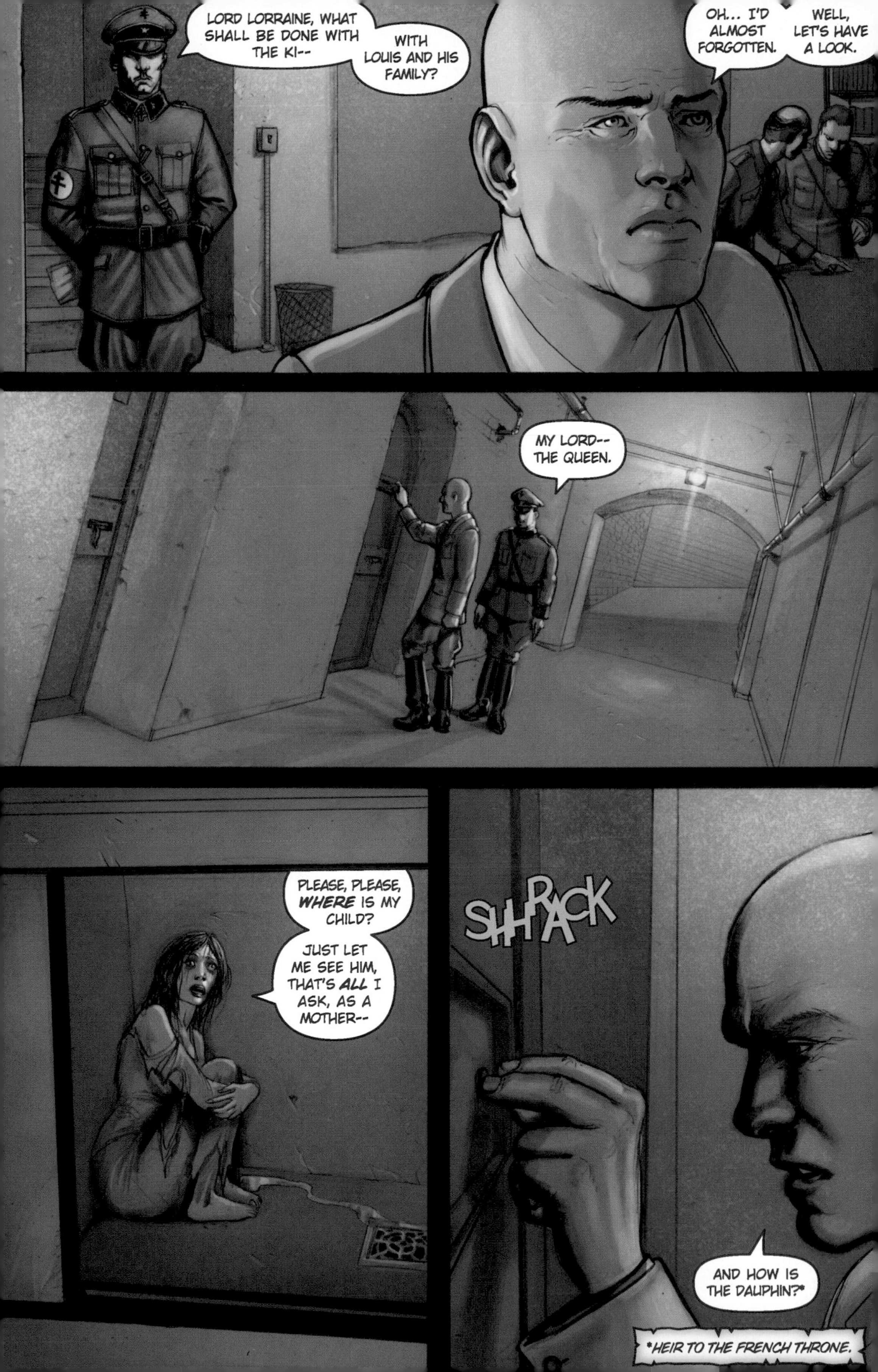

LORD LORRAINE, WHAT SHALL BE DONE WITH THE KI--
WITH LOUIS AND HIS FAMILY?
OH... I'D ALMOST FORGOTTEN.
WELL, LET'S HAVE A LOOK.
MY LORD-- THE QUEEN.
PLEASE, PLEASE, *WHERE* IS MY CHILD?
JUST LET ME SEE HIM, THAT'S *ALL* I ASK, AS A MOTHER--
SHHRACK
AND HOW IS THE DAUPHIN?*
*HEIR TO THE FRENCH THRONE.

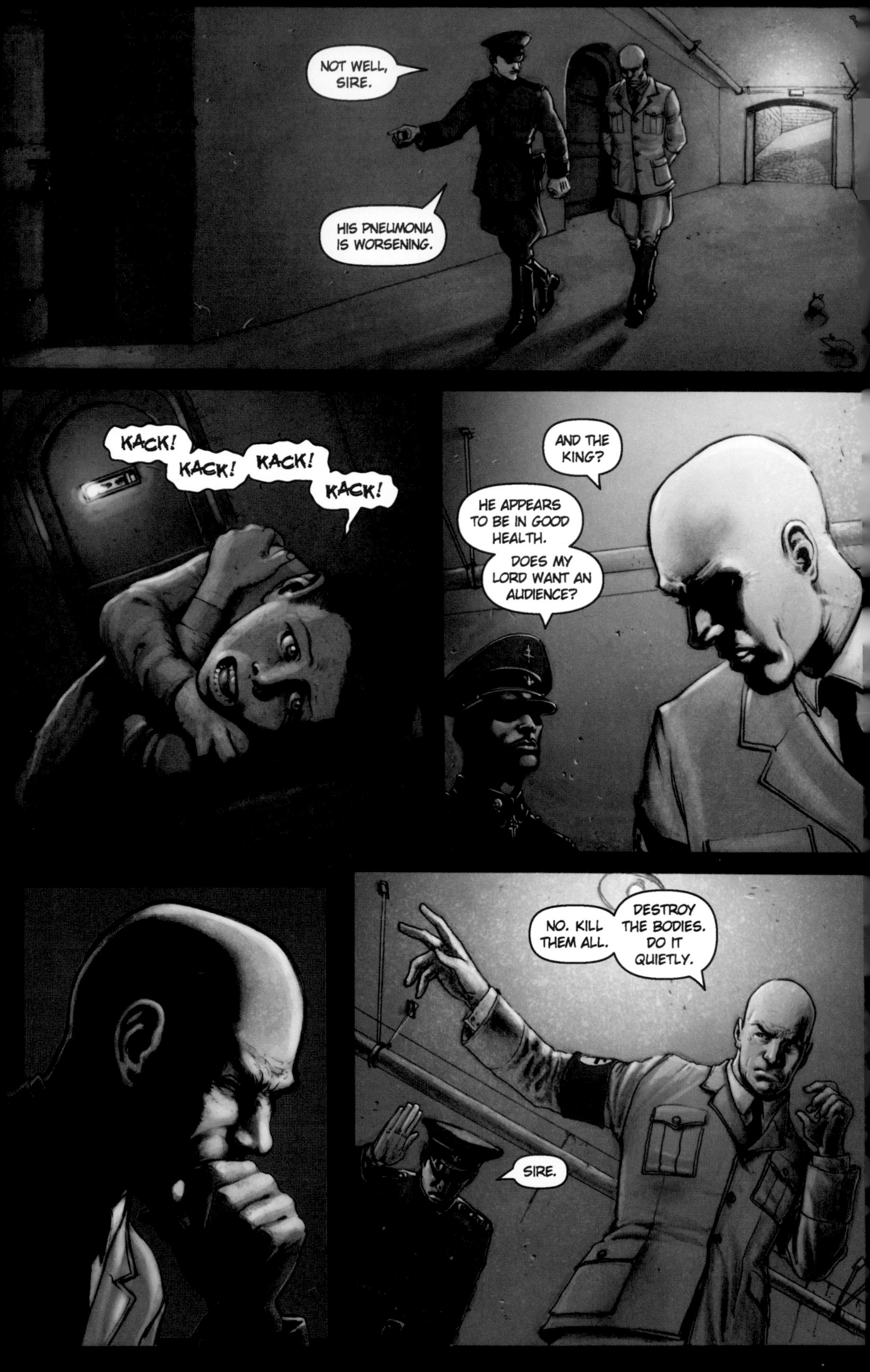
NOT WELL, SIRE.
HIS PNEUMONIA IS WORSENING.
KACK!
KACK!
KACK!
KACK!
AND THE KING?
HE APPEARS TO BE IN GOOD HEALTH.
DOES MY LORD WANT AN AUDIENCE?
NO. KILL THEM ALL.
DESTROY THE BODIES. DO IT QUIETLY.
SIRE.

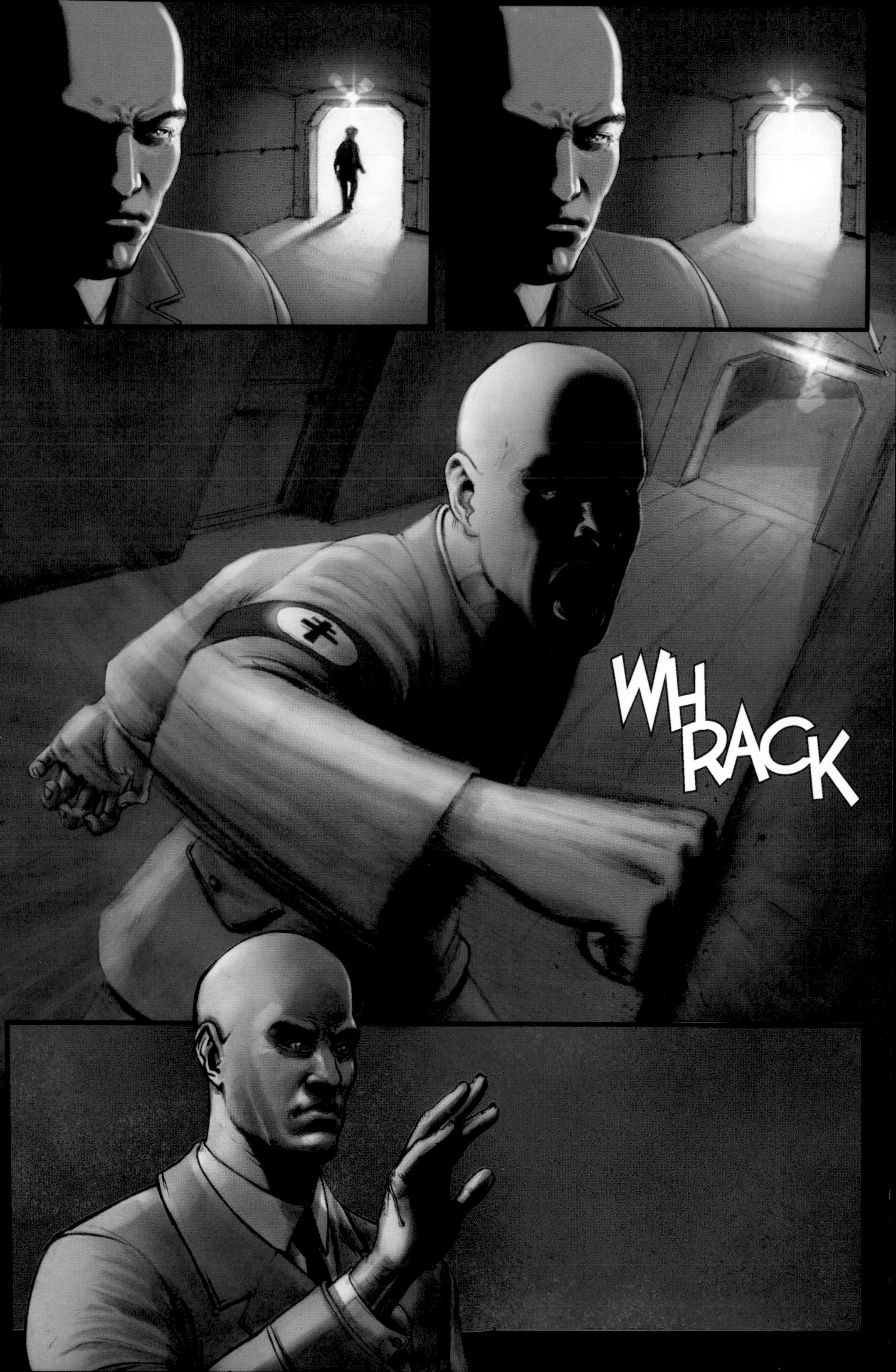
WHRACK

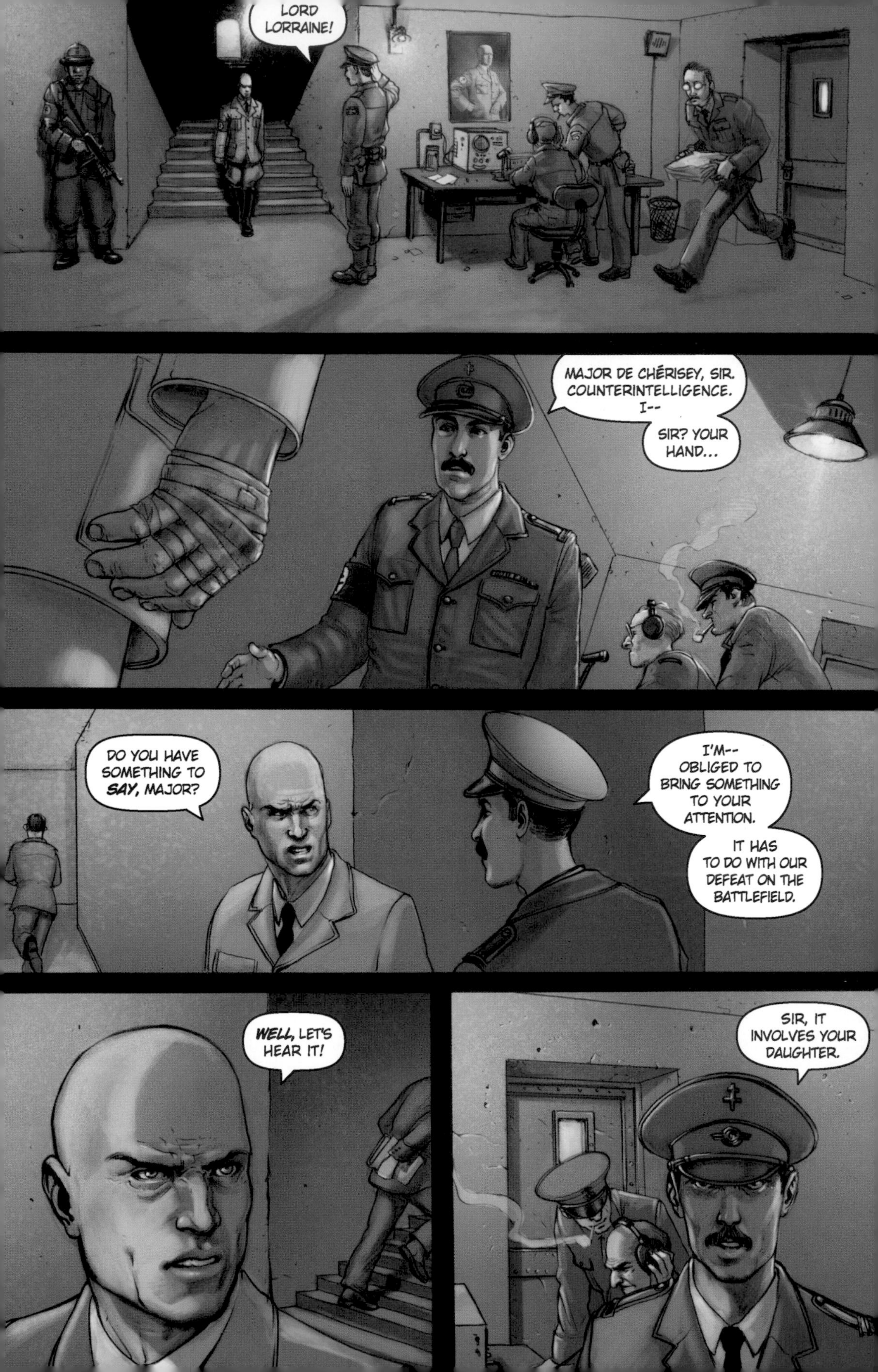
LORD LORRAINE!
MAJOR DE CHÉRISEY, SIR. COUNTERINTELLIGENCE. I--
SIR? YOUR HAND...
DO YOU HAVE SOMETHING TO SAY, MAJOR?
I'M-- OBLIGED TO BRING SOMETHING TO YOUR ATTENTION.
IT HAS TO DO WITH OUR DEFEAT ON THE BATTLEFIELD.
WELL, LET'S HEAR IT!
SIR, IT INVOLVES YOUR DAUGHTER.

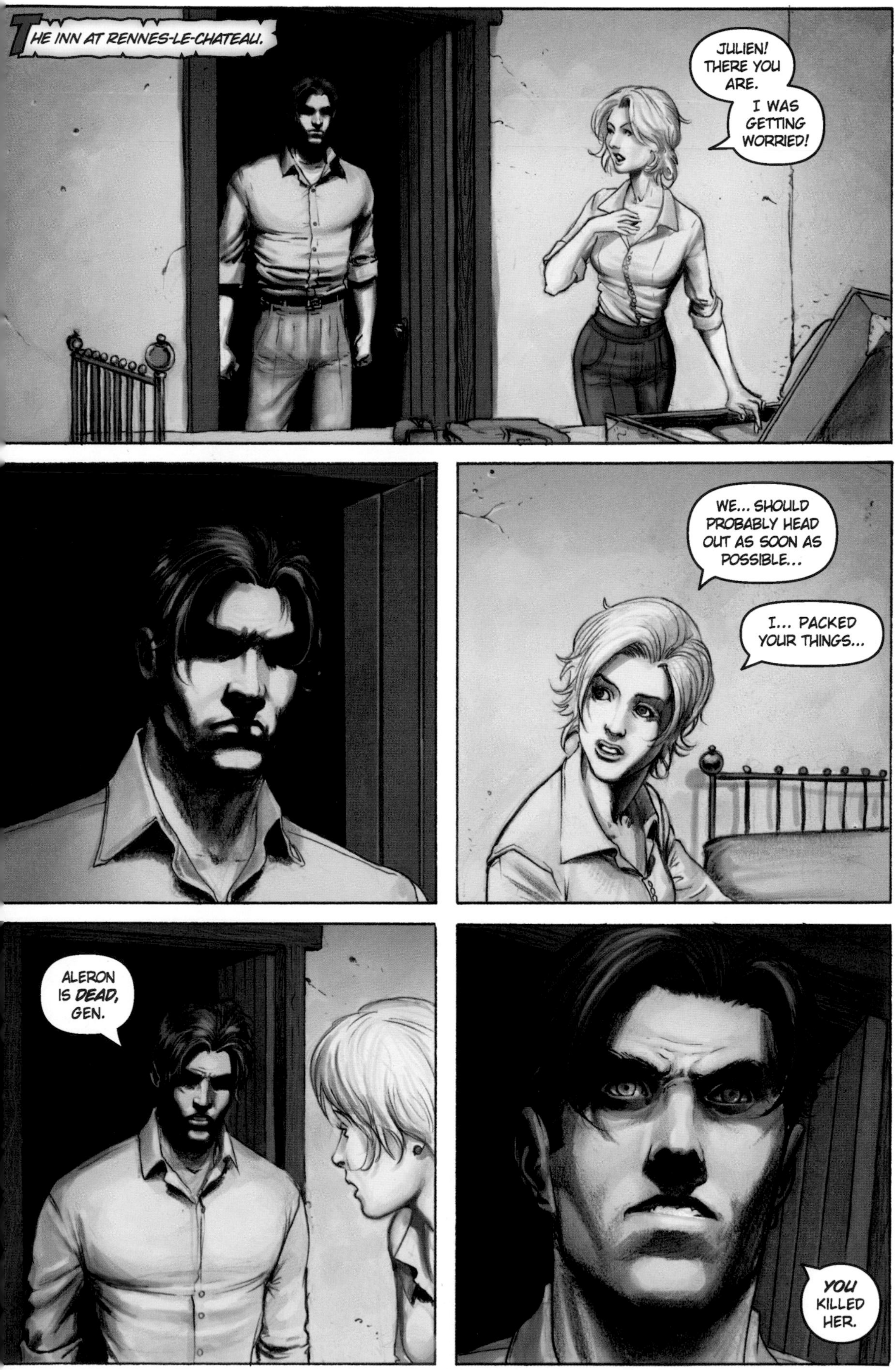
THE INN AT RENNES-LE-CHATEAU.
JULIEN! THERE YOU ARE.
I WAS GETTING WORRIED!
WE... SHOULD PROBABLY HEAD OUT AS SOON AS POSSIBLE...
I... PACKED YOUR THINGS...
ALERON IS DEAD, GEN.
YOU KILLED HER.

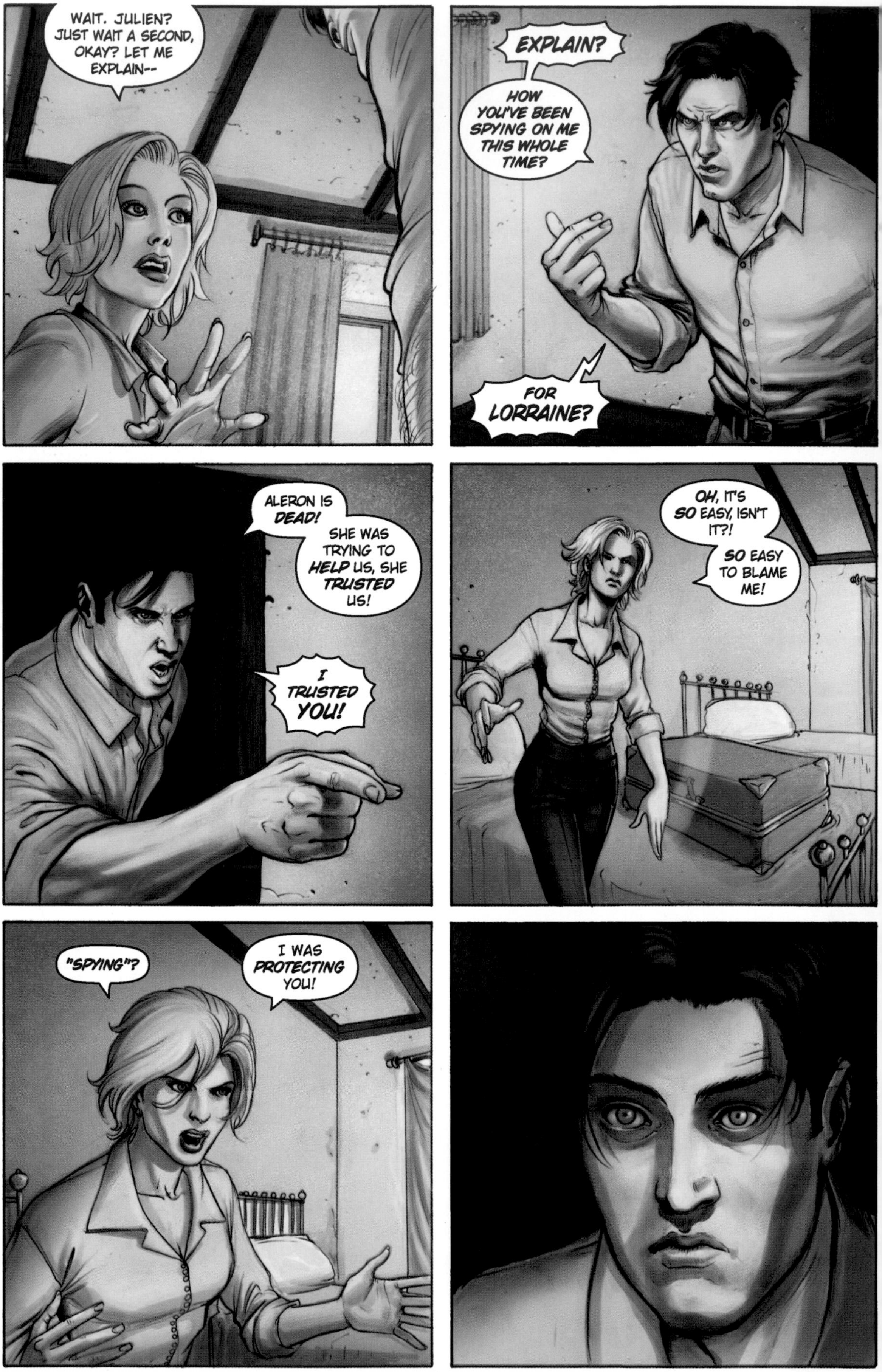
WAIT. JULIEN? JUST WAIT A SECOND, OKAY? LET ME EXPLAIN--
EXPLAIN?
HOW YOU'VE BEEN SPYING ON ME THIS WHOLE TIME?
FOR LORRAINE?
ALERON IS DEAD!
SHE WAS TRYING TO HELP US, SHE TRUSTED US!
I TRUSTED YOU!
OH, IT'S SO EASY, ISN'T IT?!
SO EASY TO BLAME ME!
"SPYING"?
I WAS PROTECTING YOU!

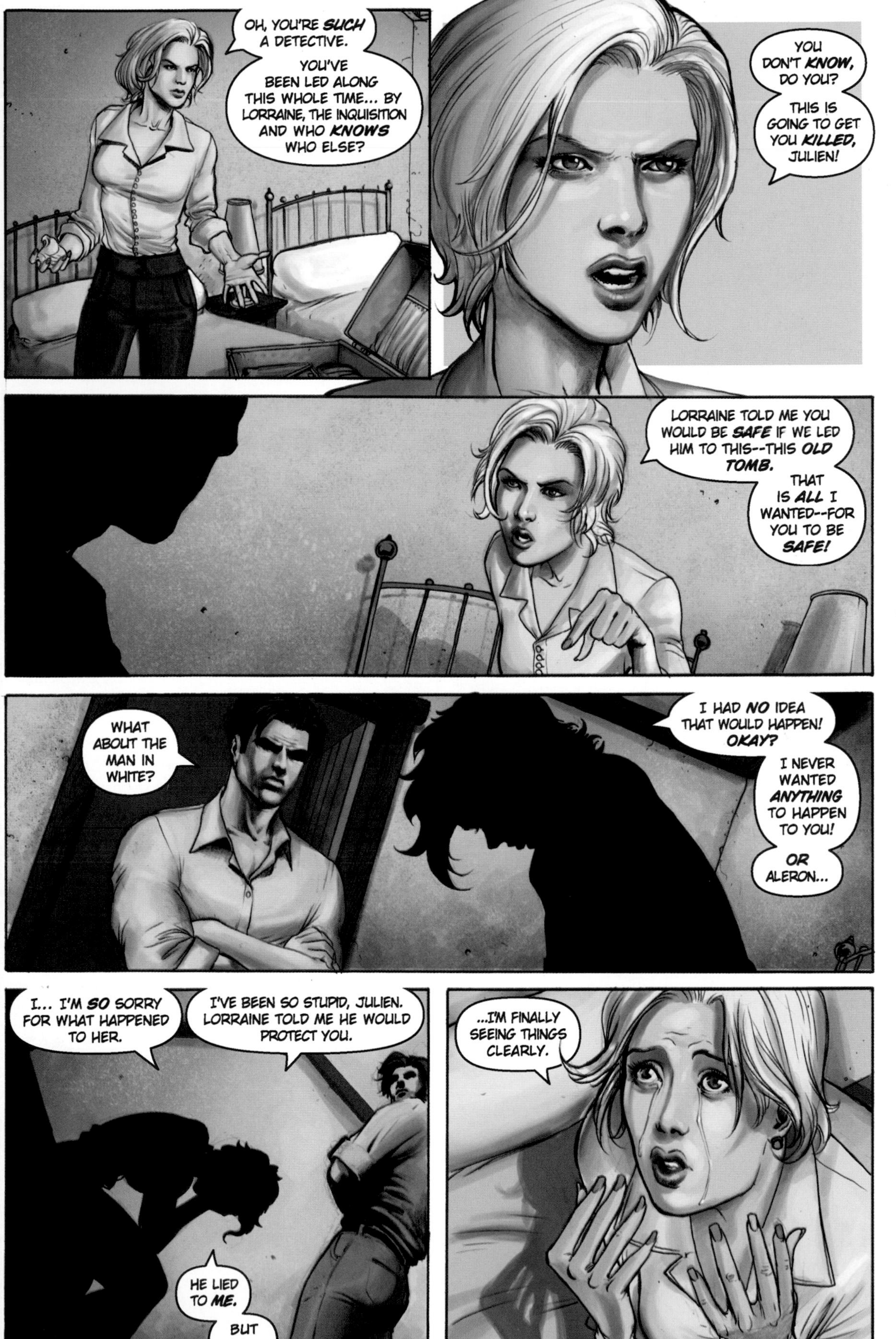
OH, YOU'RE SUCH A DETECTIVE.
YOU'VE BEEN LED ALONG THIS WHOLE TIME... BY LORRAINE, THE INQUISITION AND WHO KNOWS WHO ELSE?
YOU DON'T KNOW, DO YOU?
THIS IS GOING TO GET YOU KILLED, JULIEN!
LORRAINE TOLD ME YOU WOULD BE SAFE IF WE LED HIM TO THIS--THIS OLD TOMB.
THAT IS ALL I WANTED--FOR YOU TO BE SAFE!
WHAT ABOUT THE MAN IN WHITE?
I HAD NO IDEA THAT WOULD HAPPEN! OKAY?
I NEVER WANTED ANYTHING TO HAPPEN TO YOU!
OR ALERON...
I... I'M SO SORRY FOR WHAT HAPPENED TO HER.
I'VE BEEN SO STUPID, JULIEN. LORRAINE TOLD ME HE WOULD PROTECT YOU.
HE LIED TO ME.
BUT NOW...
...I'M FINALLY SEEING THINGS CLEARLY.

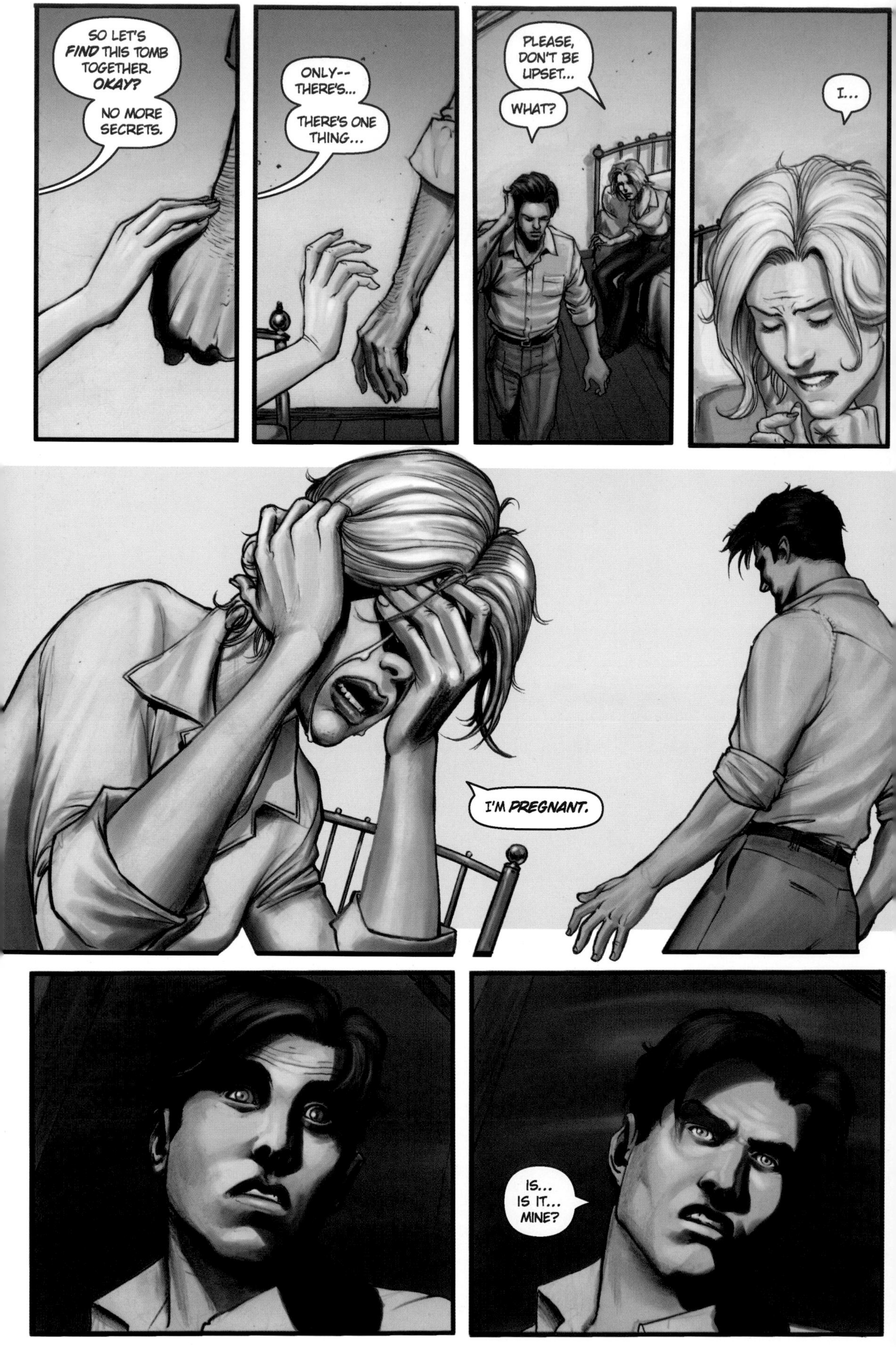

SO LET'S *FIND* THIS TOMB TOGETHER. ***OKAY?***
NO MORE SECRETS.
ONLY-- THERE'S...
THERE'S ONE THING...
PLEASE, DON'T BE UPSET...
WHAT?
I...
I'M ***PREGNANT.***
IS... IS IT... MINE?

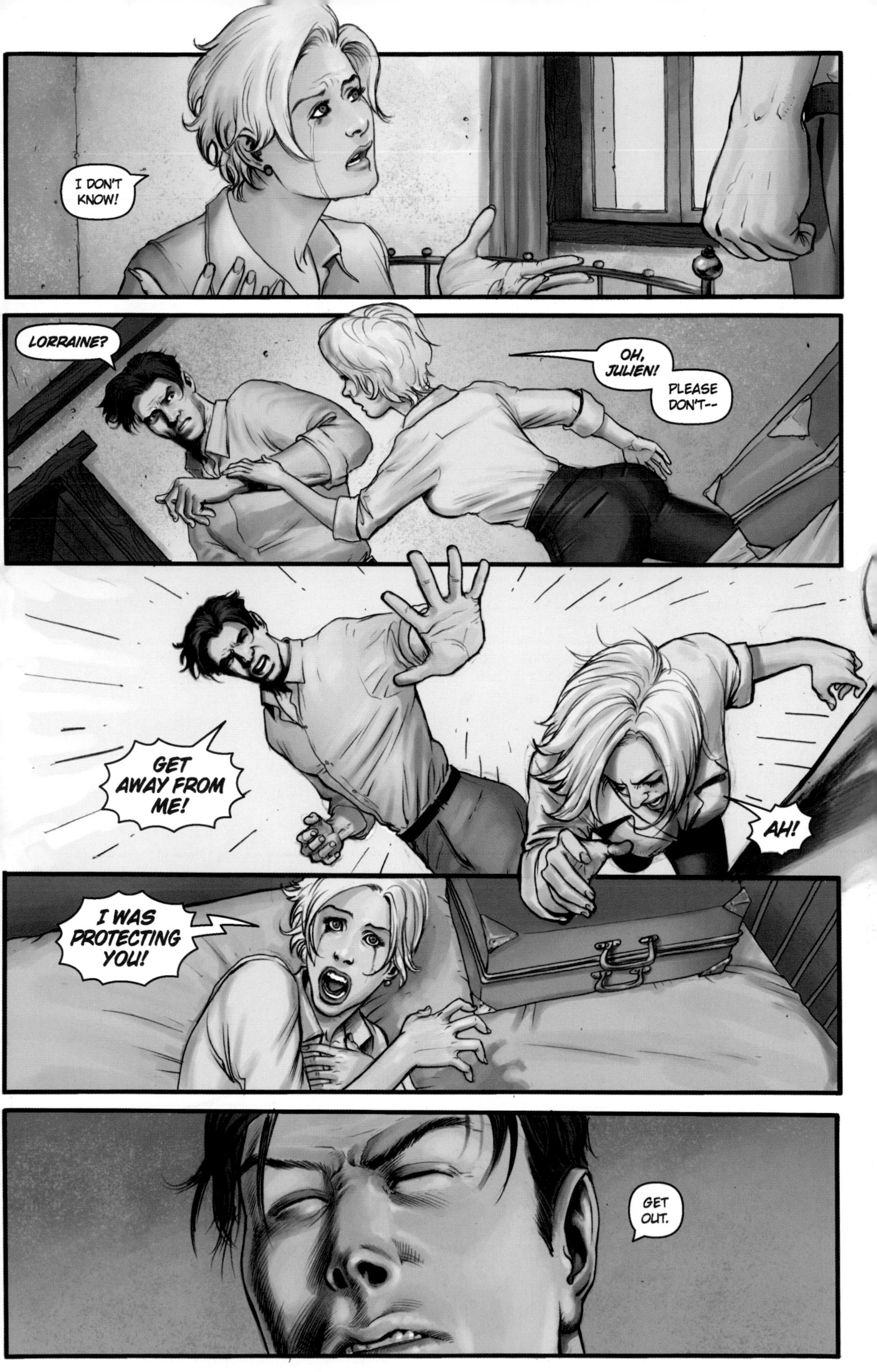
I DON'T KNOW!
LORRAINE?
OH, JULIEN!
PLEASE DON'T--
GET AWAY FROM ME!
AH!
I WAS PROTECTING YOU!
GET OUT.

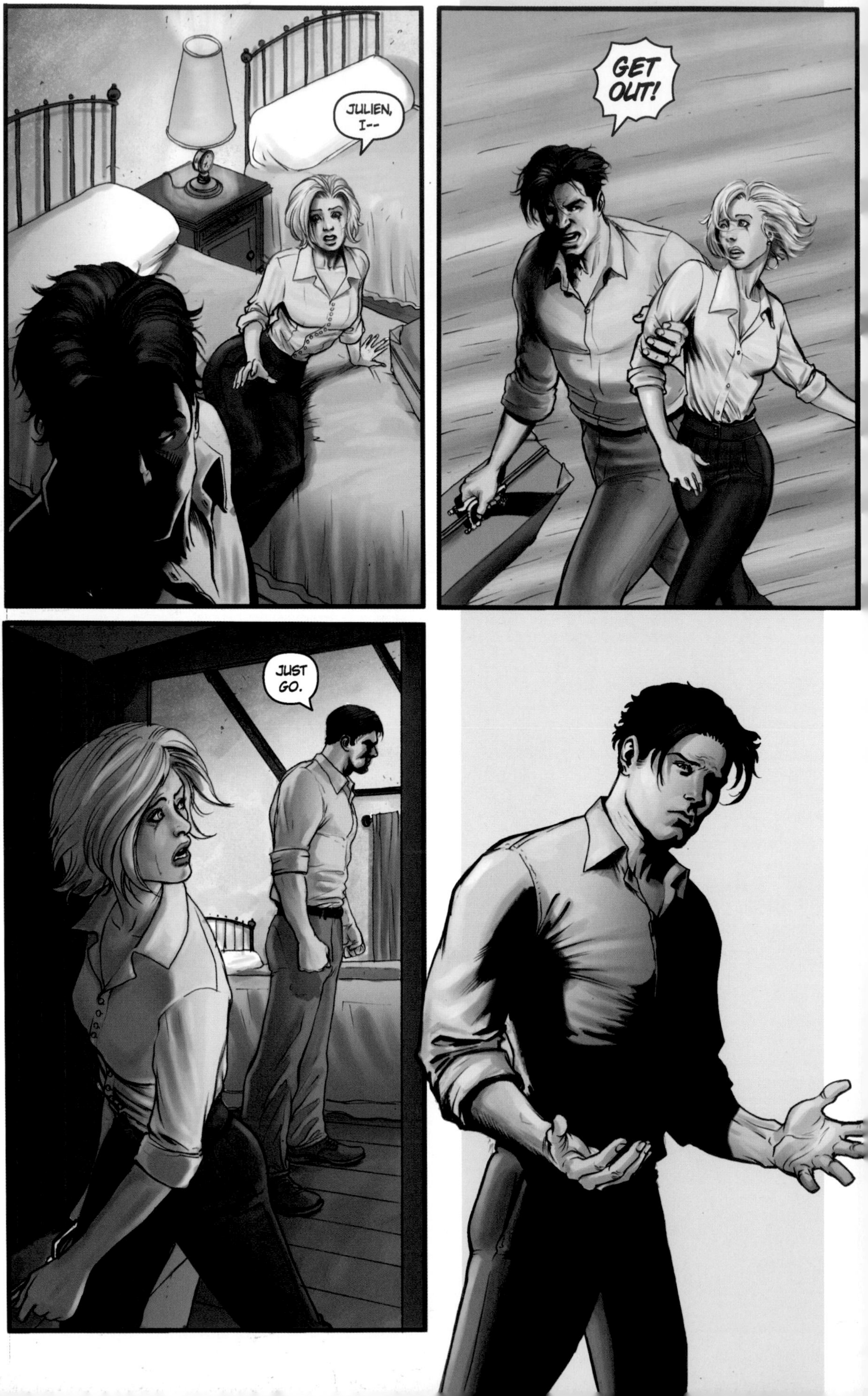
JULIEN, I--
GET OUT!
JUST GO.

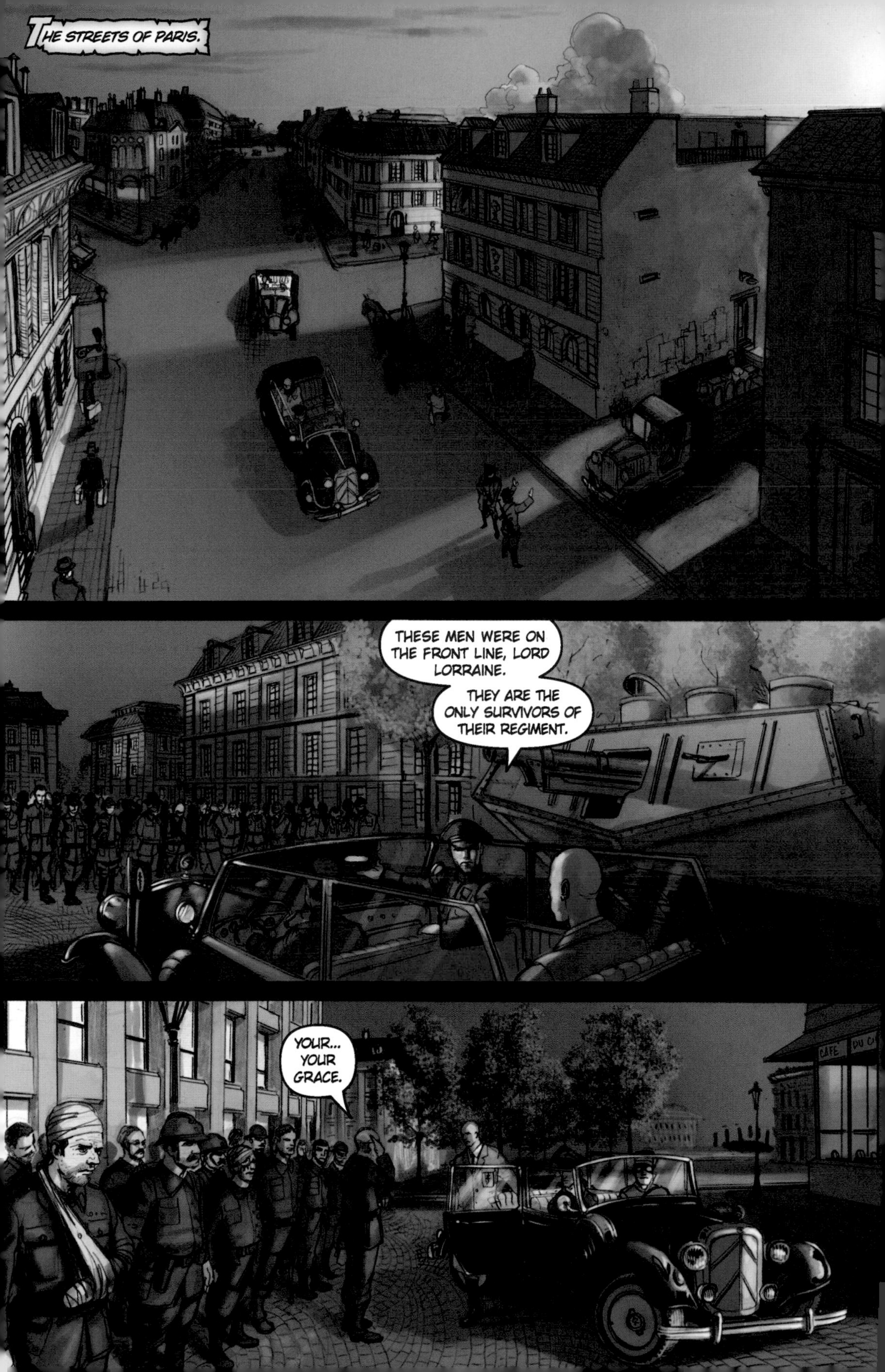
THE STREETS OF PARIS.
THESE MEN WERE ON THE FRONT LINE, LORD LORRAINE.
THEY ARE THE ONLY SURVIVORS OF THEIR REGIMENT.
YOUR... YOUR GRACE.
CAFE

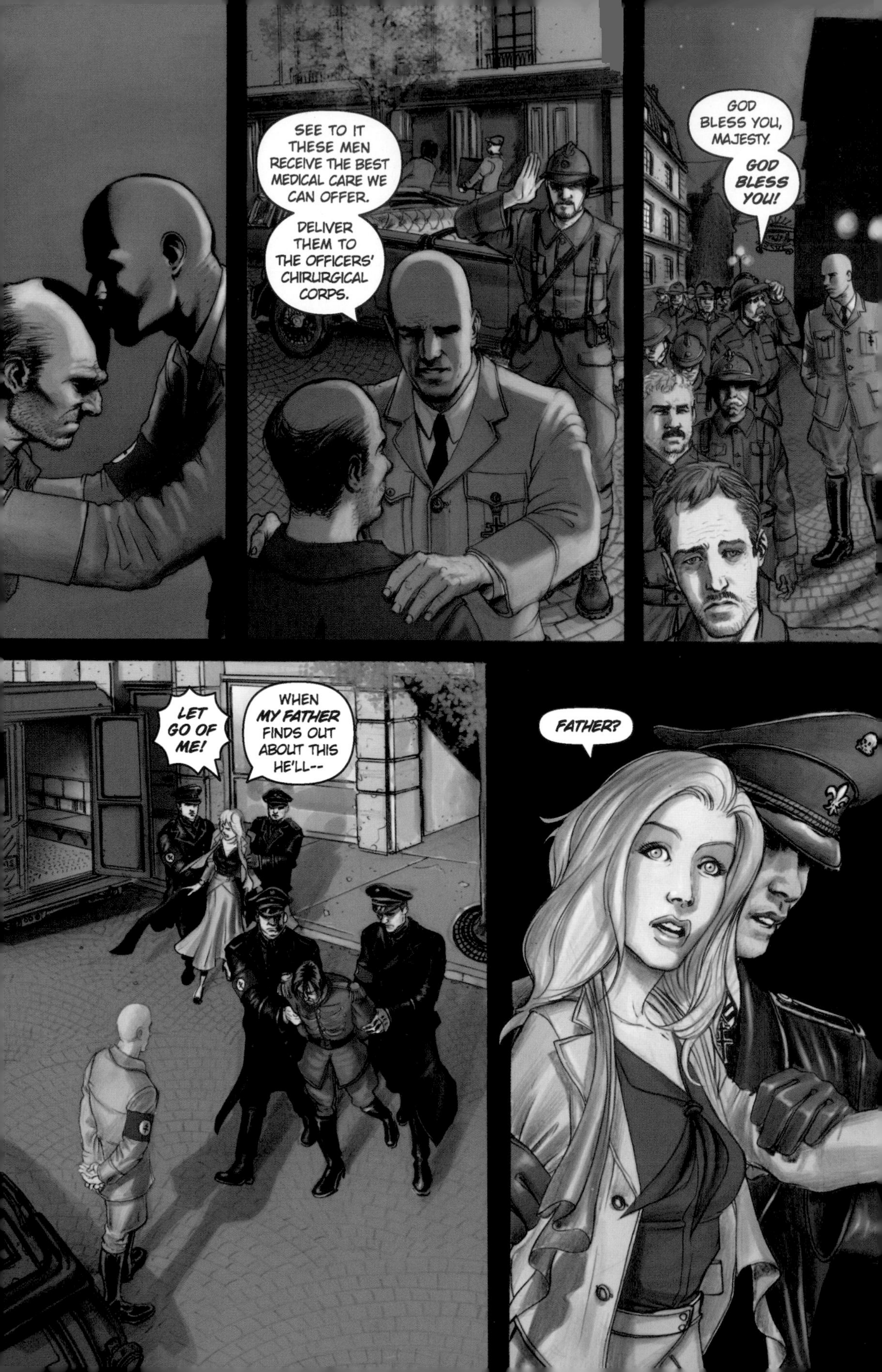
SEE TO IT THESE MEN RECEIVE THE BEST MEDICAL CARE WE CAN OFFER.
DELIVER THEM TO THE OFFICERS' CHIRURGICAL CORPS.
GOD BLESS YOU, MAJESTY.
GOD BLESS YOU!
LET GO OF ME!
WHEN MY FATHER FINDS OUT ABOUT THIS HE'LL--
FATHER?

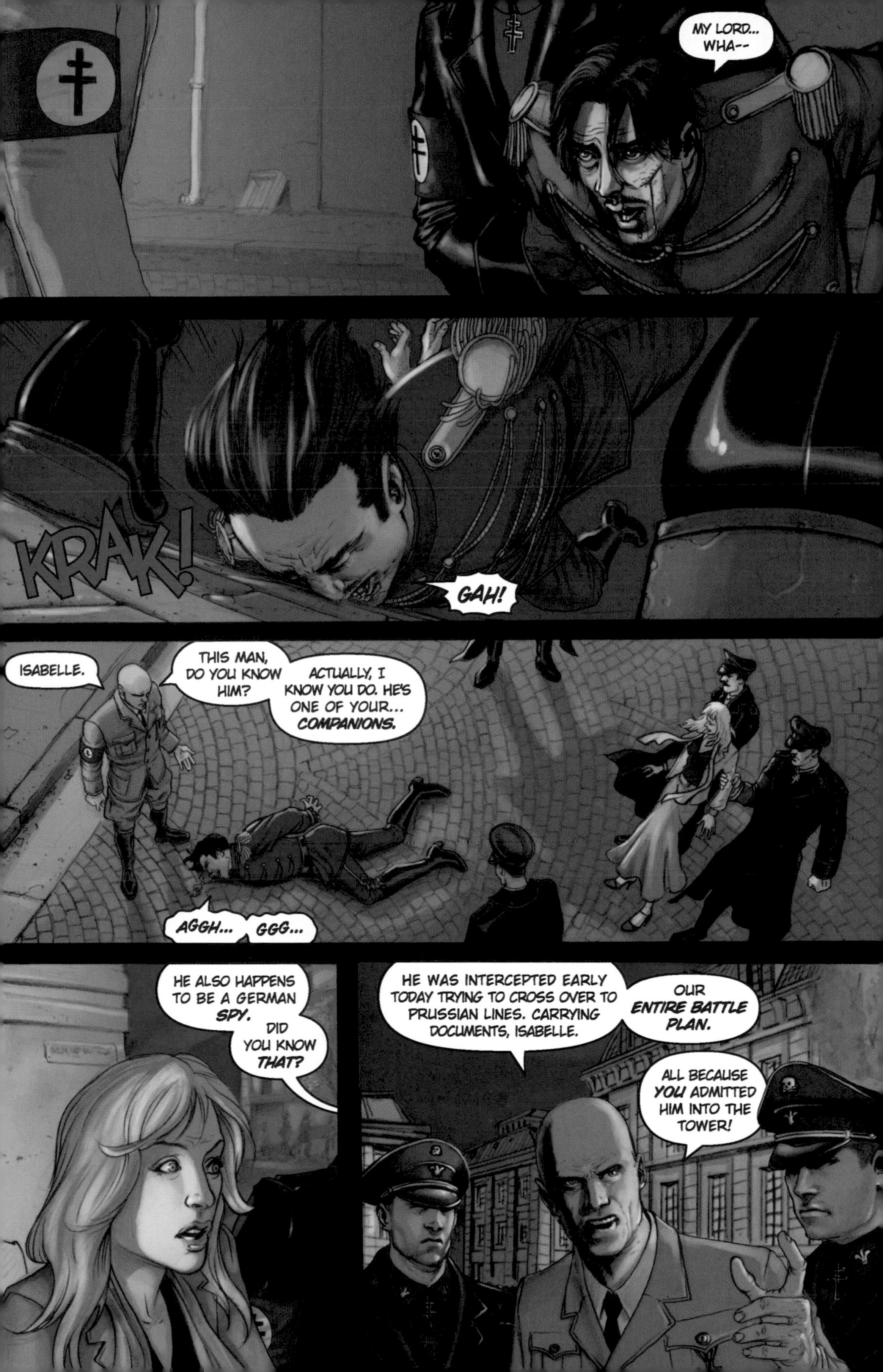

MY LORD... WHA--
KRAK!
GAH!
ISABELLE.
THIS MAN, DO YOU KNOW HIM?
ACTUALLY, I KNOW YOU DO. HE'S ONE OF YOUR... COMPANIONS.
AGGH... GGG...
HE ALSO HAPPENS TO BE A GERMAN SPY.
DID YOU KNOW THAT?
HE WAS INTERCEPTED EARLY TODAY TRYING TO CROSS OVER TO PRUSSIAN LINES. CARRYING DOCUMENTS, ISABELLE.
OUR ENTIRE BATTLE PLAN.
ALL BECAUSE YOU ADMITTED HIM INTO THE TOWER!

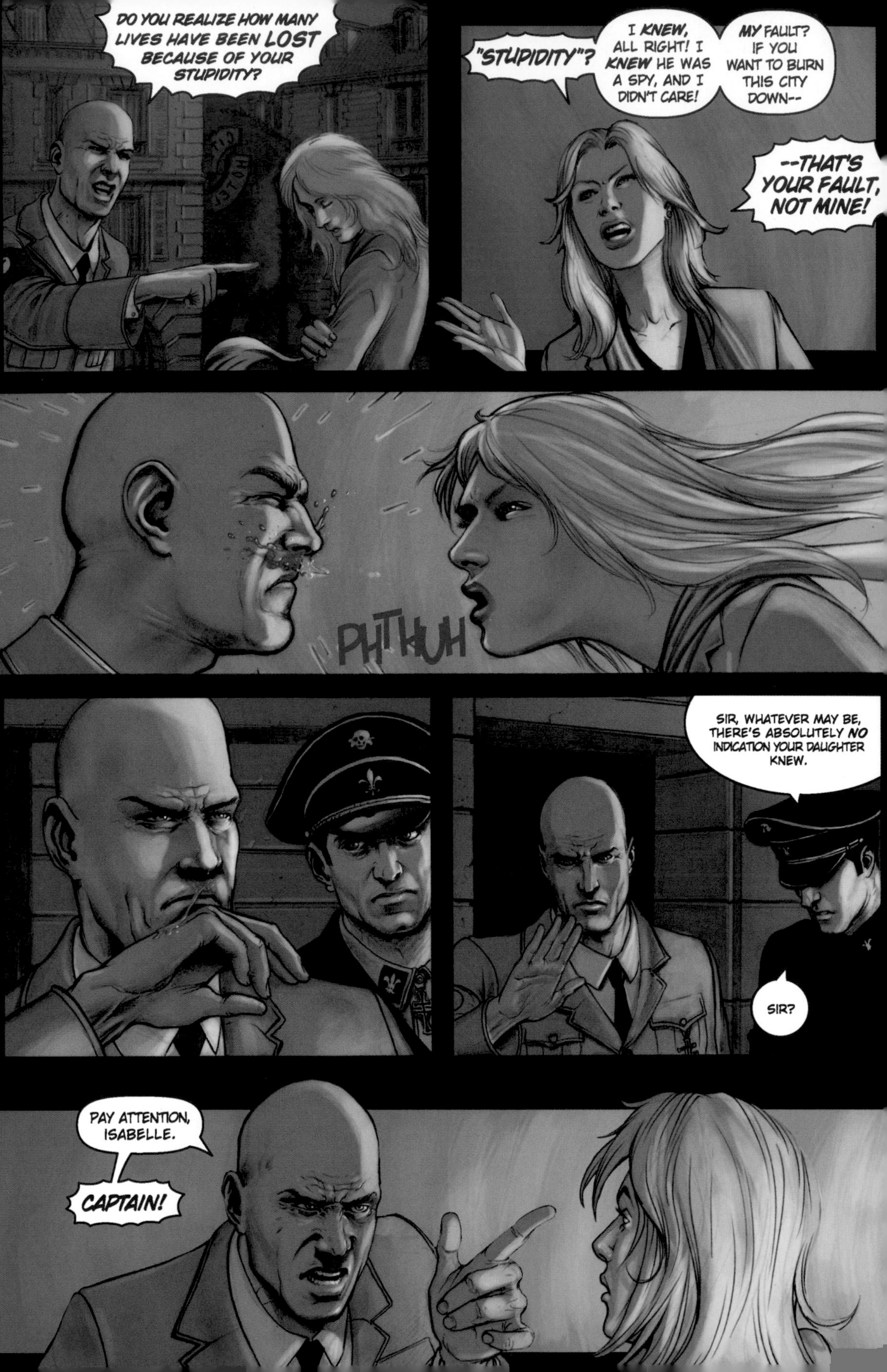
DO YOU REALIZE HOW MANY LIVES HAVE BEEN LOST BECAUSE OF YOUR STUPIDITY?
"STUPIDITY"?
I KNEW, ALL RIGHT! I KNEW HE WAS A SPY, AND I DIDN'T CARE!
MY FAULT? IF YOU WANT TO BURN THIS CITY DOWN--
--THAT'S YOUR FAULT, NOT MINE!
PHTHUH
SIR, WHATEVER MAY BE, THERE'S ABSOLUTELY NO INDICATION YOUR DAUGHTER KNEW.
SIR?
PAY ATTENTION, ISABELLE.
CAPTAIN!

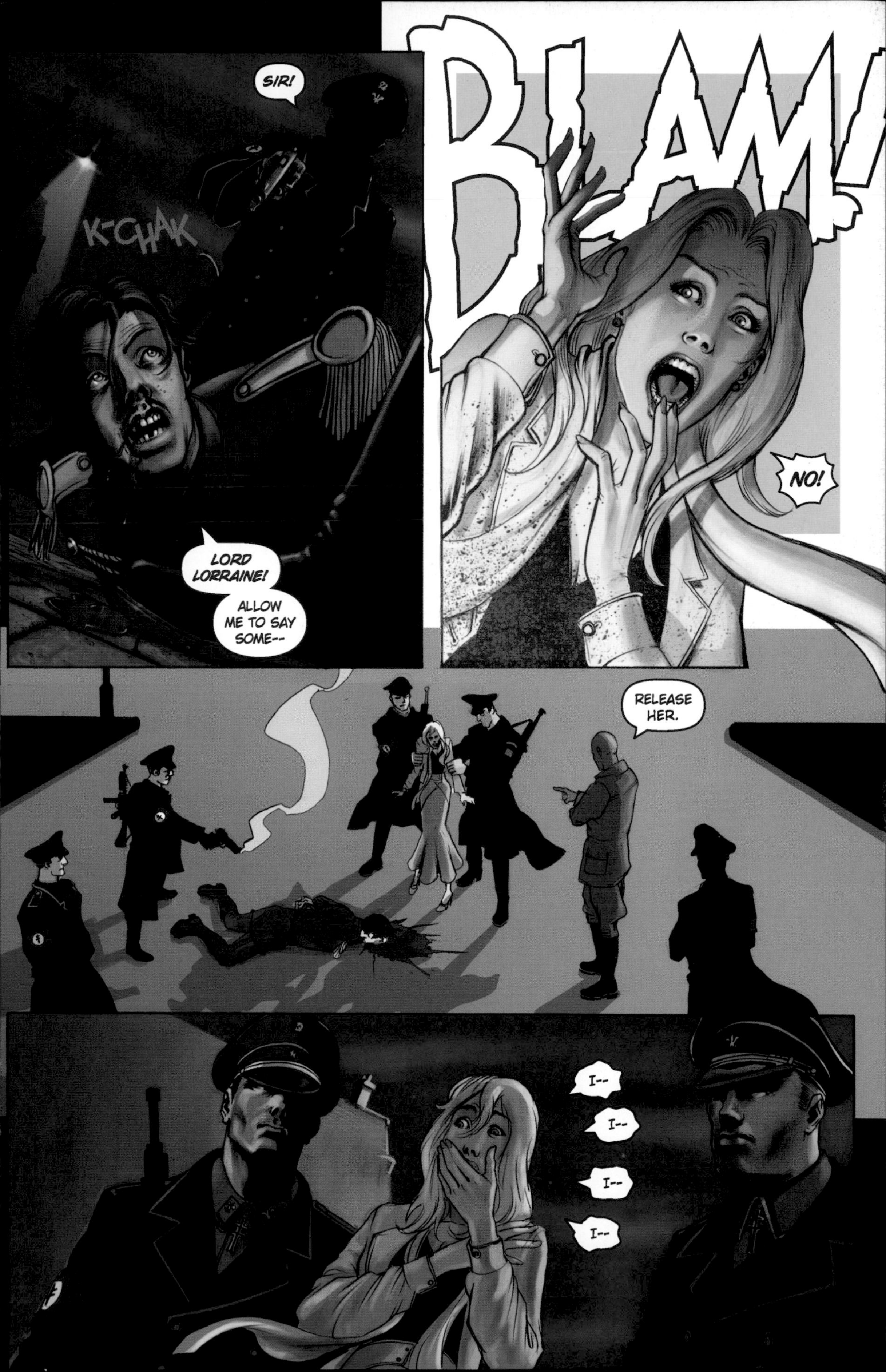
SIR!
K-CHAK
LORD LORRAINE!
ALLOW ME TO SAY SOME--
BLAM!
NO!
RELEASE HER.
I--
I--
I--
I--

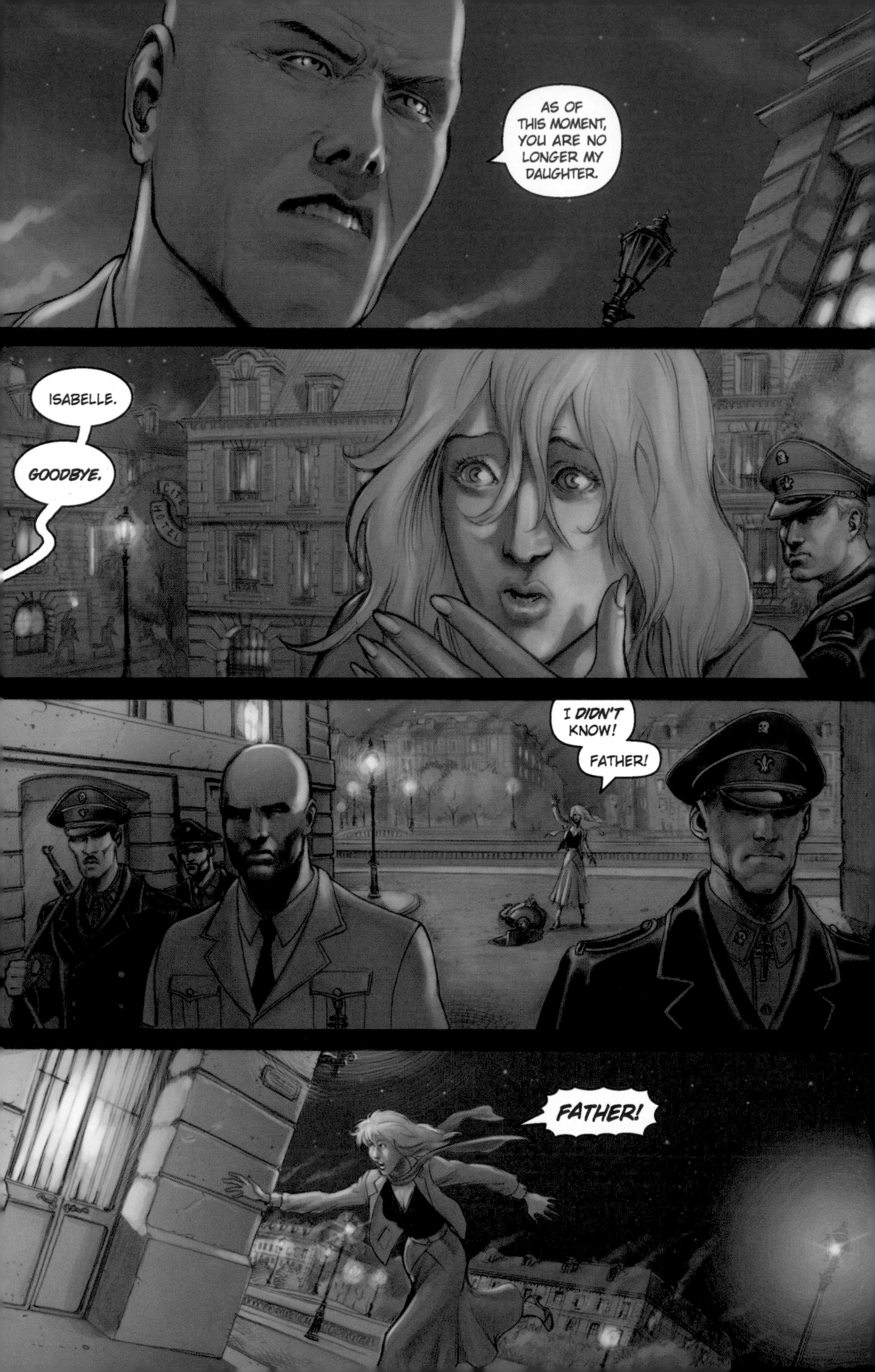
AS OF THIS MOMENT, YOU ARE NO LONGER MY DAUGHTER.
ISABELLE.
GOODBYE.
I DIDN'T KNOW!
FATHER!
FATHER!

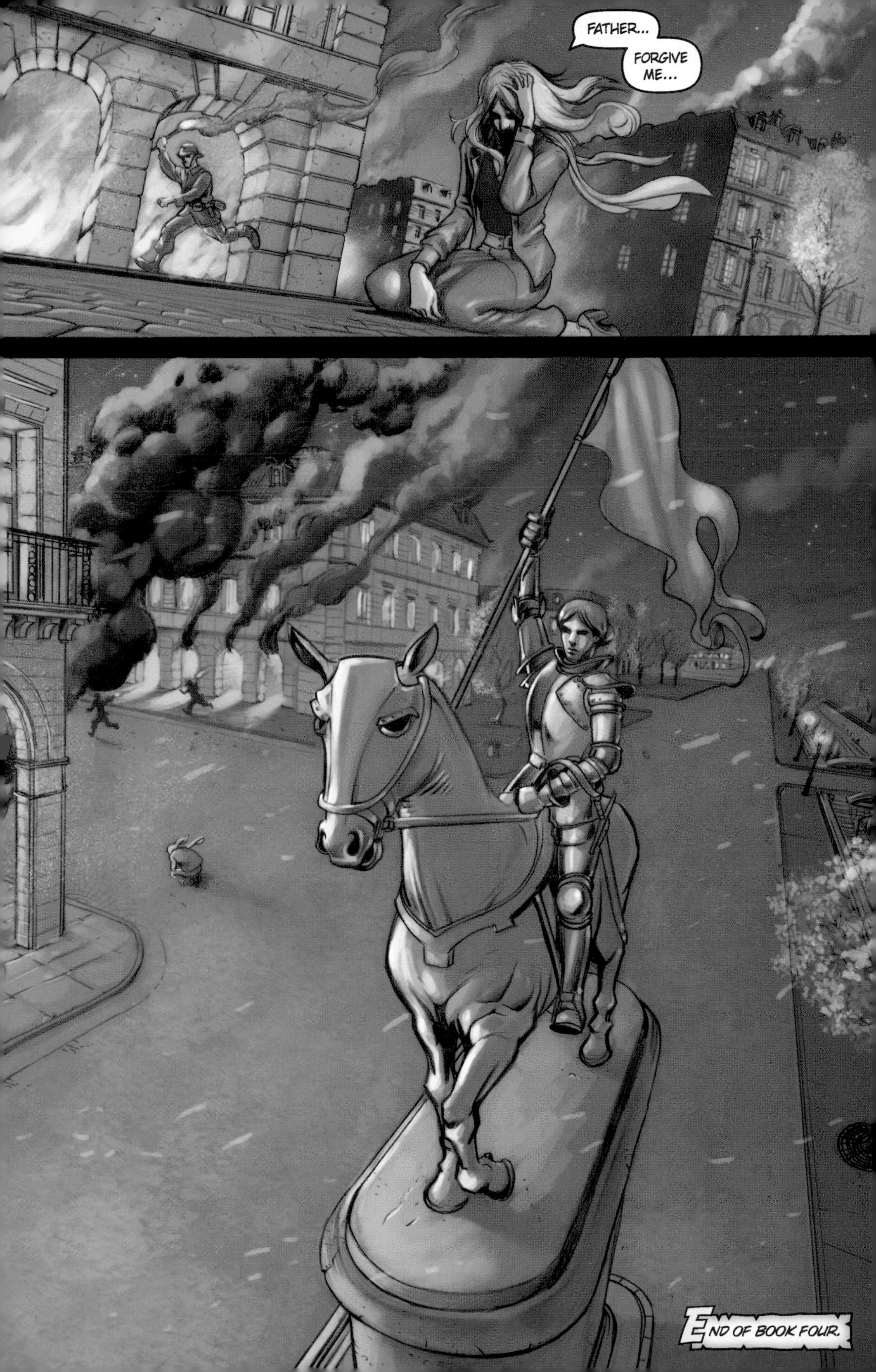
FATHER...
FORGIVE ME...
END OF BOOK FOUR.

Le Journal de la Liberté

Paris's leading anglophone newspaper • vol. 205, no. 106 • Nov. 20, MCMXXXIII

Editors in Chief: M. Tait Bergstrom, M. Matthew Pasteris. **Story Editor:** M. Arvid Nelson.
Art Editor: M. Juan Ferreyra. **Photography Editor:** M. Alexander Waldman.
Layout Supervisor: M. William Kartalopoulos. **Editors Emeritus:** M. Clark A. Smith,
M. Howard P. Lovecraft, M. Robert E. Howard. Redacted under the direction of His Excellency
Archbishop Emile-Jean Ireneaux. *Le Journal de la Liberté* is printed under the benign auspices of his
eminence David-Louis Plantard de St. Clair, Duke of Lorraine and First Consul of the Empire of France.

Papal seal

of Approval

PARIS FALLS

For seven centuries, Notre Dame de Paris has been a monument to Christian civilization. Badly damaged by Prussian artillery, its future is now uncertain.

Paris – The artillery bombardment came without warning, and not all the clergy were able to evacuate Notre Dame in time.

"We heard a whistling sound. Of course we had no idea it was an artillery fire," Brother Jean, a Carmelite monk visiting Notre Dame, said. "By the time the first shells impacted, it was too late."

A dozen members of the clergy are reported to have died in an errant Prussian artillery barrage that turned Notre Dame into a scene of death and carnage.

"I have truly gazed into the depths of Hell," Brother Jean said. "There were limbs, blood and gore everywhere."

A Prussian occupation of Paris is all but inevitable now, following the defeat of the Anglo-French forces defending the city.

The Prussians, supported by their Austrian allies, routed the defenders in a daring surprise assault across the "no-man's land" between the trenches of the two sides.

The Duke of Nevers was in charge of Paris's defence. Sources close to Lord Nevers report espionage might have played a role in his defeat. Rumors of a spy inside the French command headquarters are widespread.

"The attack was just too well planned. They knew exactly where to strike, and exactly how many forces to commit. That kind of luck doesn't exist," Col. Grégory Dorol, in charge of a section of the French trenches, said.

Prussian and Austrian forces also had a significant numerical advantage in the surprise attack, in some places outnumbering the defenders two-to-one.

This is because French forces are spread thinly, fighting in the Iberian Peninsula against the Cordovan Emirate in addition to defending Paris against the German advance.

Whether insufficient manpower or spies are to blame, the loss is an utter disaster for the French. Lord Lorraine, supreme commander of the French forces, had no choice but to abandon the city to the Prussians.

Shortly before withdrawing, Lorraine set the city on fire, thereby denying the Prussians the opportunity to recover from their relentless drive west.

Over 70 percent of the city is now a smoking ruin.

A tide of refugees is fleeing the Prussian advance – women, children and old men carrying valuables by any means available. They throng southward, hungry, weary, and facing an uncertain future.

The exact number of fleeing civilians is unknown, but estimates range into the hundreds of thousands.

The few citizens who choose to remain in Paris face the uncertainty of a Prussian occupation.

The Duke of Lorraine is responsible for the strategic decision to divide the French forces

to the south and north. High ranking military officials are now privately questioning the wisdom of his plan.

"We have been taken off guard by the ferocity of the German offensive because we didn't have enough troops to commit to the defense of Paris," a senior officer said. "Too many men have been diverted to the campaign in the South."

The scattered remnants of the defenders of Paris are regrouping, possibly in the city of Toulouse.

"This war is far from over and victory may still be ours," the Duke of Guise, one of Lorraine's closest military confidantes, said.

Lorraine is unapologetic about his decision to divide the French forces, he said.

Indeed, the campaign in the south against the Mohammedan Cordovans is faring much better than the contest against the Prussians in the north.

The Duke of Orleans, commander of the southern forces, said he expected to capture Cordova "within days," but the question being debated now amongst the French high command is whether or not Orleans' troops will be able to redeploy to aid the shattered northern army.

continued on next page

A flood of refugees from Paris flees the Prussian advance.

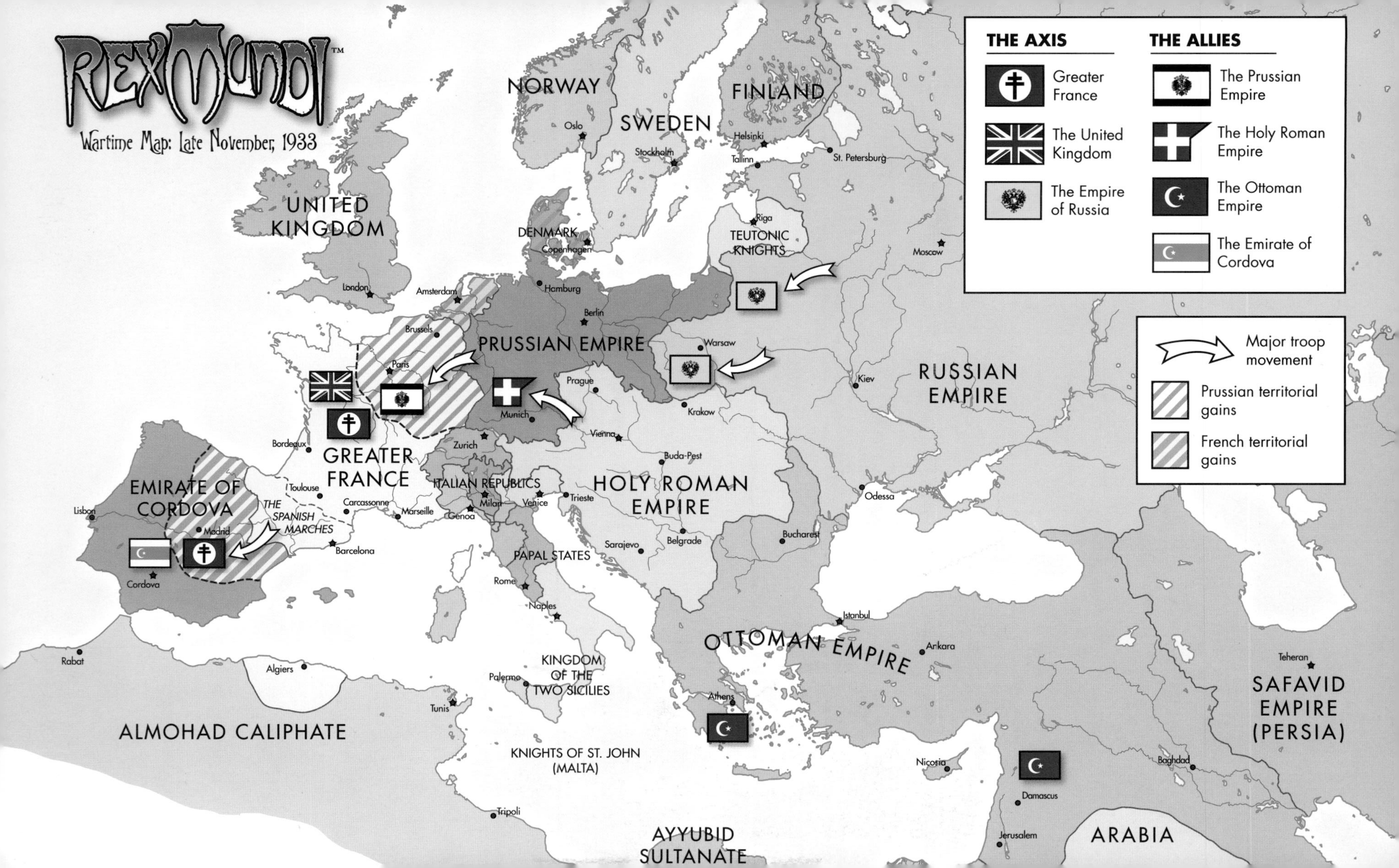

Rex Mundi™
Wartime Map: Late November, 1933
THE AXIS
Greater France
The United Kingdom
The Empire of Russia
THE ALLIES
The Prussian Empire
The Holy Roman Empire
The Ottoman Empire
The Emirate of Cordova
Major troop movement
Prussian territorial gains
French territorial gains
NORWAY
SWEDEN
FINLAND
UNITED KINGDOM
DENMARK
TEUTONIC KNIGHTS
PRUSSIAN EMPIRE
RUSSIAN EMPIRE
GREATER FRANCE
EMIRATE OF CORDOVA
THE SPANISH MARCHES
ITALIAN REPUBLICS
HOLY ROMAN EMPIRE
PAPAL STATES
KINGDOM OF THE TWO SICILIES
OTTOMAN EMPIRE
SAFAVID EMPIRE (PERSIA)
ALMOHAD CALIPHATE
KNIGHTS OF ST. JOHN (MALTA)
AYYUBID SULTANATE
ARABIA
Oslo
Stockholm
Helsinki
Tallinn
St. Petersburg
Riga
Moscow
Copenhagen
Hamburg
Berlin
London
Amsterdam
Brussels
Paris
Warsaw
Prague
Kiev
Munich
Krakow
Vienna
Bordeaux
Zurich
Buda-Pest
Toulouse
Carcassonne
Marseille
Genoa
Milan
Venice
Trieste
Odessa
Lisbon
Madrid
Barcelona
Sarajevo
Belgrade
Bucharest
Cordova
Rome
Naples
Istanbul
Arkara
Rabat
Algiers
Palermo
Tunis
Athens
Teheran
Nicosia
Baghdad
Damascus
Tripoli
Jerusalem

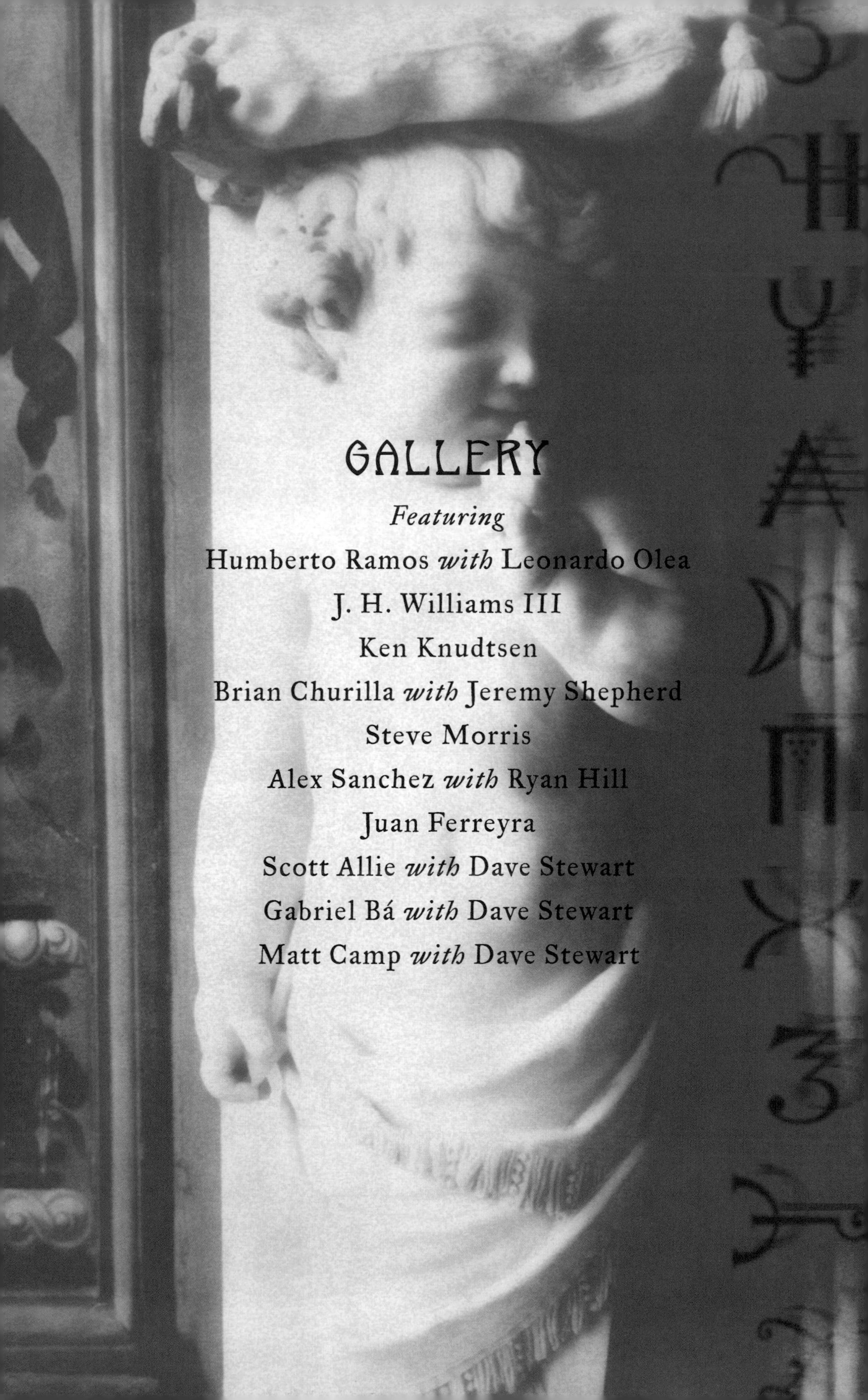

GALLERY

Featuring

Humberto Ramos *with* Leonardo Olea

J. H. Williams III

Ken Knudtsen

Brian Churilla *with* Jeremy Shepherd

Steve Morris

Alex Sanchez *with* Ryan Hill

Juan Ferreyra

Scott Allie *with* Dave Stewart

Gabriel Bá *with* Dave Stewart

Matt Camp *with* Dave Stewart

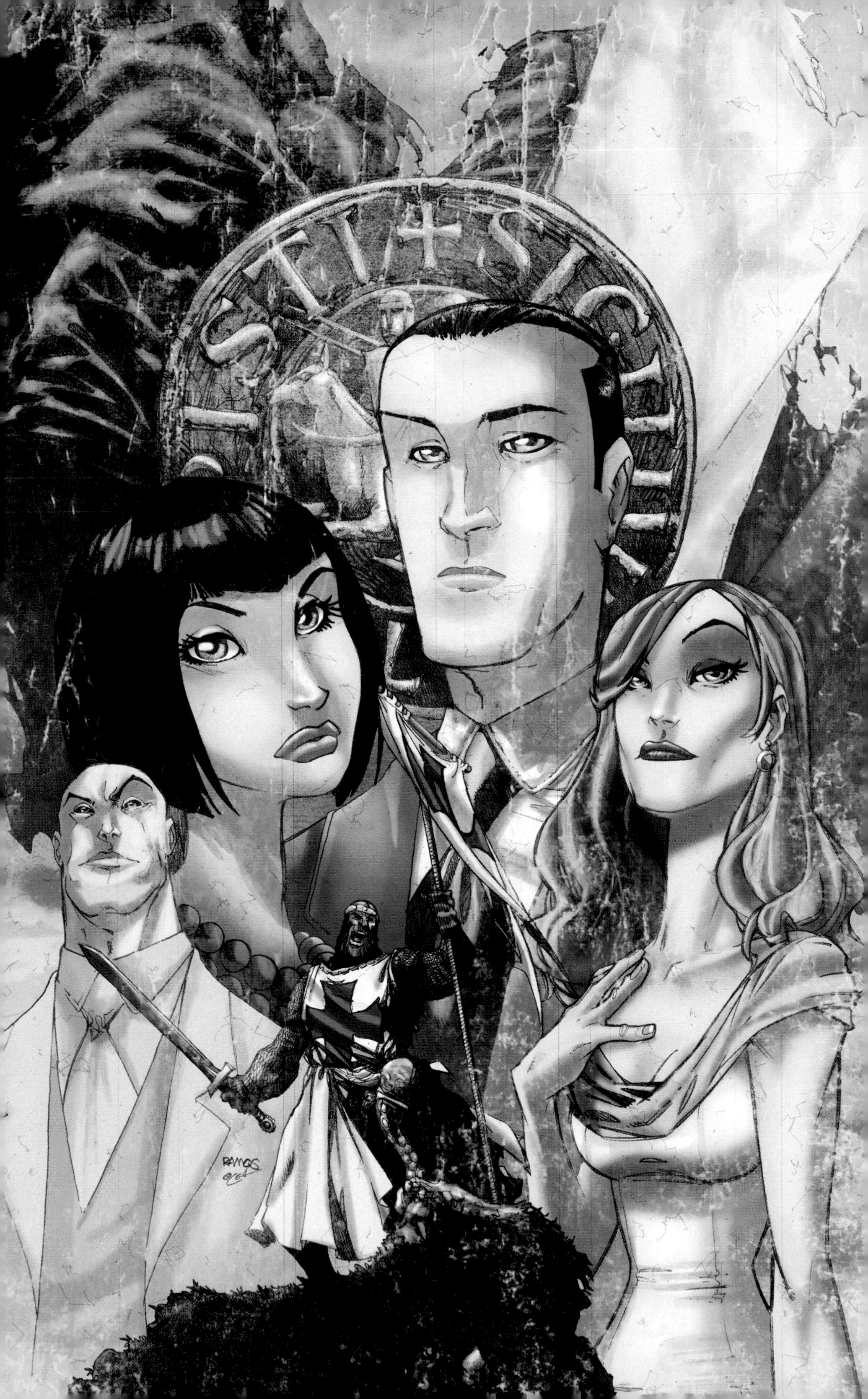
RAMOS

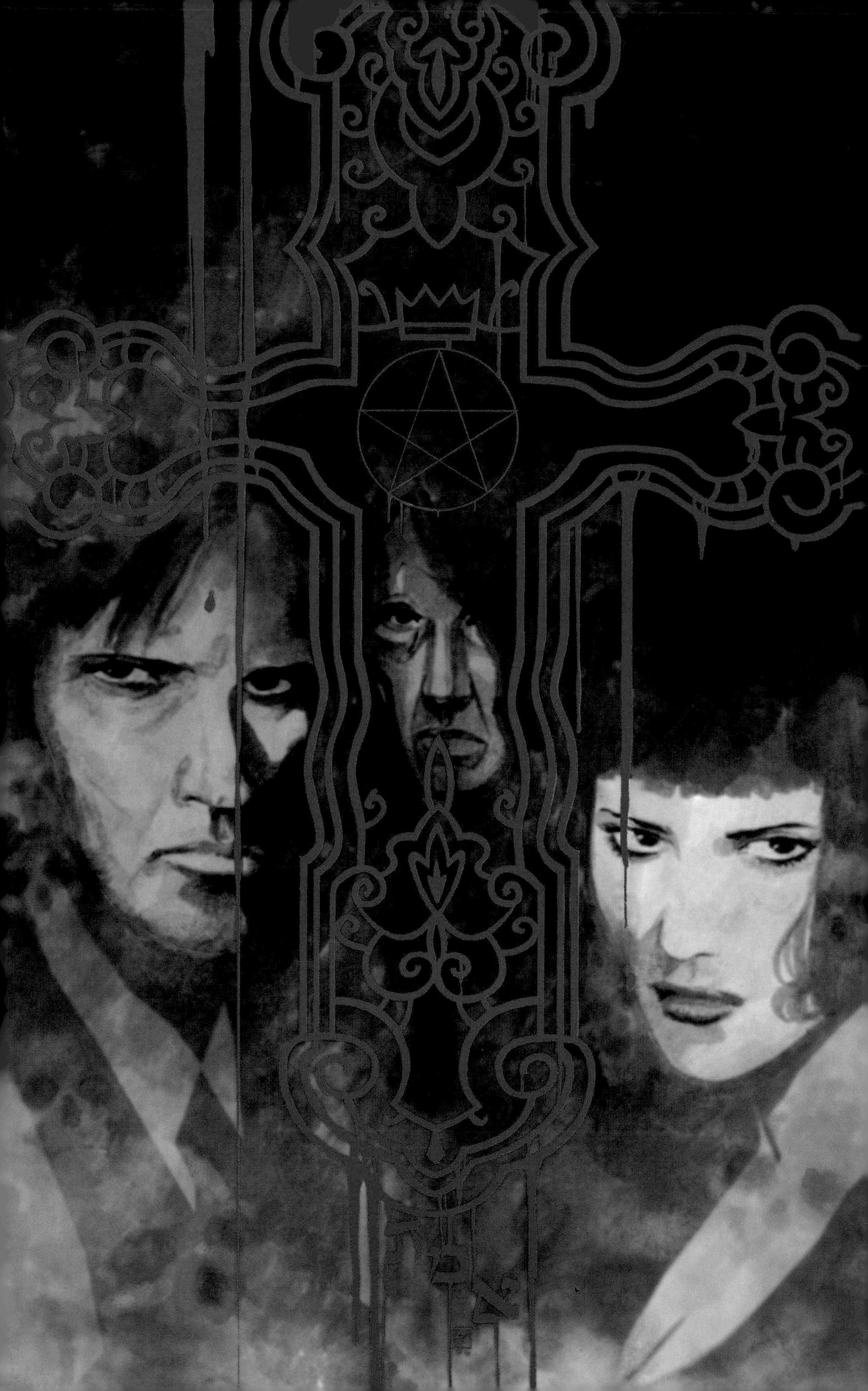

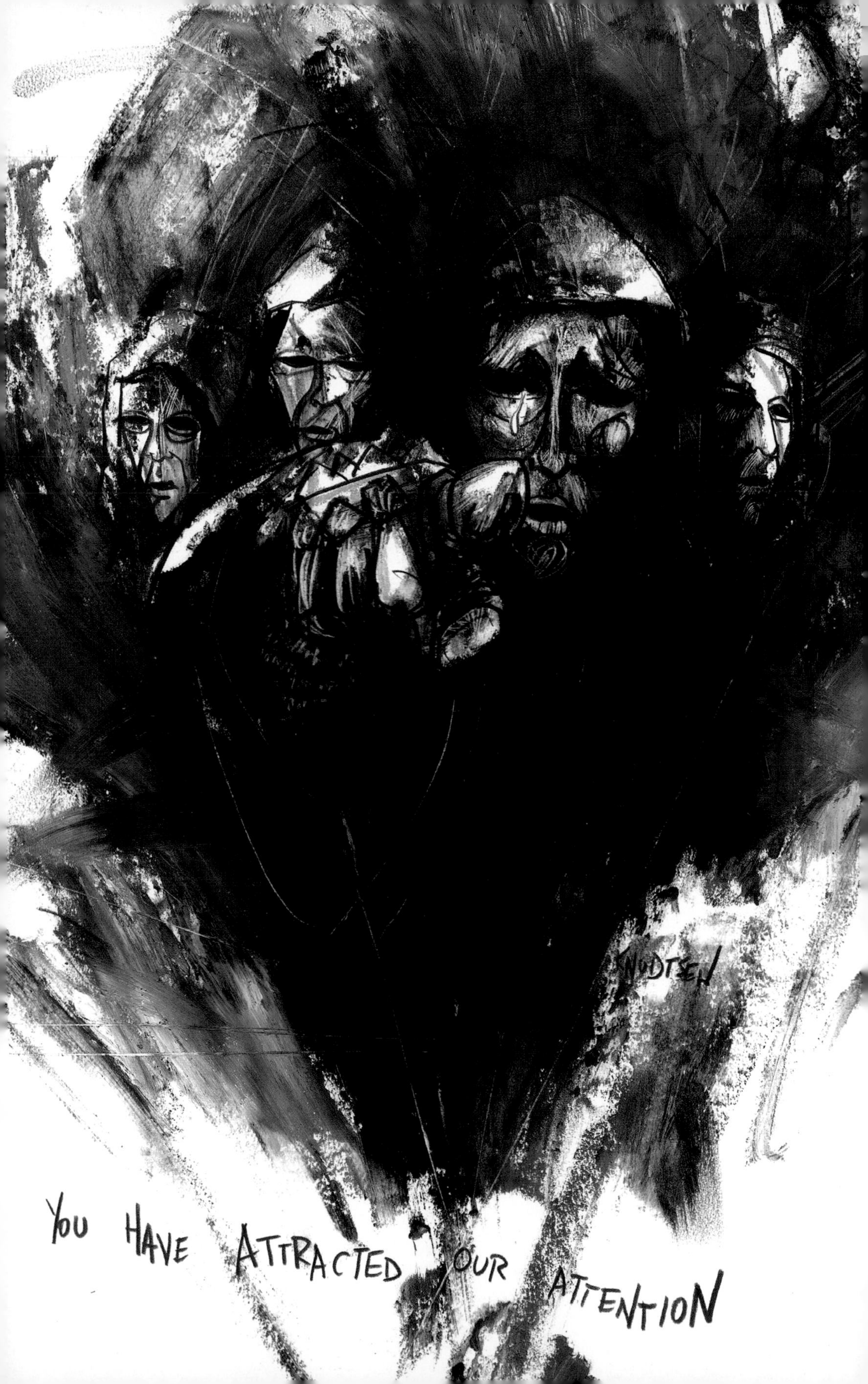
KNUDTSEN
YOU HAVE ATTRACTED OUR ATTENTION

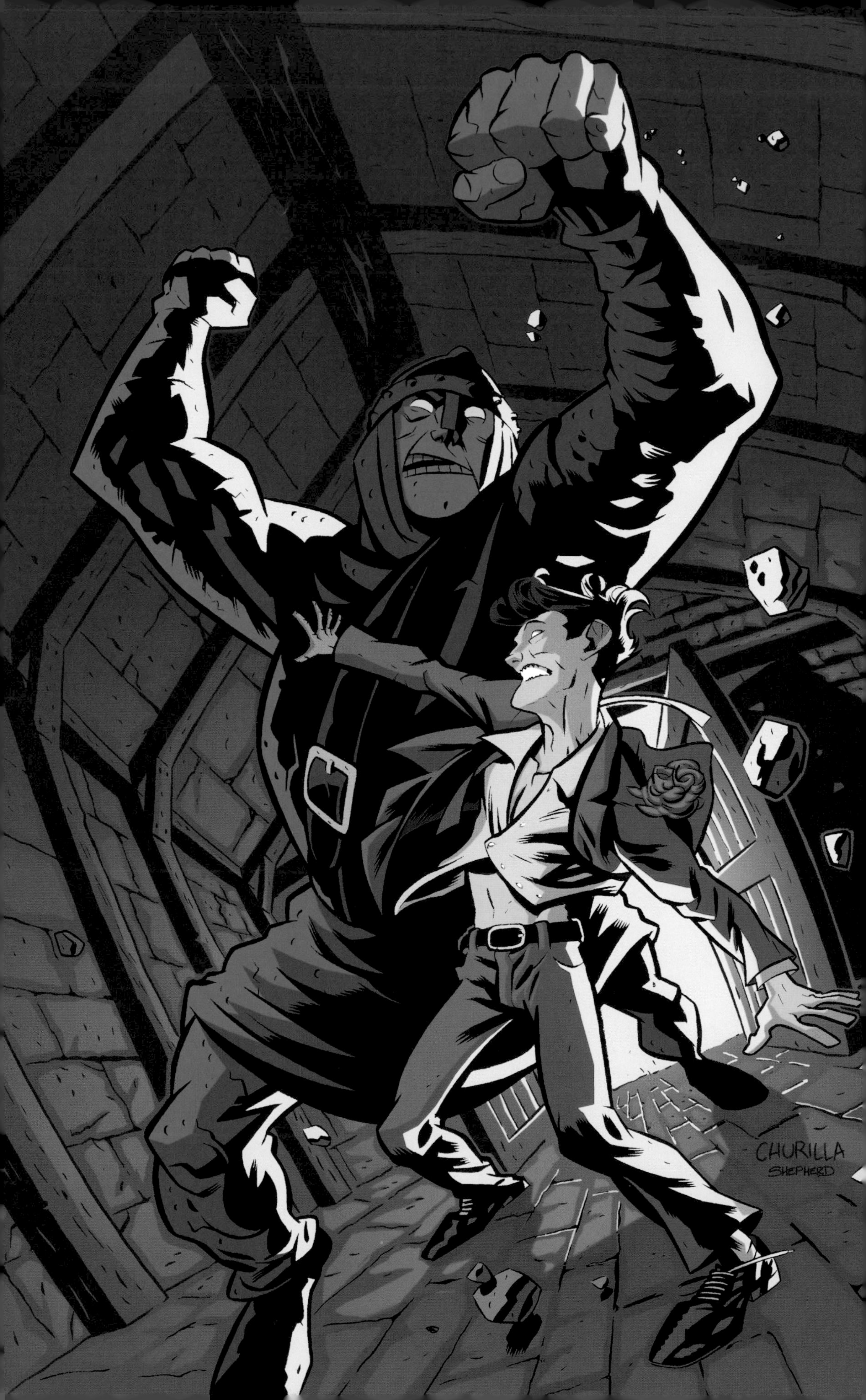
CHURILLA
SHEPHERD

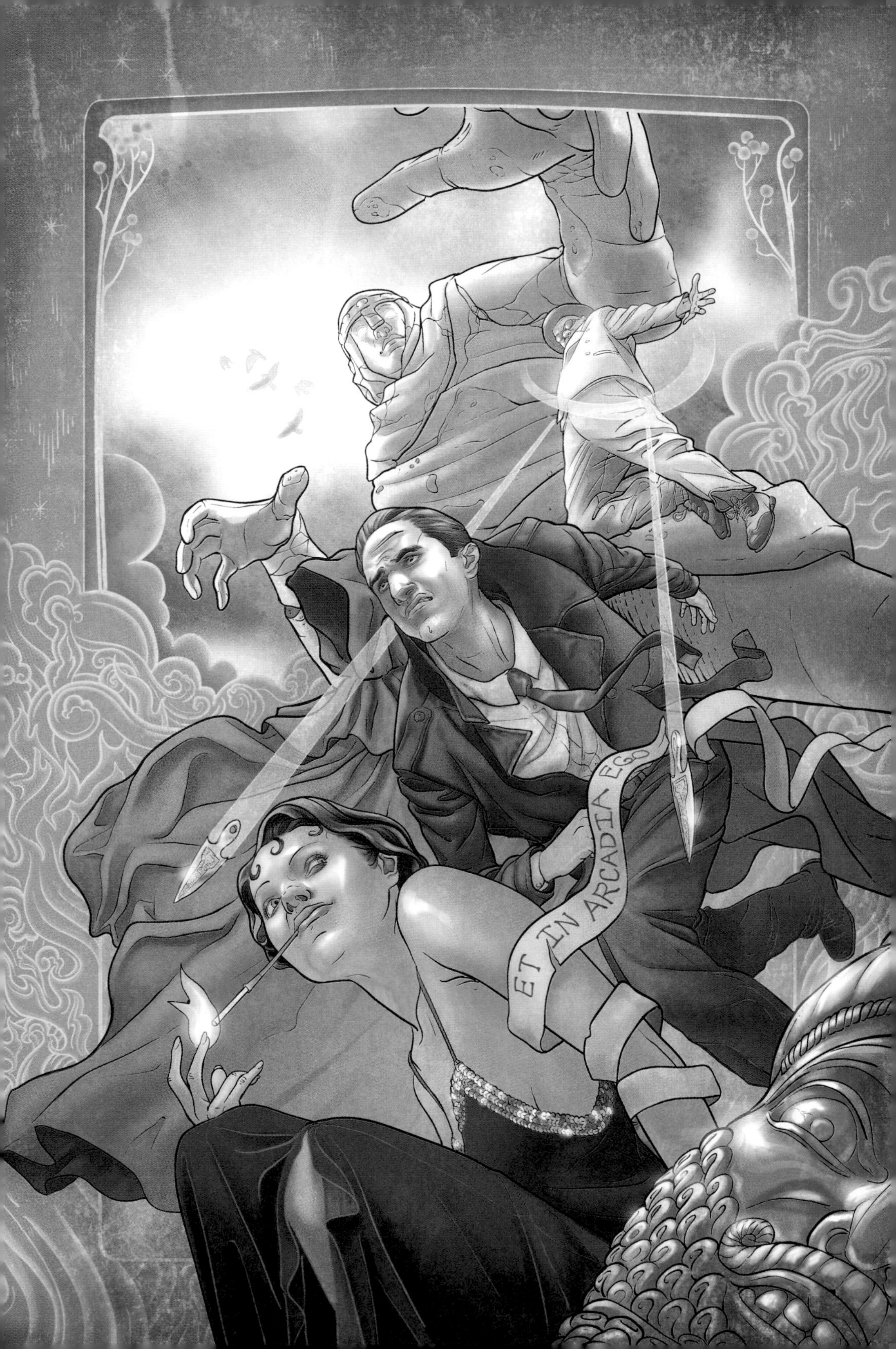
ET IN ARCADIA EGO

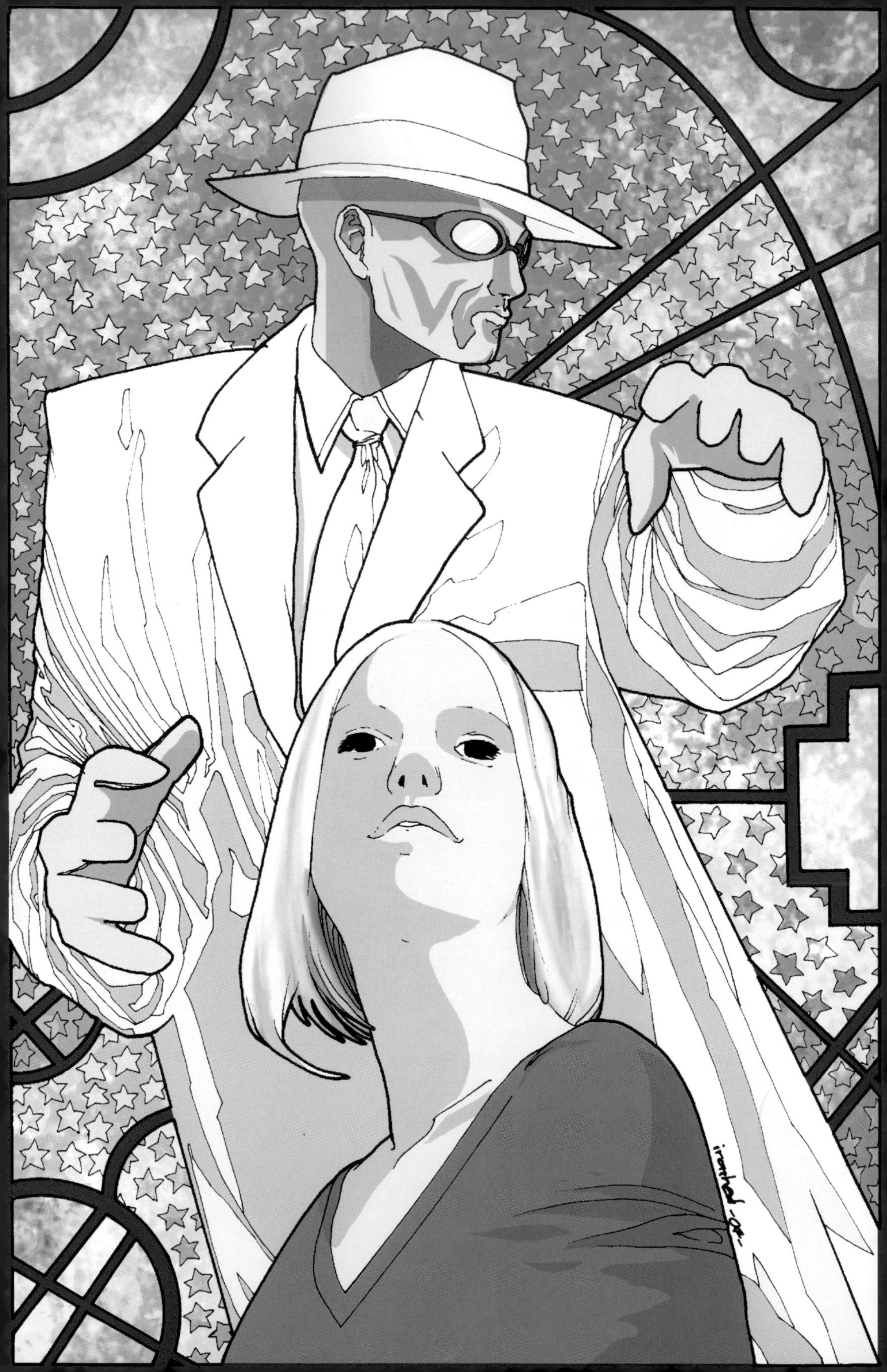

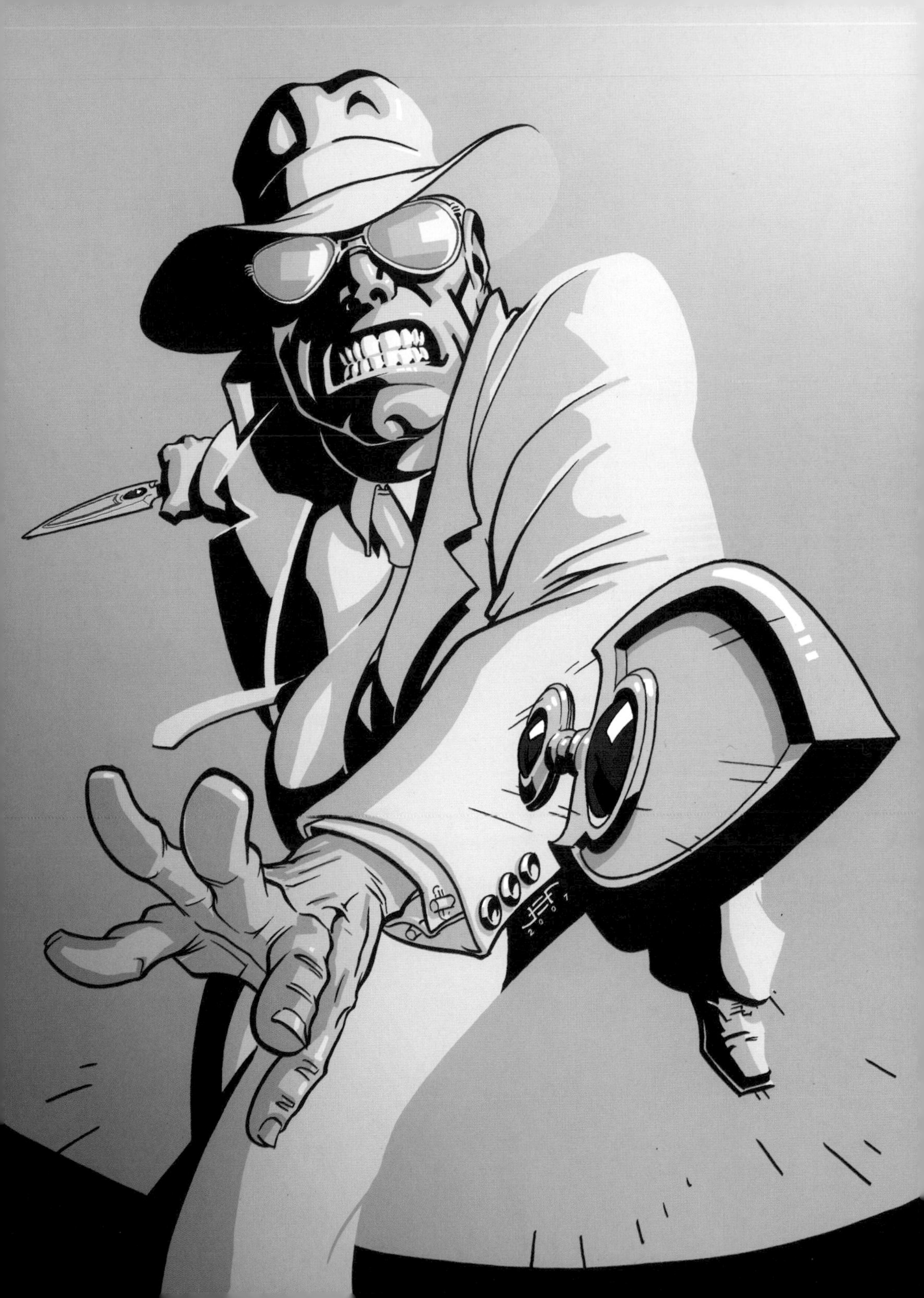

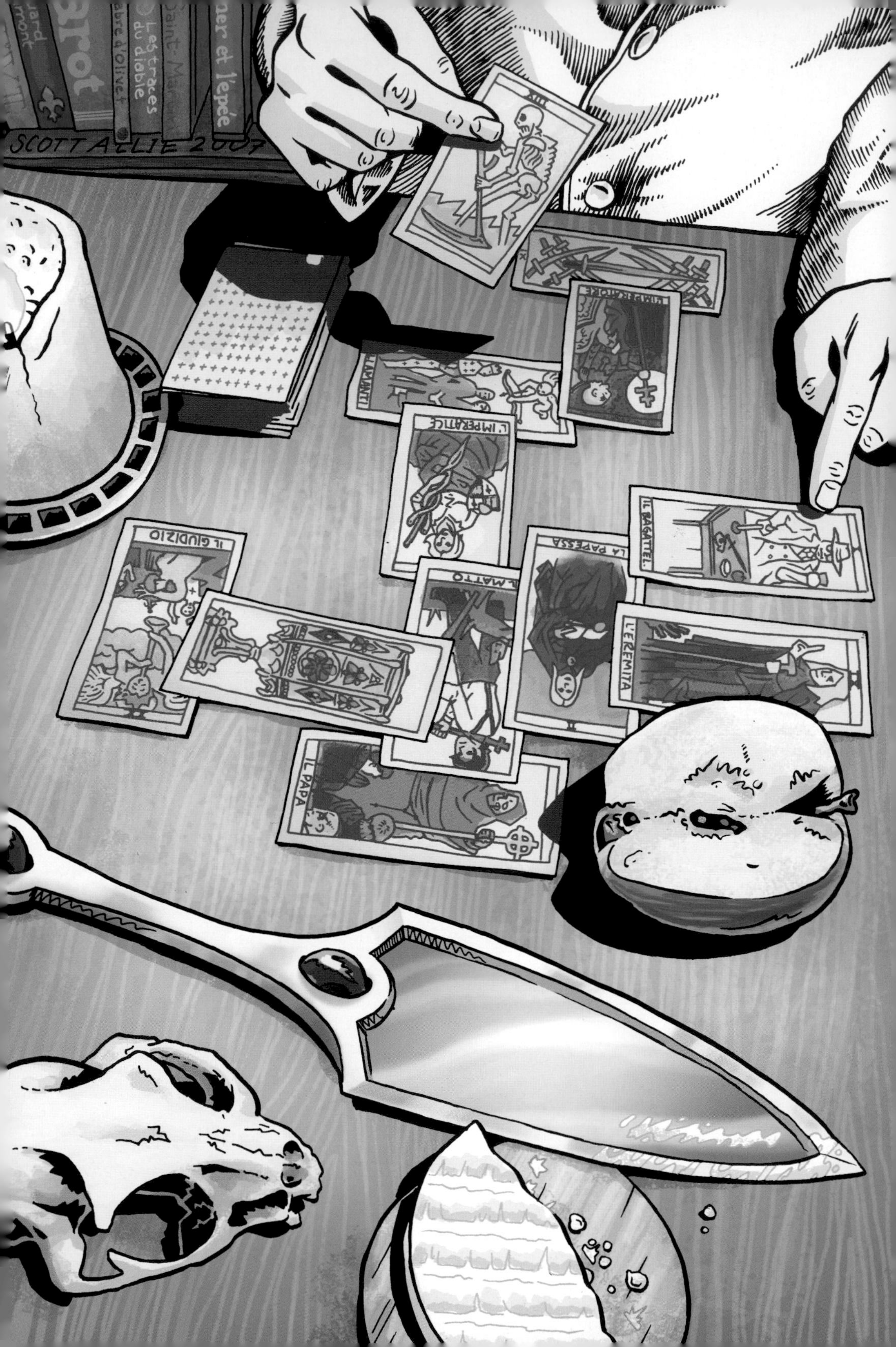

Les traces du diable
SCOTT ALLIE 2007
IL GIUDIZIO
L'IMPERATRICE
LA PAPESSA
IL MATTO
IL BAGATTEL
L'EREMITA
IL PAPA

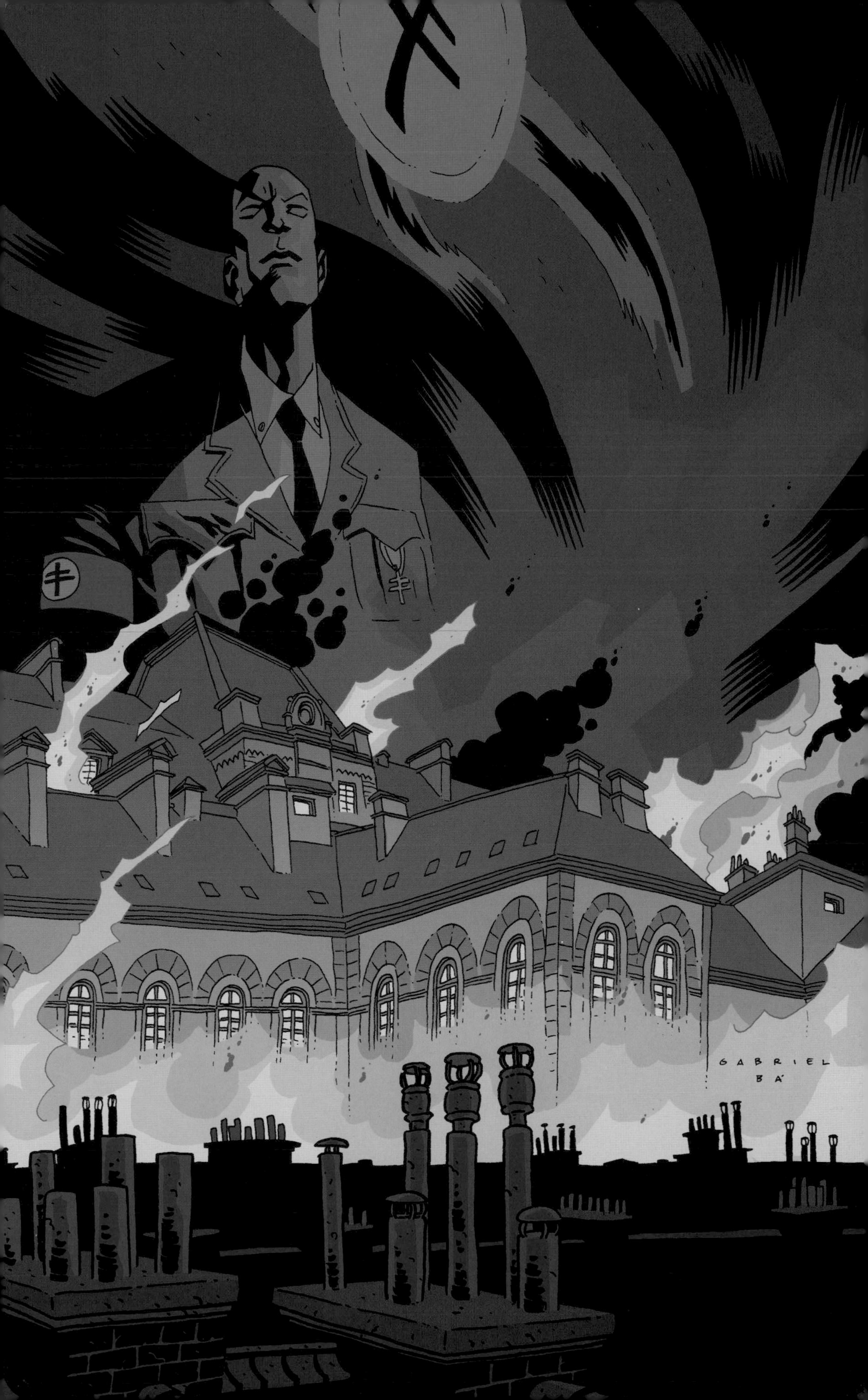
GABRIEL
BÁ

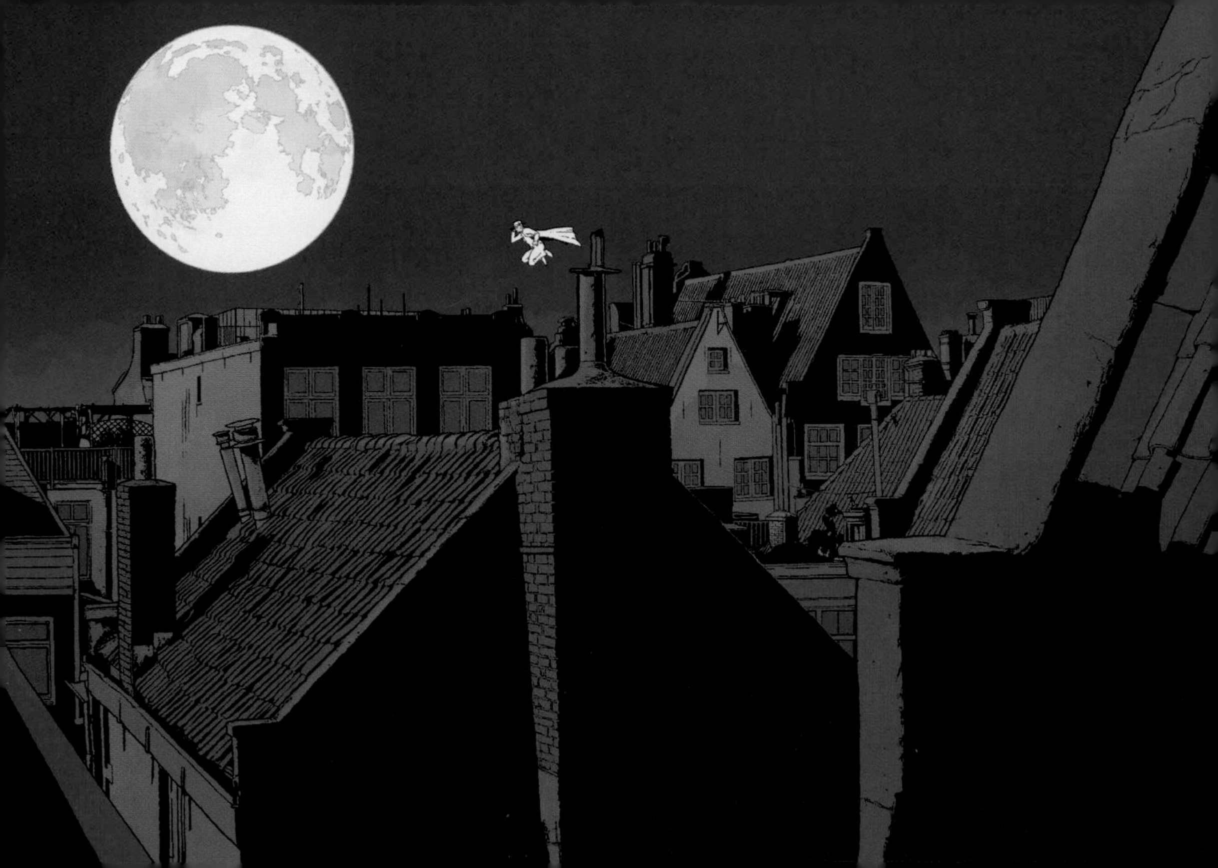

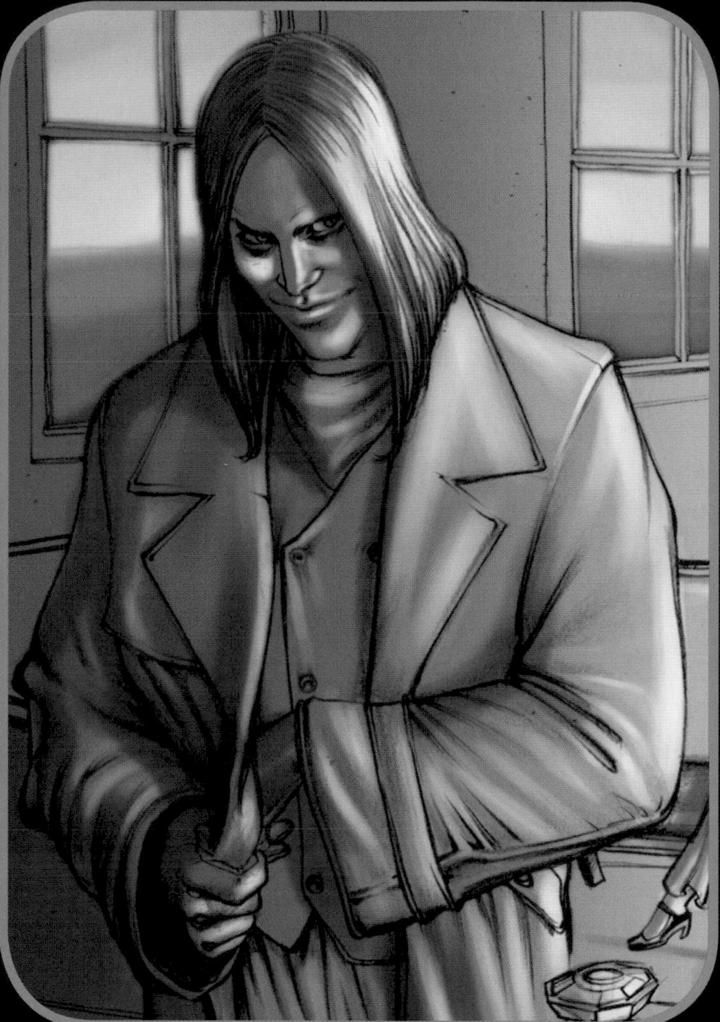

TO WEAVE A LOVER

TO WEAVE A LOVER

introduction by Arvid Nelson

Welcome, Dear Reader, to the end of *Crown and Sword*. This is the first volume of *Rex Mundi* to feature original Dark Horse content, and the first completely filled with Juan Ferreyra's art. The previous volume, *The Lost Kings*, was time spent beating my fists against the inside of a cocoon. Producing *Crown and Sword* has been a breakout experience. Sharing all the growth with Juan is one of the greatest pleasures I've ever experienced as a writer.

Inadvertently, "To Weave a Lover" became the epicenter of the transformation. It all started when Scott Allie, *Rex Mundi*'s editor, offered me a story in the *Dark Horse Book of Monsters*. I had just switched from Image Comics, and he was looking for ways to expose *Rex Mundi* to a wider audience, something it's always needed. The idea: a story set in Julien and Genevieve's past. One of the parameters, of course, was that the story involve monsters. The result: the pages that follow, which first saw print in the *Dark Horse Book of Monsters*.

Scott spent a lot of time going over every aspect of *To Weave a Lover* with me, from the scripting to the lettering. I learned as much through the process as I did from six years of writing *Rex Mundi* on my own. Best of all, I was able to apply what I'd learned to *Rex Mundi* itself. It all started here, Dear Reader.

The idea behind *To Weave a Lover* was to tell a monster story without ever naming the monster itself. After all, just using the word "vampire" or "werewolf" is equivalent to letting the air out of your bicycle tires. Virtually everyone knows what vampires and werewolves are, the "rules" binding them, how to stop them, what their weaknesses are. It's not so much storytelling as prescribing penicillin.

Monsters are scariest when they're not so easy to vanquish. They're forces of nature, completely beyond the bounds of human laws and morality. They're evil. I tried to create that impression in the story that follows. Only you, Dear Reader, can judge my success or failure.

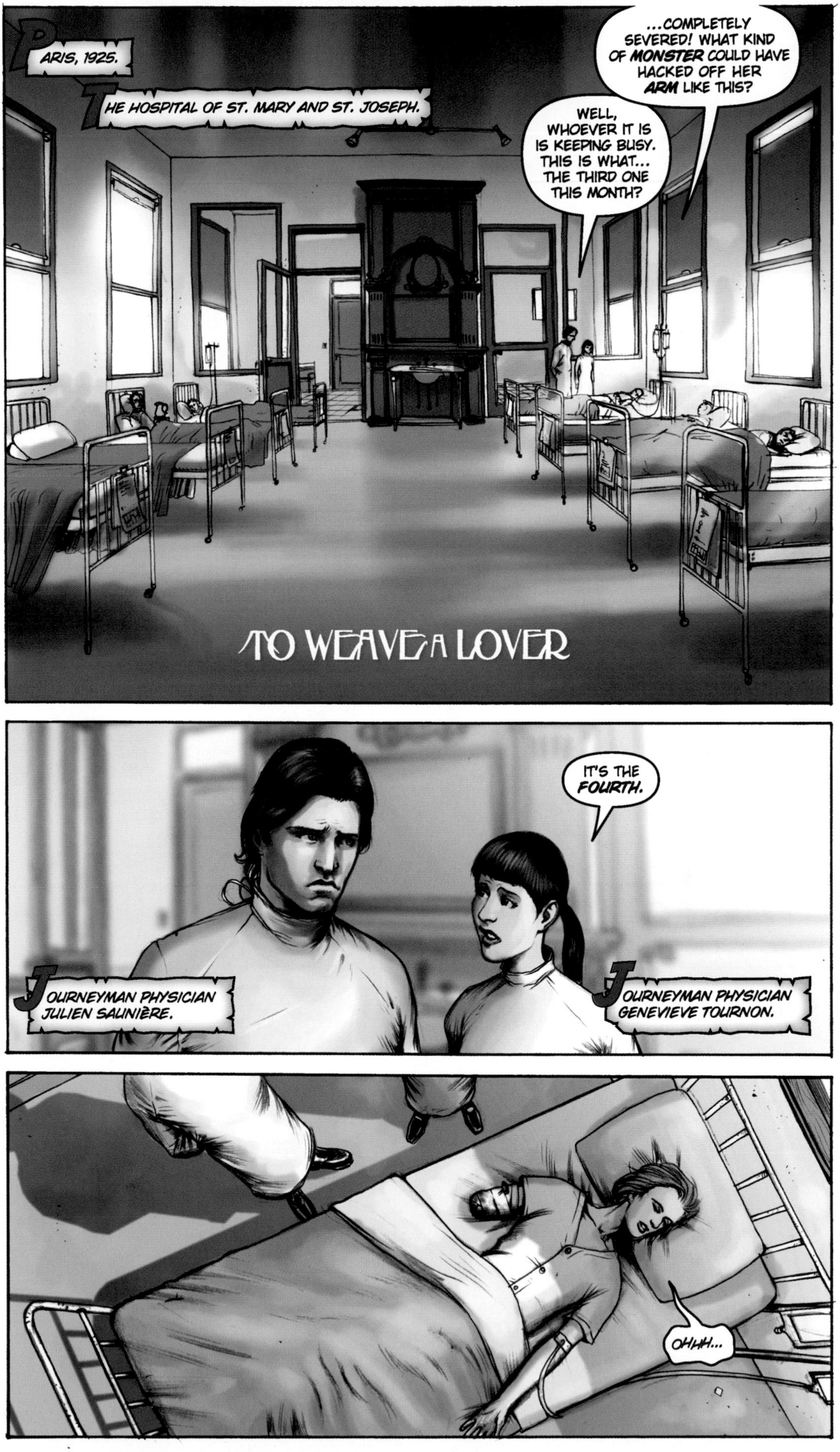
PARIS, 1925.
THE HOSPITAL OF ST. MARY AND ST. JOSEPH.
...COMPLETELY SEVERED! WHAT KIND OF MONSTER COULD HAVE HACKED OFF HER ARM LIKE THIS?
WELL, WHOEVER IT IS IS KEEPING BUSY. THIS IS WHAT... THE THIRD ONE THIS MONTH?
TO WEAVE A LOVER
IT'S THE FOURTH.
JOURNEYMAN PHYSICIAN JULIEN SAUNIÈRE.
JOURNEYMAN PHYSICIAN GENEVIEVE TOURNON.
OHHH...

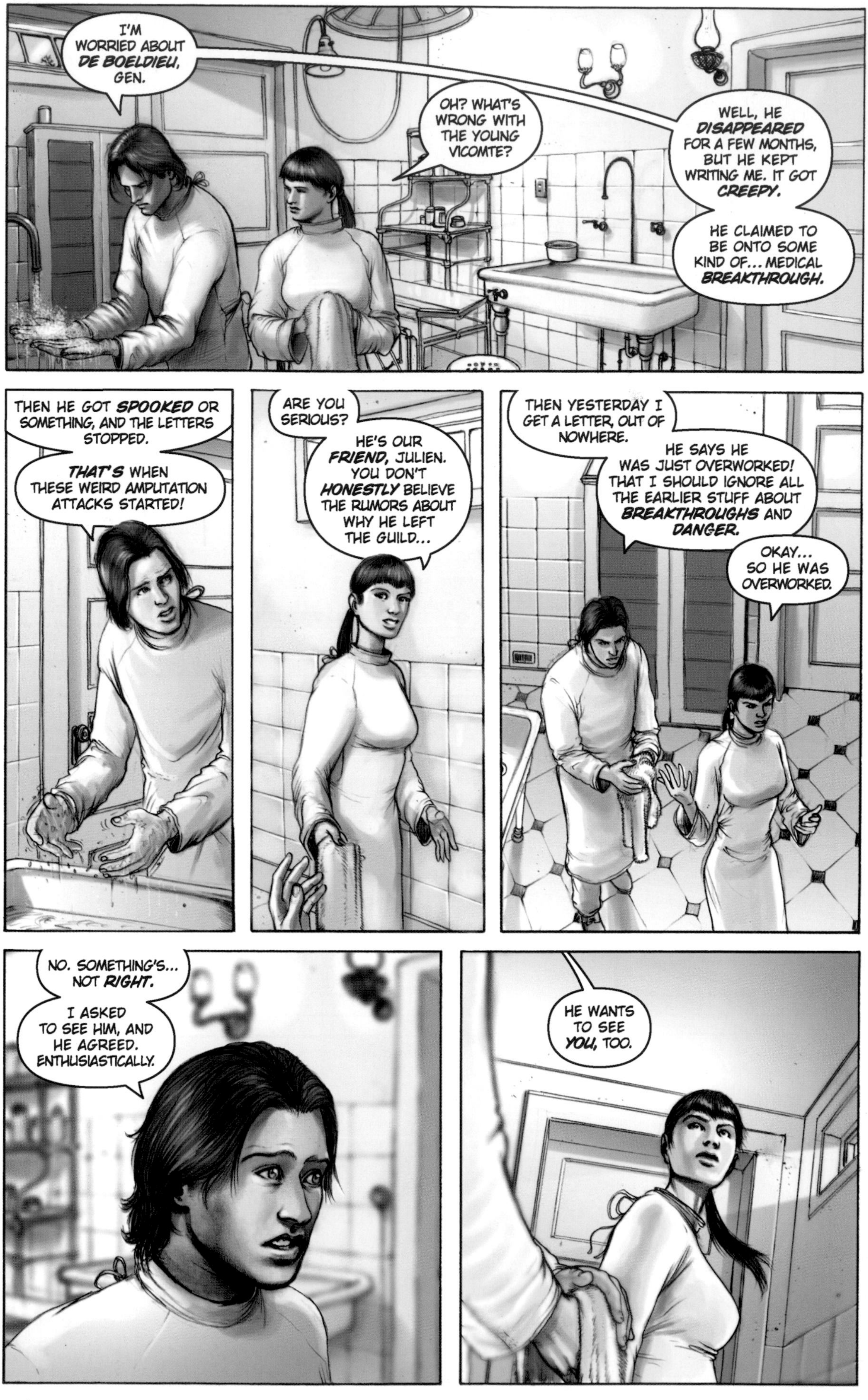
I'M WORRIED ABOUT DE BOELDIEU, GEN.
OH? WHAT'S WRONG WITH THE YOUNG VICOMTE?
WELL, HE DISAPPEARED FOR A FEW MONTHS, BUT HE KEPT WRITING ME. IT GOT CREEPY.
HE CLAIMED TO BE ONTO SOME KIND OF... MEDICAL BREAKTHROUGH.
THEN HE GOT SPOOKED OR SOMETHING, AND THE LETTERS STOPPED.
THAT'S WHEN THESE WEIRD AMPUTATION ATTACKS STARTED!
ARE YOU SERIOUS?
HE'S OUR FRIEND, JULIEN. YOU DON'T HONESTLY BELIEVE THE RUMORS ABOUT WHY HE LEFT THE GUILD...
THEN YESTERDAY I GET A LETTER, OUT OF NOWHERE.
HE SAYS HE WAS JUST OVERWORKED! THAT I SHOULD IGNORE ALL THE EARLIER STUFF ABOUT BREAKTHROUGHS AND DANGER.
OKAY... SO HE WAS OVERWORKED.
NO. SOMETHING'S... NOT RIGHT.
I ASKED TO SEE HIM, AND HE AGREED. ENTHUSIASTICALLY.
HE WANTS TO SEE YOU, TOO.

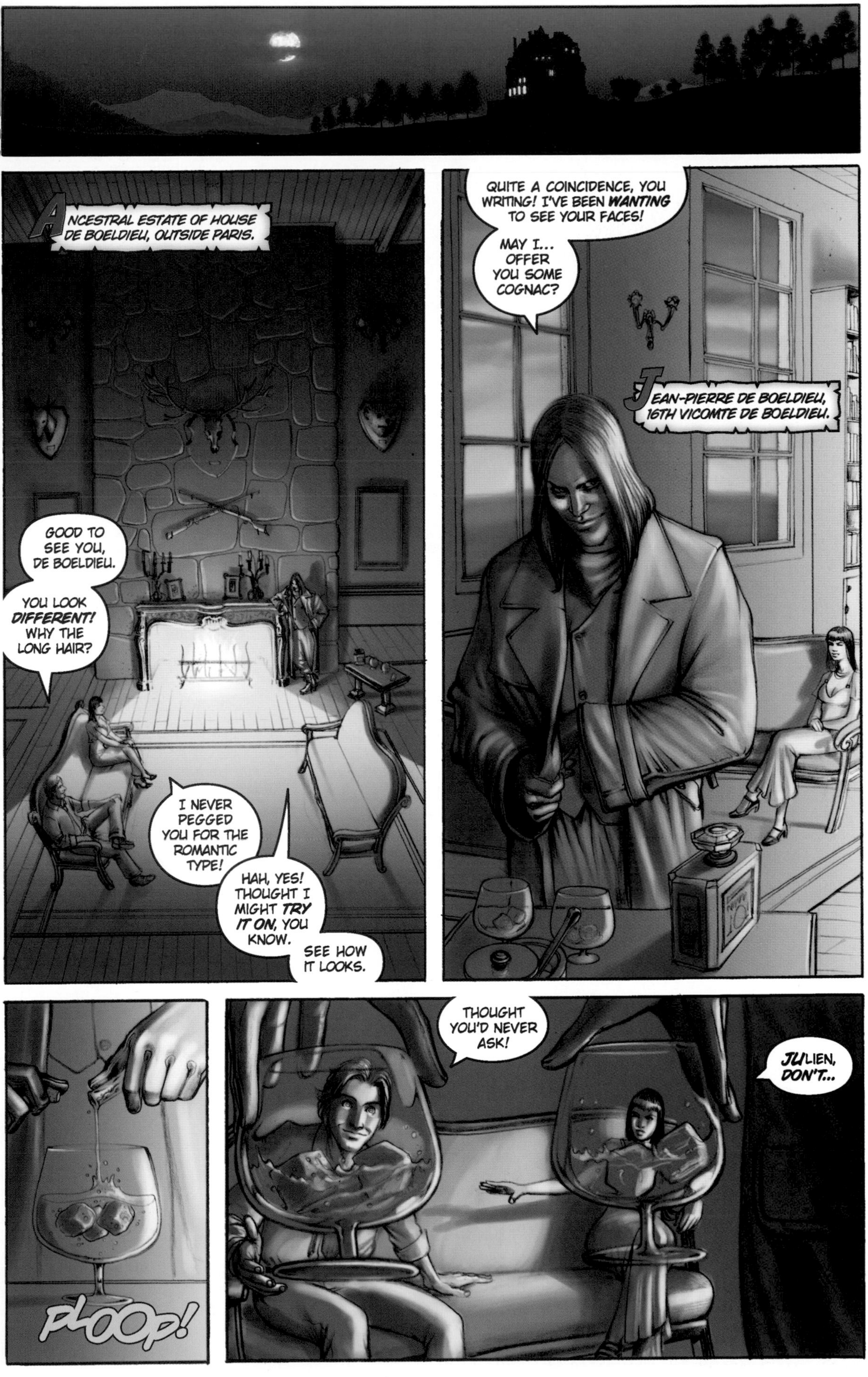
ANCESTRAL ESTATE OF HOUSE DE BOELDIEU, OUTSIDE PARIS.
GOOD TO SEE YOU, DE BOELDIEU.
YOU LOOK DIFFERENT! WHY THE LONG HAIR?
I NEVER PEGGED YOU FOR THE ROMANTIC TYPE!
HAH, YES! THOUGHT I MIGHT TRY IT ON, YOU KNOW.
SEE HOW IT LOOKS.
QUITE A COINCIDENCE, YOU WRITING! I'VE BEEN WANTING TO SEE YOUR FACES!
MAY I... OFFER YOU SOME COGNAC?
JEAN-PIERRE DE BOELDIEU, 16TH VICOMTE DE BOELDIEU.
PLOOP!
THOUGHT YOU'D NEVER ASK!
JULIEN, DON'T...

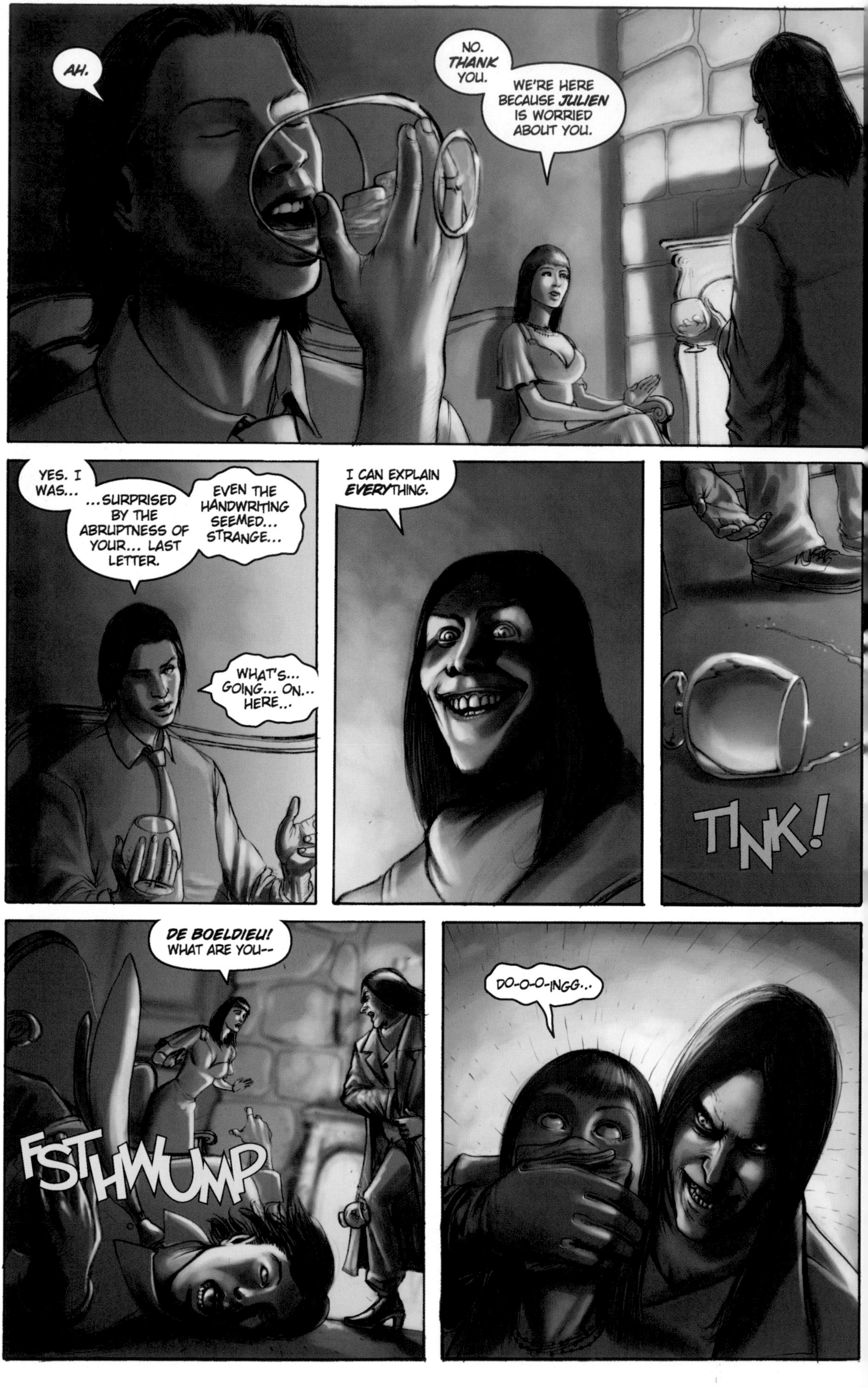
AH.
NO. THANK YOU.
WE'RE HERE BECAUSE JULIEN IS WORRIED ABOUT YOU.
YES. I WAS...
...SURPRISED BY THE ABRUPTNESS OF YOUR... LAST LETTER.
EVEN THE HANDWRITING SEEMED... STRANGE...
WHAT'S... GOING... ON... HERE...
I CAN EXPLAIN EVERYTHING.
TINK!
DE BOELDIEU! WHAT ARE YOU--
FSTHWUMP
DO-O-O-INGG...

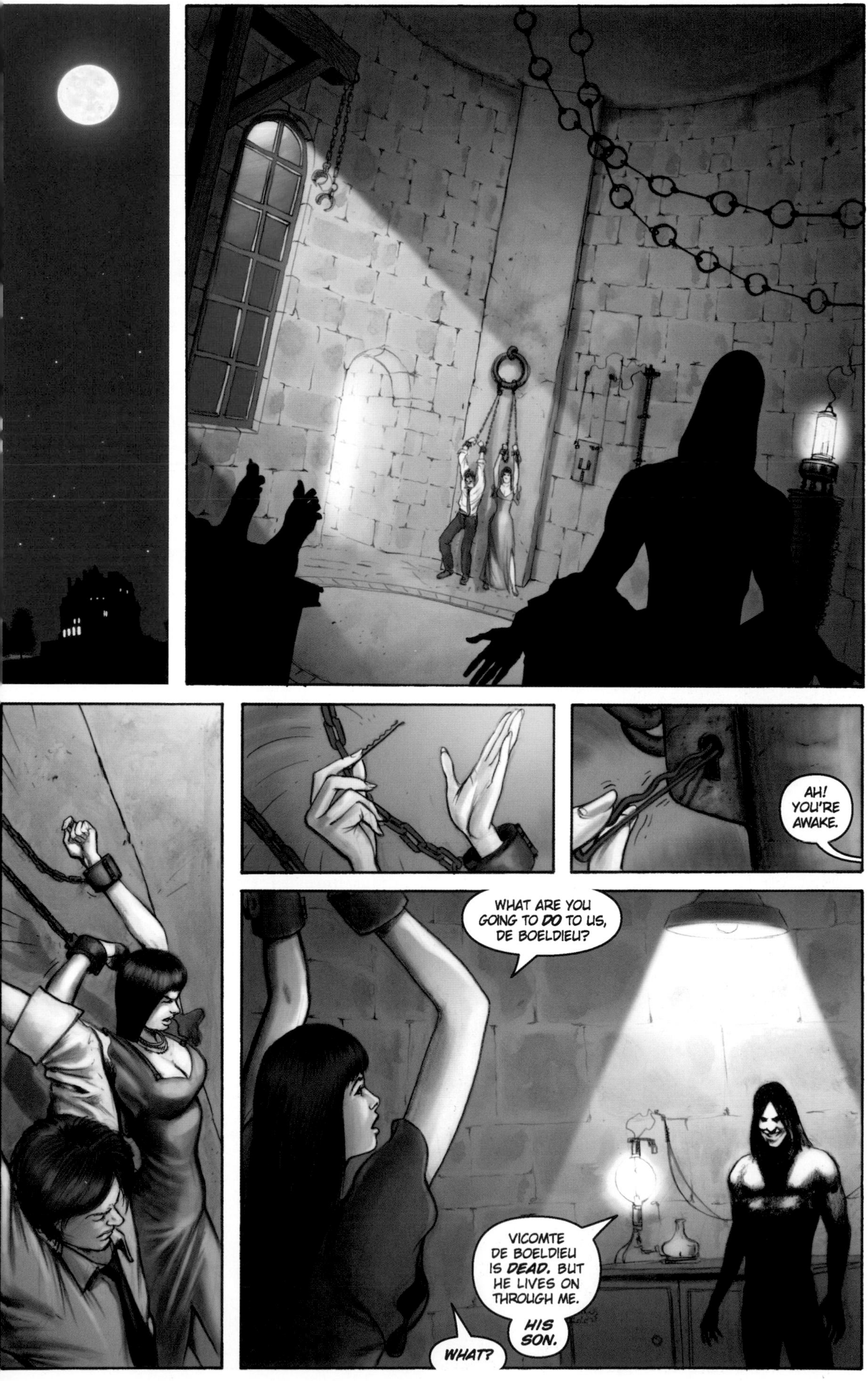
AH! YOU'RE AWAKE.
WHAT ARE YOU GOING TO DO TO US, DE BOELDIEU?
VICOMTE DE BOELDIEU IS DEAD. BUT HE LIVES ON THROUGH ME.
HIS SON.
WHAT?

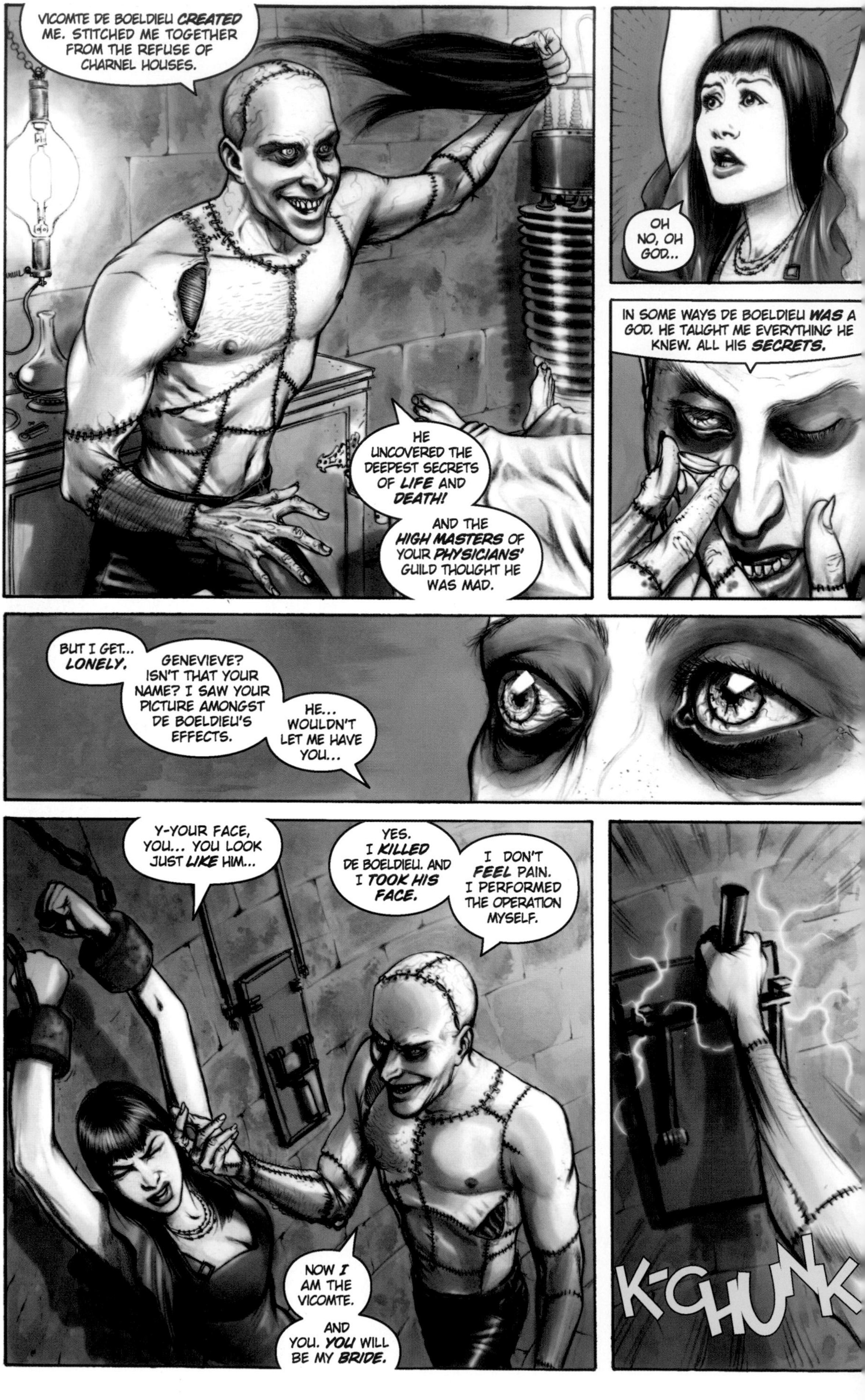
VICOMTE DE BOELDIEU CREATED ME. STITCHED ME TOGETHER FROM THE REFUSE OF CHARNEL HOUSES.
HE UNCOVERED THE DEEPEST SECRETS OF LIFE AND DEATH!
AND THE HIGH MASTERS OF YOUR PHYSICIANS' GUILD THOUGHT HE WAS MAD.
OH NO, OH GOD...
IN SOME WAYS DE BOELDIEU WAS A GOD. HE TAUGHT ME EVERYTHING HE KNEW. ALL HIS SECRETS.
BUT I GET... LONELY.
GENEVIEVE? ISN'T THAT YOUR NAME? I SAW YOUR PICTURE AMONGST DE BOELDIEU'S EFFECTS.
HE... WOULDN'T LET ME HAVE YOU...
Y-YOUR FACE, YOU... YOU LOOK JUST LIKE HIM...
YES. I KILLED DE BOELDIEU. AND I TOOK HIS FACE.
I DON'T FEEL PAIN. I PERFORMED THE OPERATION MYSELF.
NOW I AM THE VICOMTE.
AND YOU. YOU WILL BE MY BRIDE.
K-CHUNK

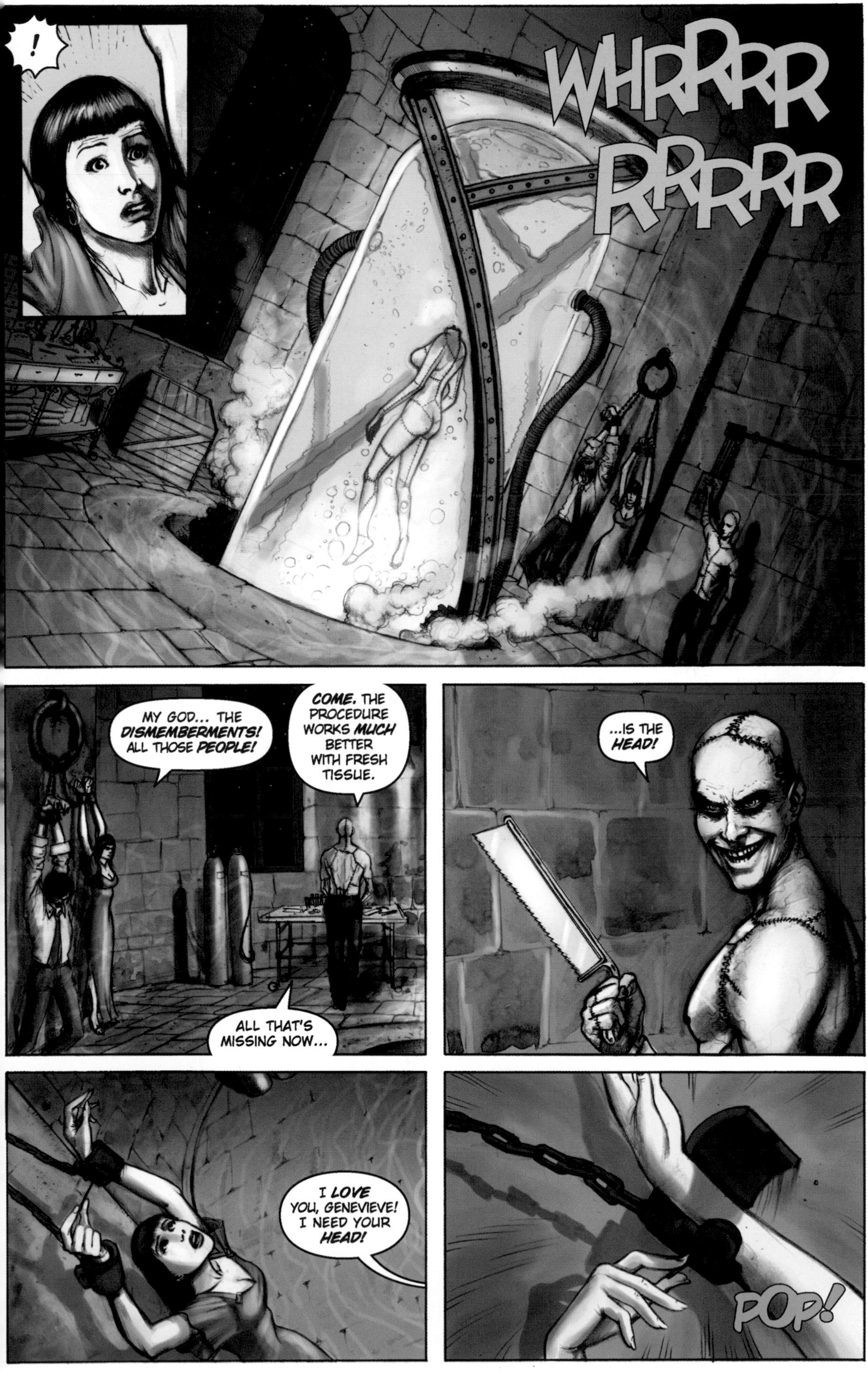
!
WHRRRR RRRRRR
MY GOD... THE DISMEMBERMENTS! ALL THOSE PEOPLE!
COME. THE PROCEDURE WORKS MUCH BETTER WITH FRESH TISSUE.
ALL THAT'S MISSING NOW...
...IS THE HEAD!
I LOVE YOU, GENEVIEVE! I NEED YOUR HEAD!
POP!

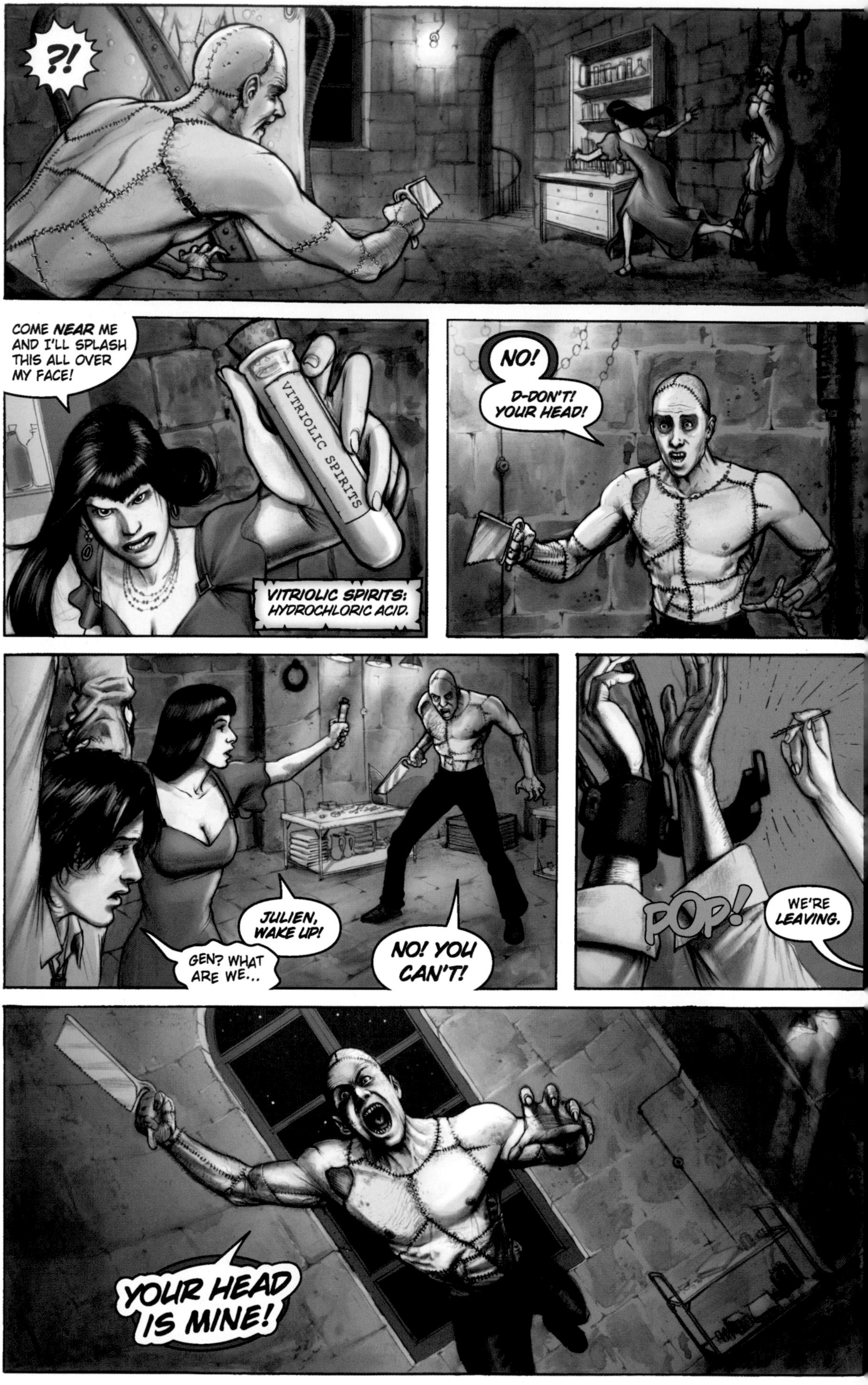
?!
COME NEAR ME AND I'LL SPLASH THIS ALL OVER MY FACE!
VITRIOLIC SPIRITS
VITRIOLIC SPIRITS: HYDROCHLORIC ACID.
NO!
D-DON'T! YOUR HEAD!
JULIEN, WAKE UP!
GEN? WHAT ARE WE...
NO! YOU CAN'T!
POP!
WE'RE LEAVING.
YOUR HEAD IS MINE!

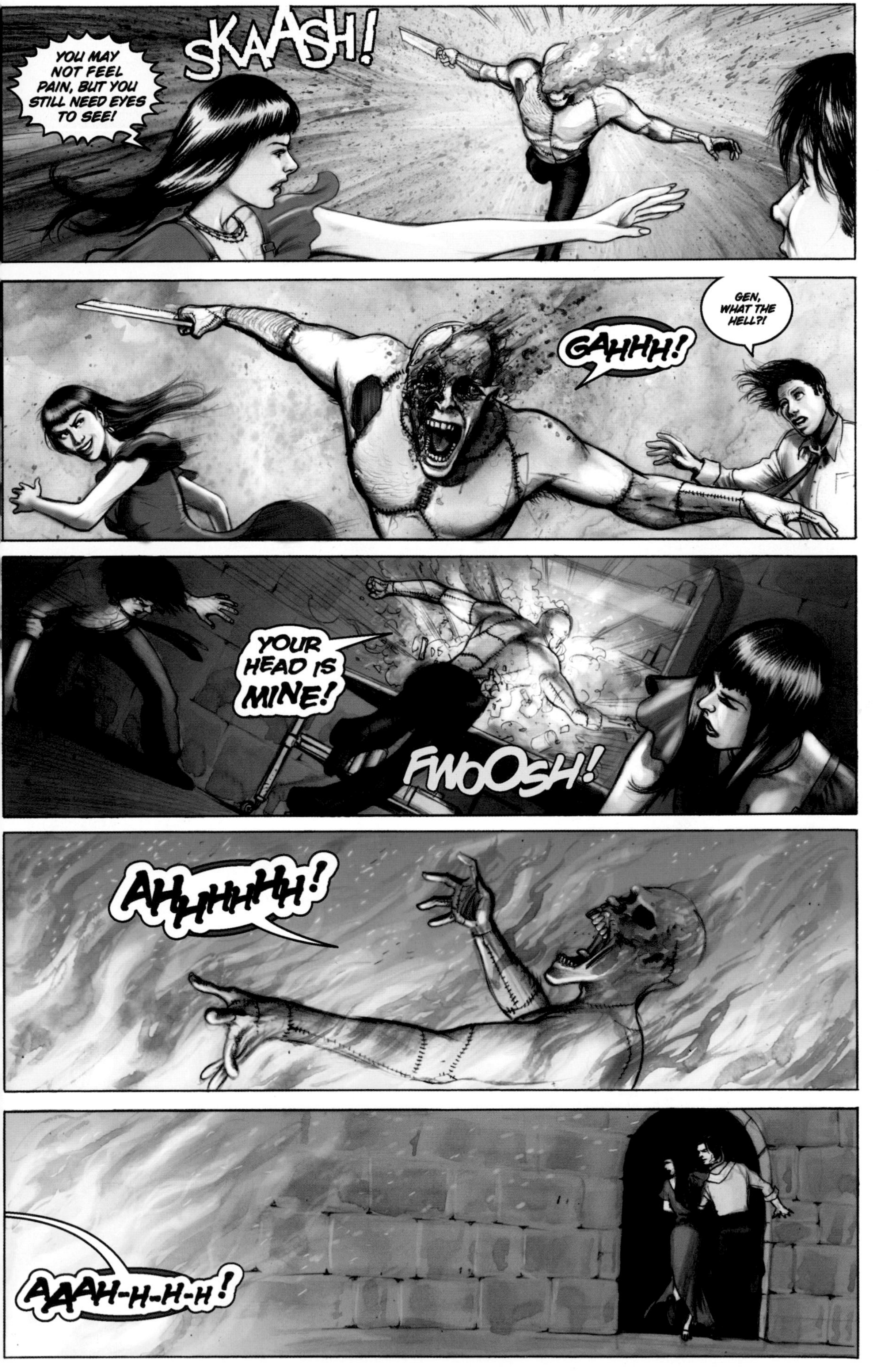
YOU MAY NOT FEEL PAIN, BUT YOU STILL NEED EYES TO SEE!
SKAASH!
GAHHH!
GEN, WHAT THE HELL?!
YOUR HEAD IS MINE!
FWOOSH!
AHHHHHH!
AAAH-H-H-H!

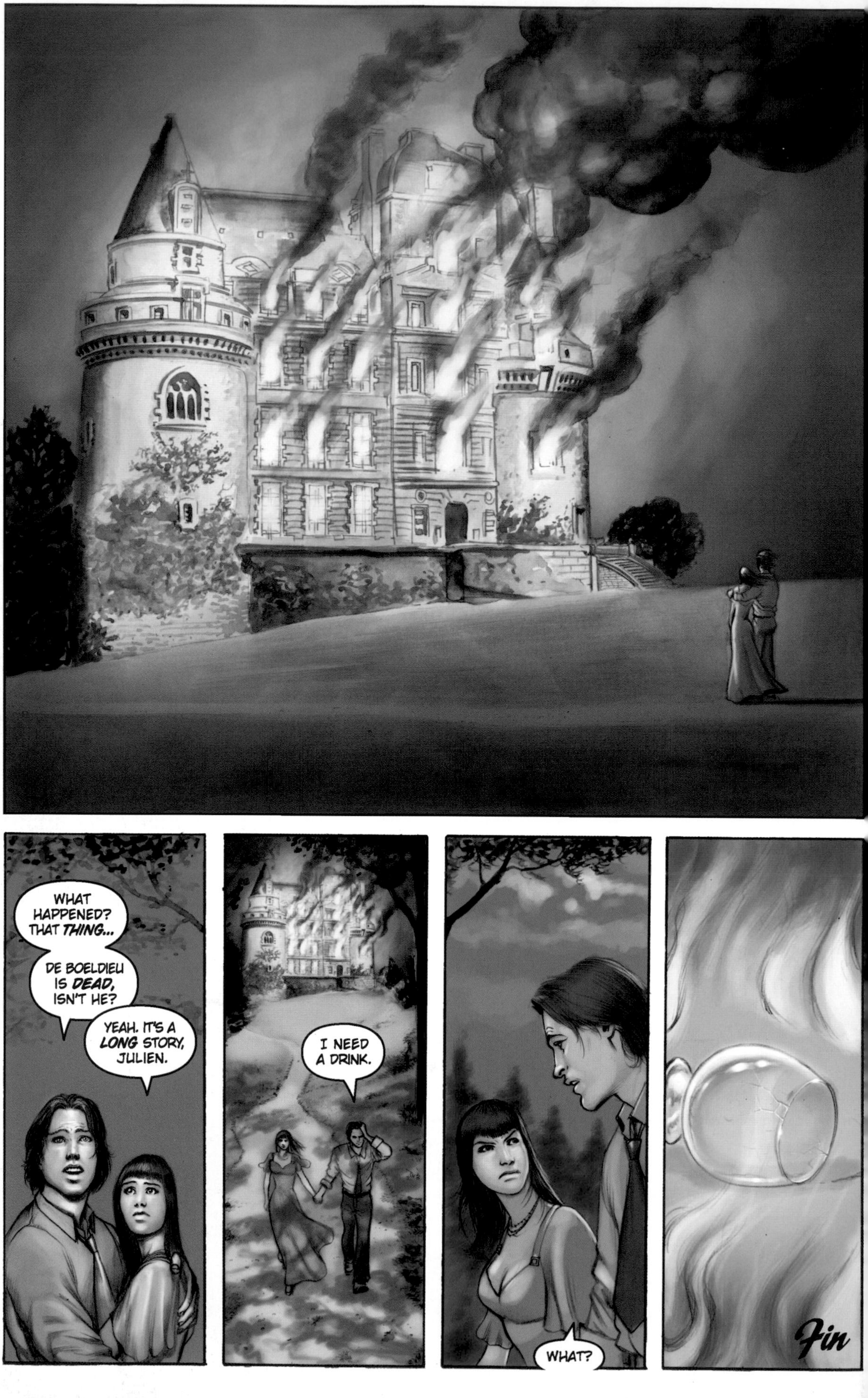
WHAT HAPPENED? THAT THING...
DE BOELDIEU IS DEAD, ISN'T HE?
YEAH. IT'S A LONG STORY, JULIEN.
I NEED A DRINK.
WHAT?
Fin

REX MUNDI

**THE GUARDIAN OF
THE TEMPLE**
ISBN: 978-1-59307-652-8
$16.95

THE RIVER UNDERGROUND
ISBN: 978-1-59307-682-5
$16.95

THE LOST KINGS
ISBN: 978-1-59307-651-1
$16.95

CROWN AND SWORD
ISBN: 978-1-59307-824-9
$16.95

AVAILABLE AT YOUR
LOCAL COMICS SHOP
OR BOOKSTORE

TO FIND A COMICS
SHOP IN YOUR AREA,
CALL 1-888-266-4226. For more
information or to order direct: •On the
web: darkhorse.com •Email: mailorder@
darkhorse.com •Phone: 1-800-862-0052
Mon.-Fri. 9 A.M. to 5 P.M. Pacific time.
Rex Mundi™ © 2007 Arvid Nelson.
[BL6052]

ALSO FROM DARK HORSE BOOKS

THE 13TH SON
THE BOOK SAYS HE'S REAL, AND HE KILLS MONSTERS!
HOW MANY TIMES DO I NEED TO TELL YOU — THERE'S NO SUCH THING AS THE 13TH SON!
WORSE THING WAITING

13TH SON: WORSE THING WAITING
Kelley Jones
The 13th Son is a creature like nothing this world has seen before. Humans are not his target. It's the other monsters who walk this earth who live in fear of his enormous and terrifying powers.
ISBN-10: 1-59307-551-0 / ISBN-13: 978-1-59307-551-4
$12.95

a cal mcdonald mystery
LAST TRAIN TO DEADSVILLE
steve NILES
kelley JONES

LAST TRAIN TO DEADSVILLE: A CAL MCDONALD MYSTERY
Steve Niles and Kelley Jones
It's supernatural private eye Cal McDonald's most spine-chilling (and side-splitting) case yet, as some Beverly Hellbillies take him into the heart of a Southern California backwater brimming with monsters and mullets.
ISBN-10: 1-59307-107-8 / ISBN-13: 978-1-59307-107-3
$14.95

Mike Mignola
Jill Thompson
Evan Dorkin
Kelley Jones
Eric Powell
Gary Gianni
and others
The Dark Horse
BOOK OF THE DEAD

THE DARK HORSE BOOK OF THE DEAD
Kelley Jones, Mike Mignola, Jill Thompson, Evan Dorkin, Eric Powell, Gary Gianni, and others
The latest in Dark Horse's line of horror anthologies, *The Dark Horse Book of the Dead* features tales of the risen and hungry dead from comics notables including Mike Mignola, Gary Gianni, and Conan creator Robert E. Howard.
ISBN-10: 1-59307-281-3 / ISBN-13: 978-1-59307-281-0
$14.95

THE FOG
Scott Allie
Todd Herman
Andy Owens
Dave Stewart

THE FOG
Scott Allie and Todd Herman
Fourteen years ago, a group of Shanghai traders fled their native land and the curse that haunted it. But the curse has found them again, as a sinister fog wreaks terrible changes on their small, seaside town in this chilling prequel to the 2005 film.
ISBN-10: 1-59307-423-9 / ISBN-13: 978-1-59307-423-4
$6.95

AVAILABLE AT YOUR LOCAL COMICS SHOP OR BOOKSTORE! • To find a comics shop in your area, call 1-888-266-4226.
For more information or to order direct visit darkhorse.com or call 1-800-862-0052 Mon.-Fri. 9 A.M. to 5 P.M. Pacific Time. Prices and availability subject to change without notice.

DARK HORSE COMICS *drawing on your nightmares*
darkhorse.com

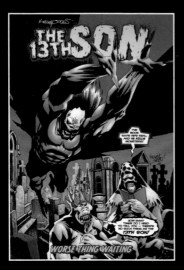

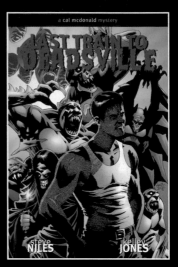

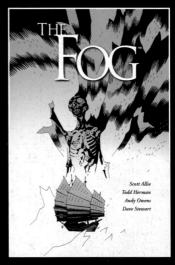

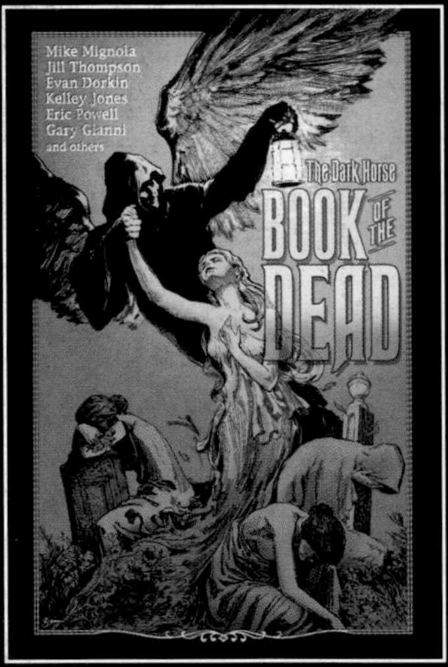